THE PROCESS OF FINANCIAL PLANNING:

DEVELOPING A FINANCIAL PLAN

RUTH H. LYTTON
JOHN E. GRABLE
DEREK D. KLOCK

5081 Olympic Boulevard
Erlanger, KY 41018
800-543-0874
www.nuco.com

The National Underwriter Company
A Unit of Highline Media
The Leader in Insurance and
Financial Services Information

Acquisition / Lead Editor: Sonya E. King, J.D., LL.M.
Technical Editor: William J. Wagner, J.D., LL.M., CLU

ISBN 0-87218-692-X

Library of Congress Control Number: 2006934882

THE NATIONAL UNDERWRITER COMPANY

Copyright © 2006
The National Underwriter Company
P.O. Box 14367
Cincinnati, Ohio 45250-0367

First Edition

Dedications

Ruth H. Lytton

"To Mom—
You didn't want me to do this and died before it was completed.
I hope I made the right choices."

John E. Grable

"To Emily and Sarah"

Derek D. Klock

"To Doc—
You made this and me better than anyone thought. I will forever be grateful."

About the Authors

Ruth H. Lytton

Ruth H. Lytton, Ph.D., RFC is Associate Professor of Financial Planning and the Director of the Certified Financial Planner™ Board of Standards, Inc. and the International Association of Registered Financial Consultants registered undergraduate program at Virginia Tech. Dr. Lytton has been recognized with various student association, university, and national professional association awards for her contributions as a teacher, researcher, and career/academic advisor, including the College of Human Resources Certificate of Teaching Excellence, College of Human Resources and Education Excellence in Undergraduate Student Advising Award, and the Virginia Tech Award for Excellence in Career Advising. She has over 20 years of experience teaching financial management and is the co-author of the student study guide, instructor's manual and other print and Internet resources for multiple editions of a leading personal finance textbook. Her personal finance course is a popular elective for students across the Virginia Tech campus and attracts over 400 students annually. Dr. Lytton is an active contributor to research and education in the area of personal financial planning and management, and publishes and speaks for academic, professional, and consumer audiences. Honorary memberships include Phi Upsilon Omicron, Phi Sigma Society, Kappa Omicron Nu, Phi Kappa Phi, and Golden Key National Honor Society. Dr. Lytton is an academic member of the Financial Planning Association (FPA), the National Association of Personal Financial Advisors (NAPFA), and the International Association of Registered Financial Consultants (IARFC), for whom she currently serves on the Board of Directors.

John E. Grable

John E. Grable, Ph.D., CFP®, RFC holds the Vera Mowery McAninch Professor of Human Development and Family Studies professorship at Kansas State University. He received his undergraduate degree in economics and business from the University of Nevada, an MBA from Clarkson University, and a Ph.D. from Virginia Tech. He is the Certified Financial Planner™ Board of Standards, Inc. and International Association of Registered Financial Consultants registered undergraduate and graduate program director at Kansas State University. Dr. Grable also serves as the director of The Institute of Personal Financial Planning at Kansas State. Prior to entering the academic profession he worked as a pension/benefits administrator and later as a Registered Investment Advisor in an asset management firm. Dr. Grable is the founding editor of the *Journal of Personal Finance*, a rigorous peer-reviewed research journal sponsored by the International Association of Registered Financial Consultants (IARFC). His research interests include financial risk-tolerance assessment, financial planning help-seeking behavior, and financial planning practice standards. He has been the recipient of several research and publication awards and grants, and is active in promoting the link between research and financial planning practice where he has published more than 60 refereed papers. Dr. Grable has served on the Board of Directors of the IARFC, as Treasurer for the American Council on Consumer Interests (ACCI), and on the Research Advisory Council of the Take Charge America Institute (TCAI) for Consumer Education and Research at University of Arizona. In 2004 he won the prestigious Cato Award for Distinguished Journalism in the Field of Financial Services, and in 2006 he was honored with the IARFC Founders Award.

Derek D. Klock

Derek D. Klock, MBA, RFC is an instructor of finance and career advisor in the Pamplin College of Business at Virginia Tech and an instructor of business at Hollins University. He has taught a variety of courses including financial skills and concepts, introduction to business, corporate finance, investments, and personal finance. Prior to working in education, Mr. Klock worked for several years in both bank management and as a personal and small business investment consultant. He either currently or has previously held the Virginia State Life and Health Agents License, and the National Association of Security Dealers (NASD) Series 6, 7, and 63 Registrations. Since leaving banking, Mr. Klock has worked as an independent financial advisor and consultant. He has developed print and Internet financial education tools, including the co-development of ancillary student and instructor materials and a personal financial planning educational software package for a leading collegiate-level textbook. He serves on the Board of Directors of the International Association of Registered Financial Consultants. Honorary recognitions include being a R.B. Pamplin Student Fellow and membership in Beta Gamma Sigma.

About the Peer Reviewers

Michael E. Kitces

Michael E. Kitces, MSFS, CFP®, CLU, ChFC, RHU, REBC, CASL, CWPP™ is Director of Financial Planning for Pinnacle Advisory Group, a private wealth management firm located in Columbia, Maryland that oversees more than $450 million of client assets. He is an active writer and editor and has been featured in publications including *Financial Planning*, the *Journal of Financial Planning, Journal of Retirement Planning, Practical Tax Strategies, Leimberg Information Services*, and recently co-authored his first book The Annuity Advisor with John Olsen. Michael also speaks regularly at local and national conferences, has been a guest on *CNBC PowerLunch, NBC Nightly News, CNN Live*, and *NPR*, and has been quoted in numerous articles in numerous publications, including *The Wall Street Journal, Newsweek, BusinessWeek, The Washington Post, USA Today, Investment News, Journal of Financial Planning, and Financial Planning magazine.*

Michael was recognized as one of only five financial planning practitioner "Movers and Shakers" for 2006 by Financial Planning magazine for his active work in the financial planning community, serving as a member of the Editorial Review Board for the *Journal of Financial Planning*, a Moderator for the discussion boards on *Financial-Planning.com*, a commentator on retirement distribution and retirement planning issues for *Leimberg Information Services, Inc.*, an expert on the Financial Services Council for Gerson Lehrman Group, and for his work as an active member of the Financial Planning Association as a member of the Board of Directors of his local Maryland chapter and on several committees at the National FPA level. Michael is also a co-founder of NexGen, a community of the next generation of financial planners that aims to ensure the transference of wisdom, tradition, and integrity, from the pioneers of financial planning to the next generation of our profession.

Charles K. Re Corr

Chuck Re Corr is a Vice President and a discretionary Portfolio Manager with Merrill Lynch Private Client Group. He has been a Financial Advisor to individuals, and institutional clients for most of his thirty-three years with Merrill Lynch. He has taught finance courses at Rutgers, the State University of New Jersey and at North Carolina State University. In addition to his professional responsibilities, he is on the Board of Directors of the North Carolina Securities Industry Association. He was formally the Chairman of the Board of the Institute for Certified Investment Management Consultants. He is a Certified Investment Management Analyst (CIMA), a Certified Investment Management Consultant (CIMC), a Certified Professional Forecaster (CPF), and a member Arbitrator for NASD Board of Arbitrators. He has written, been published, and developed software on the topic of quantifying investor risk tolerance.

Chuck is the founder and current Volunteer Executive Director of the Research Triangle Chapter of the National Association of Corporate Directors (RTC-NACD), and has written articles for the NACD on advisory boards, and board decision-making process. Information on the RTC-NACD can be found on their website at www.rtc-nacd.org with links to the national website.

Chuck can be contacted at http://fa.ml.com/moore_recorr, or by calling him at (919) 829-2012.

Preface

The growth of financial planning from 1969 until today represents a phenomenal trend that has impacted the delivery of financial products and services as well as the financial and personal lives of countless Americans. The impact is now spreading around the world where growth of financial planning professionals outpaces the growth in the United States. In its purest sense, financial planning *can* make clients' dreams come true. But regardless of the significant contributions of financial planning professionals, financial planning is, in 2006, plagued by disillusionment and disagreement among those affiliated with the profession, the American public, and the various groups that stand ready to regulate or set standards for operation. No doubt financial planning will continue to evolve over the next 30-plus years, just as it has to date. We can only guess that the evolution will continue in response to: marketplace changes (i.e., economic, financial, legal, tax, regulatory); changes in financial products; demographic and social changes among consumers; and other factors that we cannot begin to anticipate.

The myriad of factors that affect the "delivery" of financial planning, as well as the need for product and service delivery that is uniquely personalized, provide a unique challenge to the profession. Central to the profession is the six-step process proffered by the Certified Financial Planner Board of Standards, Inc., which many authors have explained or adapted. But our experiences as educators, practitioners, and observers of financial planning suggested that there was a need for a more definitive explanation. As a result, the vision for this book was threefold. One objective was to offer a more in-depth and multidisciplinary explanation of the *process* of financial planning that might be used to ground the *practice* of financial planning and the education of future professionals. Ideally, such a process could serve as a framework for the practice of financial planning, regardless of the business model or method of compensation chosen by the advisor. The second objective was to surround the process with an introductory *discussion of concepts* central to everyday practice: the ethical, legal and regulatory environment; planner-client communication; and planner-client decision making. The third objective was to provide an *explanation of the components* of a model financial plan, whether comprehensive or modular, to document and guide the process for the advisor and the client.

As authors, we fully expect this book to foster disagreement over the explanations and examples offered. But out of that dialogue—and we encourage you to engage us in these discussions—we hope will come continued development of the process and practice of financial planning. Development that will benefit students and practitioners whose contributions will shape the continued evolution of financial planning. Nevertheless, errors, omissions, and/or oversights are our responsibility.

Ruth H. Lytton
John E. Grable
Derek D. Klock

Acknowledgements

This book would not have been possible without the contributions of numerous Virginia Tech and Kansas State University students who helped us learn about financial planning; financial planning professionals who shared their experiences; anonymous reviewers who challenged us to make the manuscript stronger; and Sonya King (Assistant Editor), Debbie Miner (Editorial Director), and others at the National Underwriter Company that supported this project through countless delays and obstacles. Whether named or unnamed, each of you contributed to the overarching mission of financial planning—to make clients' dreams come true. Thank you for your assistance.

Special Acknowledgement: We wish to thank Pinnacle Advisory Group, Inc. of Columbia, Maryland for allowing us to use their Privacy Policy and Investment Management Agreement.

Ruth H. Lytton
John E. Grable
Derek D. Klock

Contents

The Profession of Financial Planning

The Process of Financial Planning

The Product of Financial Planning

Appendices

Chapter *1*

What Is Financial Planning

1. Review the history of financial planning.

2. Recognize examples of financial planning membership and certification organizations as well as the designations, credentials, and registrations offered.

3. Describe the traits of successful financial planners.

4. Explain the terms "financial planning" and "life planning."

5. Differentiate between a comprehensive and a targeted, or modular, financial plan.

6. Identify the reasons why consumers seek financial planning.

7. Identify why someone might consider a career in financial planning.

8. Explain the different methods of compensation commonly used by financial planners.

9. Describe the different business models or outlets for financial planning products and services.

10. Identify National Association of Securities Dealers (NASD) and Securities and Exchange Commission (SEC) requirements for employment as a Registered Representative, Registered Principal, or Registered Investment Advisor.

11. Describe career options for those trained in financial planning.

Key Terms

Certificate

Certified Financial Planner
  Board of Standards, Inc.

Certified Financial Planner
  (CFP®) certificant

Comprehensive financial
  planning

Designees

Fiduciary

Financial planning

Financial planning process

Goal

Life planning

National Association of
  Securities Dealers (NASD)

Objective

Principal

Professional practice standards

Qualitative

Quantitative

Registered Investment Advisor
  (RIA)

Registered Representative
  (Registered Rep)

Securities and Exchange
  Commission (SEC)

Suitability

Targeted, or modular, financial
  plan

A Brief History of Financial Planning

Financial planning, as it is practiced today in its multiple forms, is significantly different from financial planning as it was practiced almost 40 years ago. While it is important to know that the future of financial planning is quite promising, it is equally important to understand its historical roots.

Financial planning has been called the "first broad-scope service profession to emerge in recent years."[1] Its history can be traced to a meeting in 1969 that led to the founding a year later of the International Association of Financial Planners (IAFP) trade association. The name was later changed to the International Association for Financial Planning (IAFP), but the objective of bringing together professionals representing the variety of specialized financial products and services remained the same. The premise that integrated the group was an emphasis on service and not sales, although it was the latter which served as the foundation.

Only a handful of people practiced what might be considered a type of financial planning prior to 1969. Nearly all financial services professionals at that time were engaged in stock, bond, or insurance sales. Some practitioners sold products door-to-door, while others sold from storefront locations to individuals or more broadly to companies and their employees. Very few firms used a process of (1) establishing a relationship with the client, (2) gathering broad-based financial data, (3) examining the data to develop a plan, (4) recommending and implementing a solution that included product sales, and (5) monitoring the client's situation into the future. The idea of hiring an individual or a firm to serve a client as a comprehensive financial planner was something that few practitioners or consumers envisioned at the time.

The meeting that occurred in 1969 literally changed the face of financial services forever. It did not take long for consumers to realize that there was more to achieving financial success than simply purchasing a product. Success could better be achieved if a professional advisor were hired to help establish goals and objectives and then develop a comprehensive financial plan to meet those very aspirations. The 1969 meeting also helped practitioners realize that a process of financial planning could be used to both improve the financial lives of clients and enhance career and income opportunities for planners by offering greater income stability, and allowing practitioners to create a business that could be sold at retirement. Neither of these outcomes was widely available to salespersons prior to 1969.

With the goal of integrated services—the birth of comprehensive financial planning—came the need for education and the establishment of the College for

Financial Planning in 1971. Designation of the first 42 Certified Financial Planner (CFP®) certificants occurred in 1973. Today, there are more than 40,000 CFP® **certificants**. Although not without discord and competition from other professional designations that have emerged, the CFP® certification is nevertheless recognized as the premiere designation or consumer standard for qualified financial planners in the United States, and efforts are underway to expand that acceptance internationally.

In 1985 the College for Financial Planning became an independent entity with an educational mission, and the **Certified Financial Planner Board of Standards, Inc.** (CFP Board) was formed to administer the certification and to register academic programs that offered education leading to a certificate or a Bachelor's degree or graduate degree (M.S. or Ph.D.) focused on financial planning. In 1987, the first 20 universities were approved for offering registered educational programs. By 1992, the modular, or topical, examination schedule was replaced with a 10-hour comprehensive, integrated exam. The recent pass rate for the exam has averaged less than 60%, which is a testament to the rigor of the preparation and examination process. Furthermore, effective in 2007 a Bachelor's degree will be a required prerequisite to earning the CFP® certification.

However, the road from where financial planning began, with only 42 CFP® certificants, to where financial planning is today was not a smooth one. Early adopters of the phrase "financial planning" were dominated by advisors whose primary objective was selling products and assisting clients in avoiding paying high taxes. The use of tax shelters, annuity products, limited partnerships, and hard asset investing captured the attention of financial planners and their clients through the 1970's and early 1980's. It was only after the tax law changes of 1986 and the significant reduction in inflation during the Reagan presidency that the focus of financial planning turned towards a more holistic and comprehensive view of a client's financial affairs.

The 1990's witnessed record numbers of people entering the field of financial planning. Much of the growth was attributable to the good economy and rising securities prices of the last decade of the 20th century. From that growth emerged a unified organization, the Financial Planning Association (FPA), established to develop and promote the financial planning profession. The FPA was formed in 2000 from the merger of the Institute of Certified Financial Planners (ICFP), an organization of CFP® certificants established by 36 of the initial 42 program graduates, and the original integrative trade association formed in 1970, the International Association for Financial Planning (IAFP). The FPA, with over 27,000 members, has positioned itself as the "heart of financial planning" with the intent of representing the profession and the consumers served without regard to the business model used or method of compensation employed. In fact the growth of fee-only financial planning, as an alternative to the commission-based sales oriented model from which financial planning originated, resulted in the National Association of Personal Financial Advisors (NAPFA) becoming the preeminent organization of comprehensive fee-only financial planners. Currently, NAPFA has approximately 1,300 members and affiliates.

The diversity of professionals, services, products, and consumers served within the broad umbrella of financial planning has resulted in widespread growth in membership and certification organizations. Today, there are over 87 North American professional associations and 89 certifications and designations available.[2] Figure 1.1 provides a partial list of membership organizations active in the United States and Canada[3]. Figure 1.2 presents a selected list of the most widely recognized professional designations, credentials, and registrations. Both lists point to the diversity of specialties and the richness of the training and ongoing continuing education that is available to enhance career prospects and enable planners to better serve their clients.

As financial planning has entered the new millennium, financial planners have had to retrench as a result of the bear market following the Internet stock bubble and increased regulatory scrutiny on financial services firms and providers. Financial planning practitioners, policy makers, and regulators continue to debate each other over the role of financial planning, the need for regulation, and the standards that should be applied to those practicing financial planning. The next decade promises to be one of challenge and progress. The one thing that is unlikely to change is the continued conversion of financial planning from a product sales emphasis to a service-oriented process of helping clients to define and achieve life-fulfilling financial goals.

Clients have a strong desire to work with financial planning professionals who can deliver value to their lives. Financial planning as a service is not inexpensive in terms of time, money, and/or personal vulnerability. Clients demand that the benefits outweigh the costs of engaging a planner. Furthermore, both clients and planners want the planning relationship to be pleasant. For the process to succeed, clients must share their hopes and dreams for the future. They must trust the planner to expertly guide their financial lives through the best and worst events that life and the economy may present. In a recent survey of consumers, when asked to identify the ten most important factors when choosing a financial planner, traits such as trustworthiness, listening skills, problem solving abilities, proven performance and expertise were at the top of the list. Other traits included professionalism, allowing clients to choose the degree of control over decisions, reasonable costs, technological competence, and professional accreditation.[4]

Individuals seriously considering entry into the financial planning profession ought to ask themselves if they have, or can attain, these client-identified traits. If the answer to these questions is yes, the chance of success in the profession will be significantly enhanced. There must also be a commitment to continuing professional development and lifelong learning. Furthermore, a commitment to these principles will almost certainly help resolve the nagging question of whether financial planning truly is a profession. Many consider financial planning to be a profession in its infancy, while others question *whether* financial planning *is* a profession. The focus on product *and* service delivery, and not just product *sales*, is a central issue to that debate. Many continue to believe that salesmanship should be a primary trait of new entrants; however the ability to foster strong client relationships and technical competence top the list of client-identified traits. These traits will contribute to professional success whether promoting an idea (e.g., a change in household spending to yield savings) or a

Figure 1.1 Selected Listing of Financial Planning Membership Organizations

AFS – Academy of Financial Services

ACAT – Accreditation Council for Accountancy and Taxation

ABA – American Bankers Association

ABA – American Bar Association

AICPA – American Institute of Certified Public Accountants

ARIA – American Risk and Insurance Association

AALU – Association for Advanced Life Underwriting

AFCPE – Association for Financial Counseling and Planning Education

CAFP – Canadian Association of Financial Planners

CAIFA – Canadian Association of Insurance and Financial Advisors

CFA Institute – Certified Financial Analyst Institute

CIFP – Canadian Institute of Financial Planning

CIMA – Chartered Institute of Management Accountants

FPA – Financial Planning Association

FMA – Financial Management Association

GAMA – International General Agents and Managers Association

IRF – Institute of Business and Finance

ICFE – Institute of Consumer Financial Education

IIAA – Independent Insurance Agents of America

IAQFP – International Association of Qualified Financial Planners

IARFC – International Association of Registered Financial Consultants

IFP – Institute of Financial Planning

InFRE – International Foundation for Retirement Education

IMCA – Investment Management Consultants Association

LUTC – Life Underwriter Training Council

MDRT – Million Dollar Round Table

NAEA – National Association of Enrolled Agents

NAEPC – National Association of Estate Planners and Councils

NAFEP – National Association of Financial and Estate Planning

NAIFA – National Association of Insurance and Financial Advisors

NAPFA – National Association of Personal Financial Advisors

NAPIA – National Association of Professional Insurance Agents

NICCP – National Institute of Certified College Planners

NICEP – National Institute of Certified Estate Planners

RFPI – Registered Financial Planners Institute

SCSA – Soceity of Certified Senior Advisors

SFSP – Society of Financial Service Professionals

Figure 1.2 Selected Professional Designations, Credentials, and Licenses[1]

Acronym	Title	Granting Organization	Website
AAMS	Accredited Asset Management Specialist	College for Financial Planning	Info6.cffp.edu
ATP	Accredited Tax Preparer	Accreditation Council for Accountancy and Taxation	www.acatcredentials.org
BCE	Board Certified in Estate Planning	Institute of Business and Finance	www.icfs.com
CDP	Certified Divorce Financial Analyst	Institute for Divorce Financial Analysts	www.institutedfa.com
CEBS	Certified Employee Benefit Specialist	International Foundation of Employee Benefit Plans	www.iscebs.org
CFA	Chartered Financial Analyst	Certified Financial Analyst Institute	www.cfainstitute.org
CFP®	Certified Financial Planner	Certified Financial Planner Board of Standards, Inc.	www.cfpboard.org
CFS	Certified Fund Specialist	Institute of Business and Finance	www.icfs.com
ChFC	Chartered Financial Consultant	The American College	www.theamericancollege.edu
CLU	Chartered Life Underwriter	The American College	www.theamericancollege.edu
CIMA	Certified Investment Management Analyst	Investment Management Consultants Association	www.imca.org
CPA	Certified Public Accountant	American Institute of Certified Public Accountants	www.aicpa.org
CRC	Certified Retirement Counselor	International Foundation for Retirement Education	www.infre.org
CSA	Certified Senior Advisor	Society of Certified Senior Advisors	www.society-csa.com
EA	Enrolled Agent	Internal Revenue Service	www.irs.gov
LUTCF	Life Underwriter Training Council Fellow	The American College	www.theamericancollege.edu
PFS	Personal Financial Specialist	American Institute of Certified Public Accountants	www.aicpa.org
RFA	Registered Financial Associate	International Association of Registered Financial Consultants	www.iarfc.org
RFC	Registered Financial Consultant	International Association of Registered Financial Consultants	www.iarfc.org

[1] **RIA**, or **Registered Investment Advisor**, is not a professional designation, credential or license, although often confused as such. The term cannot be used after a professional's name. Registration as an RIA with the Securities and Exchange Commission or state securities regulator(s) is discussed later in this chapter and also in Chapter 2.

product (e.g., investment or insurance) that the projected savings could be used to fund. Unmistakable is the fact that financial planning has grown from a small group of people in 1969 to what it is today—a multi-billion dollar service industry that is evolving to better meet the needs of all consumers.

What is Financial Planning?

There are no national standards defining what is meant by the term "financial planning." However, there have been attempts to create a common definition. The following definition is advocated by the CFP Board: "**Financial planning** denotes the process of determining whether and how an individual can meet life goals through the proper management of financial resources."[5] Specifically, the **financial planning process** entails six steps, according to the *CFP Board's Standards of Professional Conduct*, which include:

1. "Establishing and defining the client-planner relationship;

2. Gathering client data, including goals;

3. Analyzing and evaluating the client's financial status;

4. Developing and presenting financial planning recommendations and/or alternatives;

5. Implementing the financial planning recommendations; and

6. Monitoring the financial planning recommendations."

Furthermore, these six steps serve as the foundation for **professional practice standards** promulgated by the CFP Board in 1995 through its self-regulatory function to establish a level of professional practice among CFP Board **designees**. These steps and the accompanying standards were developed to establish identifiable practice methods to promote professionalism among planners and to increase the value of financial planning relationships for consumers.

Others have defined financial planning much more broadly than the CFP Board. A *practical* definition of **financial planning** is as follows:

1. Creating order out of chaos;

2. A deliberate and continuing process by which a sufficient amount of capital is accumulated and conserved and adequate levels of income are attained to accomplish the financial and personal objectives of the client;

3. The development and implementation of coordinated plans for the achievement of a client's overall financial objectives; and/or

4. Income tax planning, retirement planning, estate planning, investment and asset allocation planning, and risk management planning.[6]

It is important to note that both the CFP Board's definition and the practical definition of financial planning are *general* in nature. Someone can follow the process, for instance, without writing a comprehensive financial plan or any plan for that matter. To do so using the CFP Board's definition requires a planner to document that an exchange of information occurred with the client, and that the recommendation made was suitable at the time of the client engagement.

For the purposes of this text, **comprehensive financial planning** is defined as the *process of helping clients achieve multiple financial goals and objectives through the application and integration of synergistic personal finance strategies*. The terms "goal" and "objective" are often used interchangeably by financial planners and their clients. However, there is a difference between the two concepts. A **goal** is a more global statement of a client's personal or financial purpose, while an **objective** is a more definitive financial target that supports a goal.[7] Goals tend to be broader and more encompassing than objectives. For example, in support of the goal of funding $1.5 million for retirement, the objective might be accumulating $250,000 in a Roth IRA. But the process of arriving at these definitive and quantifiable statements may begin with the client's generalized statements of:

- "I want a comfortable retirement";

- "I want to be able to spend time with my grandchildren who are scattered halfway across the country"; or

- "I want the freedom to do _____ as long as I'm healthy."

It is from these broad statements of life goals and dreams that the interchange between planner and client—and ultimately the process of financial planning—begins.

An increasing number of financial planners are recognizing the potential significance of a broader exploration of a client's life goals, dreams, and aspirations, and are choosing to expand, or integrate, financial planning with **life planning**. A review of the literature on life planning reveals concepts such as: exploration of attitudes toward life and money; the emotional, experiential, and spiritual concerns that influence life choices and the use of money; the "soft issues" surrounding money; and the significance or legacy of the individual that supersedes a focus on net worth or assets. In essence, life planning offers the planner and client a richer foundation for asset-focused financial planning by more broadly exploring the *person* for whom the planning is being done. Stated another way, attention to life planning reminds the client and planner to build a financial plan grounded in the life—past, present, and future—of the client. Life planning is not psychological self-help or relationship counseling; it is a guided exploration of what is most meaningful in the client's life relative to money.

Regardless of the planner-client commitment to a broader personal exploration of the role of money within the client's life, the central purpose of financial planning is to position the client to achieve goals and objectives.

Accordingly, the financial planning process typically involves a review of at least seven broad areas in a client's financial life:

1. current financial position;

2. income taxes;

3. risk management;

4. retirement;

5. investments;

6. estate management; and

7. education planning and other special needs issues.

It is important to note that these are broad categories of inquiry. Whereas baseline analysis should be conducted for every client, the scope of the planning services must be tailored to the individual planner-client situation.

Often, comprehensive financial planning results in a written plan delivered to the client that addresses each of these core topics. Those who practice comprehensive financial planning typically review *all* areas of a client's financial situation before making a recommendation on any single topic. Rather than focus on one service or product line, a comprehensive financial planner incorporates multiple products and service recommendations into a plan that is designed to enhance a client's total financial wellness. Comprehensive financial planners believe that this approach offers clients the best opportunity to meet short- and long-term financial goals and objectives, rather than attempting to build a lifetime plan in a piecemeal manner using services and products gathered over time from different advisors.

Nonetheless, some clients' needs may be met most effectively through a single focus, **targeted**, or **modular financial** plan. According to the College for Financial Planning, who conducted the 2005 *Survey of Trends in the Financial Planning Industry*, consumers continue to show an interest in having investment, college education funding, tax, estate, elder care, and insurance single focus plans written. Consistent with survey results from 2002 through 2005, investment plans were requested more than any other single focus plans.[8] These plans concentrate analysis and recommendation development on the targeted area. Although broad questions about the client's financial situation may be considered, a comprehensive analysis of the seven financial areas is not conducted. The fact that a financial planner may not actually be engaged in conducting comprehensive reviews of a client's financial situation does not mean that writing financial plans is on the decline. In fact, the opposite is true. According to results reported from that same survey in 2004,[9] the average number of targeted financial plans written by practitioners increased by almost 43% from 2003 to 2004. Financial planners reported writing nearly 28% more comprehensive financial plans during the same time.

Suitability issues and litigation, based on the presumed failure of the advisor to recommend products "suitable" to the client's financial limitations and investment objectives, can arise more easily when financial strategies are implemented without documentation. Whether the financial professional is providing an analysis of suitablity or a modular or comprehensive plan, any source that documents the situation analysis protects the advisor. Without a plan in hand, a client can more easily assert that an advisor acted without adequately evaluating the client's situation. Increasingly, financial advisors are encouraged to use written financial plans or suitablity analysis documents (and in fact some documentation is required by either the NASD or the SEC) when working with clients because doing so limits a firm's liability exposure. A written financial plan, whether comprehensive or targeted to a specific client need, is one of the single best methods available to reduce future disputes over recommendations or product selection. Drafting the plan requires the planner to systematically complete and document each step in the process. Delivering a written plan also ensures that the client must give explicit approval of the strategies and recommendations provided in the plan prior to implementation.

Why Consider a Career in Financial Planning?

Financial planning, as a career option, is perennially ranked as one of the top professional choices.[10] In 2006, *Money* and Salary.com ranked financial advisors as third on their list of the 50 best jobs in America based on salary, job prospects, and characteristics of the career.[11] There are several reasons for this. First, financial planning is based on a helping relationship. Financial planners strive to help their clients achieve personal and financial success and, as a result, the career offers the reward of personal fulfillment. Second, financial planning offers significant earnings potential and job security as the future demand for personal financial advisors is strong. Using data from the Bureau of Labor Statistics and the Internet site Salary.com, *Fast Company* magazine reported that the need for advisors showed "very strong job growth—almost 35% through 2012. A college degree is a must and salary prospects are among the very best, ranging between $28,330 and $145,600. And that's just as high as the BLS data goes; a personal financial (sic) advisor could earn millions."[12]

Undergraduate or graduate students studying financial planning in collegiate programs, and those making a career change after completing a certificate program, are in a unique position to benefit from these opportunities in the financial planning profession. *Money* magazine reported a nearly 26% 10-year job growth rate and an average salary of $122,462.

In addition to societal trends (e.g., the aging of the baby boomers), the complexity and uncertainty within the financial marketplace, and the time-starved lives of Americans, the projected demand reflects the diverse market opportunities for financial planning services. Financial planners serve markets ranging from middle America to the ultra wealthy. In fact, there are financial planning opportunities whenever services and products are appropriately matched to the geographic and demographic profile of the clients to be served. Unlike financial counselors—also called debt counselors, who work with clients as they react to stressful financial situations, and attempt to recover from too much debt accumulated in the past—financial planners typically work with clients in a proactive, future-oriented manner. Debt management may still be an issue for a household seeking financial planning, but it is typically not the primary concern. The 10 reasons people seek help, as reported in a recent survey of financial planners, include the following:

1. retirement funding;

2. paying for health care;

3. investment and asset growth;

4. tax planning;

5. longevity planning;

6. money management;

7. estate planning;

8. funding education;

9. managing personal debt; and

10. planning for job loss or downsizing.[13]

A survey of consumers, conducted by the CFP Board, provides a different look at the reason people seek help from financial planners. Interestingly, developing a plan to fund retirement is number one on both lists, as indicated below:

1. retirement funding;

2. home purchase planning;

3. building an emergency fund;

4. managing debt;

5. planning for a vacation;

6. funding education;

7. accumulating capital;

8. insurance planning;

9. tax planning; and

10. generating current income.[14]

The planner and consumer lists above indicate an obvious need for truly comprehensive financial planners who can synthesize multiple client wishes into a single detailed plan for the future. The ability to evaluate a client's comprehensive financial situation, combined with the skill to write a financial plan that not only details the current situation, but also provides procedures to implement (and monitor) recommendations, are traits that are in high demand by both employers and consumers. However, note that opportunities for writing modular plans are growing as well. The lists point to the need for planners who can create targeted financial solutions to meet specific client needs. This helps explain why the *practice* of financial planning is so diverse.

Data shown in Exhibit 1.1 highlights the fact that even those individuals indicating financial planning as their primary profession often provide services beyond what may typically be considered comprehensive financial planning. Results of a 2005 survey of FPA members who also hold the CFP® certification revealed that while 82% classify what they do as "financial planning," the multiple affiliations reported by the respondents cannot be overlooked. Forty-four percent were affiliated with the investment planning industry. These results did not vary greatly from responses to the same survey one year earlier. However, the responses for both the securities and insurance affiliations dropped significantly. Twenty-nine percent of respondents indicated a securities affiliation, a decline from 36% reported in 2004, while only 24% reported an insurance affiliation as compared to 30% a year earlier. It may be safe to assume that this decline can be attributed to more financial professionals embracing a more comprehensive approach to their practice, or it could be that fewer financial planning pro-

Exhibit 1.1 Industry Affiliation for Respondents with CFP Designation and FPA Membership

Numbers do not aggregate to 100 due to multiple affiliations reported by planners.

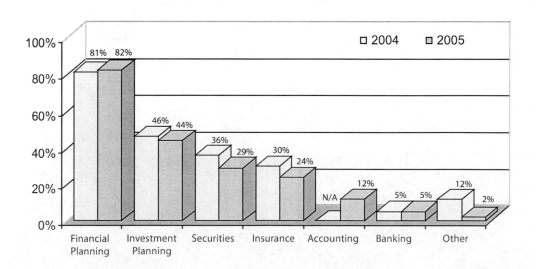

Sources: *2004 Survey of Trends in the Financial Planning Industry and 2005 Survey of Trends in the Financial Planning Industry.*
Reprinted with permission from the College for Financial Planning.

Figure 1.3 Financial Advisors by Channel

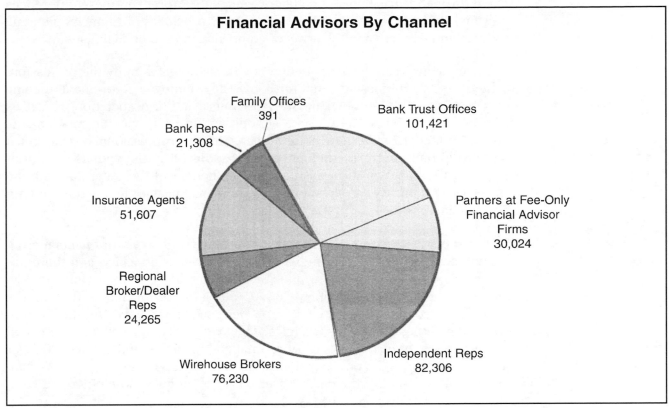

Financial Advisors By Channel

Family Offices
391

Bank Trust Offices
101,421

Bank Reps
21,308

Insurance Agents
51,607

Partners at Fee-Only
Financial Advisor
Firms
30,024

Regional
Broker/Dealer
Reps
24,265

Independent Reps
82,306

Wirehouse Brokers
76,230

Note: Another source indicated that there were 350,000 CPAs, 60,000 wirehouse brokers, 50,000 indepedent reps, 50,000 regional broker/dealer reps, 15,000 partners at fee-only financial advisor firms, and 3,000 pension consultants; another source indicated that there are 500,000 financial advisors across all channels.

Source: 2/04 Registered Representative; 11/24/03 Cerulli Edge; 2/9/00 Prima Capital Meeting (Watson); 1/00 Prima FA, CPA, & FO interviews; 12/10/99 Prima Capital Conversation (McColl); Tiburon Research & Analysis.

Reprinted with permission of Tiburon Strategic Advisors.

fessionals are reporting secondary or terciary affiliations. Another 19% reported being employed in 2005 in accounting, banking or other fields, such as benefits administration. In other words, although guided by the CFP Board definition of financial planning and the six-step process, the delivery of financial planning *services* and *products* occurs through a variety of venues and business models as illustrated in Figure 1.3.

Central to an understanding of the practice of financial planning is paying attention to the line that divides *and* integrates financial planning business models. The delivery of financial planning *service*—in other words, the collaboration of planner and client to identify goals and implement and monitor recommendations—may be detached from the *products* required for the plan's implementation. For example, insurance, investment, retirement, or other ancillary financial planning products are fundamental building blocks of plan implementation. In fact, in its truest sense, a comprehensive plan or a modular plan is a deliverable, sometimes saleable, *product* that resulted from the *service* of financial planning. Although the nuances surrounding the delivery of financial products versus financial services range from glaring to subtle, the perceptions affect both financial professionals and consumers. And in fact, the differences are in some cases upheld through legislative and regulatory mandate. Moreover, these differences often fuel the debate over the fiduciary role of providers of financial planning products and services and the array of compensation methods in use.

A fiduaciary relationship is defined by the actions taken by the professional; therefore definitions are put forth by The Employee Retirement Income Security Act of 1974 (ERISA), the SEC, the American Bar Association, as well as many others, to define appropriate actions within each specific relationship. Loosely defined, to act as a **fiduciary** means that the professional has entered a relationship built on trust, confidence and responsibility and will, as a result of ethical, professional, or legal duty, act for the benefit of the other party. In the legal sense, a fiduicary has a responsibilty for managing another person's or entity's financial, business, or property assets.

Some planners assert that anyone involved in the delivery of financial products and services in an advisor-client relationship *is* a fiduciary, and therefore must act in the best interests of the *client*. Others allege that in some employment situations, the professional has a fiduciary responsibility first to the *employer* to promote products and meet sales goals that must be fulfilled in concert with meeting the client's interests. The availability of sales incentives and commissions may bias the delivery of financial products and services, further threatening the fiduciary responsibility of the advisor to the client. This contention is at the core of the debate over business models and methods of compensation.

Financial planners are typically compensated by one or more of the methods listed in Exhibit 1.2, which also loosely parallels financial planning outlets and business models. Points of professional entry as well as requirements for employment or advancement may be differentiated by the firm's business model and method of compensation.

Individuals who enter the financial planning profession by selling products are typically compensated by *commission* (with or without salary), and need to be licensed. Insurance licenses are issued by the state(s) in which the person does business and are differentiated by the types of products sold (e.g., life, health, long-term care, property and casualty, etc.). Those who provide investment advice may be either licensed with the **National Association of Securities Dealers (NASD)** or registered with the **Securities and Exchange Commission (SEC)** or a state securities office in all states where clients reside. The basis for differentiating the need for NASD licensure or SEC registration is whether or not the advice is the primary aspect of the client-professional relationship. Those professionals, known as **registered representatives** who represent the broker-dealer in securities transactions with the public to sell securities, and who only provide advice that is incidental to the sale, must be licensed with the NASD. The commonly required NASD exams for entry and advancement are shown in Figure 1.4. To advance into the role of **principal**, a manager who supervises registered representatives, additional NASD exams are required as outlined in Figure 1.5. Professionals that are compensated for providing advice, whether or not a product sale results from that advice, must register with the SEC or equivalent state board as an RIA.

Exhibit 1.2 How Financial Planners Are Compensated

Method of Compensation	Example[1]
Commission	Varies with the product, but an example might be 5% of initial product purchase is paid as a front-end load
Flat Fee	Less than $1,000 to $5,000 or more for preparation and delivery of a financial plan; less than $100 to $1,500 or more for a modular plan
By-the-Hour	Less than $100 to $300 or more per hour to work on specific client projects
Assets Under Management (AUM)	Annual fee for assets actively managed by the planner (typically a sliding scale such as 0.25% to 1.50% based on the dollar value of assets managed)
Retainer Fee	Flat $5,000 or higher fee provides year-round access to a planner and may include preparation of a plan
Planning Fee Plus Fee for Investment Services or Commissions	Plan preparation fee is charged in addition to AUM or other fee structure for investment management services *or* commissions earned on sales of financial products (e.g., investments, insurance)
Fee-Offset[2]	Charge $3,000, for example, for a comprehensive plan, but use commissions earned on plan implementation (e.g., products sold) to offset initial planning fee

[1] Some of the examples noted are based on Powell, R. (2005, September/October) *How Much are Consumers Paying for Financial Plans? Solutions*, 3, Denver, CO: FPA.

[2] Proper disclosure and explanation is very important due to possible NASD ramifications and confusion with the illegal practice of rebating. For more information see Chapter 2, Ethics, Laws and Regulations.

The stock brokerage industry has taken a growing interest in the way the financial planning process can be used to achieve client goals. The largest brokerage firms often actively recruit individuals trained in financial planning and those with a CFP® certification and experience are highly sought after. Merrill Lynch, for example, has stated publicly that it supports the financial planning process.

Contingent on the place of employment and the range of securities represented, not all of the exams listed in Figure 1.4 or 1.5 would be required. As illustrated in Figure 1.6, for example, retail sales of mutual funds in a banking or insurance environment may require only a Series 6 exam, not a Series 7, since stocks or other securities may not be represented. The same is true for state insurance licenses, with the required licenses dependent upon the products being represented. Or in some cases an independent financial planning firm may specialize in a particular product, such as long-term care. Also of note, assistants or paraplanners employed with multi-product financial planning firms (e.g., Ameriprise or AXA Advisors) could be subject to the same licensing requirement as the advisor. The primary determination for the need for licensing is whether or not the assistant or paraplanner facilitates financial product transactions.

Banks, brokerage firms, and insurance companies may have other financial planning professionals who develop comprehensive financial plans (in support of insurance or investment product sales) based on a "fact finder" or customer questionnaire conducted by the registered representative, or product provider. Upon completion, the plan is returned to the professional for presentation to the client. These "remote" planners are typically paid a salary. In some instances, the availability of the financial planning services is dependent on account holdings, net worth, or some other combination of factors, with the plan provided as a free service or for a fee. The financial planning services provide a comprehensive means for helping clients reach their goals as well as the delivery of other products necessary for implementation.

Independent financial planners may practice in solo firms or in small-to-large group practices that are referred to as "ensemble" firms because of the varied professionals that are working together as a group. Small practices composed of planners and support staff are sometimes referred to as "boutique" financial planning firms, an analogy drawn from retailing because of the specialized products and services being offered to a niche market. The method of compensation as outlined in Exhibit 1.2 may distinguish these firms, their methods of operation, and their requirements for employment as shown in Figure 1.6. For example, some firms may charge *hourly fees*, an *annual retainer*, or a combination of both depending on the planning services sought or the scope of the work to be done. An hourly fee might be charged for a targeted plan or resolution of a particular problem (e.g., retirement planning), while for the retainer a client might get a comprehensive plan, implementation and monitoring services, and access to a planner throughout the year. If this entry point is taken, the person will most likely need to register as a Registered Investment Advisor (RIA) with the SEC or the state in which they practice or the states where their clients live. Although the rules leave some room for interpretation (e.g., existence of a state investment advisor statute, number of client accounts, amount of assets under management), generally $25 million under management is the dividing line between registering with the state or with the SEC. A full range of financial planning services may be offered or coordinated, depending on the size of the firm and client capacity, but a constant stream of firm revenue may be generated through the investment management services. As shown in Exhibit 1.2, charges for these services are typically based on assets under management (AUM) or a variation of this approach that considers a combination of factors such as net worth, income range, or other factors with or without AUM.

Firms choosing hourly, retainer, or AUM-based methods of compensation may hold themselves out to the public as fee-only *if* no commission-based products are sold directly to clients. Should products be required to implement the

Figure 1.4 Entry-Level ("Registered Rep") NASD Licensing Exams[1]

Series Number	Series Title
6	Investment Company Products / Variable Contracts Representative Exam This exam qualifies an individual to sell only investment company securities, variable annuities, and variable life insurance mutual funds.
7	General Securities Representative Examination This exam qualifies a representative to sell any type of security. This exam covers information contained on exams 6, 22, 42, 52, and 62.*
11	Assistant Representative - Order Processing Exam This exam qualifies an individual associated with an NASD member firm to accept unsolicited telephone orders and give quotes to customers.
52	Municipal Securities Representative This exam qualifies an individual to sell only municipal securities of qualifying government issuers.
55	Equity Trader Limited Representative The exam qualifies an individual to trade equity and convertible debt securities on a principal or agency basis. Only for those persons holding the NASD Series 7 or 62 license.
63	Uniform Securities Agent State Law Examination This exam qualifies individuals to sell securities across state lines. These laws are sometimes called "Blue Sky" laws.
65	Uniform Investment Adviser Law Examination This exam qualifies a representative to act as an investment adviser and receive a fee.
66	Uniform Combined State Law Examination This exam qualifies an individual to be both an "agent" of a broker-dealer and an "investment adviser" representative in each state. Only for those persons holding the NASD Series 7 license.
86/87	Research Analyst Qualification Examination / Analysis and Regulations Modules This exam qualifies an individual to produce written or electronic communications that analyze equity securities or individual companies/industry sectors, and provide reasonably sufficient information upon which to base investment decisions.

* The NASD Series 22, 42, and 62 are little used limited representative examinations for representing Direct Participation Programs, Options, and Corporate Securities, respectively.

[1] http://www.nasd.com/web/idcplg?IdcService=SS_GET_PAGE&ssDocName=NASDW_011051.

Figure 1.5 Advanced-Level ("Principal") NASD Licensing Exams[1]

Series Number	Series Title
4	Registered Options Principal Examination This exam qualifies an individual to manage supervising option sales personnel or individuals supervising options compliance. Only for those persons holding the NASD Series 7, 42, or 62 license.
9/10	General Securities Sales Supervisor / Options Module & General Module This exam qualifies an individual to register as principals to supervise sales activities in corporate, municipal, and options securities; investment company products, variable contracts and direct participation programs. Only for those persons holding the NASD Series 7 license. This exam covers information from the 4, 24, and 53 exams.
23	General Securities Principal Sales Supervisor Module This exam qualifies an individual to be an officer, partner, or supervisor of sales personnel with a NASD member firm. Only for those persons holding the NASD Series 9/10 license.
24	General Securities Principal Examination This exam qualifies an individual to be an officer, partner or supervisor, of sales personnel with a NASD member firm. Only for those persons holding the NASD Series 7 license.
26	Investment Company Products / Variable Contracts Principal This exam qualifies an individual to supervise the sale of investment company securities and variable contracts. Only for those persons holding the NASD Series 6 or 7 license.
27	Financial and Operations Principal This exam qualifies an individual to be a financial officer of a NASD member firm.
53	Municipal Securities Principal Examination This exam qualifies an individual to be an officer, partner, or supervisor of a municipal securities dealer. Only for those persons holding the NASD Series 7 or 52 license.

[1] http://www.nasd.com/web/idcplg?IdcService=SS_GET_PAGE&ssDocName=NASDW_011051.

Figure 1.6 Employment Opportunity Comparisons for Financial Services Students

Entry Level Position Within This Type of Firm or Sector	Job Oppor-tunities	Career Advance-ment	Compen-sation Method	First Year Compen-sation	Long-Term Compen-sation	Required Education and Licensing	Optional Education and Licensing
Brokerage Firm							
Client Services/Sales							
Assistant	5	1	S+B	$	$$	11	BA+7+63
Retail Broker	4	1	C	$	$$$$	7+63+65	BA
Institutional							
Broker/Trader	2	4	S+C	$$	$$$$$	7+63+65	BA
Education and Outreach	3	3	S+B	$$	$$$$	BA	M+7+63+CFP
Analyst	1	3	S+B	$$$	$$$$$	BA+86+CFA	M+87
Management	2	3	S+B	$$	$$$	BA+7+63+65	M+10+24+CFP
Insurance Firm							
Retail Sales	5	1	C	$	$$$$	6 or 7+63	65
Institutional Sales	2	3	C+B	$$$	$$$$$	6 or 7+63	65
Management	1	3	C+B+S	$$$	$$$$	6 or 7+65	BA+10+26
Financial Planning Firm							
Paraplanner	4	4	C+S	$	$$	7+63	BA+65
Financial Planner	3	3	C	$$	$$$$	BA+7+63+65+CFP	M
Fee-Only Planning Firm							
Paraplanner	3	2	S	$	$$	IAR	BA
Financial Planner	1	2	S+B	$$	$$$	BA+RIA+CFP	M
Mutual Fund Firm							
Client Services	5	5	S	$$	$$$	6 or 7+63	BA+65
Internal Sales	1	5	C+S	$$$	$$$$	6 or 7+63	BA
Wholesaler	1	4	C	$$$	$$$$$	BA+7+63	
Education and Outreach	2	4	S+B	$$	$$$$	BA+7	M+CFP
Human Resources	2	2	S	$$	$$$	BA	M
Analyst	1	5	S+B	$$$	$$$$$	BA+86+CFA	M+7+87
Accounting	5	2	S	$$	$$$	BA	M+7
Banking Firm							
Customer Relations	4	4	S	$	$$		BA+6+63
Bank Management	2	3	S	$$	$$$	BA	M+6+63
Trust Management	2	4	S	$$	$$$	BA	CFP+CFA
Securities Sales	5	2	C	$$	$$$$	BA+7+63	M+65+CFP
Financial Counseling Firm							
Counselor	2	2	S	$	$$	BA	AFC
Manager	1	1	S	$	$$$	BA	M+AFC
Consulting Firms							
General Consultant	4	5	S+B	$$$	$$$$	BA	M
Benefits Consultant	2	5	S+B	$$$	$$$$	BA	M

Key:

Opportunity: 1 = Low; 3 = Average; 5 = High

Compensation method: B = Bonus; C = Commission; S = Salary

Compensation amount: $ = Low Salary; $$$ = Average Salary; $$$$$ = High Salary

Education: BA = Bachelor's Degree; M = Master's Degree; CFP = Certified Financial Planner Certification; CFA = Certified Financial Analyst; AFC = Accredited Financial Counselor; RIA = SEC and/or State Securities Registered Investment Adviser; IAR = Investment Adviser Representative

NASD Licenses: 6, 7, 10, 11, 24, 26, 63, 65, 86, 87

NASD Note: For those persons holding the NASD Series 7 license, the NASD Series 66 license can substitute for both the Series 63 and Series 65.

plan, fee-only firms refer the client to no-load providers or other financial product providers who can meet the client's product needs. As shown in Figure 1.6, employment requirements differ for a planning firm and a fee-only firm. Furthermore, about half of the states have a license or other requirement, based on experience, education and/or examination, to be able to offer fee-based insurance advice.

Depending on the compensation philosophy, some firms use a combination of *planning fees and commissions*, or *planning fees plus fees for investment services* (typically AUM) to determine client charges. The former may be referred to as "fee-based" planning, and would not be available in a firm that is strictly fee-only because of the commissions. However, some firms use both approaches to give the planner the latitude to choose the most cost effective approach for the client, particularly if the commission-based approach would be more cost effective for a smaller portfolio. A variation on this approach is the *fee-offset* method, where commissions generated by the sale of products used in the plan implementation reduce the charge initially assessed for the financial plan. Note that whenever product sales are involved, applicable state insurance and NASD licensing requirements must be met.

As financial planning continues to evolve, the dissension over business models and compensation can be viewed as yet another opportunity for those entering the profession. Although opinions vary, a primary characteristic of success in financial planning is the ability to look at the world from an entrepreneurial perspective and to see income as a byproduct of providing a useful service. While entreprenuer by defininion means *to undertake* or *begin anew*, what may be more important than the *actions* of an entreprenuer are the *traits* exhibited by entreprenuers. Many entreprenuers are innovative risk takers that enjoy developing or transforming products, services, or delivery methods. These are the same characteristics exhibited by many persons in the financial services industry. Individuals who are willing to endure the financial challenges of establishing, growing, or merging a business are generally well rewarded—for themselves financially and for their loved ones through a legacy of a financial planning firm that can serve families for generations into the future. The challenge for the future lies in the continued development of product and service delivery models, grounded in the process of financial planning, that can effectively serve a broader range of consumers and the life transitions they face.

Chapter Summary

In response to the question, "what is financial planning?," this chapter has introduced the idea that it is a profession, a process, and a product. And, although arguments can be made against these assertions, consider the broader view. Professions are characterized by intensive training, specialized knowledge and/or concentrated academic study. The history of financial planing supports this claim, albeit the fact that financial planning attracts professionals from a variety of disciplines, designations, credentials, and licensures, all of whom are embracing the process of financial planning and developing the required integrative, specialized study. Consistent with this diversity is a variety of business models and compensation methods, which are also grounded in the process of financial planning. This process, summarized by the six steps offered in the *CFP Board's Standards of Professional Conduct*, serves to integrate the products and services offered by financial planners in response to the seven broad categories of inquiry within a client's financial life. As such, financial planning can be defined as a deliverable product or service, ranging from the 'service' of exploring life and financial planning issues to the product, ranging from a discrete financial product to a modular or comprehensive financial plan. Understanding these concepts will help students and novice planners to match their skills, interests, and personality to the appropriate career path within this multifaceted career field, which everyone agrees offers much opportunity for the professionals, but more important, for the families and individuals they serve.

Figure 1.7 The Building Blocks of Financial Planning Pyramid

Chapter Endnotes

1.   Rattiner, J. H. (2000). *Getting Started as a Financial Planner*. Princeton, NJ: Bloomberg Press.

2.   A complete listing can be found at: http://www.iarfc.org/coninfo/FA.SHTML.

3.   A more complete listing of organizations can be found at: http://www.iarfc.org/coninfo/FPO.SHTML.

4.   CFP Board. (2004). *CFP Board's 2004 Consumer Survey*. Available at: http://www.cfp.net/media/survey.asp?id=4.

5.   Certified Financial Planner Board of Standards, Inc., *CFP Board's Standards of Professional Conduct: www.CFP.net*.

6.   Leimberg, S. R., Satisnky, M. J., LeClair, R. T., & Doyle, R. J. (2004). *The Tools and Techniques of Financial Planning,* 7th Edition. Erlanger, KY: National Underwriter.

7.   For simplicity, references to clients throughout the text will typically appear in the singular. Readers are cautioned to remember that a client may be an individual, couple, multi-generational family, or legal entity (e.g., trust, estate, business).

8.   College for Financial Planning. (2005). *2005 Survey of Ttrends in the Financial Planning Industry*. Denver: College for Financial Planning.

9.   Mason, D. A. (2004). *2004 Survey of Trends in the Financial Planning Industry*. Denver: College for Financial Planning.

10. Krantz, L. (2002). *Jobs Rated Almanac* (6th ed.) Fort Lee, NJ: Barricade Books. Krantz, L. (2001) *Jobs Rated Almanac* (5th ed.) NY: St. Martin Press.

11. Kalwarski, T., Mosher, D., Paskin, J. & Rosato, D. (2006, May). *The 50 Best Jobs in America.* Money, 35, NY: Time, Inc.

12. Fast Company, (2005). *Fast Company, 25 Top Jobs for 2005.* Available at: http://biz.yahoo.com/special/bestjobs05.html.

13. College for Financial Planning. (2005). *2005 Survey of Trends in the Financial Planning Industry*. Denver: College for Financial Planning.

14. CFP Board. (2004). *CFP Board's 2004 Consumer Survey*.

Chapter Review

The Basics: Review Questions

Discussion Questions

1. Describe the 6-step process that serves as the foundation for professional practice standards promulgated by the CFP Board of Standards, Inc., through its self-regulatory function. What is the purpose of the professional practice standards?

2. Why is financial planning ranked as one of the top professional choices?

3. Describe the difference between a goal and an objective. How does each relate to life planning, financial planning, or suitability of a product recommendation?

4. Which seven core content areas should be included in a comprehensive financial plan?

How do they relate to client goals and objectives?

5. Describe the basic differences between fee-only and commission-based financial planners. Explain the various ways that financial planners may be compensated.

6. Describe the differences and similarities between a targeted, or modular, financial plan and a comprehensive financial plan.

7. Why are there so many membership organizations, designations, credentials, and licenses available to financial advisors? For each, give an example and describe.

8. How has the practice of financial planning changed since 1969?

9. What are the goals of the Financial Planning Association (FPA), and how has it positioned itself as the "heart of financial planning"?

10. What does it mean to act as a fiduciary?

Chapter 2

Ethics, Laws, and Regulations: How Standards Impact the Plan, Process, and the Profession

Learning Objectives

1. Describe the two approaches used to define ethical behavior.

2. Review the federal regulatory framework that impacts financial planning practice.

3. Understand the role of Form ADV as a disclosure statement.

4. Review the types of client records investment advisors must retain.

5. Explain how state securities regulations differ from federal regulations.

6. Describe the role of NASAA and NAIC in regulating financial planners.

7. Explain the purpose of self-regulatory organizations.

8. Compare and contrast Investment Advisor Representatives and Registered Representatives.

9. Understand the differences between certifications and designations.

10. Identify characteristics of the leading professional certification and membership organizations.

11. Describe who is likely to be classified as a fiduciary.

12. Identify ethical requirements for financial planners.

13. Describe the various continuing education requirements and understand their benefits.

14. Explain the role of errors and omissions insurance in a financial planning practice.

15. Describe the NASD arbitration process.

"Believe it or not, we are in the peace of mind business...character is critical. Trusting a financial advisor to behave ethically when no one is looking is the single most important factor on a consumer's mind. Clients are begging for someone they can trust. We can build that good faith and reliance by showing them that our integrity is beyond reproach."

Katherine Vessenes[1]

The Building Blocks of the Financial Planning Pyramid

Key Terms

Accredited Business Accountant (ABA)

Arbitration

"Blue Sky Laws"

Certification

Certified Financial Planner (CFP®)

CFP® Board Code of Ethics

Chartered Financial Analyst (CFA)

Chartered Financial Consultant (ChFC)

Chartered Life Underwriter (CLU)

Chief Compliance Officer

Competence

Confidentiality

Continuing education

Custody

Deontological

Descriptive ethics

Designation

Diligence

Errors and Omissions (E&O) Insurance

Ethics

Fairness

Fidelity bond

Fiduciary

Fiduciary liability insurance

Financial Planning Association (FPA)

Financial Privacy Rule

Form ADV

Form U-4

Gramm-Leach-Bliley Act (GLBA)

Integrity

Investment Advisor Registration Depository (IARD)

Investment Advisors Act of 1940

Investment Advisor Representative (IAR)

Investment discretion

Maloney Act of 1938

Mediation

Membership organization

Million Dollar Round Table (MDRT)

Model Prudent Man Rule Statute

NAPFA Fiduciary Oath

NAPFA-Registered Financial Advisor

National Association of Insurance Commissioners (NAIC)

National Association of Personal Financial Advisors (NAPFA)

National Association of Securities Dealers (NASD)

Normative ethics

North American Securities Administrators Association (NASAA)

Objectivity

Personal Financial Specialist (PFS)

Practice standards

Professionalism

Quasi-Certification

Rebating

Registered Financial Associate (RFA)

Registered Financial Consultant (RFC)

Registered Financial Planner (RFP)

Registered Investment Advisor (RIA)

Registered Representative

Rule 1120

Safeguards Rule

Securities Act of 1933

Securities Exchange Act of 1934

Securities and Exchange Commission (SEC)

Self-Regulatory Organization (SRO)

"Selling away"

Series 65 examination

Teleological

Uniform Investment Advisor Law Examination

Uniform Prudent Investor Act (UPIA)

Values

The Ethical Foundations of Financial Planning

Financial planners are faced with ethical choices in almost all aspects of their business. Consider the situation where an advisor recommends a product that has not been approved by the advisor's firm (e.g., broker-dealer). The advisor argues that the product is more suitable for the client than any particular product from the "approved product list." Does this action violate ethical and regulatory standards? What about a situation where an insurance agent uses commissions earned on the sale of life insurance to offset fees associated with writing a financial plan? Is this ethical? These are just two examples where a financial planner may innocently cross the line into unethical conduct. The first case is called "**selling-away**," and is a violation of Rule 3040, established by the **National Association of Securities Dealers (NASD),** a **self-regulatory organization (SRO)** that oversees stockbroker activities.[2] This rule requires NASD associated persons to obtain written approval from their firms before they sell any security. Although the advice may have been in the best interest of the client, the action still violates the rule, which is in place to ensure that clients are sold only products that meet the standards of the planner's broker-dealer. Selling-away can subject a broker-dealer to claims of product unsuitability, unnecessary fees, and regulatory sanctions.

The second case is an example of **rebating**, defined as the discounting or waiving of a commision by an agent to induce a client to purchase a security or insurance product. The essence of the situation described above is that the insurance agent was attempting to coerce the client into purchasing another product by offering a discount on either the service or the product. Rebating is both unethical and, in most states, is also illegal, because it might cause a planner to sell products that are not in the client's best interest to increase the planner's income or to entice a client to engage in additional services. Rebating can be a violation of NASD Rule 2470,[3] as well as numerous state insurance regulations.

As these two examples illustrate, the line that separates legal and ethical financial planning actions from those that are unethical and sometimes illegal is at times hard to distinguish. In order to fully understand how ethics, standards, regulations, and laws influence the daily life of financial planners, it is first necessary to define certain key terms. To begin with, it is essential to understand what the term **ethics** really means. According to Hansen, Rossberg, and Cramer, "ethics are suggested standards of conduct based on an agreed-upon set of values," where **values** are preferred attitudes and behaviors.[4] The study of ethics has its foundations in Western moral philosophy. Ethics, when viewed from the perspective of philosophers such as Aristotle, Locke, Kant, and Hume, can be categorized as either teleological or deontological.[5]

A **teleological** or consequential approach to ethics is based on relativism, where actions are deemed to be right or wrong based on the consequences of the actions. Sometimes this is refered to as "situational ethics." Acting in one's own interest is ethical from a teleological perspective as long as another party is not hurt or put at a disadvantage. Ethics from a **deontological** approach are based on absolutism, the concept of universally accepted rights and wrongs. The ethical perspective that enslavement is wrong is based on the notion that this action is intrinsically wrong at all times, regardless of the outcomes or consequences. Ethical codes used by financial planners tend to be based on a deontological foundation; however, everyone should be able to recognize that very few situations are universal in intent and outcome. In other words, right and wrong actions can be predetermined, and prescribed proceedings can be taken against a violator regardless of the outcome, but mitigating circumstances may affect the severity of the sanction or punishment. This ethical framework provides the only foundation for the practice management standards used in the industry today; in practice the application of ethical values tends to be more fluid.

A **practice standard** is defined as a behavior that is deemed "acceptable" by a certain segment of society or society as a whole, and is typically codified in a code of ethics or statement of standard practices. For the financial planning industry, practice standards reflect **normative ethics**, as defined by the governing bodies (such as the NASD) and membership organizations (such as the Financial Planning Association (FPA)) of the financial planning industry. Examples of this codification of ethics and standards are shown throughout the chapter. A normative standard signals what a financial planner should do in a given situation. Standards serve as benchmarks for ethical behavior. "Stealing from clients is wrong," is an example of a normative standard.

While nearly all financial planning rules and regulations have a deontological ethical foundation—that is, where practitioners and regulators have predetermined which activities are acceptable and which are not—many other situations are "judgment calls," meaning that a more teleological approach is warranted. To that end, practice standards can also be **descriptive**, where actions are "right" or "wrong" based on their outcomes (i.e., relativism). In order for a practice standard to come into existence and to be enforced, certain groups of people must agree on what is inherently right and wrong. This means that normative standards must be practiced. While it is not necessary for all practitioners and regulators to be in agreement with a standard, standards cannot be enforced if behaviors are evaluated solely on relative outcomes.

Federal Regulations

The financial world of the early 1900's was a wild and dangerous place. Practically anyone could provide advice and guidance to others about saving and investing. The lack of laws, rules, regulations, and general standards of practice made the saying "caveat emptor" (i.e., buyer beware) absolutely true. The lack of standards meant that frauds and rip-offs were almost as common as legitimate investment and financial advice activities. It was only during the aftermath of the stock market crash of October 1929 that policymakers, legitimate investment advisors, and citizens banded together to enact legislation to protect consumers against illegal, unethical, and fraudulent securities schemes. In effect, it was these early acts of regulation that helped codify the ethical standards that dominate today's financial planning profession.

The **Securities Act of 1933** (also known as the "Paper Act") was the first major securities legislation and set the foundation for the federal oversight[6] of securties trading. This law requires full disclosure to investors of any new security offered for sale.. **The Securities Exchange Act of** 1934 (also known as the "People's Act") was a major step forward in establishing ethical standards within the practice of corporate and personal finance. The 1934 Act was responsible for creating the **Securities and Exchange Commission (SEC)**, which was specifically established to regulate the securities markets so that the investing public would have a higher level of trust in the market system. Under the 1934 Act, publicly traded companies were required to provide more information to investors, including quarterly and annual reports. The 1934 Act was strengthened by the **Maloney Act of 1938.** The Maloney Act added Section 15A to the Securities Exchange Act of 1934, allowing for the establishment of registered securities associations to promote self-regulation of the securities industry. The primary outcome of the Maloney Act was the establishment of the NASD.

By the late 1930's, all securities markets in the United States were under federal regulation. Stock brokers and others who earned a commission on the purchase and sale of securities were regulated through the NASD, with oversight by the SEC. However, it was still possible for those who only charged a fee for service to avoid federal regulation. Up to that point, there were no practice standards in place for individuals who marketed investment advisor services for a fee. This changed in 1940 with the passage of the **Investment Advisors Act of 1940**, which has had the greatest impact on the way financial planning has been and is currently practiced. The Investment Advisors Act initially set the stage for all individuals who provide investment advice for a *fee* to be registered with the SEC; however, it left the regulation of broker-dealers in the hands of the NASD. The Investment Advisors Act created two new terms for those that provide investment advice for a fee: **Registered Investment Advisor (RIA)** and **Investment Advisor Representative (IAR)**. The definition of an investment advisor is found in Title 15 of the United States Code, and states that an:

> "Investment advisor is any person who, for compensation, engages in the business of advising others, either directly or through publications or writings, as to the value of securities or as to the advisability of investing in, purchasing, or selling securities, or who, for compensation and as part of a regular business, issues or promulgates analyses or reports concerning securities."[7]

Therefore, to be called an RIA a person or firm must meet at least one of three tests:

1. provide advice or analysis on securities either by making direct or indirect recommendations to clients or by providing research or opinions on securities or securities markets;

    2.   receive compensation in any form for the advice provided; or

    3.   engage in the regular business of providing advice on securities.

Exceptions to this test include, but are not limited to: (1) banks and bank holding companies; (2) lawyers, accountants and the like whose investment advice is solely incidental to their business; (3) publishers; and (4) persons whose advice is limited to direct obligations of the United States government.[8]

An IAR is defined as an individual who performs services on behalf of or works for an RIA. It may be possible for a person to be both an RIA and IAR. This would be true, for example, if the person was the sole owner of a corporation that was registered as an RIA. The owner would then need to be registered as an IAR.

The Investment Advisors Act of 1940 was amended in 1997. Starting in 1997, those advisors with assets under management less than $25 million are required to register with their state securities regulator, while those with assets greater than $25 million are allowed to register directly with the SEC. In addition to the $25 million rule, all of the following advisors must also register with the SEC:

- advisors to investment companies under the Investment Company Act of 1940;

- those that provide services in 30 or more states; and

- anyone eligible for an exemption by rules or orders under the Investment Advisors Act of 1940.

The main document in the registration process, **Form ADV**, is an advisor's most important document. This two-part form is about 75 pages long. Part I asks for information about the advisor's business, the persons who own or control the advisor, and whether the advisor or certain personnel have been sanctioned for violating the securities laws or other laws. Beginning in 2001, RIAs are required to register with their home state or the SEC electronically through an automated system called the **Investment Advisor Registration Depository (IARD)**. Once an IARD account has been established, Form ADV Part I can be accessed, completed, and updated (Part II is not yet available for electronic completion). If filed with the SEC, the advisor will be notified within 45 days after receipt of the Form ADV if the registration has been accepted or rejected. The SEC and the individual states rely on Part I to identify which investment advisors warrant more immediate examinations or those who may pose a risk to clients or the general public. Part II is a written disclosure statement (most often a brochure) that provides information about an advisor's business practices, fees, and conflicts of interest. Items that must be addressed in Part II include the following:

- education;
- certifications;
- types of investments;

- fees charged;

- methods of analysis;

- investment strategies; and

- descriptions of legal problems.

Part II, a disclosure statement, must be given to all clients and potential clients. Specifically, the Investment Advisors Act of 1940 requires delivery of a copy of Part II or a brochure containing comparable information to prospective clients, and that a copy of the document (or brochure) be offered annually to all clients. Figure 2.1 illustrates how information can be disclosed using a disclosure statement/brochure. Figure 2.2 provides an example of a letter of confirmation that can be used to document that required information was delivered to and received by the clients.

Writing Tip: Going beyond the Basics

In recent years, more financial planners have begun packaging their introductory materials on CDs. In addition to the materials presented in the financial plan, the software provides links to the planner's Internet home page, the home pages of relevant professional organizations, and other useful links. For example, one planner showed her innovation by providing clients with a 3½ inch floppy disk formatted with links to the Certified Financial Planner Board of Standards, Inc., and the regulatory complaints pages of the Securities and Exchange Commission (SEC). She also provided a link to find her Form ADV. The planner had enough confidence in her practice to highlight to clients exactly where to go to find information about her past practices. She was also smart in doing this because she was subliminally prompting clients to check out the competition as well. Be creative and innovative; but be sure that you have your compliance officer's approval.

It may be possible to provide investment advice for a fee but not be required to register as an RIA. Specifically, there are eight RIA exemptions allowed under the law. Those employed as bankers, lawyers, accountants, engineers, and teachers whose performance of investment services is solely incidental to the practice of his/her profession can ask to be exempted from registration requirements. Certain publishers whose reporting on securities is deemed incidental to their primary business may also request exemption. Advisors whose only clients are insurance companies, and those who have fewer than 15 total clients and do not hold themselves out publicly as investment advisors, may also be exempt from registration. In general, however, anyone not listed above who advises others for compensation must register. Failing to register may result in a penalty up to $10,000 and five years in jail.

Investment advisors are required to maintain and keep practice management and client records for at least five years. At a minimum, investment advisors must retain the following documents:

- receipts and disbursements journals;

- a general ledger;

Figure 2.1 Disclosure Statement/Brochure Example

DISCLOSURE STATEMENT - PERSONAL FINANCIAL COUNSELING

As a Registered Investment Advisor, our firm is required to file with the Securities and Exchange Commission and to make the information contained in that registration available to actual and prospective advisory clients.

This is a summary of information related to our personal financial review activity. Individuals may request a copy of our SEC registration. This information is frequently referred to as a "brochure."

DESCRIPTION OF OUR SERVICES

We provide various levels of comprehensive personal financial counseling for a fixed fee, as well as various specialized analyses billed on a time and disbursements basis. We do not provide continuous monitoring of securities for individuals nor do we manage accounts on a discretionary basis or hold personal securities or funds of any kind.

COMPREHENSIVE FINANCIAL REVIEW

Comprehensive personal financial advising is provided to clients following a written agreement and fee schedule. In general, the client agrees to complete our questionnaire and provide other relevant information and authorizations. We agree to prepare a written plan that describes the current situation, identifies needs and opportunities, and makes recommendations designed to help the client achieve his or her goals.

Comprehensive personal financial advising is primarily an analytical process designed to help the client articulate and quantify goals, organize financial data, identify needs and opportunities, and evaluate alternative courses of action. It includes an analysis of current net worth, income taxes, cash flow, investments, employee benefits, estate and gift tax planning, and risk management.

Attention is directed toward restructuring existing assets to achieve the planning objectives. For example, a plan might recommend that a particular security or securities be sold to realize a tax loss, provide diversification, or to change from a growth-related investment to an income-related investment.

While comprehensive financial counseling includes investment advice concerning securities, it also includes investment advice with respect to products that may not constitute "securities," such as certificates of deposit, life insurance, and annuities. It also takes into consideration tax and estate planning issues that may not constitute "investment advice."

FEE-ONLY FINANCIAL ADVISING

Many consumers are rightfully concerned that a professional advisor render services on a truly objective basis—not influenced by potential commissions. Therefore, all of our planning is performed on that basis. Each plan concludes with a summary of recommendations and an "Implementation Checklist."

If a client wishes to take action in any area that involves the purchase of additional services or financial products, these may or may not be items that our organization or its associates can offer. Clients generally wish to use the services of others for most items. However, where no other satisfactory relationship exists, we may be able to help. In such cases, a new and completely separate relationship is deemed to exist—one that is entirely at the discretion of the client to engage or discontinue.

Figure 2.1 Disclosure Statement/Brochure Example (cont'd)

SPECIALIZED FINANCIAL ANALYSIS

In addition to comprehensive financial counseling, we provide specialized services that focus on particular client needs. These services are provided on a time and disbursements basis, pursuant to a written agreement. The kinds of services listed below are representative of those requested by our clients:

      Education funding analysis
      Analysis of life, health, and disability coverages
      Estate liquidity and survivor income analysis
      Financial advising for closely held businesses
      Formal business plans with financial projections
      Business valuation and continuation planning
      Retirement income analysis and projection
      Retirement plan disbursement option analysis
      Employee benefit plan analysis
      Employer sponsored financial counseling
      Analysis of investment portfolios

FEES, REFUNDS, CANCELLATION, ARBITRATION

For a comprehensive plan, one-half of the fee is due upon receipt of the executed engagement letter and the balance is due upon delivery of the completed plan. A client may cancel and receive a full refund of our fee if we are notified in writing within five business days after signing an agreement, or at any time before we begin work on the plan. If cancellation occurs thereafter, we have the right to retain 50% of the fee. In the event of a dispute, binding arbitration is used to avoid any litigation.

In a time and disbursements engagement, we request a deposit based on one-half of our lowest estimate of costs to be incurred. However, if it appears during the course of the engagement that total costs will exceed the top end of the estimate, we will notify the client, and will incur costs above that point only with prior authorization. A client may cancel at any time and be responsible only for expenses incurred to that point.

TYPES OF PLANNING CLIENTS

Our planning services are provided primarily to individuals of the general public, professional persons, individual executives, and employees under employer sponsored programs as well as to business entities regarding the affairs of the company and its employee benefit plans.

TYPES OF SECURITIES EVALUATED

In a comprehensive plan, we will evaluate the appropriateness of any securities or other investments owned, proposed for ownership, or which we think could assist the client in achieving personal goals. Such investments may include, but are not limited to: equities; corporate debt; municipal bonds; government securities; options; commodities; certificates of deposit; life insurance; annuities; mutual funds; and limited partnership interests designed for certain tax benefits.

METHOD OF ANALYSIS AND INFORMATION SOURCES

While we do not primarily evaluate individual securities, we do keep abreast of general business conditions and changes in the law, taxation, and various investment and insurance products. To this end, members

Figure 2.1 Disclosure Statement/Brochure Example (cont'd)

of our staff review general business publications, tax services, technical journals, and other materials relevant to the services provided.

THE INVESTMENT STRATEGIES

All types of investment strategies are considered. However, we do not assume the responsibility of continuously monitoring the performance of client investments. Selection of an investment strategy is based on the resources, objectives, and risk tolerance of each individual client.

OUR PROFESSIONAL AFFILIATIONS

The officers and staff of the organization are very active in a variety of professional associations. These organizations provide continuing education and an exchange of planning techniques. The following list does not, however, constitute an endorsement by those associations: Academy of Financial Services; Association of Financial Counseling and Planning Educators; Australian Association of Financial Planners; CFP Board of Standards; FPA - Financial Professional Association; International Association of Registered Financial Consultants; Million Dollar Round Table; National Association of Estate Planners; National Association of Life Underwriters; National Institute of Finance; and the Society of Financial Service Professionals (formerly American Society of CLU & ChFC).

OUR BUSINESS AFFILIATIONS

Our organization is affiliated with an informal international network of financial planners located throughout the UNITED STATES, Australia, Malaysia, Bermuda and Canada. Our staff members participate actively in the development of training and practice management materials, and frequently participate in regional and national conferences.

Financial Planning Consultants has associated persons that are registered representatives of Amalgamated Financial Services, Inc.

INTEREST IN SECURITIES TRANSACTIONS

If clients purchase investments through one of our associated persons, acting as a registered representative of one of the above firms, that person will receive compensation, if any, for such transactions.

For those occasions when no broker relationship exists and where the client has elected not to place transactions with one of our registered representatives, we will suggest, at the client's request, individual brokers and their firms or financial institutions that provide brokerage services.

Our Internal Compliance Officer monitors the personal trading of securities by the officers of the corporation as well as selected employees to avoid conflicts of interest.

INTEREST IN INSURANCE TRANSACTIONS

In the course of our planning, we may recommend the purchase of insurance. Clients may select our firm or an affiliated person to act as an agent who would receive compensation, if any, for such transactions. For those occasions when no agent or broker relationship exists, and where the client has elected not to place transactions with one of our associates, we will suggest, at the client's request, individual agents or agencies that can provide the recommended insurance product.

Figure 2.1 Disclosure Statement/Brochure Example (cont'd)

POSSIBLE CONFLICTS OF INTEREST

Whenever our firm, any associated person, or any family member would receive economic benefit from the transactions of clients, whether or not recommended in our plan, a "conflict of interest" exists. In all such cases we advise our clients of the circumstances, that commissions could be received, and emphasize their freedom to do business elsewhere.

THE FIRM'S HISTORY

Financial Planning Consultants, Inc., was founded in 1969 to extend estate planning and business consulting services to individuals, corporations, and institutions on a fee basis—without any requirement that they purchase financial products.

Its personnel became involved in the development of computer software for financial analysis in 1972. The firm continues to market these programs to financial advisors, accountants, estate planners, and trust departments throughout the UNITED STATES under the trade names of ProPlan, Education Funding Analysis, Business System (valuation and funding), Retirement Plan Analysis and the financial Text Library System.

Offices were originally located at 2113 Central Avenue, Middletown, Ohio. In 1977, the firm renovated a two-story building with training facilities located at 2507 North Verity Parkway, now known as the Financial Planning Building.

Financial Planning Consultants, Inc., employs individuals with various backgrounds and education. For those individuals that provide financial counseling services, in a direct or non-direct manner, we generally require either a college degree or extensive experience in related fields, such as business, finance, insurance, employee benefits, or financial services.

We require an extensive program (far beyond the minimal requirements of professional societies) of continuing education for all persons involved in financial counseling or advisory activity. The principals of the firm are:

Edwin P. Morrow:
Centre College of Kentucky, 1957-60
University of Louisville Law School, 1962-64
Chartered Life Underwriter, 1968
Certified Financial Planner, 1982
Chartered Financial Consultant, 1984
Registered Financial Consultant, 1990
President of Financial Planning Consultants, Inc., since November, 1969
Admitted to the Registry of Financial Planning Practitioners (IAFP), at its founding, 1984; Board of Governors, National Center for Financial Education, since 1985. Director of the Institute of Certified Financial Planners 1986-1988.
Academy of Financial Services, an academic association, Director 1989-1992
Practitioner in Residence, 1990-92 Finance Department, Wright State University; Purdue University, 1999

Figure 2.1 Disclosure Statement/Brochure Example (cont'd)

Other Named Individuals
Education
Specialized studies
Designations
Short bio including significant achievements

The above named individuals are shareholders of Financial Planning Consultants, Inc., serve on the Board of Directors, and are responsible for the affairs of the firm.

The above information is provided so that you might be aware of our background, operations, and personnel. If you have any questions after reading this, please do not hesitate to ask.

Please indicate your receipt of this for our records:

Received by: _____ Date: _____

Sincerely,

Source: Ed Morrow, Financial Planning Consultants, Middletown, Ohio, 2005.© Used with permission.

- order memoranda;

- bank records;

- bills and statements;

- financial statements;

- written communications and agreements (including electronic transmissions);

- list of discretionary accounts;

- advertising;

- personal transactions of representatives and principals;

- client records:

  - powers granted by clients,

  - disclosure statements,

  - solicitors' disclosure statements,

  - performance claims,

- customer information forms and suitability information, and

- written supervisory procedures.

The amount of archiving and reporting is increased dramatically if an advisor is determined to have custody over client assets. **Custody** is defined as having direct or indirect access to, or a legal responsibility for, a client's funds or securities. Generally, independent investment advisors are advised against taking custody of client assets. If an advisor is also a custodian, the advisor must prove that client assets are safeguarded. The role of the advisor as custodian must also be disclosed to clients. Furthermore, the custodian must submit to random audits by an accountant. Custodians must maintain and keep the following documents, in addition to the ones already listed above:

- journals of securities transactions and movements;

- separate client ledgers;

- copies of confirmations;

- records showing each client's interest in a security; and

- client purchases and sales history.

In addition to custodial responsibilities, many financial professionals may also face the possibility of having **investment discretion** over client's assets. Financial professionals are said to have investment discretion if they are authorized to determine the disposition of assets (e.g., what securities shall be purchased or sold) for the account of another person, whether or not another person may have responsibility for such investment decisions, or if they exercise such influence with respect to the purchase and sale of securities that they may as well have executed the transaction themselves.[9]

While a custodial relationship must be disclosed to a client prior to taking possession of an asset, discretionary investment management (or "trading authority") must be agreed to and typically requested by the client before any trading can begin. In other words, there is a very fine line between the two legal arrangements. "Custodian" means that a financial professional has physical possession of an asset, but must follow the directions of the client as to its disposition, whereas "discretion" means that the financial profession can dictate the disposition of an asset but probably does not have possession of it. Note, however, that in either instance the financial advisor has increased fiduciary responsibly.

Figure 2.2 Brochure Receipt Letter

Mr. Jonathan T. Sample
111 East Avenue
Dayton, OH 45402-4300

Dear Jon and Annie:

The federal securities laws require us to provide you with the latest version of our "brochure" which has been prepared in accordance with the Investment Advisor Act of 1940. Each year we must offer or deliver a current version of this brochure, even though there may be no substantial changes in our services or personnel.

If you have not already done so, please read this material and advise us if you would like additional information or perhaps a clarification of any item. Please acknowledge your receipt below:

By: _____   Date: _____

Please return this letter to us, as we are required to keep a copy in our file.

Sincerely,

Edwin P. Morrow, RFC, CFP®

Source: Ed Morrow, Financial Planning Consultants, Middletown, Ohio, 2005.© Used with permission.

State Regulations

The regulation of securities and investment advisors by individual states predates the creation of the federal Securities and Exchange Commission by more than two decades. Regulation of securities offerings, the licensing of broker-dealers and their agents, and investment advisor registration by individual states are governed by what are known as **blue sky laws**. The term "blue sky" refers to speculative schemes that have no more substance than so many feet of blue sky.[10]

The first modern blue sky law was adopted by the state of Kansas in 1911 and served as the nationwide model for state securities regulation. As a result of this pioneering work, the **North American Securities Administrators Association (NASAA)** was organized in the state of Kansas in 1919. Currently, NASAA membership consists of 67 state, provincial, and territorial securities administrators in the 50 states, the District of Columbia, the United States Virgin Islands, Puerto Rico, Canada, and Mexico. NASAA moved its corporate office from Topeka to Washington, D.C., in 1987.

Each state has its own unique laws governing the registration of investment advisors and Investment Advisor Representatives. In general, however, states require advisors to complete a Form ADV, obtain a passing score on a competency examination, pay a fee, and provide a bond, especially if the advisor takes custodianship of client assets. In addition, a **Form U-4** application must be filed for each Investment Advisor Representative that provides services on behalf of an advisor. Most states require an investment advisor to pass a **Series 65 exam**, also known as the **Uniform Investment Advisor Law Examination**. This test, which is administered by the NASAA, ensures that those who hold themselves out to be investment advisors have a sound understanding of securities laws, rules, and regulations.

Financial planners who use insurance products to implement recommendations also fall under state regulatory authority. The **National Association of Insurance Commissioners (NAIC)** is the national organization of state insurance regulators that develops uniform insurance regulations and agent examinations. The NAIC was created in 1871 to provide regulatory oversight of insurance companies operating in more than one state. Authority was then given to the NAIC and state regulators to provide more comprehensive consumer protection by requiring anyone selling life, health, or property insurance to be licensed in their respective state of operation.

Exhibit 2.1 lists the most common types of insurance licenses held by financial planners that use insurance products. There are eight licenses requiring an examination and six licenses that require registration with a state regulator. Note that it is possible to obtain a combined license that covers life, accident and health, property and allied lines, and casualty and allied lines insurance. If this combined license is not obtained, a financial planner will be required to take individual examinations to obtain each license separately.

Exhibit 2.1 Common Types of Insurance Licenses

Licenses That Require An Examination	Licenses Not Requiring An Examination
Life	Variable Contracts*
Accident and Health	Travel
Property and Allied Lines	Auto Club
Casualty and Allied Lines	Viatical Settlements
Personal Lines	Reinsurance Intermediary
Crop	Excess Lines
Title	
Bail Bond	

*Financial planners who sell variable contracts must be licensed through the NASD and have a life agent license.

In order to obtain an insurance agent's license, a person must meet the following eight criteria:

1. be at least 18 years of age;

2. submit a NAIC Uniform Application to his or her state insurance regulator;

3. submit an application fee;

4. notify the state regulator if an insurance license is held in another state;

5. provide evidence of Series 6 or Series 7 NASD registration if selling variable contracts;

6. pass a licensing examination;

7. secure an insurance company certification showing where business will be transacted; and

8. meet ongoing continuing education (CE) requirements.

Insurance license continuing education requirements are set forth by the state that holds the primary licensing authority for the agent, typically the state of residence, and can vary greatly by state. For example, the Commonwealth of Virginia requires that an agent with one license complete 16 credit hours every two years of which two hours must be in laws and regulations, and if the agent holds two or more licenses then the agent must complete 24 credit hours every two years. Other state-specific restrictions may apply (e.g., who provides the training, available carry-over hours for additional training completed during the period, etc.).

Self-Regulatory Organizations

The Maloney Act of 1938 made it possible for broker-dealers and other organizations involved in the financial services industry to band together to create one or more **self-regulatory organizations (SROs)**. As the name implies, SROs are managed and funded by firms participating in a particular segment of the securities markets. The primary purpose of an SRO is to provide consumers with protection against fraud while providing a mechanism to enforce rules and standards as developed by the SRO. All SROs allowed by the Maloney Act of 1938 are subject to oversight by the SEC. Exhibit 2.2 lists some of the largest SROs in the United States. Notable in its absence is an SRO for the financial planning profession. Currently, no SRO exists to provide self-regulation to those who specifically practice financial planning.

Exhibit 2.2 United States Self-Regulatory Organizations

SRO	Acronym	Industry Members
National Association of Securities Dealers	NASD	Broker-dealers
American Stock Exchange	AMEX	Securities firms
Chicago Board Options Exchange	CBOE	Options trading firms
Municipal Securities Rulemaking Board	MSRB	Municipal bond dealers
National Futures Association	NFA	Derivatives trading firms
New York Stock Exchange	NYSE	Securities trading firms
Options Clearing Corporation	OCC	Options trading firms

The NASD is, by far, the most powerful SRO that has an interest in financial service activities. The NASD oversees the activities of more than 5,100 brokerage firms, approximately 99,000 branch offices, and nearly 675,000 registered securities representatives (stockbrokers). The NASD licenses individuals to sell securities, admits firms to the industry, writes rules to govern stockbroker and firm activities, conducts regulatory and ethical compliance examinations, and disciplines those who fail to comply with rules. The NASD also oversees and regulates equity, corporate bond, futures, and options trading. In addition, the NASD operates the largest securities dispute resolution forum, and according to statistics reported by the NASD, the organization processes over 8,000 arbitrations and 1,000 mediations every year. Anyone who sells securities for a commission is required to obtain a securities license. There are numerous licenses available and each allows a specific type of activity. Exhibit 2.3 lists the most commonly held securities licenses that can be obtained through the NASAA and NASD.[11]

A person who is licensed with the NASD is known as a Registered Representative (or "Registered Rep"). A **Registered Representative** is a person associated with a broker-dealer firm who is engaged in the investment banking or securities business. This definition can include those working in a solicitation role and those who are engaged in the training of persons associated with a broker-dealer. (Note, however, that anyone acting in a training or supervisory role would also have to pass an additional licensing exam (e.g., the General Securities Principal exam, or Series 24).)

Registered Representatives are affiliated with broker-dealer firms and, to be eligible for a license, must be sponsored by a broker-dealer. The typical Registered Representative engages in arm's length transactions with clients by executing customer orders to purchase and sell securities. As such, Registered Representatives are required to hold either a Series 6 and/or Series 7 NASD license.

Exhibit 2.3 Securities Licenses and Testing Formats

Securities License	Testing Format	
	Testing Time	**Number and Format of Questions**
Investment Company Products/ Variable Contracts Limited Representative - (NASD Series 6)	2 hours and 15 minutes	100 multiple choice questions
General Securities Representative – (NASD Series 7)	6 hours total; 3 hours for each of two parts	250 multiple choice questions; two parts of 125 questions each
Uniform Securities Agent State Law Examination - (Series 63) (NASAA)	1 hour and 15 minutes	65 multiple choice questions
Uniform Investment Advisor Law Examination - (Series 65) (NASAA)	3 hours	130 multiple choice questions
Uniform Combined State Law Examination - (Series 66) (NASAA)	2 hours and 30 minutes	100 multiple choice questions

The difference between an RIA and a Registered Representative can sometimes get confusing. RIAs typically charge a fee for their advice. Registered Representatives usually execute transactions for a commission. In general, financial planners who provide investment advice to others and who are employed by another person or firm must be registered with the SEC or licensed with the NASD. In some cases, a financial planner must be registered and licensed with both regulatory agencies. Figure 2.3 provides a comparison of Investment Advisor Representatives and Registered Representatives.

Professional Financial Services Organizations

The primary role of the SEC, NASAA, and NASD is to provide regulatory oversight of those who provide investment advice to consumers through the process of registering and licensing individual practitioners. However, regulatory agencies and SROs are not professional organizations. The SEC, for example, makes this distinction clear by prohibiting those that are registered as investment advisors from using the initials "RIA" as a marketing or certification mark.

Professional organizations differ from regulatory entities in that participation is voluntary in a professional organization, whereas adherence to the rules and standards of a regulatory entity is required. People join professional organizations for a number of reasons, including continuing education, the opportunity to use a designation or certification, and camaraderie. Professional financial services organizations can be classified into one of four types: (1) credentialing organizations; (2) quasi-credentialing organizations; (3) designation organiza-

Figure 2.3 Investment Advisor and Registered Representatives Compared

INVESTMENT ADVISOR REPRESENTATIVE	REGISTERED REPRESENTATIVE
Purpose Provides investment advice or manages securities portfolios.	*Purpose* Provides advice on securities and executes transactions on behalf of the brokerage customer.
Primary Service Formulates an overall investment plan, taking into account all investment and asset information of the client.	*Primary Service* Handles orders, investment research, and plans investment activity in regard to specific investment account.
Firm Registration IAR affiliated with advisory firm registered with SEC or state.	*Firm Registration* RR affiliated with brokerage firm registered with NASD and state.*
Individual Licensing Most states require individual license to provide investment advice.	*Individual Licensing* Licensed by NASD and states. Has right to sell securities products only.
Examination No examination process required by the SEC; state specific examination such as Series 65 generally required unless waived for private certification such as the CFP® designation.	*Examination* Must successfully complete examination process administered by NASD for licensing; usually Series 6 or 7 exams.
Legal Responsibility Fiduciary duty to client. Acting as a fiduciary requires an IAR to place the client's interest above his or her own and not favor one client over another. In addition, the IAR must: render impartial advice; make suitable recommendations in light of the client's objectives, needs, and financial position; exercise significant degree of care in making representations and disclosures; and have an adequate basis in fact for recommendations, representations, or investment projections.**	*Legal Responsibility* Suitability requirement to brokerage customer. Also, there is a duty to deal fairly and honestly with clients, and to disclose material information about any recommendation. Ongoing fiduciary duty and extensive disclosure requirements of conflicts of interest and qualifications, required for an IAR, are usually not required for a RR. In certain fact-specific situations, however, a fiduciary duty may apply.

* Sometimes a brokerage firm may be dually registered as an advisory firm, and its agents dually licensed to provide both advisory and brokerage services. Some broker-dealers permit financial planners who are affiliated with them to additionally register separate advisory firms for purposes of providing independent financial planning services.

** The CFP *Code of Ethics and Professional Responsibility,* like most codes of ethics, requires compliance with applicable laws. (See Rule 606.) In addition, the *Code of Ethics* may have higher standards of professional conduct, including disclosure of material information, than is required under securities laws. (See Rules related to the Principle of Fairness: Rules 401, 402, 403, and 404.)

Reprinted with permission by the Financial Planning Association, "Investment Adviser Representatives vs. Registered Representatives," at: http://www.fpanet.org/member/practice_center/practice_services/pm/RIAvsRR.cfm.

tions; and (4) membership organizations. As of January 2005, there were 87 professional financial services organizations in the United States and Canada. Combined, these organizations offered almost 90 professional certifications and designations.

A **certification** organization is one that validates that a financial planner has met a minimum qualification and knowledge level. Certification is generally granted only after a practitioner has met stringent criteria based on experience and obtained a passing score on a knowledge competency examination. While participation in a certification organization is voluntary, the right to use a certification mark is restricted only to those that maintain good standing with the certifying body. Almost all certification organizations require members to maintain their knowledge through continuing education. One of the oldest financial services certification organizations is the American College, which was founded in 1927 to provide education and certification to those in the insurance industry. The American College created, and to this day maintains, the **Chartered Life Underwriter (CLU)** certification. The College also certifies financial planners through their **Chartered Financial Consultant (ChFC)** certification.

The certification organization most closely associated with the financial planning profession is the the Certified Financial Planner Board of Standards, Inc. (CFP Board). The CFP Board was established in 1985 to "benefit the public by establishing and enforcing education, examination, experience and ethics requirements for CFP® professionals."[12] In order to obtain the right to use the CFP® mark a financial planner must meet five requirements:

1. Before applying for the CFP® certification examination, one needs to complete educational requirements set by the CFP Board in one of three ways:

    a. Complete a CFP Board-registered education program from one of 285 academic programs at colleges and universities across the country.

    b. If eligible, apply for challenge status. Academic degrees and credentials that fulfill the educational requirements include:

        •   Certified Public Accountant (CPA) — inactive license acceptable;

        •   Licensed attorney — inactive license acceptable;

        •   Chartered Financial Analyst® (CFA®);

        •   Doctor of Business Administration;

        •   Chartered Financial Consultant (ChFC);

        •   Ph.D. in business or economics; or

        •   Chartered Life Underwriter (CLU).

c.   Request a transcript review. Certain industry credentials recognized by the CFP Board, or the successful completion of upper-division level college courses, may satisfy some or all of the educational requirements set by the CFP Board. (Beginning in January of 2007, a bachelor's degree, in any field of study or program, will be required to obtain CFP® certification.)

2.   Pass the CFP® certification examination. The comprehensive examination tests the candidate's ability to apply financial planning knowledge to client situations. The 10-hour exam is divided into three sessions, and all questions are multiple choice. The exam is administered three times a year— generally on the third Friday and Saturday of March, July, and November. There is currently a $595 examination fee.

3.   Meet an experience requirement. At least three years of qualifying full-time work experience is required for certification. Qualifying experience includes work that can be categorized into one of the six primary elements of the personal financial planning process. Experience can be gained in a number of ways including working on any portion of the financial planning process, supervising others who do planning, or teaching financial planning.

4.   Adhere to the CFP Board of Standards, Inc., *Code of Ethics and Professional Responsibility* and pass a background check. After candidates have met the education, examination, and work experience requirements, they must disclose past or pending litigation or agency proceedings and agree to abide by the CFP Board's *Code of Ethics and Professional Responsibility* and *Financial Planning Practice Standards*.[13] A background check will also be conducted.

5.   Pay certification fees. A one-time, non-refundable initial certification application fee of $100 for the background checks and a biennial certification fee of $360 will be charged.

Another highly esteemed certification is the **Chartered Financial Analyst (CFA)** certification offered by the CFA Institute (formerly known as the Association for Investment Management and Research (AIMR)). Those holding a CFA certification must pass three examinations administered by the CFA Institute. This professional certification is an appropriate designation for someone who is most interested in investment management and financial analyst work. The CFA study materials do not encompass the full range of financial planning. Those with a CFA designation must have three years of experience working in an investment decision-making capability, join the CFA Institute, and abide by its code of ethics.

There are several quasi-certification organizations that serve the interests of financial planners. **Quasi-certifications** are those that are based on a planner showing proof of completing another recognized certification or proving attainment of education through an accredited college or university. The American Institute of Certified Public Accounts (AICPA) allows CPAs who specialize in financial planning the opportunity to obtain the **Personal Financial Specialist (PFS)** designation. This certificate requires CPAs to have at least 250 hours of experience per year in personal financial planning. The examination requirement, necessary for all certifications, is fulfilled by completion of the CPA education requirement. The **Registered Financial Consultant (RFC)**, which is offered by the International Association of Registered Financial Consultants (IARFC), is another example of a quasi-certification. The RFC emphasizes continuing education rather than a one-time examination. The IARFC waives its own examination requirement for financial planners that can show three years of experience and completion of a recognized financial planning certification, such as the CFP® certification or the CLU certification. Planners with fewer than three years of experience may obtain a **Registered Financial Associate (RFA)** certification after completing educational requirements from a registered college or university academic program.

Designation organizations make up another category of professional organizations. In order to obtain a designation, a person simply needs to meet standards as established by the designation granting board. Designations differ from certifications in that one need not pass an examination to obtain a designation, but an examination must be passed to obtain a certification. The **Accredited Business Accountant (ABA)** is an example of a designation. This designation is awarded by the Accreditation Council for Accountancy & Taxation to individuals who have demonstrated technical proficiency in financial accounting, compilation services, accounting, taxation, business law, and ethics. The **Registered Financial Planner (RFP)** mark is another example of a designation. The RFP is awarded by the Registered Financial Planners Institute. Members of the organization must have a college degree, license, or a minimum of 75 classroom hours of financial planning education from a college, university, or preparatory school with a passing grade and a minimum of two years experience in their respective field. RFPs must also receive 15 hours of continuing education every three years.

Membership organizations make up the last important category of professional financial services organizations. Membership organizations are voluntary associations of individuals with shared interests, practice management techniques, and practice management objectives. Generally, membership organizations do not offer certifications or designations. The **Financial Planning Association (FPA)** is the largest pure financial planning membership organization in the United States. Anyone may join the FPA by paying an annual fee and agreeing to abide by the organization's *Code of Ethics*. Thus, members need not be financial planners. Some membership organizations are voluntary but open only by invitation. The **Million Dollar Round Table** (MDRT) is an example of a membership group that has stringent restrictions on who may join the organization. This group is made up of primarily very financially successful insurance agents and brokers.

Some organizations do not fit neatly into any one category. The **National Association of Personal Financial Advisors (NAPFA)** is such an example. NAPFA is an organization established to further the cause of "fee-only" financial planning. NAPFA has several categories of membership, and in general, anyone who pays a membership fee and agrees to abide by the group's Code of Ethics may join. But in order to be a **NAPFA-Registered Financial Advisor**, one must meet several additional standards, which makes the organization more like a quasi-credentialing organization than a pure membership organization. Full NAPFA members must agree to be bound by the NAPFA *Code of Ethics*, Fiduciary Oath, and Standards of Membership and Affiliation. Additionally, members must meet the following standards:

1. Hold a bachelor's degree, in any discipline, from an accredited institution of higher learning.

2. Possess specialized education or training with a minimum of three (3) credits (at least 36 hours) of formal academic course work in each of the following five areas: (1) income tax planing; (2) estate planning; (3) retirement planning; (4) investments; and (5) risk management. This requirement may be satisfied by completion of a graduate or undergraduate degree in financial planning from an accredited institution, or by attainment of any of the following credentials: CFP®; ChFC; CPA; or PFS.

3. Obtain a minimum of 60 hours of approved continuing education every two years, and attest to completion of this requirement and submit documentation no later than February 15th of the required reporting cycle.

4. Offer comprehensive financial planning services to consumers. This means offering or supervising others who offer consultation in all areas of comprehensive financial planning to his/her clients. This requirement does not imply that every client must receive comprehensive financial planning services, but only that such services are made available by the member to clients. NAPFA defines comprehensive financial planning advice to require consideration of each of the following areas for a client: income tax planning; cash flow; retirement planning; estate planning; investments; risk management, and any special needs planning. NAPFA-Registered Financial Advisors are required to attest to the continuing availability of comprehensive services in each annual membership renewal.

5. Applicants for NAPFA-Registered Financial Advisor or Provisional Member status must submit a comprehensive financial plan for peer review. The plan, which must have been prepared within the last 12 months prior to submission of the application, must address all of the following factors: income tax planning; cash flow; retirement planning; estate planning; investments; risk management; and any special needs planning. The plan must apply a comprehensive approach to advisory services and include: collection and assessment of all relevant data from the client; identification of client goals; identification of client financial problems; provision of recommendations; assistance in implementation of the recommendations; and the offer of periodic review. The plan must also be the author's original work product and follow current guidelines. The applicant has full accountability and responsibility for the plan. It may reflect an actual client case or a fictional case—including a plan based on a NAPFA-provided case study.

6. The individual must have had at least 36 months of experience being primarily engaged in the provision of comprehensive financial planning services. This experience must have been attained within the past 60 months, and must include the most recent 12 months.

Fiduciary Rules

A **fiduciary** includes anyone who provides financial services and acts in a position of trust on behalf of, or for the benefit of, a third party.[14] Titles signaling a fiduciary capacity include trustee, executor, administrator, registrar of stocks and bonds, transfer agent, guardian, assignee, receiver, or custodian. But generally, a financial planning fiduciary is anyone who: (1) provides specific recommendations regarding securities; (2) is paid to provide ongoing financial advice; or (3) works with unsophisticated clients that rely on the advisor's advice. A financial planner becomes a fiduciary when the advice given to a client becomes comprehensive and continuous.[15]

Defining who is a fiduciary and which fiduciary responsibilities are applicable when working with clients has a long history in the United States. Fiduciary standards, also known as prudence standards, can be traced back to a landmark lawsuit is 1830.[16] The ruling stated that trustees should "observe how men of prudence, discretion and intelligence manage their own affairs, not in regard to speculation, but in regard to the permanent disposition of their funds, considering the probable income, as well as the probable safety of the capital to be invested." This became the foundation of **The Model Prudent Man Rule Statute** that was adopted in 1942. The "prudent man" standard is based on the following statement: "The trustee shall observe the standards in dealing with the trust assets that would be observed by a prudent man dealing with the property of another ..." In 1959, the "prudent man rule" was restated to include the following statement: "In making investments of trust funds the trustee is under a duty to the beneficiary ... to make such investments and only such investments as a prudent man would make of his own property having in view the preservation of the estate and the amount and regularity of the income to be derived ...."[17]

The **Uniform Prudent Investor Act (UPIA)**, as adopted in 1994, was a further update of the prudent man statute. While the Act is primarily concerned with the management of trust and foundation assets, most states apply the Act much more broadly. As such, any financial planner who is also acting as a fiduciary will find that the Act is applicable. Investment professionals who advise charities and pensions also fall under the scope of the UPIA. The Act specifically states that "in making investments of trust funds the trustee of a charitable trust is under a duty similar to that of the trustee of a private trust." The **Employee Retirement Income Security Act (ERISA)**, the federal regulatory scheme for corporate pension trusts enacted in 1974, also requires investment professionals to follow the UPIA through the prudence standard of ERISA. The Supreme Court of the United States has stated: "ERISA's legislative history confirms that the Act's fiduciary responsibility provisions 'codify and make applicable to [ERISA] fiduciaries certain principles developed in the evolution of the law of trusts.'"[18]

The UPIA also applies to executors, conservators, and guardians of property. The UPIA has five fundamental components (shown as written in the text of the Act[19]):

1. "The standard of prudence is applied to any investment as part of the total portfolio, rather than to individual investments. In the trust setting the term "portfolio" embraces all the trust's assets.

2. The tradeoff in all investing (i.e., between risk and return) is identified as the fiduciary's central consideration.

3. All categorical restrictions on types of investments have been abrogated; the trustee can invest in anything that plays an appropriate role in achieving the risk/return objectives of the trust and that meets the other requirements of prudent investing.

4. The long familiar requirement that fiduciaries diversify their investments has been integrated into the definition of prudent investing.

5. The much criticized former rule of trust law forbidding the trustee to delegate investment and management functions has been reversed. Delegation is now permitted, subject to safeguards."

The UPIA requires a trustee to adhere to the following strict rules when making investments:

1. "A trustee shall invest and manage trust assets as a prudent investor would, by considering the purposes, terms, distribution requirements, and other circumstances of the trust. In satisfying this standard, the trustee shall exercise reasonable care, skill, and caution.

2. A trustee's investment and management decisions respecting individual assets must be evaluated not in isolation but in the context of the trust portfolio as a whole, and as a part of an overall investment strategy having risk and return objectives reasonably suited to the trust.

3. Among circumstances that a trustee must consider in investing and managing trust assets are any of the following that are relevant to the trust or its beneficiaries:

    a. general economic conditions,

    b. the possible effect of inflation or deflation,

    c. the expected tax consequences of investment decisions or strategies,

    d. the role that each investment or course of action plays within the overall trust portfolio, which may include financial assets, interests in closely held enterprises, tangible and intangible personal property, and real property,

e. the expected total return from income and the appreciation of capital,

f. other resources of the beneficiaries,

g. needs for liquidity, regularity of income, and preservation or appreciation of capital, and

h. an asset's special relationship or special value, if any, to the purposes of the trust or to one or more of the beneficiaries.

4. A trustee shall make a reasonable effort to verify facts relevant to the investment and management of trust assets.

5. A trustee may invest in any kind of property or type of investment consistent with the standards of the UPIA.

6. A trustee who has special skills or expertise, or is named trustee in reliance upon the trustee's representation that the trustee has special skills or expertise, has a duty to use those special skills or expertise."

The effect of the UPIA on financial planners is potentially significant. The Act requires anyone who falls under the scope of the Act to act in the best interest of the client. Specific duties include: being objective; monitoring investments; investigating investments; diversifying portfolios; maintaining loyalty to the client; remaining impartial; reducing costs to maximize portfolio efficiency; and maintaining regulatory compliance. These are the minimum requirements a "prudent person" would expect of a financial planner.

The anti-fraud provisions of the Investment Advisors Act of 1940 clearly imply that investment advisors must act as fiduciaries when dealing with clients. Because of this, investment advisors may also fall under the scope of the UPIA, and therefore as fiduciaries are expected to:

1. "Hold the client's interest above all other matters.

2. Use the highest standards of care when working with clients.

3. Avoid conflicts of interest.

4. If conflicts of interest cannot be avoided, be diligent in disclosing such information to all interested parties.

5. Disclose compensation methods.

6. Ensure client confidentiality.

7. Select broker-dealers based on their ability to provide the best execution of trades for accounts where the advisor has authority to select the broker-dealer.

8. Make recommendations based on a reasonable inquiry into a client's investment objectives, financial situation, and other factors."

The burden of proof regarding a breach of fiduciary duty always lies with the advisor. Financial planners individually, as well as the firms they work for, can be held financially liable for a breach of fiduciary duty. In some cases, a financial planner can also face criminal charges for a fiduciary breach.

The fiduciary standards required by the SEC apply only to those individuals who are RIAs and RIA representatives at the federal level (although almost all states tend to follow the federal guidelines, making the rules *de facto* universal). However, the SEC exempts broker-dealers and broker-dealer representatives from the fiduciary and ethics rules. Stockbrokers are required to meet only three standards when working with clients. First, the NASD requires the broker to know a client's investment goals and objectives. Second, investment recommendations must be suitable to meet the client's objectives. Third, trades must be made accurately. Based on these standards, stockbrokers currently are not considered to be fiduciaries. On the other hand, financial planners are almost always considered to be fiduciaries. Under SEC rules, *stockbrokers cannot call themselves financial planners*. They may, however, use terms such as financial consultant or wealth manager. As such, stockbrokers are exempt from most disclosure rules. Brokers need only disclose that brokerage accounts are different from managed advisory accounts, and that the broker may receive incentive income from third parties.

Rules Governing Communication

Special consideration must be given to all communication from financial professionals to the public regardless of whether the recipient of the communication is an actual client. The rationale behind this is that an implied level of knowledge is given to a person who is credentialed or licensed to practice a certain type of business. The manner in which a financial professional conducts business (e.g., insurance agent, Registered Representative, RIA) dictates the guidelines and regulations for public communication and advertising.

The NAIC defines advertising as any material designed to create public interest in a product, or induce the public to purchase, increase, modify, reinstate, borrow on, surrender, replace, or retain a policy.[20] Advertising under this broad definition includes everything from business cards to brochures and also includes any other communication used to enhance sales. The language used in such advertising pieces must be clear, easily understood, and not worded in such a way as to mislead the reader or misrepresent the product. Though the NAIC is working on nationalizing some of the requirements, currently the individual states control the maintenance schedule requirements for the advertising file that must be kept by agents and insurance companies. Holding requirements range from two or three years on the lower end to as much as seven to 10 years on the upper end.

The NASD also defines advertising very broadly. Anything that is likely to make its way into the hands of a consumer is considered advertising. This includes newspapers, radio and television ads, signs and billboard messages, and voice recordings. The key to whether information will be considered advertising is the level of control the purveyor of the information has over who receives it. In the examples above, the purveyor or publisher of the information has no control over who sees and reads the advertisement.

The other form of written communication with the public is sales literature, defined as any written communication distributed to customers or the general public upon request—meaning that the publisher has some control over who is receiving the information. This type of communication includes research reports, form letters, and educational seminar materials. Whether the communication is classified as advertising or sales literature, the NASD requires the materials to be approved by a registered principal of a NASD member firm prior to distribution.[21]

All pieces of broker-dealer advertising (including electronic advertising) must also be filed with the NASD. The exception is prospectuses and other similar documents used in conjunction with the offering of securities that have already been filed with the SEC. In addition to the approval and filing requirements, written communication pieces must be kept on file by the issuing party for a period of not less than three years from the initial use date, and must include the name of the people who prepared and approved its use.

Of course when it comes to the last word concerning public communication for the purposes of solicitation or facilitation of financial transactions, the practitioner must look to the SEC. According to the SEC it is unlawful for any person to use the mail or any other form of interstate commerce (including telephone and email) to employ manipulative or deceptive practices in conjunction with the purchase or sale of any security.

Regulations do not stop with written communication; telephone and electronic communication are also regulated. In addition to their other responsibilities, most SROs and some other membership organizations also control telephone communication in accordance with the Telephone Consumer Protection Act of 1991. This Act (administered by the Federal Communication Commission (FCC)) protects consumers from unwanted telephone calls for the purpose of soliciting business. Specifically, it limits the hours that a person may be called (8:00 a.m. to 9:00 p.m. local time), and requires the maintenance of a "Do Not Call" list. However, exceptions exist for parties who have already established a working relationship and the recipient of the call has given prior permission.

For electronic communication, the SEC, FCC, and the FTC have banded together to attempt to control the amount and content of email communication and solicitation. The SEC requires that email communications between broker-dealers (or other financial intermediaries) and their clients or the general public be archived. The SEC's authority to enact this requirement is grounded in the Securities Exchange Act of 1934. Rules 17a-3 and 17a-4 of this Act require financial intermediaries to create, and preserve in an easily accessible manner, a comprehensive record of each securities transaction they effect and of their securities business in general for at least three years. This is done for the purposes of monitoring compliance with applicable securities laws and financial responsibility standards. In 1997, the SEC amended paragraph (f) of Rule 17a-4 to allow broker-dealers to store records electronically in a non-rewriteable, non-erasable format.[22]

Although it is quite evident that communication *with* the public is very highly regulated, in fact, communication *about* the public is just as highly regulated. The **Gramm-Leach-Bliley Act (GLBA)**, signed into law November 12, 1999, eliminated legal barriers between the securities, insurance, and banking industries. One of the major components of the legislation was the development of privacy laws and regulations. The GLBA gives authority to eight federal agencies and the states to administer and enforce the **Financial Privacy Rule** and the **Safeguards Rule**. These two regulations apply to "financial institutions," which includes not only banks, securities firms, and insurance companies, but also companies providing many other types of financial products and services to consumers. Among these services are: lending, brokering or servicing any type of consumer loan; transferring or safeguarding money; preparing individual tax returns; providing financial advice or credit counseling; providing residential real estate settlement services; collecting consumer debts; and an array of other activities. Section 504 of the GLBA requires the SEC and other organizations to adopt rules implementing notice requirements and restrictions on a financial institution's ability to disclose nonpublic personal information about consumers. Under this Act, a financial institution must provide its customers with a notice of its privacy policies and practices and must not disclose nonpublic personal information about a consumer to nonaffiliated third parties without proper disclosure and consent. In accordance with the GLBA, the SEC has adopted Regulation S-P. As it relates to brokers, planners, and other investment professionals, the regulation states that as a general rule, the initial privacy notice must be given to a customer or proposed customer no later than when the registered advisor provides the client with a written disclosure statement or investment advisory contract.

Ethical Requirements for Financial Planners

The SEC, most state securities agencies, and financial services professional organizations require financial planners to abide by a code of ethics. Rule 204A-1 amended the Investment Advisors Act of 1940 so that every advisor must now have a code of ethics that sets forth standards of conduct expected of advisory personnel. The focus of the rule was to reduce conflicts of interest between advisors and clients by requiring RIAs and RIA representatives to report personal securities transactions, including purchases and sales in any mutual fund managed by an advisor. Under this rule, a code of ethics must, at a minimum, include a:

- requirement that the RIA maintain and enforce the code by appointing a chief compliance officer;

- requirement that standards of business conduct, which reflect a firm's fiduciary duty, be written;

- provision that the chief compliance officer and supervised persons comply with federal securities laws;

- mechanism for reporting and reviewing an advisor's personal investment transactions;

- provision that requires a supervisor's approval before an RIA representative invests in an initial public offering or private placement;

- provision for the prompt internal reporting of any violation of the code of ethics;

- requirement that all of a firm's employees receive subsequent amendments to the code;

- requirement that the advisor keep copies of the code, records of violations of the code, and actions taken as a result of any violation of the code; and

- requirement that a copy of the receipt from all RIA representatives, acknowledging receipt of the code of ethics, be kept on file.

Information as found at: http://www.law.uc.edu/CCL/InvAdvRls/rule204A-1.html.

The SEC also adopted two additional rules to further refine how a firm's code of ethics should be written, reviewed, and enforced. Rules 206(4)-7 and 204-2 require any RIA registered with the SEC to have written policies and procedures, annual reviews, and a chief compliance officer. Written policies and procedures must include the following 11 points:

1. identification of conflicts of interest and risks facing the RIA;

2. a description of the portfolio management process used by the RIA, including allocation practices, consistency of investment objectives, disclosures made by the investment advisor, and any applicable regulatory restrictions;

3. a description of trading practices, including best execution obligations, use of soft dollars, and allocation of aggregated trades;

4. a description of the policies for proprietary trading of the RIA and RIA representatives;

5. a policy on the accuracy of disclosures made to clients, including account statements and advertisements;

6. a policy on safeguarding clients' assets;

7. a description of the books and records maintained by the RIA, the security of books and records, and protection of client information;

8. a description of marketing policies, including the use of solicitors;

9. a process for valuing client holdings and calculating fees;

Figure 2.4 Privacy Statement Example

<Firm Name>

Privacy Policy

Our relationship with you is our most important asset. We understand that you have entrusted us with your private financial information, and we do everything we can to maintain that trust. This notice is being provided to you in accordance with the Securities and Exchange Commission's rule regarding the privacy of consumer financial information ("Regulation S-P"). Please take the time to read and understand the privacy policies and procedures that we have implemented to safeguard your nonpublic personal information.*

We collect personal information to do financial planning and to perform our investment management responsibilities.

1.   **We do not sell your personal information to anyone.**

2.   **We do not disclose any nonpublic information about our customers or former customers to anyone, except as permitted by law.**

     *   In accordance with Section 248.13 of Regulation S-P, in limited circumstances where we believe in good faith that disclosure is required or permitted by law, we may disclose all of the information we collect, as described above, to certain nonaffiliated third parties such as attorneys, accountants, insurance brokers, auditors and persons or entities that are assessing our compliance with industry standards. We enter into contractual agreements with all nonaffiliated third parties that prohibit such third parties from disclosing or using the information other than to carry out the purposes for which we disclose the information.

         Outside of this exception, we will not share your personal information with third parties unless you have specifically asked us to do so.

         We collect personal information in the normal course of business in order to provide planning and investment management services.

     *   *New client information.* We collect information that you provide to us when you become a client. The information we collect includes name(s), address, phone number, email address, Social Security number(s), and other information about your investing and financial planning needs.

3.   **We protect the confidentiality and security of your personal information.**

     *   We restrict access to personal information to our staff and for business purposes only.

     *   We maintain physical, electronic, and procedural safeguards to guard your personal information.

4.   **We continue to evaluate our efforts to protect personal information and make every effort to keep your personal information accurate and up to date.**

     *   If you identify any inaccuracy in your personal information, or you need to make a change to that information, please contact us so that we may promptly update our records.

5.   **We will provide notice of changes in our information sharing practices.**

     *   If, at any time in the future, it is necessary to disclose any of your personal information in a way that is inconsistent with this policy, we will give you advance notice of the proposed change so that you will have the opportunity to opt out of such disclosure.

---

* Nonpublic personal information means personally identifiable information and any list, description or other grouping of consumers that is derived using any personally identifiable financial information that is not publicly available.

10. a description of safeguards for the privacy of client records and information; and

11. a disaster recovery and business continuity plan.

Information as found at: http://www.law.uc.edu/CCL/InvAdvRls/rule206(4)-7.html.
Information as found at: http://www.law.uc.edu/CCL/InvAdvRls/rule204-2.html.

The rules also require an annual review of policies and procedures. RIAs must maintain documentation of annual reviews and of actions taken to rectify any deficiencies. The role of the **chief compliance officer** is to administer compliance policies and procedures. The SEC requires the compliance officer to be competent and knowledgeable about the Investment Advisors Act of 1940, and to be in a position of power to take full responsibility and authority for developing and enforcing appropriate policies and procedures.

Although the SEC's ethical requirements are commendable, it is important to note that those requirements apply only to RIAs and RIA representatives registered at the federal level (and in certain cases, when also adopted at the state level). Stockbrokers, insurance agents, and other financial advisors are exempt from these ethical guidelines. Professional organizations help fill this ethical void by establishing, maintaining, and enforcing ethical standards within the profession. The CFP Board has made the greatest strides in defining and formalizing a code of ethics for financial planning practitioners. The process to define financial planning ethics and standards began in 1985. At that time, the CFP Board undertook the task of defining competency within financial planning. From this assignment emerged the CFP Board's *Code of Ethics and Professional Responsibility*. Ten years later, in 1995, the CFP Board created a Board of Practice Standards, which was charged with the responsibility of drafting financial planning standards. Since the late 1990's, all CFP® certificants have been required to follow both the practice standards and the *Code of Ethics*.

The **CFP Board Code of Ethics** consists of seven principles (as shown in Figure 2.5) and specific rules related to each principle.[23] According to the CFP Board materials, "Principles are statements expressing in general terms the ethical and professional ideals that CFP Board designees are expected to display in their professional activities. As such, the Principles are aspirational in character but are intended to provide a source of guidance for CFP Board designees."[24] Anyone who is either certified to use the CFP® mark or who may be entitled to someday use the mark, as well as candidates for CFP® certification, must follow the ethics rules. For instance, this means that any student enrolled in a CFP Board approved undergraduate, graduate, or certificate program at a university is required to follow the standards and rules.

Almost all professional financial services organizations require their members to abide by a code of ethics. The FPA went so far as to adopt the CFP Board *Code of Ethics*; this sharing of ethical statements is unique however. While the CFP Board has established the standard for ethics, the CFP Board's principles are by no means universally accepted or used. Other organizations typically have statements of ethics that are more general in nature. For example, the International Association of Registered Financial Consultants (IARFC)

Figure 2.5 CFP Board of Standards Ethical Principles

Principle 1 – Integrity

A CFP Board designee shall offer and provide professional services with integrity.

As discussed in "Composition and Scope," CFP Board designees may be placed by clients in positions of trust and confidence. The ultimate source of such public trust is the CFP Board designee's personal integrity. In deciding what is right and just, a CFP Board designee should rely on his or her integrity as the appropriate touchstone. Integrity demands honesty and candor which must not be subordinated to personal gain and advantage. Within the characteristic of integrity, allowance can be made for innocent error and legitimate difference of opinion; but integrity cannot co-exist with deceit or subordination of one's principles. Integrity requires a CFP Board designee to observe not only the letter but also the spirit of this *Code of Ethics*.

Principle 2 – Objectivity

A CFP Board designee shall be objective in providing professional services to clients.

Objectivity requires intellectual honesty and impartiality. It is an essential quality for any professional. Regardless of the particular service rendered or the capacity in which a CFP Board designee functions, a CFP Board designee should protect the integrity of his or her work, maintain objectivity, and avoid subordination of his or her judgment that would be in violation of this *Code of Ethics*.

Principle 3 – Competence

A CFP Board designee shall provide services to clients competently and maintain the necessary knowledge and skill to continue to do so in those areas in which the CFP Board designee is engaged.

One is competent only when he or she has attained and maintained an adequate level of knowledge and skill, and applies that knowledge effectively in providing services to clients. Competence also includes the wisdom to recognize the limitations of that knowledge and when consultation or client referral is appropriate. A CFP Board designee, by virtue of having earned the CFP® certification, is deemed to be qualified to practice financial planning. However, in addition to assimilating the common body of knowledge required and acquiring the necessary experience for certification, a CFP Board designee shall make a continuing commitment to learning and professional improvement.

Principle 4 – Fairness

A CFP Board designee shall perform professional services in a manner that is fair and reasonable to clients, principals, partners and employers, and shall disclose conflict(s) of interest in providing such services.

Fairness requires impartiality, intellectual honesty and disclosure of conflict(s) of interest. It involves a subordination of one's own feelings, prejudices and desires so as to achieve a proper balance of conflicting interests. Fairness is treating others in the same fashion that you would want to be treated and is an essential trait of any professional.

Principle 5 – Confidentiality

A CFP Board designee shall not disclose any confidential client information without the specific consent of the client unless in response to proper legal process, to defend against charges of wrongdoing by the CFP Board designee or in connection with a civil dispute between the CFP Board designee and client.

A client, by seeking the services of a CFP Board designee, may be interested in creating a relationship of personal trust and confidence with the CFP Board designee. This type of relationship can only be built upon the understanding that information supplied to the CFP Board designee will be confidential. In order to provide the contemplated services effectively and to protect the client's privacy, the CFP Board designee shall safeguard the confidentiality of such information.

Figure 2.5 CFP Board of Standards Ethical Principles (cont'd)

Principle 6 – Professionalism

A CFP Board designee's conduct in all matters shall reflect credit upon the profession.

Because of the importance of the professional services rendered by CFP Board designees, there are attendant responsibilities to behave with dignity and courtesy to all those who use those services, fellow professionals, and those in related professions. A CFP Board designee also has an obligation to cooperate with fellow CFP Board designees to enhance and maintain the profession's public image and to work jointly with other CFP Board designees to improve the quality of services. It is only through the combined efforts of all CFP Board designees, in cooperation with other professionals, that this vision can be realized.

Principle 7 – Diligence

A CFP Board designee shall act diligently in providing professional services.

Diligence is the provision of services in a reasonably prompt and thorough manner. Diligence also includes proper planning for, and supervision of, the rendering of professional services.

Professional Code of Ethics requires IARFC members to abide by the following statements:

- "I will at all times put my client's interests above my own.

- I will maintain proficiency in my work through continuing education.

- When fee-based services are involved, I will charge a fair and reasonable fee based on the amount of time and skill required.

- I will abide by both the spirit and the letter of the laws and regulations applicable to financial planning services.

- I will give my client the same service that I would apply to myself in the same circumstances."

The above quote, from the IARFC Code of Ethics (http://www.iarfc.org//content_sub.asp?n=16), was reprinted with permission from the International Association of Registered Fianancial Consultants.

The National Association of Personal Financial Advisors, the nation's largest "fee-only" financial planning organization, also requires its members to abide by a strict code of ethics. The NAPFA *Code of Ethics* states the following:

"Recognizing our fiduciary responsibility to clients and the public, NAPFA Members uphold the highest standards of care in the industry by espousing and practicing:

- Objectivity;

- Complete Disclosure;

- Integrity and Honesty;

- Competence;

- Confidentiality;

- Fairness and suitability;

- Professionalism; and

- Regulatory Compliance."

All NAPFA members must also take what is known as the **NAPFA Fiduciary Oath,** which is as follows:

"The advisor shall exercise his/her best efforts to act in good faith and in the best interests of the client. The advisor shall provide written disclosure to the client prior to the engagement of the advisor, and thereafter throughout the term of the engagement, of any conflicts of interest, which will or reasonably may compromise the impartiality or independence of the advisor.

The advisor, or any party in which the advisor has a financial interest, does not receive any compensation or other remuneration that is contingent on any client's purchase or sale of a financial product. The advisor does not receive a fee or other compensation from another party based on the referral of a client or the client's business.

What the Fiduciary Oath means to you - the client:

- I shall always act in good faith and with candor.

- I shall be proactive in my disclosure of any conflicts of interest that may impact you.

- I shall not accept any referral fees or compensation that is contingent upon the purchase or sale of a financial product."

The about quotes, from the NAPFA Code of Ethics (http://www.napfa.org/about/CodeofEthics.asp) and the NAPFA Fiduciary Oath (http://www.napfa.org/consumer/NAPFAFiduciaryOath.asp) were reprinted with permission from the National Association of Personal Fianancial Advisors.

Professional Practice Issues

As this chapter indicates, ethical standards have a wide ranging impact on the way financial planners work with clients. The ethical foundations of financial planning directly influence the way client data is gathered and used, and the way in which recommendations are implemented. Opportunities exist at every step of the financial planning process to cross the line from an ethical approach to one that is shaded by a questionable standard. Federal, state, and organizational regulators stand ready to enforce rules and standards, but these entities can only do so after a prohibited act has taken place. Thus, financial planners, to a large extent, are responsible for monitoring their own actions to ensure that ethical standards are not crossed. While the majority of this chapter has been focused on describing the myriad types of rules a financial planner must follow to protect consumers, this section looks at how financial planners can take steps to improve their practice methods in order to limit their fiduciary and ethical standard liabilities.

Continuing Education

One of the first and best ways to ensure that a planner is continuing to act in accordance with the multitude of industry regulations is by participating in and taking seriously the continuing education requirements imposed by the various governing bodies and membership organizations. All credentialing and designating organizations require their members to stay current in the profession via **continuing education (CE)**. (Ancillary service providers, such as insurance agents and lawyers, also spend a great deal of time ensuring that they meet the state required minimums for continuing education for their respective licenses.) Current CFP Board rules direct that all CFP® certificants complete at least 30 hours of continuing education every two years, of which two hours must be from a CFP Board-approved program on the *Code of Ethics* and Professional Standards. Organizations such as IARFC and NAPFA have more stringent continuing education requirements than the CFP Board. NAPFA requires that 60 hours of CE be completed every even-year biennial, and the IARFC requires 40 hours per year—and these are just the minimum requirements. But to quote a prominent figure in the industry "How can [an advisor] stay current in this profession on just [a couple] days." To be the best in the industry on service, product delivery, and compliance, a financial planning professional should count on spending much more time than the required minimum in class, regardless of whether the class or other educational activity counts for CE credit.

As for the NASD and Registered Representatives, the SEC created CE requirements in 1995. The requirements consist of two parts: (1) the regulatory element; and (2) the firm element, known together as **Rule 1120**. The regulatory element requires regular participation in computer-based training on topics including licensing and registration, communications with the public, product suitability, and professional conduct. This training program must be completed within 120 days of a representative's second anniversary of his/her registration approval date and every three years thereafter. The firm element requires that a broker-dealer establish a formal training program to keep employees up to date on job- and product-related subjects.

So what happens if a financial planner or investment representative fails to comply with an organizational or regulating body's CE requirement? Failure to comply with the regulatory element of the NASD requirement results in a Registered Representative's registration being deemed inactive until all program requirements are fulfilled. Similar to the individual punishment for the NASD,

NAPFA requires that a member who becomes "CE deficient" relinquish all benefits of and reference to membership in the organization. And the CFP Board of Standards will not renew the certificant's CFP® certification, therefore precluding any use of the CFP® marks. So penalties are severe, even if not monetary. However, the organization for which the financial professional works also bears responsibility for the noncompliance and is subject to penalties as well. According to a 1996 press release, the NASD censured and fined Citicorp Securities, Inc. $25,000 and ordered it to comply with an undertaking to disgorge $300,000 for violating NASD Regulation's CE requirements—and this was for only 19 employees.[25]

Professional Liability Insurance

Maybe even more important than keeping up to date with continuing education is protecting one's financial planning practice and livelihood in the event of a mistake that leads to a lawsuit. Financial planners operate in an environment that is conducive to litigation. In some cases, a financial planner may be required to provide a bond or insurance to protect clients. Although not required, a growing number of planners are turning to **errors and omissions (E&O) insurance** to protect themselves against claims from clients. E&O insurance provides protection against claims arising out of acts, errors, or omissions of a planner (or any other covered person for whom the financial planner is legally liable) in the rendering of professional services. However, E&O insurance does not cover acts of fraud.

In some cases, financial planners are required by the SEC or state securities regulator to post a **fidelity bond**. This is most often the case when a financial planner has custody of a client's assets. Financial planners who fall under the reach of ERISA also need to post a bond. Fidelity (fiduciary) bonds cover dishonest acts by a financial planner. E&O insurance, on the other hand, provides advisors with coverage against losses due to any actual or alleged negligent act, error, or omission committed in the scope of performing their professional services. E&O insurance protects a financial planner's business, corporation, business officers, directors, and employees from claims arising out of acts, errors, or omissions in rendering or failing to render professional services. **Fiduciary liability insurance** is a subcategory of E&O insurance. This type of insurance provides *additional* coverage against claims arising from fiduciary breaches.

Before purchasing E&O insurance, advisors should consider the coverage in relation to the following factors:

1. **Will the insurance cover prior acts?** Prior acts coverage protects the planner from claims of a practice error that may have occurred prior to taking out the E&O coverage. Prior acts coverage can be acquired for an extra premium.

2. **Will all legal expenses be paid?** Some policies include legal expenses as part of the maximum liability limit of the policy. If, for instance, the liability plus legal fees exceeds the policy limit, the planner will be responsible for paying the excess. Some policies, on the other hand, will pay legal expenses above the policy liability limit.

3. **Where is the policy in force?** Planners who do business in several states, or in Mexico or Canada, need to determine if there are restrictions on where E&O coverage applies.

4. **What is covered?** Financial planners who perform other services, such as tax preparation, need to determine if these ancillary services are covered in a basic E&O policy. Sometimes professional activities related to limited partnerships, private placements, syndicated investments, and real estate investments are excluded from E&O policies.

One of the best ways to avoid a claim of professional misconduct is to manage a financial planning practice using the highest level of professional ethical standards. Abiding by a code of ethics is a good starting point. Using disclosure and practice management standards as they apply to fiduciaries, regardless of how one is paid or what type of planning one does, is another way to reduce possible errors and omissions claims. Figure 2.6 indicates the types of items a financial planner ought to disclose to prospective and current clients. It is similar in content to the ADV (if one is required of the advisor), but broader in scope. These items need to be disclosed to, received by, and confirmed in writing by a client prior to implementing recommendations, or in some cases even establishing a professional relationship.

It is also important to obtain a client's written agreement regarding financial planning and investment management services prior to gathering data or making a recommendation. Although this seems like common sense, a surprisingly large number of financial planners enter into working arrangement with clients without contracts only to find later, usually after an investment reversal, that the client holds the planner responsible. Figures 2.7 and 2.8, respectively, illustrate how a financial planning agreement and an investment advisory agreement can be worded.

Finally, the best method to use to avoid claims of misconduct, errors, and omissions is to know the applicable laws that relate to one's profession, disclose any and all items that might be considered a conflict of interest with clients, and avoid actions that might be deemed unethical, illegal, or below commonly accepted practice standards. Some of the most common actions financial advisors sometimes engage in that later lead to claims of misconduct include the following: implementing recommendations and failing to follow-up with a client, borrowing money from a client, failing to disclose investment risks, hiding fees, and rebating insurance premiums to clients. Exhibit 2.4 shows how selected case types were arbitrated from 2001 through 2005.

Exhibit 2.4 Types of Arbitration Cases[1]

Type of Controversy	2001	2002	2003	2004
Margin Calls	375	366	244	168
Churning	784	824	665	449
Unauthorized Trading	884	930	789	520
Failure to Supervise	1,968	2,633	3,230	2,743
Negligence	2,275	2,522	3,500	3,398
Omission of Facts	692	1,178	1,949	2,195
Breach of Contract	1,921	1,958	2,328	2,723
Breach of Fiduciary Duty	3,458	4,236	5,565	5,426
Unsuitability	1,524	2,644	3,198	2,697
Misrepresentation	1,895	2,623	3,280	3,230
Online Trading	155	95	74	4

[1] NASD Arbitration Case Types (2001-2004); as found at http://www.nasd.com/web/idcplg?IdcService=SS_GET_PAGE&nodeId=516.

Unfortunately, however, sometimes, no matter how diligent a financial planner is, something goes wrong. So what happens? Again, it depends.

Regulation, Arbitration, and Litigation

Financial planners must file a U-4 Form upon being hired by an NASD member firm when acting as a Registered Representative, or when engaging in the securities industry as a NASD licensed member. According to NASD Rule 3080, and as disclosed on the U-4 Form, any NASD member is "agreeing to arbitrate any dispute, claim or controversy that may arise between you and your firm, or a customer, or any other person, that is required to be arbitrated under the rules of the self-regulatory organizations with which you are registering."[26] However, while this ruling compels the *professional* to seek resolution through arbitration, it does not compel a client to follow the same process.

To level the playing field, almost all investment contracts and brokerage account applications require *clients* to pursue actions against advisors through an arbitration process. **Arbitration** is a dispute resolution process that takes the place of traditional court system lawsuits. The arbitration process involves taking a case before a trained expert (i.e., the arbitrator) who imposes a final solution to resolve a conflict. In such cases, the parties agree that the arbitrator's solution is bilaterally binding. (In simpler, or less egregious cases, clients and planners may use **mediation**, which involves working with a trained conflict resolution expert to help two or more parties reach agreement on an issue. Unlike arbitration, a mediator's solution is not binding.) The process of arbitration is shown in Figure 2.9.

The arbitration process is begun by the claimant, usually a client, filing a Statement of Claim and a Submission Form with the appropriate arbitration authority. While the fees associated with arbitration may cost thousands of dollars, it is normally cheaper for the client and the advisor than pursuing remuneration in the court system. Once the claim has been filed, a very court-like

Figure 2.6 Certificant Disclosure Form

CFP® CERTIFICANT DISCLOSURE FORM (FORM FPE) – SAMPLE FILLED-IN FORM

For Use in Financial Planning Engagements

This disclosure form gives information about the CFP® certificant(s) and his/her/their business. This information has not been reviewed, approved or verified by CFP Board or by any governmental or self-regulatory authority. CFP Board does not warrant the specific qualifications of individuals certified to use its marks, nor does it warrant the correctness of advice or opinions provided.

PART I. GENERAL INFORMATION:
(Code reference - Rule 401)

A. Business affiliation:

B. Address:

C. Telephone number:

D. Information required by all laws applicable to the relationship (e.g., if the CFP certificant is a registered investment adviser, the disclosure document required by laws applicable to such registration):

PART II. MATERIAL INFORMATION RELEVANT TO THE PROFESSIONAL RELATIONSHIP
(Written disclosures required to be provided <u>prior to</u> the engagement)
(Code reference - Rule 402)

A. Basic philosophy of the CFP certificant (or firm) in working with clients:

Our approach to personal financial planning is to obtain from you significant financial and other information including your attitudes, goals and objectives; to analyze the information obtained in order to develop alternatives for your consideration; to educate you about the implications of selecting a particular alternative; to implement the alternative selected by you; and to periodically update the plan adopted. It is our goal to become your chief financial adviser and to coordinate the efforts of your other advisers in your best interests. We want you to be educated about your own financial affairs and to take an active role in managing them.

B. Philosophy, theory and/or principles of financial planning which will be utilized:

Our philosophy of financial planning is to gather adequate reliable information about a client's personal financial situation; to determine the client's goals and objectives, time horizon, and risk tolerance; to analyze all of the foregoing information in an objective manner and to develop recommendations for our clients based upon this thorough analysis and in the interest of rendering disinterested advice. In a personal financial planning engagement, we endeavor to consistently act in the interest of our client and to place his or her interest ahead of our own. Moreover, we believe that a client should be both informed and proactively involved in his or her personal financial affairs. Accordingly, we believe in holding frequent meetings with our clients to educate them about the financial planning process and their own financial situation.

Figure 2.6 Certificant Disclosure Form (cont'd)

C. Attached to this disclosure form, or summarized in the space provided below, are résumés of principals and employees of the CFP® certificant's firm who are expected to provide financial planning services:

   1. Educational background:

   John Doe:
   > *Bachelor of Science degree in accounting from Hofstra University, 1971.*
   > *Master of Business Administration degree in Financial Services from Golden Gate University, 1975.*

   2. Professional/employment history:

   John Doe:
   > *Was employed as a stockbroker for DEF Brokerage for nearly ten years before becoming a partner in Comprehensive Financial Planning Services, Inc., in 1986 (see attached résumé).*

   3. Professional certifications and licenses held:

   John Doe:
   > *CERTIFIED FINANCIAL PLANNER™ practitioner*
   > *NASD Series 7 (General Securities) license - 1974*
   > *Life & Health insurance licenses - 1978, State of Arkansas*

D. Description of the financial planning services to be provided by the CFP certificant:

   Example 1:
   This engagement is limited in scope to retirement planning only. Other types of personal financial planning services will not be performed by us, unless they directly affect your retirement plan, and you give us your express permission prior to performing such additional services.

   Example 2:
   You have expressed interest in asset management services. These services include:
   - *Analysis of your current financial condition, goals and objectives, and development of a personal financial plan.*
   - *Design of an investment portfolio appropriate to your individual circumstances, needs, goals, risk tolerance, investment experience and time horizon.*
   - *Quarterly written reports on the status of your investment portfolio.*
   - *Two meetings each year to review and update your objectives and financial status and provide an evaluation of your investment portfolio.*
   - *Ongoing monitoring of your investment portfolio.*
   - *Recommendations involving investment repositioning and current opportunities for new investments.*
   - *Availability of our professional staff to answer questions.*

E. Conflict(s) of interest and source(s) of compensation:

   1. Conflict(s) of interest:

   Example 1:
   John Doe represents Larry Peters, your business partner.

Figure 2.6 Certificant Disclosure Form (cont'd)

Example 2:
My broker/dealer permits me to sell only those securities products which it has approved.

2. Source(s) of compensation:

   Example 1: Fees from clients

   Example 2: Commissions from third parties

3. Contingencies or other aspects material to the certificant's compensation:

   I will not receive a commission unless you purchase the financial products recommended by me.

F. Agency or employment relationships:

   1. Material agency or employment relationships with third parties:
      Life & Health Insurance Broker for DEF Insurance Company

   2. Compensation resulting from such agency or employment relationships:
      50% commissions on first year life insurance premiums and 0.25% commission upon annual renewal.

G. Other material information relevant to the professional relationship:
   John Doe is licensed only for the sale of mutual funds and variable annuities.

Part III. ADDITIONAL NOTIFICATION

A. As a client or prospective client, you have the right to ask me, as a CFP® certificant, at any time for information about my compensation related to the services I provide you. I will communicate the requested information in reasonable detail as it relates to our financial planning engagement, including compensation derived from implementation. This disclosure of compensation:

   1. May be expressed as an approximate dollar amount or percentage or as a range of dollar amounts or percentages;
   2. Shall be made at a time and to the extent that the requested information can be reasonably ascertained;
   3. Will be based on reasonable assumptions, with estimates clearly identified, and;
   4. Will be updated in a timely manner if actual compensation significantly differs from any estimates.
   (Code reference - Rules 402 and 403)

B. As a CFP certificant's personal financial planning client, you have the right to receive annually my current SEC Form ADV Part II or the current revision of the disclosure you received when our relationship began. (Code reference - Rule 404)

I hereby acknowledge receipt of this required disclosure.

_____ / _____   _____ / _____

Client's Signature   Date   Client's Signature   Date

Form FPE   Rev. 01/03

Figure 2.7 Sample Financial Planning Agreement

LETTER OF ENGAGEMENT FOR PRO BONO FINANCIAL PLANNING SERVICES

1) We, the undersigned CERTIFIED FINANCIAL PLANNER™ certificant (hereafter CFP® certificant or "planner") and pro-bono recipient ("pro bono client"), acknowledge that we are entering into a limited pro-bono financial planning engagement for which the planner will receive no compensation, directly or indirectly, for services provided.

2) The scope of this engagement is to provide to the pro-bono client general financial planning advice and consultation that may include, but are not necessarily limited to, the following:
    a. Verbal and/or written financial planning advice from a CERTIFIED FINANCIAL PLANNER™ certificant. (CFP candidates who have passed the comprehensive exam may also be eligible. Please refer to the FPA® Pro Bono Program Guidelines.)
    b. Organization of family finances.
    c. Banking issues, payment of bills, and budget and cash flow management.
    d. Medical, disability, life, property, and casualty insurance, including information about benefits, settlements and claims administration.
    e. Review of savings and investments.
    f. Tax issues.
    g. Review of estate planning.
    h. Access to available financial benefits to which the pro-bono client and his or her family may be eligible.
    i. Consulting with other allied professionals such as accountants, attorneys and insurance professionals. (Please refer to Appendix A for the specific pro bono services to be provided by the financial planner.)

3) The scope of this pro bono engagement is not intended to be a long-term or ongoing relationship. It does not cover implementation of the advice received as described herein. The client may pursue other options to implement his/her financial plan, as described in Appendix A.

4) The planner will receive no compensation for this engagement, and will comply with all regulatory, professional and ethical obligations, including but not limited to those imposed by the Securities and Exchange Commission (SEC), state securities and insurance regulators, and, if applicable, the Certified Financial Planner Board of Standards. Further, the planner is prohibited from charging for additional services not anticipated but provided during the pro bono financial planning sessions. This financial planner will not pursue an ongoing financial planning business relationship unless proactively requested by the participant. If the participant requests such a relationship, he or she will enter into a new and separate agreement for financial services with the financial planner, with the pro bono engagement terminated prior to execution of the business agreement. The planner affirms that all professional licenses and certifications held by the planner are in good standing, and that the planner has not at any time been censored, convicted or otherwise found by competent authority to be guilty of any fraudulent activity or professional misconduct.

5) The financial planner participating in this letter of engagement is a member of the Financial Planning Association. The undersigned planner is bound by the Financial Planning Association's Code of Ethics, as well as the Certified Financial Planner Board of Standards *Code of Ethics and Professional Responsibility*. Neither FPA nor its officers, members or staff assume responsibility or liability for the accuracy or appropriateness of the advice given by said planner. By accepting assistance, the pro bono client acknowledges and agrees that FPA does not purport to provide or hold itself out as providing any financial advice to the participant and FPA, nor any of its directors, officers, employees, agents or members, has any professional or business relationship with, or has or assumes any responsibility or liability for the accuracy or appropriateness of any advice or assistance provided by the planner. The pro-bono client acknowledges that he or she must make an independent judgment regarding a particular planner's qualifications and suitability for the pro-bono client's needs and circumstances.

6) All personal financial advice and assistance provided by the undersigned financial planner is provided solely by the individual financial planner and not by or on behalf of FPA. The financial planner is solely responsible for his or her professional advice and services. Both the planner and pro bono client agree to hold FPA as well as its directors, officers, employees, agents or members (other than the financial planner) harmless from any loss, damage, cost or liability in any way arising from such advice, acts or omissions.

7) The terms of this agreement are limited to those items described in Appendix A, and this agreement will terminate upon the completion of the services described in Appendix A or the time allotted in Appendix A, or written notice of either planner or client.

Figure 2.7 Sample Financial Planning Agreement (cont'd)

8) The pro bono client understands that the responsibility for financial planning decisions are his/her own and that he/she is under no obligation to follow, either wholly or in part, any recommendation or suggestion provided by the pro-bono planner.

9) Should any concern arise regarding this advisory relationship, it is agreed that the parties will consult with each other to resolve such issues. Any unresolved issue shall then be submitted to non-binding mediation under the Commercial Mediation Rules of the American Arbitration Association. Any dispute still unresolved may then be submitted to binding arbitration under the Securities Industry Arbitration Rules of the American Arbitration Association.

_____, CFP® / _____   _____ / _____
(Planner signature)   (Date)   (Pro Bono Client signature)   (Date)

_____   _____

_____   _____

_____   _____

_____   _____

_____   _____
(Print name, firm, address and telephone number)   (Print name, address and telephone number)

Figure 2.7 Sample Financial Planning Agreement (cont'd)

Appendix A

*(Copies to be provided to pro bono client, planner, sponsoring organizations, and FPA chapter
at conclusion of the engagement.)*

Pro-bono Advisory Services Provided (check appropriate categories):

___ Verbal and/or written financial planning advice from a CERTIFIED FINANCIAL PLANNER™ certificant
___ Organization of family finances
___ Banking issues, payment of bills, and budget and cash flow management
___ Medical, disability, life, property, and casualty insurance, including information about benefits, settlements and
     claims administration
___ Review savings and investments
___ Tax issues
___ Review estate plan
___ Access to available financial benefits to which the pro-bono client and his or her family may be eligible
___ Consulting with other allied professionals such as accountants, attorneys and insurance professionals
___ Other (specify) _____

Time allocated to Pro-bono Engagement: _____ hours.

Next Steps:

☐   Client has been referred to Planner Search on the Financial Planning Association's website at
     www.fpanet.org.
☐   Client has received referrals to allied professionals (accountants, attorneys, insurance professionals).
☐   The undersigned client understands the terms of this agreement and has elected to pursue a
     relationship with the pro bono planner on a compensation basis, as discussed with the planner and
     under a separate agreement.
☐   Client has decided to seek advice and/or implementation with another financial planner or financial firm.
☐   Client has decided not to pursue any further financial planning services.
☐   Other _____

Signed: _____, CFP®   Date: _____
           (Pro bono financial planner)

Signed: _____   Date: _____
           (Pro bono client)

Figure 2.8 Sample Investment Advisory Agreement

INVESTMENT MANAGEMENT AGREEMENT

This *AGREEMENT* sets forth the investment advisory engagement entered into by and between *<Firm Name>*, a duly registered advisor and

_____ (Client).

SERVICES OF <FIRM>: <Firm> shall provide Investment Management to the Client. Client appoints <Firm> as the investment manager of those assets designated to be held in the Managed Investment Portfolio.

TRADING AUTHORIZATION AND ESTABLISHMENT OF ACCOUNTS: Client hereby constitutes and appoints <Firm> as its true and lawful agent for the selection of securities to be bought and sold and the amount of securities to be bought and sold that <Firm> deems, in its sole and unrestricted discretion and judgment, to be consistent with Client's investment objectives and to take all actions necessary to the execution of any purchase, sale or trade of securities. **<Firm> is not granted authority, and shall have no power, to withdraw funds from Client's account or to take custody of client's funds or securities.** Client retains the right to make deposits or withdrawals from his/her account at any time, however, Client is advised to notify <Firm> of each withdrawal or deposit before it occurs. The term "securities" herein means stocks, bonds, notes, or any other types of instruments defined as a security under the federal securities law.

BASIS OF ADVICE: Client acknowledges that <Firm> obtains information from a wide variety of publicly available sources and that <Firm> has no sources, and does not claim to have, sources of inside or private information. The recommendations developed by <Firm> are based upon the professional judgment of <Firm> and its individual professional counselors and on information received from Client and neither <Firm> nor its individual counselors can guarantee the results of any of their recommendations. Client at all times shall elect unilaterally to follow or ignore completely or in part any information, recommendation or counsel given by <Firm> under this Agreement. <Firm> is not responsible for tax reporting of gains and losses. Client should keep trade confirmations, account statements, or other correspondence supplied by the custodian for this purpose.

INVESTMENT POLICY: The Managed Investment Portfolio is to be managed according to the risk parameters as set by the client. An investment policy with more detailed risk parameters will be developed specifically for the client after completion of the financial plan. <Firm> will not make investments on behalf of the Client until such Investment Policy is complete. If the Client wishes to change the investment objective at any time, Client agrees to provide written instruction to <Firm>.

CUSTODY: Advisor does not maintain custody of client funds or securities, nor is it authorized to hold or receive any stock, bond or other security or investment certificate or cash (except in the payment of its advisory fee) that is part of the Client's account. Custody of Account assets will be maintained with the independent custodian, as determined by <Firm>, (the "Custodian"), and Client will be solely responsible for paying all fees or charges of the Custodian.

LIABILITY OF <FIRM>: The Client agrees that <Firm> will not be liable for any recommendation, act or omission, including but not limited to any error in judgement, with respect to the Managed Investment Portfolio, so long as such recommendation, act or omission does not constitute a breach of fiduciary duty to the Client. Nothing contained herein shall in any way constitute a waiver or limitation of any rights which the Client may have under applicable federal or state securities laws. <Firm> shall not be liable for complying with any directive or instruction of the Client that is not in writing. <Firm> shall not be liable for any act or omission of any custodian, broker or other third party with respect to the Managed Investment Portfolio, so long as the same is retained in good faith by <Firm>.

SERVICES TO OTHER CLIENTS: Client understands and agrees that Advisor performs investment advisory services for various other clients. Client agrees that Advisor may give advice or take action in the performance of its duties with respect to any of its other clients, or for the Advisor and/or its employees' own accounts, which may differ from advice given to or action taken on behalf of Client. Advisor is not obligated to buy, sell or recommend for Client any security or other investment that Advisor or its employees may buy, sell or recommend for any other client or for their own accounts.

[1] This contract must be reviewed by an attorney to conform to applicable state and federal laws. This example is for educational purposes only, and is not intended to be legal advice.

Figure 2.8 Sample Investment Advisory Agreement (cont'd)

COMPENSATION: Fees for Investment Management are computed based on the attached fee schedule. Management fees are based upon a percentage of the assets under management and are payable in advance three times per year: January, May and September. The first payment is due and payable when the account is opened and will be assessed pro rata in the event the account is opened other than the first day of the month when billing occurs. Fees for subsequent billing periods are due and will be assessed on the first day of each billing period based on the value of the portfolio as of the last business day of the previous billing period.

Client agrees to the fee schedule as attached and authorizes the Custodian (Brokerage Firm or Fund Sponsor) to deduct these fees from the Client's account. Client understands he/she will receive an invoice showing the amount of the fee, the value of the assets on which the fee was based, and the specific manner in which the <Firm>'s fee was calculated.

TRANSACTION COSTS: All commissions and other transaction fees with respect to transactions for the Managed Investment Portfolio shall be payable by the Client.

LEGAL AND ACCOUNTING SERVICES: It is understood and agreed that <Firm> and its employees are not qualified to and will not render any legal or accounting advice nor prepare any legal or accounting documents for the implementation of Client's financial and investment plan. Client agrees that his/her personal attorney shall be solely responsible for the rendering and/or preparation of the following: (i) all legal and accounting advice; (ii) all legal and accounting opinions and determinations; and (iii) all legal and accounting documents.

PROXY: Client shall maintain all proxy voting authority over all securities managed by <Firm>.

CONFLICT OF INTEREST DISCLOSURE STATEMENTS: <Firm> is an investment advisor registered with the Securities and Exchange Commission under the Investment Advisors Act of 1940. <Firm> has delivered information providing disclosures regarding <Firm>'s background and business practices. The Client acknowledges receipt of such information.

In the course of services to Client an advisor/employee may receive other commissions, consideration and fees from insurance carriers. In the event an employee of <Firm> is acting in the capacity of registered representative, he/she shall disclose any fees or commissions as are required by existing federal and state securities laws and regulations.

REPRESENTATIONS BY CLIENT: Client represents that the terms hereof do not violate any obligation by which Client is bound, whether arising by contract, operation of law or otherwise, and that, if required, (i) this contract has been duly authorized by appropriate action and is binding upon Client in accordance with its terms, and (ii) the Client will deliver to <Firm> such evidence of such authority as it may reasonably require, whether by way of a certified resolution, trust agreement, or otherwise. A trustee or other fiduciary entering into this Agreement represents that the proposed investment objective designated by client in the investment policy statement is within the scope of the investments and policies authorized by the governing instrument.

ARBITRATION: Any dispute, controversy or claim, including but not limited to, any claim relating to errors and omissions arising out of, or relating to, this Agreement, the breach thereof, or the purchase or sale of any security, the handling of funds or any other matter relating to the handling of Client's account, shall be settled by arbitration in accordance with the Code of Commercial Arbitration of the American Arbitration Association, and judgement upon the award rendered by the arbitrator(s) may be entered in any court having jurisdiction thereof. Client understands that this agreement to arbitrate does not constitute a waiver of the right to seek a judicial or other forum where such waiver would be void under the federal and state securities laws. Arbitration is final and binding on the parties.

MISCELLANEOUS PROVISIONS: The Agreement shall be governed by the laws of the State of _____ and in compliance with the Federal Securities Laws, including the Investment Advisors Act of 1940 and any regulations promulgated thereunder. The Agreement shall inure to the benefit of any successor of <Firm> and shall be binding upon the successors and assigns of Client. <Firm> shall not assign this Agreement without written consent of the Client. <Firm> will notify Client of any change in the legal ownership of <Firm> within a reasonable time after such change. This Agreement shall not become effective until acceptance by <Firm> as evidenced by the signature of an authorized representative below. No modification or amendment to this Agreement shall be effective unless made in writing and signed by Client and an authorized representative of <Firm>. The parties hereto acknowledge and agree that this Agreement alone constitutes the final written expression of the parties with respect to all matters contained herein, and the parties further acknowledge and agree that there are no prior or contemporaneous Agreements different or distinct from those contained herein, and all such prior and contemporaneous Agreements, if any, are merged herein, and this Agreement alone constitutes the final understanding between parties. Client certifies that he or she has read this Agreement in its entirety before executing it and understands it terms.

Figure 2.8 Sample Investment Advisory Agreement (cont'd)

TERM OF AGREEMENT AND TERMINATION: This Agreement shall be valid for one (1) year from the effective date and will be automatically renewed annually for one (1) year terms. However, either party may terminate this Agreement at any time by giving <u>written</u> notice to the current addresses of each party. Upon termination, <Firm> will not liquidate the account(s) unless Client provides written instructions to the contrary. Termination of this Agreement shall not affect any liability for <Firm> resulting from sales or exchanges initiated prior to written notice of such revocation. Transactions in progress will be completed in the normal course of business. Upon termination, Client shall receive a pro-rata refund of that portion of any prepaid advisory fees that have yet to be earned by Advisor. Such refund will be calculated from the date of receipt of the written termination notice or other agreed upon date.

SEVERABILITY: It is understood by the parties hereto that if any term, provision, duty, obligation or undertaking herein contained is held by the courts to be unenforceable or illegal or in conflict with the applicable state law, the validity of the remaining portions shall not be affected, and the rights and obligations of the parties shall be construed and enforced as if such invalid or unenforceable provision was not contained herein.

NOTICE: All written notices required hereunder shall be deemed effective when received by <Firm> at its office at 1234 Main Street, City, State, Zip Code, or by the Client at the address shown on the Client Information Form. Each party shall be entitled to presume the correctness of such address until notified in writing to the contrary.

CONFIDENTIALITY: Except as otherwise agreed in writing or as required by law, Advisor will exercise the highest degree of due diligence and care with respect to keeping confidential all Client information. However, by signing this agreement, Client authorizes Advisor to give a copy of this Agreement to any broker, dealer or other party to a transaction for the Account, or the Custodian as evidence of Advisor's limited power of attorney and authority to act on Client's behalf. In addition, Client grants Advisor authority to discuss, disclose and provide confidential Client information to outside attorneys, auditors, consultants and any other professional advisors retained by Advisor to assist in the management of this Agreement and Client's Account. It is <Firm>'s policy to make available client's account information to the client's spouse. A client may restrict such availability to client's spouse by notifying <Firm> in writing.

PRIVACY: In compliance with the Securities and Exchange Commission's Regulation S-P (Privacy of Consumer Financial Information), which was adopted to comply with Section 504 of the Gramm-Leach-Bliley Act (the "G-L-B Act"), Advisor has disclosed to Client its policies and procedures regarding the use and safekeeping of personal information, including, if applicable, how such Client may avoid ("opt out" of) having his/her information shared. By signing below, Client acknowledges that it has read and understands that initial delivery of Advisor's annual privacy notice.

ACKNOWLEDGMENT OF RECEIPT OF BROCHURE AND FORM ADV PART II: Client hereby acknowledge(s) that they have received and have had an opportunity to read <Firm>'s Form ADV Part II as required by Rule 204-3 of the Investment Advisors Act of 1940. Notwithstanding anything to the contrary herein, Client shall have the right to terminate this Agreement within five (5) business days of the effective date of this Agreement at no financial cost.

Dated _____   Client _____   Print Name _____

Dated _____   Client _____   Print Name _____

Dated _____   Client _____   Print Name _____

Figure 2.8 Sample Investment Advisory Agreement (cont'd)

<Firm Name>
Asset Management
Fee Schedule

Management Fees:

Management fees are based upon a percentage of the assets under management and are invoiced and paid prorata in January, May and September.

The ongoing management fees based upon assets are as follows:

For managed assets that are less than $500,000, a fee of 1.3% annually will be assessed.

For managed assets that are $500,000 or more, the below schedule of fees shall apply.

- 0 - $499,999   1.1% annually

- $500,000 - $999,999   .90% annually

- $1,000,000 - $1,499,999   .80% annually

- $1,500,000 - $1,999,999   .70% annually

- $2,000,000 +   .50% annually

Example: A $1,250,000 Management Account would be billed 1.1% annually on the first $500,000, .90% on the next $500,000 and .80% on the next $250,000; this equates to 0.96% annually in this example.

Dated _____   Client _____   Advisor _____

Client _____

Management fees are paid in advance at the beginning of billing period. They are assessed on the account asset value on the last business day of the previous billing period. When an account is established, the management fee is charged for the remainder of the current billing period and is based upon the initial contributions.

Figure 2.9 Arbitration Case Flow[1]

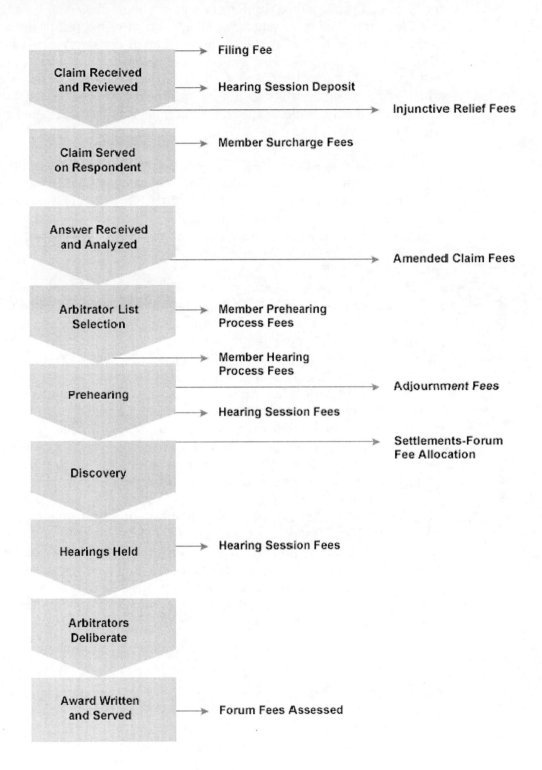

[1] NASD Arbitration Case Flow; as found on http://www.nasd.com/arbitrationmediation/arbitration/arbitrationcaseflow/index.htm.

process ensues. First, a response in the form of an Answers Statement is filed by the financial professional. In this statement, the professional being scrutinized can file counter claims against the client as part of his or her defense. Once a hearing location has been chosen and a limited discovery process completed (the discovery process is the collection and sharing of evidence), the hearing will begin. Hearings are typically scheduled for two days at the conclusion of which the 3-member arbitration panel will deliberate for up to 30 days. At the conclusion of deliberations, the panel will render its verdict (called an award) to which the parties previously agreed.

From 1995 until 2004, the NASD received an average 6,555 arbitration filings per year, but for 2003 and 2004, the NASD received over 8,200 per year. So, while the threat of arbitration should not overwhelm a financial planner's thought processes, it should serve as a reminder to do the best possible job for each client. For more information about arbitration procedures, view the NASD *Code of Arbitration Procedure* on the NASD website.

If a case involves violations of NASD rules, federal securities laws, rules, and/or regulations, the NASD can take disciplinary actions against firms or individuals. These cases can result in the censure, fining, suspension, or barring of a professional or organization found in violation. At one end of the spectrum, censuring involves publicly admonishing the financial professional; at the other end of the spectrum is barring, where a professional can be permanently prohibited from working in the financial industry. In 2005, a penalty was handed down by the National Adjudicatory Council that barred an individual from NASD membership and required restitution of more than $275,000.[27] In the most serious of cases (i.e., those involving criminal offenses such as fraud, embezzlement, extortion, or theft), the SEC or other authority can turn over the case to the appropriate state or federal court for resolution.

The penalties for acting in an unethical or illegal manner can be very severe—as they should be—considering the level of trust and responsibility bestowed on financial professionals. However, by adhering to the laws and regulations, placing the client's welfare first, and documenting every aspect of the client/planner relationship, most financial professionals will not have to worry about defending their actions to either an arbitration panel or court of law.

Chapter Summary

The primary requirement for all professions is that any persons who are affiliated with, or hold themselves out as members of, that profession must conduct business in an ethical manner. While that is a fairly innocuous statement, adhering to all of the rules, regulations, and professional standards of the member's chosen profession can be a very daunting task. This is especially so in financial planning. Prior to the 1930's, caveat emptor was the moniker that guided financial transactions in the United States. However, as a result of the financial instability of the Great Depression, numerous Congressional acts were passed that began regulating the financial industry and its participants. Though much has changed in the 70 years since those first acts were passed, the financial planning profession must still abide by this legal foundation.

However, today's financial planning environment is dictated as much by its current representatives as it is by its original legal foundation. Many different credentialing and membership organizations have developed practice standards and ethical codes to help direct and guide the profession. While the current standards are not more important than the laws on which they are based, it is to these standards that clients can most readily hold their planning professional accountable. Therefore, it is incumbent on all professionals—regardless of their chosen business model—to understand the ethical and legal requirements of the financial planning profession, and to understand the ramifications of failing to follow those standards.

Chapter Endnotes

1. Vessenes, K. (1997). *Protecting Your Practice. Princeton*, NJ: Bloomberg Press.
2. NASD Rule 3040 as found at: http://nasd.complinet.com/nasd/.
3. NASD Rule 3040 as found at: http://nasd.complinet.com/nasd/.
4. Hansen, J. C., Rossberg, R. H., & Cramer, S. H. (1994). *Counseling Theory and Process*. Boston: Allyn and Bacon, 362.
5. White, J., & Taft, S. (2004). "Frameworks for Teaching and Learning Business Ethics within the Global Context: Background of Ethical Theories." *Journal of Management Education*, 28, 463-477.
6. The Act of 1933 required new securities to be registered with the Federal Trade Commission (FTC); however, this was short-lived as the Act of 1934 transferred both the registration and oversight of publicly traded securities to the newly created Securities and Exchange Commission.
7. 15 USC §80b-2(s)(11); as found on the Cornell University Law School Website http://www4.law.cornell.edu/uscode.
8. 15 USC §80b-2(s)(11)a-f ; as found on the Cornell University Law School Website http://www4.law.cornell.edu/uscode.
9. 15 USC §78c-2(b)(35); as found on the Cornell University Law School web site: http://www4.law.cornell.edu/uscode.
10. The first use of the term is found in a written opinion by Justice McKenna of the United States Supreme Court in 1917. Justice McKenna wrote: "The name that is given to the law indicates the evil at which it is aimed, that is, to use the language of a cited case, "speculative schemes which have no more basis than so many feet of 'blue sky'"; or, as stated by counsel in another case, "to stop the sale of stock in fly-by-night concerns, visionary oil wells, distant gold mines and other like fraudulent exploitations." Even if the descriptions be regarded as rhetorical, the existence of evil is indicated, and a belief of its detriment; and we shall not pause to do more than state that the prevention of deception is within the competency of government and that the appreciation of the consequences of it is not open for our review." *Hall v. Geiger-Jones Co.*, 242 U.S. 539 (1917).
11. For additional license information visit www.nasd.org.
12. Certified Financial Planner Board of Standards, Inc. (2003). *CFP Board's Standards of Professional Conduct*. Denver. CFP Board.
13. At the time this text was going to print, the CFP Board of Standards had just released a proposal for the revision of their *Code of Ethics*. Given that the changes had just opened for public vetting, the decision was made to retain the previous version of the *Code* within this book. To ensure understanding of any possible changes that occurred since publication, readers are encouraged to independently research the final version.
14. Trone, D. B., Allbright, W. R., & Taylor, P. R. (1996). *The Management of Investment Decisions*. New York: McGraw-Hill, p. 20.
15. See "Don Trone on the Fiduciary State of Mind," in Voice, *Journal of Financial Planning*, (2005, February), 10-14.
16. *Harvard College v. Amory*, 26 Mass. (9 Pick.) 446 (1830).
17. Restatement of Trusts 2d § 227 (1959).
18. Firestone Tire & Rubber Co. v. Bruch, 489 U.S. 101, 110-11 (1989).
19. National Conference of Commissioners on Uniform State Laws (1994), *Uniform Prudent Investor Act*, as found at: http://www.law.upenn.edu/bll/ulc/fnact99/1990s/upia94.htm.
20. National Association of Insurance Commissioners (2002) *Interstate Insurance Compact*.
21. National Association of Securities Dealers Manual, Section 2200 – Communication with the Public.
22. Securities and Exchange Commission, 17 CFR Part 24, Release No. 34-47806, Electronic Storage of Broker-Dealer Records.
23. At the time this text was going to print, the CFP Board of Standards had just released a proposal for the revision of their *Code of Ethics*. Given that the changes had just opened for public vetting, the decision was made to retain the previous version of the *Code* within this book. To ensure understanding of any possible changes that occurred since publication, readers are encouraged to independently research the final version.
24. Certified Financial Planner Board of Standards, Inc. (2003). *CFP Board's Standards of Professional Conduct*. Denver. CFP Board.
25. http://www.nasd.com/web/idcplg?IdcService=SS_GET_PAGE&ssDocName=NASDW_010578.
26. NASD Rule 3080 Arbitration Disclosure Statement, http://www.nasd.com/web/idcplg?IdcService=SS_GET_PAGE&nodeId=993.
27. NASD Monthly Disciplinary Actions (June 2005); as found at http://www.nasd.com/web/idcplg?IdcService=SS_GET_PAGE&nodeId=1185.
28. Certified Financial Planner Board of Standards, Inc. (2003).

Chapter Resources

Securities Lawyer's Deskbook, Published by The University of Cincinnati College of Law, available at:http://www.law.uc.edu/CCL/xyz/sldtoc.html.

Chapter Review

The Basics: Review Questions

Discussion Questions

The Certified Financial Planner Board of Standards, Inc. defines a client as follows:

"A person, persons, or entity who engages a practitioner and for whom professional services are rendered. For purposes of this definition, a practitioner is engaged when an individual, based upon the relevant facts and circumstances, reasonably relies upon information or service provided by that practitioner."[28]

Use this definition to answer questions 1 through 3 below:

1. If a CFP® certificant were at a party and was overheard by someone he or she did not know talking about the sale of a stock, and the person acted on the information, would the CFP® Board consider the person to be the financial planner's client? Why or why not?

2. Must a person pay for services to be considered a client under this definition?

3. Are all financial planners required to use this definition of client?

4. How do teleological and deontological approaches to ethics differ?

5. How are ethics and values related?

6. How do practice standards differ from statements of ethics?

7. What are the differences between certifications, quasi-certifications, and designations?

8. Describe the five fundamental components of the Uniform Prudent Investor Act.

9. List and briefly describe the eight SEC fiduciary requirements.

10. Briefly describe the NASD arbitration process.

Chapter 3

A Fundamental Tool in the Process: Client Communication

1. Explain why financial planning requires a mix of technical and counseling skills.

2. Describe how verbal, nonverbal, and paralanguage cues contribute to communication.

3. Explain how privacy, comfort, and control influence planner-client communication.

4. Explain the role of experiential maps, heuristics, and emotions in the communication process.

5. Identify the three preferred information processing styles for learning and communicating.

6. Explain and demonstrate the use of active listening, clarification techniques, questioning, and silence.

7. Explain how different communication techniques can be used to better understand or modify client objections or resistance.

8. Identify and explain how ongoing communication efforts are used for planner marketing.

The Building Blocks of the Financial Planning Pyramid

Key Terms

Active listening	Level one probe
Attending	Level two probe
Auditory communicator/learner	Marketing
Body language	Mirroring
Comfort	Paralanguage
Communication	Paraphrase
Congruence	Privacy
Content	Prospecting
Control	Rate
Direct marketing	Restate
Drip marketing	Servicing
Experiential map	Space
Heuristic	Summarization
Indirect marketing	Tone
Kinesthetic communicator/ learner	Visual communicator/learner
	Volume

Financial Planner: Technician or Counselor?

Financial planning is built on a sound technical knowledge of a range of financial products and services coupled with the quantitative skills necessary to analyze the client's situation. In essence, a financial planner diagnoses the problem and then recommends the products or strategies with the greatest probability of success. However, this perspective of financial planner as technician neglects the critical role of the client as the foundation for the financial planning process. In fact, it is communication, and the evolving planner-client relationship, that contextualizes the client's reasons for seeking financial planning. Both clients and planners must recognize a client's attitudes, feelings, and emotions about money as well as how those attitudes, feelings, or emotions may affect financial actions or inaction.[1] To accomplish the client's goals, change may be necessary, but changing attitudes and behaviors involves incremental steps rather than a command of action. Moreover, it is often the changes that life brings—both expected and unexpected—that clients are trying to prepare for or to respond to.

Recall that a list of the 10 most important factors identified by consumers when choosing a financial planner was presented in Chapter 1. A review of those traits confirms the perception that a financial planner is a blend of counselor and technical expert who can solve problems *with* the client, but not necessarily *for* the client. In other words, the client wants to be involved. Although multiple theories and approaches to counseling abound, the seminal definition of counseling was provided by Geis when he asserted that counseling:

> "[I]s an activity in which a person who is trained and experienced in the psychological theory and practice of understanding and changing human behavior seeks to influence, mainly but not exclusively by the techniques of talking, the perceptions, thinking, feelings, emotions and actions of one or more counselees, with the intention of producing short- and/or long-range changes in the counselee and/or in his reality situation which are more self-benefiting and self-actualizing and less self-defeating and self-inhibiting, with regard to what the counselee and/or counselor define as the counselee's self-interest as it relates to his personality and/or his reality problems."[2]

Given this definition, it is evident that financial planners are not counselors. Few financial planners have academic training in personality assessment, psychotherapy, or behavioral change theory—although attention to these applications within financial planning is on the rise. In fact, some firms have added professionals with this expertise to their team. But the apparent differences should not suggest that the traits associated with successful counseling are completely inapplicable to financial planning. In fact, the opposite is true. The way in which a counselor achieves communication breakthroughs with a client should be similar to the method by which a financial planner optimizes communication with clients. In fact, the traits associated with successful counselors are easily adaptable to financial planning as shown in Figure 3.1, and should be characteristics of accomplished financial planners.

Figure 3.1 Financial Planner Communication Traits

Trait	Example
Regards Clients as Persons of Worth	Unconditional acceptance of the client and the client's past actions
Non-Possessive Warmth	Reflects genuine concern for the client with overtones of personal caring while at the same time fostering client independence and professional boundaries
Competence and Confidence	Presents an image through appearance and communication methods that highlights personal strengths and professionalism
Sincerity and Openness	Displays sincere openness and respect for the client as an individual
Empathy and Understanding	Strives to fully understand and respect the client's paradigms and share the client's concerns
Sensitivity	Acknowledges the importance of the client's emotional as well as financial needs and respects personal values, morals, and ethics
Objectivity	Provides neutral, suitable advice in the best interest of the client
Flexibility	Is willing to explore new planning strategies and to adapt previous recommendations to new client, market, or economic situations
High Intelligence	Values the role of continuing professional education and life-long learning
Absence of Emotional Disturbance or Instability	Avoids biases or moods that might distort or disrupt the planner-client relationship or the client's financial situation
Absence of Disruptive Personal Values	Screens religious, political, social, and philosophical personal differences when values are not shared by client, *or* works only with clients who share personal values
Personal Style	Comfortably uses body language, humor, stories, and emotion when working with clients
Miscellaneous Aspects	Presents a congruent message consistent with age, gender, appearance, and habits

Table and Concepts Adapted from Geis (1973).

Financial planners are almost always better served in the roles of counselor, educator, and coach than authoritative expert or financial technician. Counselors ask probing questions. Educators inform and offer new insights from which others can make sound rational decisions. Coaches promote success through disciplined actions, perseverance, and motivation. Authoritative expert planners focus on facts and presuppose what is right or wrong for a client. But a truly effective financial planner—either individually or through the combined efforts of a team of professionals—brings together the roles of technician and counselor. An effective financial planner has personality and communication traits *similar* to successful counselors in other helping professions. A great counselor or planner is open to the client's needs. Effective counselors blend empathy, compassion, and warmth with professional expertise. Planners must demonstrate similar qualities as they help prepare clients and their families to cope with the unknown. In these roles, they have the opportunity to share in the joys of dreams come true as well as the disappointments and despair that life brings. Ongoing client communication is the mechanism that makes this possible.

Perfecting the *craft* of effective client communication is built on practice, experience, and training that goes far beyond the very basic review presented in this chapter. But a thorough grounding in the communication skills necessary to initiate and foster long-term planner-client relationships is fundamental to the process of financial planning.

The Multifaceted Aspects of Client Communication

Communication, in its broadest sense, is defined as the exchange of information among two or more parties. Verbal, nonverbal, and **paralanguage** cues contribute to communication. Tone, rate, and volume of speech are sometimes referred to as paralanguage. Although it is important to individually consider the meaning or message sent in each of these different modes of communication, in reality attention to all three will likely yield the most accurate interpretation.

Communication goes well beyond a person's words, or verbalizations. In fact, the message sent by the combination of nonverbal and paralanguage cues is particularly important. Experts suggest that less than 10 percent of communication is truly conveyed by the verbal message. Over-reliance on the specific words used to relay information, referred to as the **content** of communication, can be misleading. While content is important, the manner in which the words are delivered may be more important. Understanding paralanguage or other nonverbal communication is important to interpreting the client's feelings or emotions. For example, a client may state "This is huge!" If this is said loudly with a frown, the meaning will be interpreted differently than if said loudly but with a smile.

Emotions or feelings can often be interpreted through a client's **body language**, another example of a nonverbal cue. Body language typically refers to the facial expressions, gestures, body positioning, or movements of individuals as well as the use of space between the parties. A client who sits leaning slightly back in the chair with arms folded across his or her chest is sending a message of reluctance, skepticism, and/or annoyance. On the other hand, a client who sits forward taking notes while the planner describes the recommendation is sending another message, one of engagement and interest. Body language that enhances the communication process includes leaning forward to hear, presenting an image of active engagement with the other person, avoiding overly expressive facial movements, and minimizing nervous or distracting mannerisms.

Gender, ethnic, or cultural differences must also be accounted for in nonverbal communication. Women tend to display more nonverbal cues than men, especially cues that suggest affirmation or support for the speaker, regardless of the actual level of agreement. Consistent with this message, women typically display more direct eye contact than men. Also the volume of conversation between men and women can vary dramatically. Tonal and volume differences can also come into play when a planner and client share different ethnic backgrounds. What one person considers yelling, for instance, may be another person's form of daily expression. In the Northeastern United States, people talk considerably faster than residents of the South or Midwest. It is possible for an otherwise friendly and caring planner from the East to be considered rude or pushy in the Midwest. It is also possible for someone from the South to be considered less confident, capable, or sophisticated to someone in New York City.

In terms of body proximity, most North Americans like to maintain distance between each other (at least one arm's length distance or three to four feet) while talking. Sitting too close or touching may make some clients uncomfortable. For example, in the United States it is common to provide those with who you are in close contact sufficient personal space. This is not the case in some other countries where "personal space" is a foreign concept. Spatial differences are less of a factor between women than they are with men. Men, for instance, are not as comfortable making physical contact in emotional situations.

According to Somers-Flanagan and Somers-Flanagan, non-Hispanic Whites prefer to maintain eye contact throughout an interview or meeting session.[3] Native Americans, African-Americans, and Asians, on the other hand, prefer less eye contact. Some Native American groups are offended by continued eye contact. Eye-to-eye contact between two men is appropriate in a Middle Eastern culture, but is not permitted between a man and a woman. General rules suggest that a planner maintain eye contact when listening and less contact when speaking. In the United States, increased eye contact has been associated with sincerity, self-confidence, friendliness, and maturity, while less eye contact suggests a lack of confidence, defensive, indifference, coldness, or immaturity.

It is important for planners to also assess the congruence or consistency of their own as well as their client's communication. **Congruence** refers to the consistency between *how* something is said and *what* is said. For example, a client could say "I think this will work," to reflect uncertainty with the effectiveness of a strategy. On the other hand, a different client might use the same phrase to express strong agreement with the planner's recommendation. Again, the client's tone, paralanguage, and body language can tell an astute planner much about the client's state of mind. The nonverbal message is often assumed to be the most accurate when the messages are incongruent. Rather than make assumptions, the more effective communicator will—with sensitivity—explore the discrepancy or comment on it by saying "your words say this will work, but *you* don't seem to be fully convinced." The effective interpretation and use of communication strategies is central to promoting a trusting environment for the planner-client relationship.

The synergistic combination of verbal and nonverbal cues constitutes **attending**, or attentiveness, a very important component of effective communication. Attending behavior typically focuses on maintaining comfortable *eye contact*, a comfortable *distance* between speakers, and a relaxed but comfortable *posture* with *gestures* used appropriately to "punctuate" the message. Effective verbal attending behavior prohibits the listener from asking questions that do not directly fit the topic, focus, or context of the speaker's message; changing the direction of the conversation; interrupting the speaker; or adding new meaning or explanation to the speaker's message. Recommended verbal statements include simple confirmations, such as "I see what you mean," "I understand," or restatement of a word or phrase used by the speaker. Attending behavior reinforces, supports, and encourages the speaker to continue talking about experiences, ideas, or feelings. Attending behavior validates the speaker and sends the message that the speaker and the topic are important.

Messages to Clients

Messages beyond the explicit content of the words are constantly being sent by planners and clients. Consider the initial meeting, which provides a unique opportunity to present an image to the client that will define the working relationship from that moment forward. First impressions are very important; they affect interaction and communication. Every planner needs to take an unbiased look at the type of image presented to clients. Unless the environment is safe, comfortable, and representative of the firm, the client may misinterpret the planner's abilities. Somers-Flanagan and Somers-Flanagan report that physical factors directly influence communication interactions.[4] They suggest that three elements must be present to make an interview effective: (1) **privacy**; (2) **comfort**; and (3) **control**.

Clients are often unwilling to share confidential financial and personal information in informal settings. It is because of this that a planner should take the time to design an office environment that sends a message of competence, orderliness, diligence, professionalism, and **privacy**. This explains one reason why so many financial planning and private banking offices are decorated with dark, heavy, traditional-looking furniture and fixtures. The look of dark cherry or mahogany with subdued lighting, for example, can create a mood of confidence, trust, and stability as well as success. Some clients prefer this environment, while other clients prefer a more informal, home office environment. Regardless of the office design, it is important that the office or room where the interview occurs should offer soundproofing so that clients cannot hear others nor be heard in adjacent spaces. Also, it may be appropriate to provide a private exit or meeting facility for clients, especially if the office is busy and the work being done is of a very confidential nature or for highly visible members of the community who desire privacy.

Assuming that an office provides optimal privacy, it is also important for clients to feel comfortable. Just as when counselors from other helping relationships work with clients, it is essential for financial planners to cultivate a feeling of trust. One of the best ways to do this is to design an office and interview sessions to maximize **comfort**. While every planner needs to create a work space that maximizes performance, there are a few simple ways to communicate trust and professionalism to a client that do not interfere with a planner's work needs. For example, is the office environment neat, clean, and organized? Is the space aesthetically pleasant and well maintained? Are important diplomas and certificates framed and prominently displayed? Are a variety of refreshments (if offered) available? Is the financial planning staff professional, courteous, and knowledgable? As these questions indicate, there are many ways a financial planner can design an office environment to provide privacy and comfort—and send a message to the client.

Control deals with the issue of creating an atmosphere that makes data collection, communication, and client acceptance of planning strategies and recommendations efficient and effective. For example, it is possible to create an authoritative relationship by maintaining a desk or other piece of office furniture between the client and planner. A more open relationship can be established by using a round or oval table for discussing issues with clients. Control means that a financial planner has created an environment that offers privacy and comfort, and one that allows the planner to manage the information flow, tempo of interview, and overall experience of the client. Somers-Flanagan and Somers-Flanagan provide excellent guidance on seating arrangements as a way to control the context of an interview.[5] They recommend that a client and advisor be seated between 90- and 150-degree angles to each other during interviews and client meetings. A 120-degree angle is sometimes preferred by financial planners. This angle allows a planner to make eye contact with a client without having to look at the client all of the time. Control issues extend as far as to where to place a clock in an office. Preferably, a client, when seated, should not be able to see a clock; however, the planner should be able to see the clock without the client noticing. This control factor allows a planner to pace the flow of a meeting and manage time more effectively.

Preparing for a client meeting goes beyond adjusting the physical environment. Developing a communication strategy is equally important. Factors such as the planner's appearance, demeanor, seating position, eye contact, communication style, and presentation of information all contribute to the total communication effort. Planners who proceed with a client meeting without addressing these and other communication issues are taking a leap of faith that their message, both personal and professional, will be received and understood by a client.

Communication Tip: Dressing for Financial Planning Success

The way a financial planner dresses communicates a great deal about the firm and the practice management style. For example, some very successful firms have adopted a business casual policy of wearing khakis and polo shirts to work. The work of the planners may be exceptional, but they have decided that promoting a comfortable environment for meeting and working with clients is more important than dressing in more formal and traditional business attire. Other planners feel that making a forceful first impression warrants wearing a suit everyday. This rule is used particularly by those seeking to work with clients who expect their financial planner to exhibit outward success. What is important is to remember that not all clients will appreciate a planner's personal or professional style. It is more important to work with clients that appreciate and are comfortable with the planner's business model than to attempt to be all things to all clients.

Assessing a Client's Information Processing and Communication Style

Clients and planners view the world differently. Too often, each assumes that their view is correct and shared by others. In fact, everyone has, in effect, an **experiential map**, which is used to help explain and define the world around them. Experiential maps are based, in part, on heuristics. A **heuristic** is a cognitive shortcut that can be used to simplify a difficult decision. An experiential map, thus, is based on the notion that individuals do what is best for them using past experience and knowledge as their guide. If someone, for instance, has consistently lost money buying and selling stock, there may be a strongly held heuristic that says stock equals loss. This person's experiential map will suggest that investing in stocks is imprudent and fruitless; while the planner with greater knowledge and experience with market trends knows that this heuristic is *not* true. A financial planner who works with this kind of client runs a risk of miscommunication and perhaps an unsatisfying planner-client relationship, as both parties may struggle to change the view of the other. If the client's beliefs, attitudes, and expectations are not thoroughly explored, the planner may draw incorrect conclusions about the client's willingness to implement recommendations or to accept the professional judgment of the planner.

Through verbal, nonverbal, and paralanguage clues, clients divulge their preferred methods for communicating and processing information. It is up to the planner to receive and interpret these signals and, to the extent possible, appropriately tailor communication to the client. The literature on information processing and learning styles is extensive. Fundamental to that study is the premise that individuals use three primary modes for learning and communication—**visual**, **auditory**, and **kinesthetic**—and that most individuals display a preference, although all three styles are typically used. For simplicity's sake, consider these information processing styles relative to the primary sensory inputs: eyes; ears; and physical and emotional experiences. This is not to suggest that experiences are not processed through all three sensory experiences in addition to smell and taste. In fact, activating one sense will likely result in activation of the other senses. By recognizing and activating the preferred sensory mode, the message is more likely to be received and the listener, or receiver of the message, is more likely to feel validated, or recognized. Placed in the context of financial planning, it is easy to see how important recognition of information processing styles can be to the planner-client relationship.

Visual learners rely on their eyes and thus prefer to watch others complete a task or skill. They find figures, graphs, charts, videos, and PowerPoint presentations to be very effective. Those with a visual preference favor learning and communicating by reading and taking notes, and favor an organized and sequenced presentation of information. Someone who prefers this style of communication will tend to read the entire plan, prospectus, or annual report and may take detailed notes during meetings. They are also likely to be quiet during a formal presentation of information, such as when a planner presents or explains the financial plan.

Auditory communicators rely on what they hear and may not directly observe the speaker or pay attention to the visual displays of information. Note taking is not likely, although auditory learners are often quite talkative. They prefer lectures or the interaction of discussions and question and answer sessions. In general, a client who prefers the auditory method of communication would rather talk to the planner than read the plan.

A kinesthetic communicator prefers involvement in the learning process, such as to touch, feel or manipulate something. Kinesthetic processing may involve affective, or emotional, reactions or physical actions—either of which engage the learner with the experience. Mental imagery, through drawing pictures, brief descriptive writing tasks, or responding to projections about feelings (e.g., "how would you feel if you could not fund half of your child's college costs?") are sometimes used by planners to more fully involve kinesthetic learners and to tap into emotional issues or personality traits that affect financial goals or actions. The physical aspect of kinesthetic processing involves direct actions and activities. Kinesthetic clients would find reading a comprehensive plan tedious and not very helpful, while interacting with computer or Internet-based financial planning applications or calculators could be very insightful.

Exhibit 3.1 Information Processing and Communication Style Comparisons

Learning and Communication Preference	Visual	Auditory	Kinesthetic
Learns by Listening		√	
Learns by Watching Others	√		
Learns by Reading	√		
Learns by Taking Notes and Writing	√		
Learns by Doing			√
Makes Decisions after Conducting Thorough Research	√		
Makes Decisions after Listening to Proposals		√	
Makes Decisions Based on Life Experiences			√

They might prefer to simply jump in and address financial issues as they arise. Their approach to learning is more haphazard or random rather than organized and sequential as preferred by the visual learner. Fidgeting during the presentation of a plan may be misinterpreted by the planner as lack of interest or commitment, while it is really an indicator of the need to be involved. Role plays and games are preferred learning methods. Exhibit 3.1 compares the three learning and communication styles.

While it is important to remember that everyone may have a preferred, or more effective, information processing style, some do not have a preferred style. Furthermore, everyone adapts to obtain information in a variety of ways. For example, someone who is primarily an auditory learner may also like to see data and conclusions presented visually. If one communication approach does not seem to be working, a financial planner should use another or multiple communication techniques. In these cases, the planner should attempt another form of communication or combine more than one style. Table 3.3 provides a sampling of words commonly used to indicate a person's preferred communication style.

Exhibit 3.2 Words Associated With Communication Styles

Word Reflecting Communication Style	Example	Visual	Auditory	Kinesthetic
Show	Show me what you mean.	√		
See	I see what you are saying.	√		
Look	Let me look it over.	√		
Perspective	That is an interesting perspective.	√		
Note	I need to make a note of that.	√		
Study	I would like to study those documents.	√		
Hear	I hear what you are saying.		√	
Sounds	That sounds like a great plan.		√	
Say	I understand what you are saying.		√	
Touch Base	Let's touch base in a month.			√
Feel	I feel very good about this decision.			√
Handle	Can you handle the implementation?			√
Tie, Found, Follow	That certainly helps to tie things together. But I found her explanation harder to follow.			√

Effective communication strategies can provide a richer understanding of the client's experiential map and emotions that influence financial decision making and actions. This information is useful to the planner, but may be even more useful to the client, who may never have had an opportunity to consider some of these life-influencing factors. As a part of the financial planning relationship, planners can help clients understand, adjust, expand, or revise their experiential maps and deeply held heuristic-based beliefs, or—if change is not to occur—to accept the consequences of the choice. This may occur through exploration of the source of the heuristic or through education or new experiences that expand the client's perspective. It is important to recognize that clients act on the basis of the information they have; expanding that information may expand their options and empower them to choose new options.

Opportunities abound for planner-client communication throughout the financial planning relationship. Direct exchange may occur through the interview process or initial meetings between the client and planner, the actual narrative of the plan, the planner's presentation of the plan to the client, or the planner's explanation of how the planning process will improve the client's life. Indirect opportunities may occur through the web site, client newsletters, periodic account updates or quarterly reports, or other informal means of communication. In other words, there are multiple opportunities for exchange and influence through various modes of communication. Planners who recognize their client's experiential maps and heuristics, and who incorporate multiple information processing styles in their various forms of client communication, significantly increase the likelihood that their message will be heard *and* understood.

A Basic Tool Box for Planner-Client Communication

A financial planner must be knowledgeable of the advantages, disadvantages and appropriate uses for a variety of financial products and strategies—what might be referred to as the financial "tools of the trade." It is equally important, and some would argue more important, to have a tool box of communication strategies. Similarly, the planner must recognize the advantages, disadvantages, and appropriate uses for each. Communication is used to initiate, build, foster, maintain, and enrich the planner-client relationship. Basic tools of communication focus on effective strategies for listening, clarifying, questioning, and using silence. Learning to use a variety of communication tools makes the process more interesting and less predictable, and provides the fuel for a planning relationship that promotes action, and when necessary change.

Listening

There are two important ratios that should serve as the foundation of any discussion on listening. First, people have two ears and two eyes but only one mouth. That ratio of 4:1 should guide most communication. Second, the typical rate of speaking and listening ranges from 125 to 400 words per minute, but most people think at a rate of 1,000 to 3,000 words per minute. Without a concerted effort, boredom or faster-paced thinking will drown out the spoken words and listening will give way to hearing. Hearing, however, is not listening, although the two are often confused. *Real* listening, or **active listening**, involves the ears as well as the face, the body, the mind and the heart. It is the total engagement of the listener that makes active listening a learned skill that is built on discipline and self-control.

Similar to the concept of attending, active listening involves both verbal and nonverbal communication. Active listening does not require agreement; however, through a combination of facial expressions, posture, and gestures the planner communicates understanding, interest, acceptance, and empathy. It is these physical efforts, involving *face* and *body*, which support active listening. By truly focusing on the client, the planner is better equipped to combine other communication strategies to help the client explore and amplify the experiential map, heuristics, or feelings surrounding the issue. It is important that the planner avoid interrupting the speaker, or pre-judging the situation and finishing the client's sentences. Instead, the planner can be most helpful by systematically helping the client to explore the topic. It is through these efforts that the planner's *mind* is involved in listening. An open mind is necessary, as is a concerted effort to limit environmental distractions or other mental "self-talk" that diverts attention away from the client.

By engaging the *heart* when listening, the planner is challenged to be empathetic and to fully assume the perspective of the client—even when their viewpoints diverge. For example, why would a client with significant wealth and an annual salary of $250,000 strongly assert that he has no intentions of paying for four years of a college education for his children? The planner's role is not to agree or to change the client's attitudes and feelings; instead, the planner's role is to use communication techniques to explore the surrounding issues in an effort to inform the planning process. Empathetically assuming the perspective of the client leads to greater understanding and acceptance of the client's feelings, values, and beliefs. Acceptance, not *personal* agreement, precludes judgment that could negatively impact or destroy the relationship.

Attention to the spoken message as well as the emotional message is a hallmark of active listening. But not every planner-client exchange requires empathetic listening. Simple factual exchanges regarding quantitative issues (e.g., the client's family, health, employment, or financial status) are not likely to have emotional overtones, although the planner should be sensitive to these messages. However, discussions of qualitative issues (e.g., the personal and social dimensions of the client, including goals, personality, interests, attitudes, and values) will likely require the planner to assume the role of active listener. In other situations, the emotions will be apparent and the reason for the communication.

Individuals, be they clients or prospective clients, tend to seek the help of financial planners when one or more of five emotions is present: (1) anger; (2) anxiety; (3) fear; (4) disappointment; and (5) enthusiasm.[6] Dealing with what Weisinger calls emotionally charged clients is one of the most challenging aspects of being a financial planner. While it is often easy to tell if someone is emotionally charged (e.g., they tell you they are angry or fearful), sometimes the only way to know is to evaluate the way in which the person is communicating.

Exhibit 3.3 Communication Clues of Emotional Stress

Clue	Indicator of Emotional Stress	
Tone of Voice	√	Higher than Normal Pitch
Volume of Voice	√	Raised
	√	Very Low
Rate of Speech	√	Faster than Normal
	√	Slower than Normal
Facial Expression	√	Frown
	√	Pierced Lips
	√	Tears
Body Gestures	√	Arms Folded Across Chest
	√	Use of Index Finger to Point at Advisor
	√	Covering of Face with Hands

Clues to emotionality include facial expressions and paralanguage (i.e., the rate, tone, and volume of speech). Exhibit 3.3 illustrates communication clues that indicate if a person is emotionally stressed.

In the end, the best strategy is to simply be quiet and listen—whether working with emotionally charged clients or clients who are trying to explore and identify emotional triggers within their experiential map. In other words, practice active listening. Rather than push forward in awkward situations or attempt to change the topic, the most effective financial planners allow the client to talk. The planner may use communication strategies to interpret and steer a conversation or to systematically explore the issue, but in almost all cases, it is best to allow the client to talk freely and openly.

Clarification

Many types of verbal communication strategies can be used when working with clients, but four stand out as being particularly useful. Each of these strategies signals to the client that the planner is listening, but moreover that the planner is taking an active role in the communication process.

Sometimes an effective strategy involves restating a client comment. (Some authors call this reflecting content.) With **restatement**, the main or primary thought of the message is restated by the planner in a condensed or more direct manner. If a client states that "I want to save money for my child's college expenses, but I don't see how I can do that and save for retirement at the same time," it may be appropriate to restate the comment back to the client. A restatement might include remarking that "You would like to save for college and retirement ... and it would be helpful if a solution could be found to accomplish both." The motto with restatement is "use the speaker's words," but avoid sounding like a parrot, while still accomplishing the central objectives of fully engaging in the client communication and clarifying the accuracy of the message. It is important to acknowledge that the restatement may be more for the benefit of the client than the advisor, as the topics explored—either individually or with couples, partners, or other family members—may not have ever been discussed or the personal views expressed.

The second strategy involves paraphrasing, or restating a client's comment, suggestion, or concern. To **paraphrase**, restate the basic message in a concise and simple statement. The common motto (with paraphrasing) is "use your own words." Then check for a nonverbal or verbal cue from the client about the accuracy of the interpretation. Suppose a client says that "I'm just not sure what to do. I know that I need to be saving for Omar's education, but the account balance in my 401(k) seems pitifully small." A paraphrase approach would have the planner state "You're concerned about accomplishing these two goals." If the client is presenting a mixed or double message, perhaps about the commitment to increased savings for goals *and* a reluctance to review lifestyle issues to increase cash flow, a paraphrased statement offers the planner an opportunity to reflect the discrepancy and to better gauge the client's response.

In other cases it is may be appropriate for the planner to **summarize** the client's comments, or to ask the client to summarize or identify major issues. Summaries may occur after an extended discussion between client and planner or after longer remarks by one party. Summarizing focuses on the main ideas but serves to integrate the ideas into a more cohesive reflection of the discussion. Summaries are used to indicate movement or progress, as in from one discussion subject to another or from one session to another. Summaries may occur naturally at the end of a meeting or at the beginning of a new session. In the latter case, the previous meeting would be summarized generally, or perhaps the results of that meeting would be summarized relative to the actions subsequently taken by the planner or client. For example, "at our previous meeting we discussed your wishes for the distribution of your estate and agreed to… In addition you were going to draft a list of all personal property that you would like to distribute to your children and grandchildren. Let's begin our meeting by reviewing that list. Then, we'll review our other plans in preparation for the meeting with the estate attorney later this week." A summary at the end of the meeting can also be used as a foundation for identifying tasks, responsibilities, or behaviors to be completed by the planner or client.

Some planners use a mirroring technique to enhance planner-client communication. **Mirroring** refers to reflecting both verbal and nonverbal communication of the client. The advisor's choice of words is one example of mirroring. A very knowledgeable client may choose very specific or technical language, while less knowledgeable clients may try to make associations between more familiar concepts and the ones presented to them in the plan. The planner should "match" the client's language, just as the planner might match the more formal or relaxed posture of a client. However, excessive mirroring can be distracting, and if the planner's attempts are too overt the client may find the technique offensive. This communication strategy is another example of building a connection with the client by establishing quite clearly that the planner is indeed listening to the client.

Mastering these clarification techniques, as well as other strategies recommended in this chapter, enhances planner-client communication, but more importantly contributes to a stronger planner-client relationship. Use of these techniques also accomplishes the following goals:

- Communicates empathy, understanding, acceptance, warmth, and a willingness to develop a personal, but professional relationship with the client;

- Fosters mutual trust, which can facilitate decision making as well as the framing of goals and objectives, the selection of recommendations, and the methods for implementing and monitoring the plan setting, problem resolution, and plan development steps within the process;

- Supports continued exploration of the topic, issue, emotion, or goal, which typically encourages the speaker to add detail through more introspection;

- Expands the planner's knowledge and understanding of the client's experiential map, heuristics, or emotions;

- Establishes a feedback loop between client and planner; and

- Encourages continuation of the discussion and promotes the planner-client relationship.

Obtaining Information Through Questioning

Questions are a staple of everyday conversation, but must be used carefully in a planning situation. Excessive use of questions can hinder the relationship; responsibility for the entire process shifts to the planner because of the implicit message that the planner is "in charge" and will ask what is necessary. In the worst case, too many questions become more like an interrogation with the technical expert in search of a quick resolution. Planners are cautioned not to use questions as an alternative for making a statement, such as "Wouldn't you agree that making periodic contributions to a 529 plan is the best alternative?" Although on the one hand the question may be meant to solicit the client's involvement in decision-making; on the other hand the question is a safer position for the planner than clearly stating "Opening and funding a 529 plan with periodic contributions is the best alternative for your situation."

Care also must be taken to avoid questions that have no apparent answer or appear to be insulting, such as "Why didn't you sign up for the insurance at work?" Although the intent of the question may have been sincere exploration of the factors that led to that decision, the question can have an accusatory tone. Better options might be "Could you tell me more about your decision not to sign up for the insurance at work?" or "What factors contributed to your decision not to sign up for the insurance at work?" Finally, planners must be careful not to ask questions that solicit the socially acceptable answer from the client, but not the client's true feelings or behaviors. Because of the cultural, ethnic, and societal expectation surrounding money and its use, planners must be particularly careful that the planner-client relationship is honest and trustworthy; communication techniques, especially questions, are critical to building that rapport. Typically, two types of probing questions—level one probes and level two probes—are helpful when seeking information. Both types of questions are similar in that each type may begin with interrogatives, such as who, what, when, where, why, or how. However, the scope and intent of the question and the typical response elicited can be quite different.

A **level one probe** is a question used to obtain factual client information. Answers to level one probes are verifiable. Answers to this type of question are often limited to providing "yes" or "no" responses or giving replies based on data or other known facts. For this reason, this type of question is sometimes referred to as a "closed-end" question. Questions that begin with "Do," "Did," "When," and "Where" typically generate level one responses. Variations focus on you, such as "Did you," "Are you," "Have you" or "Could you." While a level one probe is a useful tool during the initial client data gathering, responses to level one probes are less useful in understanding a client's motives for maintaining or changing the financial situation. However, level one probes can be helpful to limit responses of a client who is very talkative, or a client whose excessive responses limit the participation by others (e.g., spouse, partner, or others).

Level two probes are used to delve deeper into a client's knowledge and attitudes. A level two probe is the most effective method for obtaining information from a client about feelings, emotions, or reactions to a goal or some other aspect of the planning process. Also called "open-ended" questions, level two probes invite exploration. One way to solicit level two responses is to ask questions that begin with "What," "When," "Where," "How," and "Why." Level two probes can be very useful in determining a client's personal and financial goals and objectives or when significant life events have brought about changes that may impact the client's financial situation or planning efforts. However, planners are cautioned about careful use of "why" questions, which may not be as effective as questions that begin with "what" or "how." "Why" questions can become tedious, accusatory, and are simply difficult to answer, whereas questions phrased more carefully encourage clarification, expansion, or focus—all of which serve to better inform the planning process for both the planner and the client.

Silence

Although questioning is a staple of normal conversation, silence is not. Silence can be golden (or so the old adage says), but most people are not comfortable with it. Sometimes, however, silence can be an effective tool to help a client continue processing and discussing a difficult, emotional, or important topic. This may be true because people do not like to sit in silence, so they tend to continue talking. Or, the discussion may have truly allowed the individual the time and opportunity—perhaps for the first time—to fully consider the topic, and the silence is simply an extension of that reflection or introspection. Allowing silence, perhaps for 5 to 10 seconds, is a way to encourage the client to provide more detailed information about the situation or to resolve an important issue without the use of additional questions or comments. Furthermore, silence benefits the planner by allowing time for careful attention to nonverbal cues, reflection on the client's message, or the crafting of clarification statements or questions to continue the exploration. What is most important is not to interrupt naturally occurring silence, but to foster it through nonverbal messages such as gestures (head nodding), comfortable eye contact, simple vocalizations ("um-hum," "yes"), or restatement of a key word. The use of silence as a communication technique can be a challenge, but the benefits are well worth the effort to become comfortable with the uncomfortable.

Putting It All Together

Rattiner stresses three important attributes for effective communication.[7] The best planner at all times displays a positive attitude. The planner is always looking for positive outcomes, which often requires shifting a client's focus away from apparent weaknesses to hidden strengths. A great communicator is also able to establish rapport with a client. This does not mean that the planner is necessarily charismatic. If a planner is genuine, it is natural to communicate in a caring and empathetic way. Finally, all good planners tune in to their clients' needs and goals, spoken or otherwise. These planners attempt to understand the different communication styles used by clients to send messages. But in the end, the best planners simply "shut up" and listen.

Ongoing Planner-Client Communication

The communication skills that support personal, or face-to-face, communication can serve as an important background for other dimensions of planner-client communication. These skills are critical to the formative work that the planner and client must complete as part of the planning process. In addition, planners must master other communication skills necessary for initiating and managing client relationships. Specifically, two areas of planner communication should not be overlooked and are worthy of continued study and skill development. First is effectively responding to client resistance or objections. Granted, this type of communication will most likely occur face-to-face and some of the same skills of active listening, clarification, questioning, and silence are applicable. However, the significance of this dimension of planner-client communication warrants special consideration because of what it entails. "Closing the deal" for many planners and clients has a negative connotation, but failure to close the deal can have far reaching implications for both. Marketing, the second dimension of client communication, can be just as intimidating as client rejection of a plan or recommendation. But as overwhelming as these communication challenges may appear, the good news is that there is a wealth of expert wisdom to guide the student or novice planner beyond the brief summaries that follow.

Resistance and Objections

The financial salesperson may not be a good counselor; nor is the counselor likely to be a good salesperson. But one fact is unavoidable: financial planners *must market and sell products, services, or both.* When it comes right down to it, the primary role of a financial planner is to help clients optimize their financial situation to meet short- and long-term personal and financial goals. But that will not happen unless the planner can effectively provide products and/or services at a price that is satisfactory to the client *and* that will sustain the planner's business long term. This is true whether the planner is employed as an independent planner or as a salaried employee of a larger company. Central to that business relationship is the ability to prepare and present the plan in a way that cements the planner-client relationship.

One of the best ways to ensure client implementation of recommendations is to use a combination of communication strategies and effective follow up. Listening and nonverbal affirmations do not necessarily mean that the client is willing to implement recommendations. If a client presents objections or resistance it is important to listen quietly and hear the client out. There is no need to jump to defend a recommendation until the client has voiced all objections. Communication techniques, such as paraphrasing and summarizing, can then be used to isolate the client's reservations. When isolating the issues it is prudent to focus on one objection at a time, but in no way should the planner willingly accept a client's objection without first attempting to fully understand the emotional and intellectual underpinnings. Active listening, clarification techniques, and level two probes may be useful for fully amplifying the objections for the planner as well as the client.

An objection may be driven by the client's experiential map, heuristics, or a broad range of emotions. Objections can also be based on a client's comfort level, which may need to be modified if financial objectives are to be met. Client education may be one approach; however, what may be most important is for the planner to fully acknowledge, respect, and show understanding of the client's position. Replacing the planner's arguments, rationales, and facts with empathetic listening for the client's view can be an important step. It is said that good communicators and good salespeople are good listeners. Helping the client to explore the emotions that underlie the objection as well as the emotions that made the goal or objective important is likely to be more productive than using a purely factual or logical tactic.

Focusing on the benefits of the recommendation, or some possible middle ground for accomplishing the goal, may also help the client to more fully weigh the risks and rewards of the recommendation. At first consideration, a client's reasons for not buying life insurance (e.g., my spouse will remarry, or my in-laws will help out) may be humorous or simply evasive. But there may be a need for the client to fully acknowledge the sad reality of what life might be like without insurance to replace lost income. It is at this juncture that the difference between salesperson and counselor may be most evident. If a trustworthy, genuine relationship has been forged as a foundation of the planning process, it will ground the comparison of risks and rewards. "Pulling the heart strings" may be viewed as sincere concern, not just good salesmanship. Furthermore, that concern could lead to a recommendation that is more acceptable to the client, yet still provides some level of goal achievement.

Finally, it is important to keep the line of dialogue open to fully explore the client's inaction or confusion. Sometimes the process of presenting to the client is quick and easy; at other times, however, explaining the complexities of a financial proposal can take time. In addition to other communication attributes, patience can strengthen the communication process. Patience with clients as they work through the rational, emotional, and financial aspects of a plan is essential. Rather than rush a client to make a rash decision that may later be reversed, it is often better to patiently work with a client in answering questions and creating an environment of trust, which will lead to greater client commitment.

Communication Tip: Technology and Communication

"Whether it's a handwritten note or a private client page on your web site, the underlying messages to clients are the same: You're thinking of them and you're staying on top of their planning needs. A good communications strategy can accomplish both objectives."[8]

Cell phones, websites, and email have dramatically changed the way financial planners interact with current and prospective clients. Bruckenstein and Drucker argue that planners must adopt technologies that enhance communication in order to remain competitive.[9] Client newsletters may be available on-line or by mail. Tools such as email allow for greater frequency of communication. This can ensure that clients are kept up to date via monthly news bulletins, office closure dates, and market analyses. Since email is also less expensive than the postal service, lower costs can translate into reduced fees for clients. The use of email may also increase time efficiency for both the planner and the clients. Billing and reporting can be done using email or password protected websites. There are drawbacks to technology, however. Planners lose communication clues with electronic communication, but video conferencing and periodic meetings or telephone conversations offer alternatives for more personal dialogue.

Marketing: Initiating and Managing the Planner-Client Relationship

Multiple modes of communication are particularly important when marketing a planning practice. **Marketing** involves identifying the need for a product or service and then determining how to responsively deliver that product or service to consumers. Marketing for financial planners can be thought of in two ways: **prospecting** and **servicing**. Ideally, both should elicit action by the recipient. When prospecting for clients, a financial planner's primary goal is to enhance visibility and name recognition while informing potential clients of available services. Servicing (also known as relationship marketing) involves nurturing or expanding existing relationships through periodic communication. In financial planning, the communication might range from periodic account reporting to educational newsletters, or articles or cards acknowledging some other special or shared interest. From a client's perspective, all communication should be of some value to the client and add value to the relationship; otherwise, the communication will be viewed as just another piece of junk mail, SPAM, or random solicitation. While both prospecting and servicing are important, continuing communication with existing customers can result in the most beneficial marketing strategy of all: "word of mouth" or client referrals.

Exhibit 3.4 provides a sample of publications, forms, and actions financial planners use to market a practice. Each requires written, verbal, or a combination of both communication skills to be effective. For example, a well-written, informative article or newsletter sent to current clients to educate them may also be shared with potential clients and will enhance the credibility of the planner. **Drip marketing**—defined as a continuous, recurring, or ongoing flow of letters, cards, articles, newsletters, or other marketing items—may be used for both prospecting and servicing. Because of the continuous "attention," prospective clients may become clients. Thus, well-designed, client-appropriate drip marketing efforts can further solidify the planner-client relationship.

Exhibit 3.4 Financial Planning Marketing Strategies

Marketing Item	Communication Skill	Prospecting / Servicing	Direct / Indirect
Brochures	Written	Servicing	Both
Newsletters	Written	Prospecting	Both
Drip Marketing	Written	Servicing	Direct
Direct Mail Marketing	Written	Both	Direct
Email Updates	Written	Servicing	Direct
Websites	Written	Both	Indirect
CDs, Videos, and DVDs	Written and Verbal	Both	Direct
Speeches	Verbal and Written	Prospecting	Both
Books	Written	Prospecting	Indirect
Professional, Trade or Other Articles	Written	Prospecting	Indirect
Teaching	Verbal	Both	Direct
Periodic Meetings with Clients	Verbal	Servicing	Direct
Seminars	Verbal	Both	Direct
Cards of Congratulations or Recognition of Other Personal Events	Written	Servicing	Direct
Trade Show or Other Community Business Forum	Verbal	Both	Indirect
Telephone	Verbal	Both	Direct
Newspaper Columns	Written	Prospecting	Indirect
Print and On-air Advertising	Written and Verbal	Prospecting	Indirect
Radio and TV Shows	Oral	Prospecting	Indirect
Press Releases	Written	Prospecting	Indirect
Community Service or Pro Bono Work	Written and Oral	Both	Indirect

Marketing can also be categorized as direct or indirect marketing. **Direct marketing** (e.g., telephone calls, direct mailings, targeted seminars, etc.) should have a personal touch because each recipient would like to feel as if the communication was meant just for him or her. Whether a planner has said something to them, handed them something, or mailed something to them, clients want to feel that they received something "special." **Indirect marketing** (e.g., websites, newspaper columns, television advertisements, mass media, etc.) typically has a more formal or generalist viewpoint. While some tailoring is possible, a planner would want to generate widespread appeal.

Some planners may expand their expertise and time by purchasing one or more marketing items from, or outsourcing their marketing efforts to, specialized providers. Other planners may choose not to utilize certain strategies, or may find that some strategies simply are not effective or are no longer necessary as the planner's reputation and referral network expands. For planners who are not independent, some marketing materials may be provided by the parent company or other product providers. In all instances, marketing materials should be reviewed for accuracy, broad-based demographic appeal (unless a specific market segment is being targeted) and compliance-related issues. More information about the compliance and/or regulatory issues regarding communication with the public is discussed in Chapter 2 - Ethics, Laws, and Regulations.

Chapter Summary

The planner, office, client documents, marketing strategies, and even what is not said by the use of silence all *communicate* to clients and potential clients. When considered from this broad perspective, it is easier to understand the complexity, and significance, of communication in the total planner-client relationship. Attention to interpersonal communication strategies (e.g., the use of active listening, clarification, questioning, and silence), allows for an exchange of information, but more importantly builds planner-client trust and rapport. Awareness of the importance of information processing styles should impact oral and written client communication as well as marketing strategies and website design. Mastering the fundamental concepts introduced in this chapter will enable students and advisors to enhance their client relationships, and establish a foundation for continued learning about the multifaceted applications of communication within the process and practice of financial planning.

Chapter Endnotes

1. As noted in Chapter 1, for simplicity most comments throughout this book reference the client in the singular, although the plurality of couples, partners, families, or other legal entities should not be ignored. The content of this chapter is equally useful with one or more clients, but communicating with more than one client increases the complexity and challenges the planner to selectively use strategies that are mutually effective and engaging with each client. Furthermore, it may be necessary to promote communication between the clients, as well as between the clients and planner.

2. Geis, H. J. (1973). "Toward a Comprehensive Framework Unifying All Systems of Counseling," In John Vriend (ed.). *Counseling Effectively in Groups*. Englewood Cliffs, NJ: Educational Technology Publications.

3. Sommers-Flanagan, R., & Sommers-Flanagan, J. (1999). *Clinical Interviewing* (2nd ed.). New York: Wiley.

4. Sommers-Flanagan, R., & Sommers-Flanagan, J. (1999). *Clinical Interviewing* (2nd ed.). New York: Wiley.

5. Sommers-Flanagan, R., & Sommers-Flanagan, J. (1999). *Clinical Interviewing* (2nd ed.). New York: Wiley.

6. Weisinger, H. (2004). *The Emotionally Intelligent Financial Advisor*. Chicago: Dearborn.

7. Rattiner, J. H. (2000). *Getting Started as a Financial Planner*. Princeton, NJ: Bloomberg Press.

8. Newton, C. (2001). "Staying In Touch: How Planners Communicate With Their Clients," *Journal of Financial Planning*, at: www.fpanet.org/journal/articles/2001_Issues/jfp0401-art3.cfm?renderforprint=1.

9. Bruckenstein, J. P., & Drucker, D. J. (2004). *Tools and Techniques of Practice Management*. Erlanger, KY: National Underwriter, p. 27.

Chapter Review

The Basics: Discussion Questions

1. Develop a list of at least 20 expected or unexpected life changes or events that financial planners may help a client prepare for, or respond to. Identify at least five emotions or feelings that may surround each change. Challenge yourself to be more creative and descriptive by listing something other than basic emotions (e.g., happy, sad, or lost).

2. Define **experiential map** and **heuristic**. Give examples of how each might influence the financial planning process. How might they influence the way a client interprets a financial planner's recommendations?

3. What messages can eye contact convey? Why might this sometimes be misleading?

4. Explain why questions beginning with the word "why" can be problematic in planner-client communication.

5. Identify and briefly describe the cues a financial planner might use to identify an emotionally stressed client.

6. Explain how communication skills impact the way in which a financial planning practice is marketed.

7. List five strategies for overcoming a client's resistance or objections to a recommendation.

8. Identify three marketing strategies used by financial planners and describe them as servicing or prospecting, direct or indirect, and based on verbal or written communication. Try to identify strategies that are not listed in Exhibit 3.4.

9. How should an advisor design the office to help clients feel comfortable to share information? Describe how the office environment can convey an image of trust and professionalism.

10. Develop a list of methods for interacting with clients, noting for each the type of information processing or learning style for which it might be effective or ineffective. For example, email may be very effective for a visual learner, but ineffective for communicating important information to a client with a strong auditory or kinesthetic preference.

Chapter *4*

A Fundamental Tool in the Process: Decision Making

1. Describe and apply a general model of decision making.

2. Explain how decision making rules may be applied within the decision making process.

3. Understand and apply the traditional decision making approach to a financial planning decision.

4. Recognize and explain how behavioral finance concepts may impact the decisions and choices made.

5. Identify and explain the threats to the decision making process.

6. Summarize how uncertainty, intuition, and habits impact decision making.

The Building Blocks of the Financial Planning Pyramid

Key Terms

Aversion to loss	Maximization
Behavioral finance	Mental accounting
Complacency	Mental accounts
Decision	Objective probabilities
Decision making	Optimization
Defensive avoidance	Overconfidence bias
Deterministic model	Panic reactions
Framing	Prospect Theory
Gambler's fallacy	Regression to the mean
Habit	Regret avoidance
Herding	Representativeness
Heuristic	Satisficing
Hot hand fallacy	Stochastic modeling
House money	Subjective probabilities
Ignoring the base rate	Traditional decision making

Introduction

Financial planners—like medical, legal, and other professionals—are charged daily with making decisions with, or on behalf of, clients that will impact the lives of the clients and perhaps even the professional. But it is the sheer complexity of the relationships, the multitude of factors impacting the decisions, and the uncertainty surrounding the decisions that makes decision making a fundamental financial planning tool. In addition, there is the element of time. Decisions on choosing and funding retirement savings vehicles, although made today, can impact outcomes for decades into the future. And then there is the issue of the number of decision makers. A decision may involve one person or many people and may impact the decision maker or others, immediately or in the future. Cumulatively, all decisions made by a financial planner add up in ways that determine whether or not a practice will be successful for the planner and the clients served.

So, what is a decision? What is decision making? These may seem like silly questions on the surface because most anyone could provide an answer. But the volumes written and the numerous theories developed about this subject attest to the complexity of the questions that have been approached from various disciplines of study, ranging from personal self-help books to complex statistical and computer modeling. A **decision** represents a choice, resolution or conclusion arrived at after a consideration of alternatives. Assuming that there are no options, or no choices to make, removes the need to make a decision. Similarly, engaging in **habits** averts conscious decision making as individuals routinely select the same choice every time. To make a decision is synonymous with coming to a conclusion based on fact, emotion, assumptions, conjecture, interpretation, or some combination of these and other factors.

Decision making is the dynamic process of defining the problem or issue to be decided, identifying the alternatives, clarifying the criteria on which the alternatives will be evaluated, reviewing the alternatives, and making the choice. To some, decision making ends there—with the choice. Other authors assert that decision making continues through the stage of taking action on the choice and then evaluating both the choice and the process. In fact, authors writing about decision makers, the decision making process, decisions, and the outcomes of decisions use evaluative terms like "good" and "bad." "Good" decisions lead to positive outcomes, while "bad" decisions lead to results that are less than optimal. However, it is important to recognize that a "good" decision process could result in a "bad" outcome. Conversely, a bad decisison process, with luck, could result in a "good" outcome. The problem is that humans equate the success of the decision process with the outcome. This lends itself to throwing out good decision making processes sometimes when the outcome was not what was originally desired, and keeping lousy decision processes because luckily the outcome was what was wanted. Without objective analysis of the decision process and the outcome, a bad decision process may continue to be used until it fails, then the error is covered, or explained, by saying "who could have known?"

For example, a bad financial planning decision can result in a client coming up short of assets at a critical time in the future, or even to the termination of a client-planner relationship. Bad decisions can sometimes lead to professional reprimand and civil liability. Consider the case of a planner that decides, after careful deliberation, to borrow money from a client to cover cash flow deficits in the planning firm. This decision may seem like a good one. The planner wins by obtaining needed cash flow and the client wins by gaining a fair rate of return on a relatively low-risk loan. On closer inspection, however, this decision is fraught with problems. First, the client-planner relationship becomes one of a creditor-debtor interaction, which places the planner in a financially compromising position. The Certified Financial Planner Board of Standards, Inc. has concluded that this type of relationship is subject to review and reprimand. Borrowing money from a client is specifically prohibited for a CFP® certificant. As this example illustrates, what may appear to be a simple decision may not always be that simple or lead to the anticipated outcomes.

Furthermore, this example illustrates several important reasons for studying decision making within the context of financial planning. Although these concepts are further considered in Chapter 2 - Ethics, Regulations and Laws, it is important to recognize that decision making, with, for, or on behalf of a client, may invoke a fiduciary or trustee relationship. As such, the planner has an ethical, professional, and legal responsibility to act in the best interests of the client. Second, that professional responsibility may be further defined by professional or regulatory codes of conduct. Both professional standards and fiduciary responsibilities require defensible decision making practices. The advertising theme of a particular financial services company asserts "You cannot predict, but you can prepare." Sound decision making practices lay the foundation for solid planning practices that prepare clients—to the extent possible—for the uncertainty of the future. Sound decision making practices help planners to build a defensible position on the line separating prediction from preparation.

No decision making framework can ever hope to perfectly replicate the qualitative aspects of the behavioral process. Furthermore, the scope of the topic far exceeds what can be addressed in this chapter. But better understanding of the steps involved in decision making and increased awareness of some of the myriad factors that may affect decision making can yield new insights for planners and their clients.

A Generalized Model of Decision Making

One reason people sometimes make bad decisions is that they fail to use a standard model of decision making. A model can be quite helpful in illustrating the *ideal* steps to fully defining the problem, identifying the alternatives and their potential consequences, and choosing an alternative that best utilizes resources relative to this or other competing goals. But note that it may not be necessary to follow the model for every decision or choice. In fact habits, such as the choice of your favorite soft drink, are an example of a mental shortcut that alleviates the need to routinely process information to arrive at the simple selection of a beverage. The following discussion presents a generalized model of decision making, as shown in Figure 4.1, which can be applied in most decision making situations, including the financial planning process.

Step 1: Recognize the Need to Make a Decision and Define the Question, Behavior, Concern, Problem, or Goal. Every decision begins by recognizing a need to make a decision. This need may be prompted by a question, behavior, concern, problem, or goal. The issue may be threatening to the individual, such as a problem, or the issue may offer a new challenge or welcome change, such as an opportunity. There must be an evaluation of the issue prompting the need for a decision to allow the decision maker to truly identify the issue and not simply the symptoms of the issue. Questions to ask at this step include: (1) Is the issue longstanding or is it a short-term event? (2) Is the issue self-correcting? (3) If nothing is done, will harm occur? (4) If something is done, will benefit occur?

Step 2: Identify and Research Alternatives in Response to the Question, Behavior, Concern, Problem, or Goal. It is at this stage of the decision making process that a decision maker must put experience, knowledge, assumptions, and expectations to work. Some issues have obvious alternatives, while others do not. Some decision makers prefer to identify all possible alternatives—even those considered outside the realm of reasonable execution. Others limit the identification of alternatives to those that are feasible, given the available resources and subjective values, attitudes, or goals of the decision maker. Any assumptions regarding the decision problem and all alternatives must also be identified, the impact considered, and, if relevant, the probabilty, or likelihood, of occurrence assigned. For example, when deciding whether to fund a traditional IRA or a Roth IRA, one primary decision criteria is the tax implication for the current funding year vs. the future withdrawal year. Of critical imporatance to the benefit of tax deferral is the assumption of a lower tax bracket upon retirement. If the decision maker cannot reasonably assume being in a lower tax bracket when the funds are withdrawn, the Roth offers an immediate advantage over the traditional IRA, exclusive of other considerations.

The search for solutions and strategies may happen intuitively or in a more formalized manner. The choice of how to search for strategies depends on a person's knowledge, experience, and familiarity with an issue, as well the individual's willingness to conduct a search for new information that might introduce other alternatives or insights. Furthermore, the number of alternatives generated tends to vary with the importance of the decision. Decisions that are perceived to be more important typically warrant an extended information search to identify multiple alternatives. The decision maker's confusion or difficulty with processing multiple alternatives may increase with the number of alternatives. Confusion can be reduced with identification of alternatives that represent a wide range of appeal for the decision maker.

Finally, time should be invested in thinking about the potential unintended consequences of the decision. The more significant the potential for a negative consequence, the more time and work should be put into developing alternatives. Questions to ask at this step include: (1) Is the decision maker guilty of paradigm paralysis or the inabilty to see or identify alternatives that do not agree with the decision maker's perspective? (2) Has the alternative search resulted in repeated identification of the same, or similar, alternatives, suggesting that the search is exhastive *or*, conversely, that the decision maker is not open to new ideas? (3) Do the alternatives identified truly address the decision problem, and not just symptoms of the problem?

Step 3: Consider and Rank the Alternatives Relative to the Established Criteria. In the majority of cases, this is the most difficult step in the decision making process. First it requires the decision maker to consider the criteria, both subjective and objective, that are important for this particular decision. Subjective factors include tastes, preferences, values, attitudes, beliefs, needs, wants, assumptions, morals, or ethics—all of which may influence the choice. Objective factors include: availability of resources; costs and benefits associated with each alternative; attributes or characteristics of each alternative; and, when applicable, projections on the probability of the outcomes or assumptions. Second, the decision maker must identify the most important criteria for the decision in question. Third, the alternatives relative to the criteria set must be ranked. Questions to ask at this step of the process include: (1) Are the decision making criteria appropriately balanced between objective and subjective criteria? (2) Which criterion(a) will have the greatest impact on this decision situation? (3) Which alternative is least costly or offers the greatest benefit? (4) Which alternative best matches the decision maker's values, goals, and available resources?

Step 4: Choose an Alternative and Implement It. When the alternatives have been evaluated and ranked, a selection must be made. Quite frequently, a choice must be made among several alternatives to arrive at an optimal course of action. Some choices result from conscious deliberation while others result from intuition. Intuition, sometimes explained by the decision maker as "just knowing" or a "gut reaction," is not typically based on a conscious review of the alternatives, but rather on an assumed broad-based comprehension of the situation and a realization of the alternative to be selected. An optimal choice is often impossible, as the decision maker either does not, cannot, or will not have full knowledge of all alternatives, potential consequences, or the likelihood of any given consequence occurring. In addition to being the optimal, well-conceived, or "best" choice, the chosen alternative and its projected outcome should also reduce doubt and anxiety for the decision maker.

Once a course of action has been chosen, it is essential that implementation take place. Without implementation, a decision is really nothing more than a desire. The choice of action may be positive, negative, or neutral (i.e., no action). The timing of the choice of action may be determined by the severity of the client's situation, the importance placed on the need to improve the situation, or the availability of resources for meeting the need.

As a part of this step, it is also important to identify evaluative criteria, or preliminary signals—ranging from the anecdotal to the catastrophic—that the decision maker will use to assess the success, or failure, of the chosen alternative as well as the decision process. The evalutative criteria should be a valid reflection of the decision and the decision maker, and may be limited by the decision maker's knowledge, experience, and familiarity with the issue.

Questions to ask at this step of the process include: (1) Was the choice of the alternative primarily based on intuition, fact, or a combination of both? (2) Was the choice, the implementation, or the decision making process affected by the decision maker's procrastination? By the decision maker's anxiety to make a decision? (3) Were evaluative criteria identified that reflect both the objective and subjective issues that charaterize this decision, and its significance for the decision maker?

Step 5: Evaluate the Outcome and the Decision Making Process. It is important to complete the decision making process by assessing outcomes (positive, negative, or neutral) and making adjustments for future decisions by monitoring the process and outcomes of previous decisions. Not only does the decision maker have to identify and rank the criteria used to evaluate the outcome, but the decision maker must also set a standard—the yardstick used to measure the outcome. Identifying appropriate standards for comparison at this step serves as a final check on the most significant objective and subjective evaluative criteria. Without having a set standard—based on intangible measures, such as personal experience or satisfaction, or fact-based knowledge—that can be substantiated, the process fails to be repeatable.

Sometimes a person will make a bad decision, or one with negative outcomes, while at other times a decision may lead to unknown or unanticipated consequences. Remember, sometimes a good process may lead to a bad decision and other times a bad process may lead to a good decision, the difference in these two being luck, fate, or the unforeseen—all of which are beyond the decision maker's control. The objective is to identify a process that can be consistently applied with the expectation of yielding a satisfactory decision. Thus, it is important to document the: decision process; information search; criteria, and assumptions considered; alternatives identified; rationale for the choice; and evaluative criteria identified to monitor the success of the choice or, if necessary, the need for a new decision. This kind of information can be instrumental to the review of the decision outcome and process, or it can be helpful when facing a similar decision.

Questions to ask at this step of the process include: (1) What can be learned from this situation and the outcome achieved? (2) In hindsight, what information could have been useful, and may have changed either the decision making process or the outcome? Was the information available, but not included? Or, available, but ignored? (3) How should the decision making process change in the future, either in general or specifically when applied to similar situations?

A simple example may serve to illustrate the model. Consider an individual who recognized the need to save regularly for retirement through an available 403(b) plan. A review of the available investment products yielded a wealth of objective information on the returns, volatility, and risks of different mutual funds—all of which involved the stock market. Instead of taking on any market risk, the young professional chose to invest all of his monthly retirement savings into a money market mutual fund based on the single criterion of safety of principal. Although this alternative significantly reduced the fear of loss associated with funds invested in the stock market, the risk of the inflationary erosion of purchasing power associated with low-yielding investments was not one of the higher ranking criteria and was ignored in the decision process.

Was this decision flawed by a lack of information that would have enabled the individual to fully understand the alternatives and the benefits of prudently assumed investment risk? By the ranking of the criteria, particularly the strong personal conviction that the stock market was too risky for retirement savings? Because no method or standard, such as the historical average return on the stock market, was identifed for evaluating the outcome or the process? What is known is that after decades of savings, funds were insufficient to support retirement. The decision meant that the individual faced either a significantly reduced standard of living in retirement, or continued full-time or part-time employment during what had originally been planned to be the retirement years.

Figure 4.1: A General Model of Decision Making

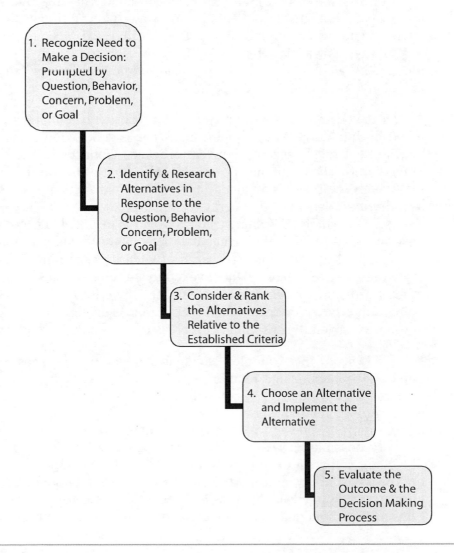

Decision Rules for Choosing Among Alternatives

There are, in fact, multiple decision making rules that can be used to reach a conclusion. The first strategy is termed **maximization**, which involves choosing the outcome with the highest unadjusted result based on the assumption that the best possible outcome of the alternative will in fact occur. For example, if a client were given two choices with one offering a 10% return and another offering a 5% return, the maximization approach would have the client choose the 10% return. This choice, as is apparent, does not take into account probabilities of success or qualitative client factors, such as risk tolerance, time frame, or experience. For example, consider the trend of investors attempting to time the market and chasing returns rather than implementing a more proven buy-and-hold strategy.

Optimization is an alternative to the maximization approach. This technique can be used when all relevant goals, data, and resources are known and more than one alternative is available. Optimization simply requires the decision maker to choose the optimum course of action, or the one that will lead to the highest level of satisfaction. But this choice is grounded on the assumptions that all the alternatives are identified and feasible (given the goal, resources, and decision making criteria), and the decision maker has the time and energy to conduct an evaluative comparison of all alternatives. Financial planners and clients that use the optimization rule must take into account a wide range of quantitative as well as subjective data in an effort to identify the optimal choice among the alternatives. Furthermore, the time and energy required for such exhaustive review should not be overlooked.

"**Satisficing**," which originated in the 1950s with economist Herbert Simon, might be summarized by the question "When is good, good enough?" For example, a client might need to reinvest proceeds from the sale of an investment immediately. The client may desire a security that offers both liquidity and relatively high returns. In any given market, these two attributes are hard to find, and there will always be uncertainty regarding the availability of such investments. A satisficing decision strategy would lead the client to choose the first best available security that adequately met the need. Once the investment had been made, little additional research or security searching would occur even though further searching might have led to a more optimal security selection. In other words, the objective is to satisfy as many criteria as possible while sacrificing some other criteria. Identification and selection of the "good enough" alternative, given the criteria identified as most important, end the search.

Aside from the examples cited, how might these decision making rules impact the planner-client relationship? Consider that each of these rules or paradigms for viewing the decision will establish a unique framework that may be counter to that employed by the others involved. For example, if the client anticipates an optimizing approach, then the client will expect extensive evaluation of every possible alternative with a clear explanation of the planner's choice. The client will want to be fully convinced that the best option is recommended, but the advisor may interpret the client's search for additional information as an effort to delay the decision or as a reflection of little confidence in the advisor. Consequently, making a recommendation that satisfies only one or two client criteria (albeit the most important ones) will likely disappoint the optimizing client.

Conversely, a client using the satisficing approach may be overwhelmed by extensive analysis and presentation of competing alternatives and wonder "Why can't we just make a decision, given our preference for X and Y, and move on?" The maximizing client may also limit the information search and decision criteria, but care must be taken that the choice of the best is, in fact, based on the criteria most likely to result in long-term success.

Typically, the most difficult challenge facing financial planners during the decision making process involves the evaluation of alternatives. Almost all of the decision making approaches discussed in the chapter can be used to make these assessments. What makes the evaluation step so challenging is the number of quantitative and qualitative factors that need to go into the assessment method. Furthermore, not every strategy lends itself to a single evaluation approach or to a defensible probability estimate. So, how does a planner or client evaluate solutions and strategies that are not easily measured statistically? Decision rules related to maximization, optimization, and satisficing certainly can be used. The problem with these evaluative tools is that they tend to be one-dimensional and focused almost entirely on one outcome measure (e.g., increasing a client's satisfaction, maximizing returns, etc.). None of these standard evaluation tools take into account behavioral processes used by individuals when making decisions, nor do they account for a full consideration of the objective, subjective, and qualitative factors that can influence the evaluative process.

The Traditional Approach to Decision Making

The **traditional decision making approach** has its roots in economics. In the world of economic decision making, individuals are assumed to be rational. It is also assumed that outcomes, or the likelihood of an alternative, can be estimated using probabilities. Under conditions of certainty, the decision maker is assumed to have full knowledge of all possible outcomes for any alternative considered. In a situation of certainty, any given outcome may not have a 100% chance of occurring, but the decision maker has a 100% chance of predicting the correct outcome. For example, consider that the weather report predicts a 60% chance of rain, consistent with the assertion that any given outcome (rain) may not have a 100% chance of occurring. But the outcome, as predicted by the individual hearing the weather report, is either 100% or 0%, such that given the weather forecast the individual has 100% chance of predicting the outcome—rain or no rain. Under conditions of uncertainty, the decision maker does not have reliable information regarding the probability of various outcomes associated with any given alternative. With uncertainty, the individual outcomes still do not have a 100% chance of occurring and the decision maker also does not have a 100% chance of correct prediction. Risk differs from uncertainty in that risk is represented by the personal or economic loss associated with the choices, while uncertainty is simply failing to make the right choice regardless of gain or loss.

The traditional decision making process relies on probabilities to arrive at a solution evaluation. There are two types of probabilities that a planner can apply when using this approach: objective and subjective probabilities. **Objective**

probabilities are those that are known with some certainty, based on experience, experiments, or results of research or study with large samples. Mortality probabilities are one example of an objective probability as are other actuarial data such as number of accidents. **Subjective probabilities** are based on a person's belief or best guess of the likelihood of an event actually occurring. For example, a market pundit's prediction may be based on history repeating itself: "this year the stock market will end up higher because 75% of the time when January is up, the market ends the year up." Conversely, another expert may conclude that the "market will be down, because of X, Y and Z, although history would predict a different outcome." It is important to understand the basis for the predictions. Both are subjective judgments, based on objective data that support the conclusions, but judgements that may or may not be supported by objective probabilities. The evaluation of financial planning strategies using the traditional decision making approach works best when probabilities are objective rather than subjective. Examples include evaluating insurance solutions where the probabilities of accidents, theft, and death are relatively well known.

Using a traditional decision making approach, it is possible to objectively value an outcome so that a decision maker can choose the optimum solution to a problem. The best way to understand this methodology is through the application of an example. Assume that a financial planner is faced with a decision to reallocate a client's portfolio. Under the first scenario, the planner could choose to do nothing. In this case, the planner estimates that the year end value of the portfolio would be $110,000. In the second scenario the planner could reallocate the portfolio to 80% stocks and 20% bonds. If successful the portfolio would be worth $125,000 at year's end. If unsuccessful the value of the portfolio value would drop to $85,000. The financial planner, who has many years of experience, believes that the chance of success is 75% while the chance of failure is 25% if the portfolio is reallocated. Should the planner reallocate the portfolio or leave it as it is?

A traditional decision making approach can be used to answer this question. An easy way to do so is to summarize the information into a table. Exhibit 4.1 illustrates how reallocating the portfolio results in a higher expected outcome compared to maintaining the current portfolio. The weighted return of achieving success ($125,000 x 75%) plus the weighted return of achieving failure ($85,000 x 25%) is $115,000, which is greater than the guaranteed return of $110,000 by doing nothing. Thus, someone using the traditional decision making approach would choose to reallocate the portfolio. (Note that if the probability of success versus failure was 50%-50% the approach would indicate that the client should hold the current portfolio.)

A relatively new branch of traditional decision making theory is known as **stochastic modeling**. A stochastic model is one in which the inputs are randomized within a certain range so that the model can account for variations and timing of returns. Essentially, stochastic models are mathematical projections that account for *multiple* variables (e.g., mean and standard deviation). A stochastic model can be compared to a **deterministic model**, where inputs are static.[1] Deterministic models are mathematical projections that account for only *one* variable (e.g., return). Hence deterministic models must use averages, which do not account for the fluctuation or timing of returns.

Exhibit 4.1 Traditional Decision Making Approach

Scenario	Ending Value	Probability	Calculation	Outcome
Maintain Current Portfolio	$110,000	100%	$110,000 x 100%	$110,000
			TOTAL	**$110,000**
Reallocate Portfolio	(A) $125,000	(A) 75%	$125,000 x 75%	$93,750
	(B) $85,000	(B) 25%	$85,000 x 25%	$21,250
			TOTAL	**$115,000**

Consider the situation of a planner who wants to evaluate a potential retirement savings strategy for a client. Using a standard deterministic modeling technique, the planner would base the evaluation on the average rate of return of each asset class corresponding to the projected client portfolio. So if the portfolio historically returned 9% on average, the planner could conclude that approximately 50% of the time the client would earn returns greater than 9%, and 50% of the time the client would earn less than 9%. In either case, the probability of achieving 9% remains constant across the evaluation period because the input is static.

Proponents of stochastic modeling argue that using just one variable (e.g., average annual rate of return over "X" years) as input to arrive at a probability estimate can result in misleading or potentially erroneous solutions. Consequently, stochastic modeling takes the actual distribution of returns over the period instead and uses this data to run hundreds or thousands of iterations to arrive at returns with specific probability estimates attached. In other words, a stochastic model can more accurately tell a planner the probability of actually earning 9% over time based on the historical data. Under stochastic modeling, the probability of achieving a straight-line 9% return (as assumed with the deterministic model) is in reality less than 50% and, depending on the standard deviation of the distribution, it could be much less!

The most common stochastic model is based on a normal distribution of one standard deviation from the mean. This model graphs the 85% probability line and the 15% probability line to illustrate that approximately 70% of the time the result will fall between the upper and lower limits. Planners find this useful because they can tell the client that 85% of the time the value under the projected scenario will be equal to or greater than the lower limit value. Obviously, this is much more conclusive than telling the client that there is a 50%-50% chance of meeting or exceeding a certain value.

Results from stochastic modeling—one example of which is called Monte Carlo Simulation—can provide very useful inputs to the traditional decision making process. Recognizing that the probabilities generated are based entirely on past returns of similar securities, and that past performance is no guarantee of future returns, the stochastic model can produce a range of expected rates of returns with corresponding probabilities.

The traditional decision making approach coupled with new stochastic modeling techniques offers financial planners an ideal way to evaluate some, but certainly not all, financial planning strategies or recommendations. Unfortunately, not all strategies lend themselves to arriving at objective probabilities. In fact, the majority of financial planning techniques do not allow probability modeling. Consider strategies of funding retirement through a 401(k) plan or a Roth IRA. What are the probabilities of success using either solution? Financial planners will most likely be willing to give estimates, but such approximations will be subjective rather than objective. Using the traditional decision making process to evaluate these types of solutions and strategies, employing only subjective probabilities is problematic at best—and dangerous at worst.

The traditional decision making approach works quite well when probabilities of outcomes can be estimated with some degree of reliability and in cases where outcomes can be quantified. Unfortunately for financial planners, very few decision outcomes can be quantified that precisely; and even when estimates can be made, the probabilities assigned to different events tend to be wrong. Evidence of this fact can be found in another approach to decision making, behavioral finance.

The Behavioral Finance Approach to Decision Making

Daniel Kahneman and the late Amos Tversky introduced the concept known as **Prospect Theory** in 1979, and many credit this as the establishment of serious study of behavioral finance. However, the origins of behavioral finance can actually be traced back to the mid-1950s.[2] Behavioral finance attempts to bridge the gap between the solely economic model of utility and the more psychological model of value. According to the classical "economic man" theory, the concept of internal motivation is based upon the condition of economic gain. Under the "rational man" theory, when given a choice man has an organized, rational, and stable system of preferences designed to maximize the utility or value received as a result of the choice.

In a review of the behavioral finance theory and research, Shefrin identified three fundamental themes:

1. Financial professionals rely on heuristics (i.e., simplified rules) when making decisions.

2. The way in which a scenario is framed can change a practitioner's perception of the risk and return involved in a decision.

3. Markets are influenced by the way financial professionals make decisions; the markets are inefficient because decisions are based, in part, on cognitive biases.[3]

Each theme will be considered in greater detail, as well as other behavioral finance themes that have emerged as having an effect on decision making.

In 1974, Kahneman and Tversky theorized that people have certain biases when making decisions that result in the formation of heuristics.[4] The preeminent bias is that people tend to avoid risk—more precisely, the kind of risk experienced when the outcome of an event is uncertain. When an event has multiple possible outcomes, each separate outcome has a probability, or range of probabilities, that it will happen; and the higher the likelihood, the higher the probability. However, the number of variables becomes overwhelming when attempting to calculate a probability when there are many possible outcomes each affected by multiple factors.

To deal with these complexities, people use experiential knowledge in order to reduce the probability equations into simpler judgments. This experiential, or common sense knowledge, results in mental shortcuts known as **heuristics** and can lead to the development of heuristic tools. An example of a commonly used heuristic tool, or general rule of practice, for retirement planning is the following equation:

100 – Client's Age = Percentage of the Portfolio in Equities

This straightforward formula simplifies portfolio development by replacing a client's personal situation, goals, time horizon, risk tolerance, attitudes, expectations, and risk capacity with a single assumption. The formula assumes that as a client ages, there is less tolerance for financial risk. Note, however, that there is no convincing empirical research to suggest that age alone causes people to become less risk tolerant. Instead, tolerance for risk is more closely linked with a client's income, net worth, education, and financial knowledge than it is directly correlated with age. In fact, some research suggests a curvilinear relationship.

As a result, although heuristics may be widely accepted, the blending of judgment and fact actually results in more subjective probabilities being assigned to the various outcomes of a choice; it does not, however, guarantee an optimal or accurate prediction of the outcome. In other words, as subjectivity increases, accuracy (at least theoretically) declines.

In addition to the problem of misconception of chance, Tversky and Kahneman identified several other reasons that heuristics and representativeness might also fail to capture the true probability. People apply heuristical judgments based on how well the current situation represents a situation with which they are familiar. This idea is known as **representativeness** (or in a social context, as a stereotype). The more representative the current situation is to the referent situation, the greater the confidence the individual has in the validity of the outcome. Unfortunately, this type of flawed thinking leads to another cause of heuristic failure: frequency of occurrence. Simply because one situation mimics another does not necessarily mean that the outcomes will be identical. A third threat is called the illusion of validity. The asset allocation illustration, above, is a case in point on how a formula can give the illusion of validity because on the surface the heuristic tool seems reasonable.

Thus, although heuristics offers some distinct benefits to decision makers, it can inadvertently bias the decision making process unless the decision maker consciously challenges the heuristics involved—especially when making decisions of great importance.

The role of heuristics in the decision making process can be quite significant. But, according to Shefrin (and others), what is less well known is how the **framing** of a question, case, or scenario can influence the way in which a person arrives at a decision.[5] Framing can occur when the decision maker frames the context of the choice by considering the possible outcomes from a particular paradigm or perspective that is representative of a set of norms, habits, or personal characteristics.

Framing may also occur when a provider of information frames or alters the context of the information in such as way as to influence the decision maker. Consequently, decision framing can be altered by the formulation of the problem or by the context of the possible outcomes. This use of information in a misleading context is readily seen when quoting a short passage from the Bible. Unless the decision maker has complete and unbiased information, the representativeness of the situation, or in this example the meaning of the quote, could be altered to suit the speaker's purpose. Therefore, changing the context has the potential to alter the prediction ability and subsequent prediction accuracy of the decision maker.

Framing may be most apparent when analyzing issues of risk. Consider the following scenario:

Please choose between the following two alternatives:

(A) Take a sure loss of $750; or

(B) Take a 75% chance where you will lose $1,000 and have a 25% chance of losing nothing.

Now consider this alternative:

Please choose between the following two alternatives:

(A) Take a sure gain of $750; or

(B) Take a 75% chance where you will gain $1,000 and have a 25% chance of gaining nothing.

Most people choose answer "B" in the first scenario and answer "A" in the second scenario. Traditional decision making theory and traditional economic theory would suggest that the same answer should be chosen in the second scenario as was chosen in the first scenario. In other words, individuals should exhibit consistent risk choices. This is true because the mathematical outcomes for each question are identical. However, behavioral decision making theory illustrates that framing a question in terms of a known guaranteed loss, the first scenario, will lead people to take risks and gamble by choosing alternative "B." When the same question is framed so that the decision maker can walk away with a guaranteed gain, the gamble is the less likely choice.

So, what does this mean in terms of decision theory? First, people tend to have a strong **aversion to loss**. People dislike losing significantly more than they like winning. Put another way, the attraction of winning is *not* as strong as the aversion for losing. Second, people are not rational (as defined in traditional economic theory) when it comes to making certain decisions. As an example, consider the frequent practice of not ackowledging an investment loss by instead asserting that a paper loss in a stock is not a loss until the stock is actually sold. This tendency is particularly true when it comes to making decisions about money. These two observations offer evidence that traditional economic decision making theory may not be as applicable to financial scenarios as once thought. Taking into account both the planner's and the client's cognitive biases appears to be one way to improve financial decisions.

Refer back to Figure 4.1, which illustrates the example of the traditional decision making approach. Decision makers who are uneasy about selecting the choice to reallocate the assets based on the mathematical outcome provided may be experiencing a behavioral bias called **regret avoidance**. In the reallocation example, above, recall that the portfolio was projected with 100% certainty to equal $110,000. By reallocating, there was the possibility of actually losing value in the portfolio. People who exhibit regret avoidance make decisions that will minimize the negative effect of making a bad or wrong decision. In other words, they will either stick with the status quo or avoid making the decision to reallocate the portfolio. If they do reallocate, it is likely that they will not be comfortable with their decision. If it is the client rather than the planner who makes the decision, it is likely that the client will be calling the financial planner on a regular basis to determine the exact market value of the portfolio. It is also likely that at the first sign of a loss in value, the client will want to return to the original portfolio allocation.

As indicated above, traditional decision making approaches require individuals to assign relatively precise probabilities to events and outcomes. Most financial planners believe that they are very good at predicting outcomes with financial data. However, the evidence suggests otherwise. Consider the now famous prediction example presented below:

> The closing price of the Dow Jones Industrial Average was 40 in 1896. By the end of 1998 the Dow stood at 9,181. Because the Dow is a price-weighted average, dividends are not shown in the closing value of the Dow. Pick a range of possible returns where you are 90% certain that the Dow would have closed had dividends been reinvested and included in the closing, price.[6]

Nearly all respondents—financial planners included—chose ranges such as 9,000 to 18,000 or 9,000 to 36,000. Few people even estimated that the real value of the Dow would have been 652,230 with dividends at year end 1998! This example illustrates how traditional decision making theory can lead to significant errors in action. People have a tendency to be overly optimistic in their own abilities to predict the future. In fact, all people are subject to psychological biases that tend to influence the way they view the world and make decisions.

How overconfident is the average person? Very overconfident indeed. Ask 100 people to rate themselves compared to other drivers on the road in terms of what kind of driver they are (i.e., average, below-average, or above-average), and most will likely offer some interesting information about overconfidence. Statistically, one-third of respondents should answer average, another third below average, and the final third above average. However, in reality it is more likely that well over 75% of those who respond will indicate being an above-average driver. How is this possible? People overestimate their own abilities and underestimate the abilities of others, and this almost always leads to overconfidence and a tendency to take risks when caution should be at the forefront of thought.

People become overconfident for a number of reasons. Investors in particular equate knowledge with control. Individuals who are subject to **overconfidence bias** believe that they can control random events simply by obtaining more knowledge and familiarity with a situation. In other words, overconfident investors believe that a risky decision can be controlled through a combination of superior knowledge, situation familiarity, and active involvement in the implementation of decision action. Again, however, history suggests otherwise. Overconfident investors tend to trade too much and earn lower returns than other investors due to increased tax liability and commissions. Overconfident investors are also more likely to subject themselves to substantially risky decisions because they underestimate the probability of failure and overestimate the probability of success.

As an example, consider the often cited 2003 update of the longitudinal *Quantitative Analysis of Investor Behavior* (QAIB) study by DALBAR, an independent research group, that revealed that the average equity mutual fund investor earned 2.57% annually, less than the comparable inflation rate of 3.14% and significantly less than the S&P 500 average annual earnings of 12.2% over the 19-year period.[7] DALBAR observes that investor fear and greed motivates poorly timed buying at market upturns and selling on market downturns.

One of the hallmarks of behavioral finance theory is the concept of **mental accounting**. Consider the following story as told by Belsky and Gilovich:

> "By the third day of their honeymoon in Las Vegas, the newlyweds had lost their $1,000 gambling allowance. That night in bed, the groom noticed a glowing object on the dresser. Upon closer inspection, he realized it was a $5 chip they had saved as a souvenir. Strangely, the number 17 was flashing on the chip's face. Taking this as an omen, he donned his green bathrobe and rushed down to the roulette tables, where he placed the $5 chip on the square marked 17. Sure enough, the ball hit 17 and a 35-to-1 bet paid $175. He let his winnings ride, and once again the little ball landed on 17, paying $6,125. And so it went, until the lucky groom was about to wager $7.5 million. Unfortunately the floor manager intervened, claiming that the casino didn't have the money to pay should 17 hit again. Undaunted, the groom taxied to a better-financed casino downtown. Once again he bet it all on 17—and once again it hit, paying more than $262 million. Ecstatic, he let his millions ride—only to lose it all when the ball fell on 18. Broke and dejected, the groom walked the several miles back to his hotel.

> 'Where were you?' Asked his bride as he entered their room.

'Playing roulette.'

'How did you do?'

'Not bad. I lost five dollars.'"[8]

Other than being an entertaining story, what does this have to do with decision making? Actually, quite a bit since this story illustrates how people tend to separate and categorize money into different **mental accounts**. Did the man in the green robe lose $5 or did he lose $262 million? If you answered $5 it is likely that you, too, rely on mental accounts as a way to manage your money and resources. Some people believe in something called **house money**. The man in the green robe mentally placed the $5 chip into one "account" and the earnings on the bets in a second "account." This cognitive bias allows gamblers and investors to operate under the illusion of controlling their losses because they feel that losing money in the house money account is not really losing. In effect, using mental accounts is one way that people reduce the feeling of regret associated with gambling and investment losses.

In fact, **mental accounting** is used by everyone in some form or another. It helps explain why some people hold high account balances in low interest earning savings accounts while simultaneously maintaining an outstanding credit card balance. While this is not logical, it can be explained by the fact that some individuals view cash in a liquid emergency fund as one "account" and their liability on a credit card as another "account." In general, few people manage their entire available resources using a global perspective. Understanding how mental accounting can influence financial planning decisions is one way of evaluating a solution to a financial question or concern. It can also be useful to explore the concept of mental accounting with clients. Helping a client who is heavily influenced by mental accounting to objectively understand this concept may lead to a needed behavioral change or even motivate a client to accomplish other goals.

For example, individuals will frequently identify "buckets" of money, or money earmarked for a particular purpose. Common examples include "this is my fun money, or my speculative fund," "this is my 'safe' money, or the kids' education fund." Frequently, however, the risk taken with each individual "bucket," when added together, would exceed the total risk ascribed for the client's situation or total portfolio. In other words, the mental accounting for each "bucket" or goal, allowed the individual to exceed, perhaps dangerously so, the previously identified *comfortable* level of aggregate risk exposure.

Gamblers often believe that a successful outcome is due after a run of bad luck. They believe that a series of independent trials with the same outcome will soon be followed by an opposite outcome. According to Shefrin in his review of behavioral finance theory and research, **gambler's fallacy** arises from the very poor understanding people have about the outcomes of independent, random events. The example most widely used to validate the gambler's fallacy is the coin toss. Suppose that an unbiased coin is flipped three times and each time the coin lands on heads. So, as of the third flip, heads has occurred 100% of the time. Therefore, if a gambler had to bet $100 on the next toss, which side of the coin would be chosen? This is a trick question because the gambler should recognize that the next toss is an independent event from the last three tosses and should have no preference between heads or tails (if the coin is honest). However, most people will choose tails anyway, which is the wrong choice. This is the concept of "they're due (to lose or win)" meaning that the individual does actually have a sense of regression to the mean, but not a clear understanding of the probabilities of each independent event. People mistakenly believe that because even odds exist for both heads and tails, the moving average should nearly reflect the actual probability in both the short-term and the long-term. The idea that regression to the mean happens on a self-correcting, continual basis is what leads people to believe in the gambler's fallacy.

The **hot hand fallacy** is another cognitive bias to which many people succumb. People often interpret accidental success to be the result of skill (i.e., don't confuse a rising stock market with being an expert investor!) and are, therefore, overconfident in their own abilities. Investors, money managers, advisors, and analysts are particularly overconfident in their ability to outperform the market because of their perceived level of knowledge; however, most fail to do so. Increasing levels of confidence frequently show no correlation with greater success—hence the term "it is better to be lucky than good."

For example, suppose that a basketball coach is designing a play and that one player must be chosen to take the final shot. There are 10 seconds left in the game and the team is down by a basket. The star player, who is a lifetime 65% shooter, is only three for ten tonight having missed several easy shots. Another veteran player, who has a 45% shooting percentage, has hit the last 10 shots attempted. For whom should the coach design the final shot? Although open for subjective argument, the coach should give the ball to the star player who has averaged 65% over the season. This example is proof that a basketball player with a "hot hand" is no more likely to make his next shot than at any other time.[9] However, most people will choose the player with the hot hand. Again, wherever independent events are concerned (i.e., shooting a basketball, flipping a coin, or selecting a stock), people are prone to overestimate the representativeness of the situation and assume that they have additional valid information.

In the gambler's fallacy and the hot hand fallacy, investors failed to fully account for the fact that independent trials regress to a mean, or assumed the regression would happen continuously. **Regression to the mean** is a statistical phenomenon pertaining to numerical data in which abnormal results tend to be followed by more average results, or at least average out over large number of attempts. In other words, extreme results in one direction are averaged by equal extremes in the opposite direction. People tend to focus on specific elements of information (e.g., a percentage) and extrapolate from what happened in the recent past well into the future. Unfortunately, this does not take into account the tendency for events, scores, and market returns to revert to their averages. For instance, suppose a stock is selling for a price-to-earnings ratio of 35 when similar stocks in the same industry are selling for a price-to-earnings ratio of 20, the historical mean for the industry. Over time an investor should expect the first stock to decline in value relative to other stocks in the industry. To assume otherwise is to discount statistical probabilities.

Regression to the mean is one example of how statistics can be misconstrued; sometimes, however, the statistical probabilities are simply unknown or ignored. Kahneman and Tversky posed the following scenario to many people over the years, but few tended to answer the question correctly:

> Steve, a thirty-seven year old American, has been described by a former neighbor as follows: "Steve is very shy and withdrawn, invariably helpful, but with little interest in people of the social world. A meek and tidy soul, he has a need for order and structure and a passion for detail." Which occupation is Steve currently more likely to have: a salesman or a librarian?

If the common assumptions are made about character traits of librarians, and the commonalities between Steve and the average librarian are compared, the predicted outcome is that Steve is a librarian. Unfortunately, people do not consider the fact that according to the Bureau of Labor Statistics, there are more than 15 million salespeople in America and there are only 180,000 librarians. Therefore, regardless of Steve's character traits, he is 83 times more likely to be a salesman. This tendency to disregard the overall likelihood of a certain outcome is known as **ignoring the base rate**.[10]

One of the financial outcomes associated with ignoring the base rate is momentum investing, a technique that can drive markets ever higher or lower than a rational model would predict. In the fall of 1987, the United States stock market crashed, falling nearly 25% and scaring away investors for nearly two years. Investors opted instead for bank accounts or bonds because of the perception of relative safety attached to these investments. This "flight to quality," as it has become known, occurred because investors and their advisors failed to remember that the base rate indicated that stocks outperform bonds. Therefore, had they remembered history rather than recent past, they would have recognized that the risk in the stock market had been reduced by the crash, not increased. For example, a review of the market returns for 1987 reveals that the market was actually *up* that year in spite of the significant correction. An interesting, but overlooked fact, given that many investors left the market.

The other cause of momentum investing stems from the fact that that nearly all investors suffer from a behavioral trait called **herding**. Herding is the tendency of animals, including people, to group together for protection. People realize that if they are going to be wrong, they would rather be wrong in a group; conversely, if the group is correct, people don't want to be left behind As described by John Maynard Keynes, "investors may be quite willing to take the risk of being wrong in the company of others, while being much more reluctant to take the risk of being right alone." In other words, people are comfortable investing in "hot" stocks and investments because everyone else is doing so. This herding effect causes a stock price to gain momentum. Generally, the price momentum is upward, but herding instincts can drive prices down as well. Other applications of herding extend to the often quoted "keeping up with the Joneses" as a rationale for consumer spending and debt, the tendency of young adults to "opt out" of health insurance because "we're all healthy," or other examples of following the trend.

In summary, behavioral finance blends the disciplines of finance and psychology into an explanation of human behavior that stands as a stark contrast to traditional economic theory. Behavioral finance theory is premised on the assumptions that when making investment and financial decisions:

- most people do not act in consistently rational ways;

- they cannot accurately predict the consequences of their choices;

- they are loss-averse and feel regret when outcomes are not as anticipated; and, maybe most importantly,

- they can be influenced by contextual changes in the presentation of information.

Furthermore, advocates of behavioral finance theory believe that people use mental shortcuts when making decisions and are often subject to cognitive biases and misplaced confidence in their abilities to anticipate outcomes. In addition, misinterpretation of statistics and knowledge inference can be problematic when trying to make accurate financial decisions.

But what does this mean for financial advisors and their clients? For some clients, biases result in no action being taken. Other clients may be prone to seemingly irrational actions, but upon further consideration can be persuaded to "stay the course" of the original plan. This discussion has introduced only some of the most widely acknowledged concepts related to behavioral finance theory and is in no way comprehensive. But it does illustrate just how many biases may significantly impact the decision processes of planners and clients. Understanding these biases provides students or novice planners a rich new perspective for interpreting their own decision making strategies as well as those of their clients.

Threats to the Decision Making Process

Financial planners are faced with a myriad of decisions daily. Some decisions are inconsequential while others can change a client's life for better or worse. Most people, financial planners included, tend to make decisions using rules that they have learned or acquired over time. The question is whether or not the use of heuristics as a decision making shortcut works effectively. The use of heuristics is a fact of life, and as such, it is important to understand when simple rules can work well and when they can lead to critical errors. When it comes to making decisions that have a low cost or little consequence, decision heuristics offer an effective way to arrive at a conclusion. However, the use of heuristics to solve more complex problems can lead to problematic outcomes. Excessive dependence on heuristics should, at the very least, call into question the method used to make the decision.

Knowing this, why are heuristic models so widespread? One reason is people are not ordinarily exposed to generalized decision making models, whereas they are exposed to heuristic models on a daily basis. Think about advertisements that are shown on television. Most, if not all, provide viewers with simplified rules for decision making. If someone has a cold they are told to simply take a particular medication. Little explanation is given as to why or what the consequences might be. It is interesting to note that selling products and services via heuristic models seems to work. People constantly look for simple solutions to what are often difficult problems.

Wheeler and Janis have identified three additional factors that can result in seriously negative decision outcomes: complacency; defensive avoidance; and panic decision making.[11] **Complacency** occurs when a person either cannot or chooses not to see approaching danger. Sometimes a person cannot see that a dangerous situation is happening, or believes that an event is more likely to occur to someone else. Common examples of complacency include an individual who fails to adopt healthier lifestyle practices (e.g., exercise, balanced diet, stress reduction) or a person who fails to take cover on a golf course during a thunderstorm. Complacency can also occur when opportunities are passed up. Consider the financial planner who chooses not to interview a recent graduate from a college financial planning program because the planner does not want to risk hiring someone without experience. In effect, the planner has missed an opportunity. The planner may hire someone with experience, but that experience may be costly in terms of salary, benefits, and the direct and indirect costs of training and retraining the individual to the firm's planning practices and procedures. Passing up the opportunity to hire a recent college graduate means that the planner may miss out on cutting-edge knowledge the graduate can bring to the practice, a willingness to learn and use the planner's techniques (no retraining required), and a higher level of enthusiasm and gratitude for a career-entry opportunity.

Defensive avoidance refers to situations where a person acknowledges a danger, but tends to deny the importance of the danger or the potential role of individual responsibility to reduce the danger. The old adage about how buggy makers failed to appreciate the competitive risk posed by automobiles is an example of defensive avoidance. Some financial planners engage in defensive avoidance when it comes to preparing a succession plan for their firm. As the average age of planners increases, the number of planners who will leave the profession also increases. What will happen to clients as planners either retire or pass away? How will retired planners draw income from their practices without a succession plan? Both of these questions are worth asking, but few planners have attempted to answer the questions. Procrastination is a symptom of defensive avoidance, and it may explain the lack of succession planning by many planners. Procrastination occurs whenever someone feels that the likelihood of a threat is minimal or too far in the future to plan for. Clients can suffer from procrastination, too. Lack of plan implementation is most closely tied with defensive avoidance and procrastination.

The third threat to the decision making process is a person's likelihood to engage in **panic reactions**. Panic occurs when people are faced with a threat that they believe is too urgent to solve using the decision making process. Panic situations related to financial planning include a sudden decline in the stock market, the bankruptcy of a large firm, the death of a loved one, deployment for active duty military service, or a major accident. Each of these situations can lead a person to frenzied searches for solutions. This often leads to minimal evaluations of the situation, and multiple courses of action being taken simultaneously. Implementation may be quick with little follow through and little effort to maintain action. Panic almost always leads to negative outcomes.

Think about the person, whom we will call Joe, who wakes up one morning to find that the stock market is in a free-fall. Commentators and stock market pundits are on television hinting that the current market drop will be the next 1929, 1987, or 2001. Panic has already set in on Wall Street and it is at this moment that Joe sees a threat. Immediately, Joe runs through his options. He never anticipated such a serious market drop. He has no plan to account for this or to lead him through the decision making process. Joe senses that time is short and that he must make a decision. Should he sell now or later? Joe is definitely not complacent, nor is he engaging in defensive avoidance. Instead, Joe is panicked. Not sure exactly what to do he logs onto the Internet. Within three minutes he has liquidated his stock holdings and moved to cash. Joe is relieved—for now. It is only a day or two later when Joe thinks through his decision. Was it really the optimal decision to sell in the midst of the downturn? Almost all of his assets were invested for retirement—in 20 years. As he checks the market returns, he is disappointed to learn that the market has corrected and is now only 2% below the record highs. Suddenly Joe realizes that he missed a grand opportunity to invest new money at low prices. He also realizes that someone else took advantage of the situation, while he did not. Someone else used a disciplined decision making approach and made money. Joe did neither.

Heuristics, complacency, defensive avoidance, and panic are all threats to decision making and an individual's proactive right to make a decision. But perhaps the biggest threat to decision making is the failure to appreciate its significance. Joe's example and others throughout this chapter illustrate the importance of understanding the decision making process as well as the spoken and unspoken (and, too often, unrecognized) influences. Regardless of the scope of their assets, most clients have limited resources, but unlimited wants and needs. It's always easier to spend more—no matter how many zeros are attached to the number that defines "more." It is unlikely that all client goals can ever be achieved, and even less likely that all alternatives can, or even should, be considered. The dilemma facing financial planners often comes down to the simplest of questions: which recommendation should be given to meet a client's goal? Without a process that balances the qualitative and the quantitative, the objective and the subjective, and the conscious and the unconscious for arriving at this conclusion, there is increased probability that the planner and client will face a disappointing outcome.

Chapter Summary

This chapter is an attempt to fill the void in financial planning decision making. The objective was not to offer students or advisors a repertoire of labels to attach to themselves or to clients. A generalized decision making model was presented to illustrate how decisions can be arrived at in a logical and practical manner. For example, for the client that is "stuck" and refusing to move forward, a simple exercise of sequentially discussing the decision making process may help the planner and client gain new awareness and insight into the client's reservations. Understanding behavioral finance concepts and how they may influence the decision maker's approach to problems and selection of alternatives can help the planner and client to more astutely explore the issue; furthermore, it may aid both in gaining a new appreciation for cognitive biases or other threats to decision making, as neither advisors nor clients are exempt from these influences. Integrating the logic of a standard approach with what sometimes appears to be the illogical behavioral influences should offer new insights to the planner-client relationship. Like other fundamental financial planning skills, continued study, training, and experience will make decision making knowledge a more comfortable tool for the planner to incorporate into daily practice.

Chapter Endnotes

1. See Kautt, G. G. (2001). *Stochastic Modeling: The New Way to Predict Your Financial Future*. Fairfax, VA: Monitor Publishing.
2. Kahneman, D. & Tversky, A. (1979). "Prospect Theory: An Analysis of Decision under Risk." *Ecometrica*, XVLII, 263-291.
3. Shefrin, H. (2000). *Beyond Greed and Fear: Understanding Behavioral Finance and the Psychology of Investing*. Boston: Harvard Business School Press.
4. Kahneman, D. & Tversky, A. (1974). "Judgment under Uncertainty: Heuristics and Biases." *Science*. *185* (4157), 1124-1131.
5. A beneficial source for behavioral decision making theory and application can be found in: Bell, D. E., Raiffa, H., & Tversky, A. (eds.) (1998). *Decision Making: Descriptive, Normative, and Prescriptive Interactions*. Cambridge, England: Cambridge University Press.
6. Nofsinger, J. R. (2001). *Investment Madness: How Psychology Affects Your Investing—and What to Do About It*. New York: Prentice-Hall.
7. DALBAR, Inc. (2003). The DALBAR study shows that market chasing mutual fund investors earn less than inflation. Available at www.dalbarinc.com/content/printerfriendly.asp?page=2003071601 retrieved 11/21/05.
8. Belsky, G., & Gilovich, T. (2000). *Why Smart People Make Big Money Mistakes—and How to Correct Them*. New York: Fireside.
9. For a more detailed description of the "hot hand fallacy" and the specific basketball example used in the original study see: Gilovich, T., Vallone, R., & Tversky, A. (1985). "The Hot Hand in Basketball: On the Misperception of Random Sequences," *Cognitive Psychology*, 17, 295-314.
10. An excellent summary of this and other heuristics, based on the work of Daniel Kahneman and Amos Tversky can be found in: Kahneman, D., Slovic, P., & Tversky, A. (eds.) (1999). *Judgment under Uncertainty: Heuristics and Biases*. Cambridge, England: Cambridge University Press.
11. See Wheeler, D. D., & Janis, I. L. (1980). *A Practical Guide for Making Decisions*. New York: Free Press.

Chapter Review

The Basics: Review Questions

Discussion Questions

1. Explain the five steps of the decision making process. Using a financial planning question, behavior, concern, problem, or goal, illustrate the five steps. Be sure to identify as many alternatives as possible and clearly define your criteria set. How does the identification of alternatives change when approached from the perspective of all possible alternatives versus only the feasible alternatives?

2. Using a financial planning question, behavior, concern, problem, or goal, explain how the choice of alternatives would vary when applying a maximizing, optimizing, or satisficing decision rule. What are the advantages and disadvantages of each rule?

3. What is the difference between objective and subjective probabilities? Identify as many financial planning questions, behaviors, concerns, problems, or goals for which objective probabilities can be applied for the alternatives.

4. Employ the traditional decision making approach to determine which of the following investments should be chosen if the most important decision criteria is to maximize the likelihood of receiving the highest return over a 10-year period. Use the data presented in the table below to answer this question:

Exhibit 4.2

Rate of Return on Investment	Future Value of $1,000 Invested for 10 Years	Probability That Rate of Return Will Be Achieved
12%	$3,105.85	50%
9%	$2,367.36	75%
5%	$1,628.89	99%

5. Explain the difference between stochastic modeling and deterministic modeling. What is the benefit to the planner and the client of knowing the probability of earning "X%"?

6. Explain the three fundamental themes commonly associated with behavioral finance. How do they impact financial planning?

7. Make a list of 5 – 10 heuristics that you use to simplify decisions in your life.

8. What does the conclusion that people dislike losing more than they like winning imply for financial planners who manage client investment assets?

9. Explain how behavioral finance merges two opposing theoretical views. Define representativeness and explain its significance in behavioral finance.

10. Identify and explain the three cognitive biases that you think are most prevalent in financial decision making. Which three are the most difficult for you to grasp or apply to actual decisions? Why?

11. Identify two relatively important decisions that you made recently, and then analyze your decision making style. Did you follow the general model of decision making? What decision rules, if any, were used? Did you use heuristics or other behavioral finance concepts? Why are values, ethics, and other personal perceptions or attitudes an important part of the decision making process?

12. Explain the four threats to decision making. For each, create an example to illustrate the threat.

13. How might the five-step decision making process be applied to diffuse the negative effects of heuristics, complacency, defensive avoidance, or panic reactions. For each threat, which step in the process is likely the most important for the decision maker to fully consider?

14. How do herding and panic reactions support the view that decision makers can impact the markets, thus adding to the claim that markets are inefficient?

15. Why is it important to understand, follow, and evaluate a decision making process? Why is it important to conduct an evaluation of the decision outcome as well as the decision making process?

Chapter 5

The Systematic Process: An Overview

Learning Objectives

1. Identify and explain the six steps in the systematic financial planning process.

2. Define and characterize professional judgment in financial planning using the criteria of stakeholders, setting, problem framing and problem resolution, and standards of practice.

2. Explain the conceptual model of professional judgment in the development of a financial plan.

3. Explain how the financial planning process may appear to be a linear process, but is really a recursive or circular process, both when applied to discreet plan development and when applied to the maintainence of the planner-client relationship over time.

4. Differentiate between the goal orientation to planning and the cash flow orientation to planning—both of which must be integrated for a proactive, sustainable plan.

Six–Step Systematic Financial Planning Process

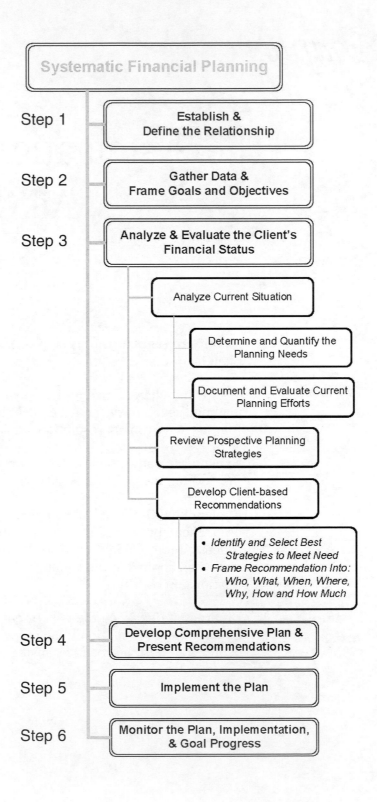

Key Terms

Cash flow orientation to planning
Goal orientation to planning
Holistic judgment
Problem framing and problem
  resolution
Professional judgment
Qualitative data

Quantitative data
Setting
Stakeholders
Standards of practice
Systematic financial
  planning process

The Systematic Financial Planning Process

The underlying premise of this book is that financial planning can be improved when the process is consistently and systematically applied to produce a financial plan that is delivered to the client. As the discussion up to this point has shown, there are a variety of financial planning practice models; and not all financial advisors write comprehensive financial plans. Some financial planners choose to work on a per-project basis or to write a single-focus, or modular, plan when writing a comprehensive plan is beyond the scope of what the client needs or the planner provides. Other financial planners focus on selling products to meet specific needs. Contingent on their business model, these planners may conduct financial planning analysis, but not prepare a plan, while others may deliver a financial plan as a method to establish product needs. Whether the final deliverable or outcome is a comprehensive plan, a modular plan, or the sale of a financial product, what should be changeless in any of those situations is the fundamental *process*. A **systematic financial planning process** is needed to guide the analytic approach as well as the presentation, implementation, and monitoring of the plan results with the client. A systematic approach is also needed to help students and novice planners develop the methods to effectively collect and utilize the required client information.

This book attempts to fill that need by presenting, describing, and illustrating a systematic, almost step-by-step, financial planning process based on the general financial planning process promoted by the CFP Board and other organizations.[1] Although the systematic financial planning process is intended for use by comprehensive financial planners, the process is equally applicable for those who write modular financial plans or simply want to conduct systematic and defensible analysis of client investment or investment-based insurance product suitability. The flow chart at the beginning of the chapter illustrates how the general six-step financial planning process can be further delineated to provide systematic guidance. What follows is a brief overview of each step, which will be further explored over the next three chapters.

Step 1: Establish and Define the Relationship. The process begins by establishing and defining the planner-client relationship. Actions taken by a planner at this stage of the process include initiating the relationship with potential clients (by referral or marketing strategies), meeting with prospective clients, and formalizing the scope of the planner-client engagement.

Step 2: Gather Data and Frame Goals and Objectives. Once the initial step of establishing and defining the client relationship has been taken, the process proceeds by gathering client data to help frame goals and objectives. Gathering data encompasses a broad range of information, contingent on the scope of the financial planning engagement. Exploring a client's financial dreams, goals, fears, current financial situation, behavioral tendencies, attitudes, and personal traits may all be included. Assessments at this stage of the process can be both **quantitative** (e.g., factual, as pertains to the client's family, health, employment, or financial status) and **qualitative** (e.g., the personal and social dimensions of the client, including personality, interests, attitudes and values), depending on the nature of the planning to be done. The primary outcome at this step in the process is framing complete, direct, and measurable client goals. In order for a goal to be measurable it must be anchored in time and have a probable and realistic cost and funding strategy.

Step 3: Analyze and Evaluate the Client's Financial Status. The step of analyzing and evaluating a client's financial situation is viewed by many as the essence of financial planning. The realities of the client's income and expenses, net worth, financial products owned, and financial strategies employed to date are scrutinized at this stage. From the narrowest view, this step is fact-based and solution-oriented. But central to this step is a perspective that goes beyond the present *factual* situation to a larger, and perhaps more multi-faceted, view of the client and the client's financial future. This exploration should have occurred in Step 2: Gather Data and Frame Goals and Objectives and should have identified issues that may influence the analysis and planning that occur during this step of the process. Too often, at this step, the "solution-focused" planner over-emphasizes the quantitative analysis to the exclusion of the *person* for whom the plan is designed. It is essential that a planner consider a client's goals and related planning assumptions during this analysis. Only by knowing a client's specific goals and using the assumptions agreed upon with the client can a financial planner anticipate, determine and quantify planning needs.

As illustrated in the flowchart at the beginning of the chapter, the three primary sub-steps involved in analyzing and evaluating a client's financial status include:

1. analyzing the current situation;

2. reviewing prospective planning strategies; and

3. developing client-based recommendations.

These steps might be summarized as *first*, "know your client" and *second*, consider the universe of strategies for meeting the client's needs. Then, using professional judgment, the advisor should match the client's situation with the available strategies to formulate client-specific recommendations that have the greatest likelihood of successfully satisfying the client's goals.

The first sub-step—analyzing the client's current financial situation—is further delineated to focus on identification and review of the planning needs and the planning efforts that are currently in place. This means that a thorough review of the qualitative and quantitative data ought to be undertaken to fully describe the client's financial situation. The planner must focus on the current situation, but must also use the information gained to anticipate present *and* future planning issues. Personal financial products and strategies that are currently in place, whether implemented by the client or in consultation with another financial services professional, must also be evaluated. Outcomes associated with this step include quantifying a client's financial strengths and weaknesses, documenting areas where the situation can be strengthened, and identifying opportunities for future planning.

The second sub-step involves reviewing prospective financial planning strategies that can be used to meet the client's needs. This might be thought of as brainstorming or reviewing the universe of strategies or possible solutions that might be applicable to the client's situation.

From this thorough review of strategies, the financial planner develops client-based recommendations. This third sub-step requires that a planner identify, select, and potentially combine the best strategies to meet a client's need. The result is a series of concise recommendations designed to optimize the client's financial situation and lead to goal achievement. As noted in the model, seven key questions must be addressed whenever a recommendation is made:

1. *Who* should implement the recommendation?

2. *What* should be done?

3. *When* should the recommendation be implemented place?

4. *Where* should the client, or other party, implement the recommendation?

5. *Why* should the recommendation be implemented? Why is it important to the client's financial future?

6. *How* should implementation take place?

7. *How much* should be purchased, saved, or invested to implement the recommendation? Specifically, what is the cost of the recommendation?

Without adequate consideration of these seven questions, it is likely that a recommendation will not be as complete as necessary for full client acceptance and implementation. Without implementation, even the very best recommendations can result in unprotected client needs or unfulfilled client aspirations.

Step 3 may also be viewed as the essence of financial planning because this step incorporates the comprehensive dimension of the planning process. This step, and the repetition of the sub-steps, must be completed for each of the following core content planning areas:

-   current financial situation;

-   income tax planning;

-   risk management (i.e., life, health, disability, long-term care, property and liability, and other insurance needs);

-   investment planning and management;

- retirement planning;

- education planning or other special needs planning (e.g., expensive purchase, second home, future support for a special needs family member, charitable giving, etc.); and

- estate planning.

At the conclusion of this step, the financial planner has prepared client-based recommendations representing the various planning components that now must be developed into a comprehensive financial plan.

Step 4: Develop a Comprehensive Plan and Present Recommendations. Developing a comprehensive plan requires a planner to integrate and prioritize recommendations for the client. It may not be possible for a client to implement all recommendations immediately, as the list may be broad and recommendations may compete for funding. Consequently, tracking the use of discretionary cash flow and changes in net worth is critical at this step in the planning process. The plan may require that the implementation of recommendations be staggered over time. The priority for funding usually centers on those recommendations that most closely match a client's goals or that provide protection from the greatest perceived risk of loss. Recommendations that are complementary in nature or that can be used to meet more than one goal may also emerge as a priority. For instance, recommending that a client fund a Roth IRA may serve the dual goals of saving for retirement and a child's college expenses. In the simplest sense, the plan must provide a realistic and workable road map for the actions required, immediately as well as in the future, to offer the client the greatest likelihood of protecting and growing assets.

Step 5: Implement the Plan. The fifth step in the process requires that a client and planner implement recommendations. Contingent on the planner-client engagement, the financial planner may assume responsibility for the action, while at other times the implementation may be directed or completed by the client.

Step 6: Monitor the Plan, the Implementation, and the Goal Progress. Sometimes it is easy to lose track of *why* a comprehensive financial plan was written. The real reason clients need a comprehensive financial plan is to ensure that their short-, intermediate-, and long-term financial goals are met. Only by looking at how each component of a client's financial life fits together can a full picture of financial threats and opportunities be drawn. Furthermore, constant tracking and monitoring of client outcomes is necessary to truly know if the client is on target to meet goals. Thus, it should be obvious that the sixth and final step in the financial planning process is of critical importance. Continued monitoring and interaction with the client allows a planner to determine the client's progress towards goals as well as the client's response to other economic or personal/life event changes. Continued monitoring also offers an opportunity for financial planners to add value to the planner-client relationship by helping the client to respond to the situation and feel in control.

Professional Judgment: From Process to Practice

Professional judgment is assumed to be central to the practice of any profession. A review of the literature describing professional judgment from professions such as accounting, medicine, and education reveals terms like "expertise," "advanced level of competence," "integrity, objectivity, and independence," "advanced level of expertise," "expertise that goes beyond competence," "fairness," and "compliance with regulations and guidelines."

But what does professional judgment really mean and how does it bridge the *process* of financial planning with the *practice* of financial planning? Like many other professional disciplines, financial planning relies on professional judgment. In the explanation of Practice Standard 400-1: Identifying and Evaluating Financial Planning Alternative(s), the CFP Board of Standards, Inc., uses the phrase "the subjective nature of exercising professional judgment." Similarly, the *Code of Ethics and Professional Responsibility* rules use the phrase "exercise reasonable and prudent professional judgment."

Writing from the perspective of a broad array of professions, Facione defined **professional judgment** as:

"[A] goal-oriented decision-making or problem-solving process carried out in the interest of one's client wherein one gives reasoned consideration to relevant information, criteria, methods, context, principles, policies and resources."[2]

Whereas this definition offers some insight, the significance of professional judgment in the practice and governance of financial planning warrants a fuller explanation as might be found in the literature of other professional disciplines. Facione, Facione, and Giancarlo offer a framework of four general characteristics of professional judgment: (1) analyzing the interests of **stakeholders;** (2) **setting;** (3) **problem framing and problem resolution;** and (4) abiding by **standards of practice.**[3] When considered from the context of the expectations of professional judgment in other disciplines (i.e., medicine, psychology, accounting, education, or law), the Facione, Facione, and Giancarlo framework is very applicable to financial planning. The examples that follow are not meant to be exhaustive or definitive; rather, they are offered as illustrations of professional judgment to help students and planners develop a richer definition of this important concept.

Stakeholders

Acting in the best interest of the client, as primary stakeholder, is a universal tenet for all professions. To do so in the context of financial planning requires not only the planner's complete engagement, but also requires the *client* to be actively involved in and fully informed of all aspects of the professional relationship. The client should be fully informed of the proposed recommendations (including the products and procedures) available for reaching the financial objectives and, whenever appropriate, should be offered alternatives. Furthermore, the planner has a responsibility to fully disclose, explain, and educate the client on the logic supporting the recommendations. Safeguarding the confidentiality of client information is yet another way to act in the best interest of the client as primary stakeholder.

Secondary stakeholders (based on the Facione, Facione, and Giancarlo framework) are other individuals or groups who may be favorably or adversely affected by the outcome of the professional relationship that must serve to maximize the client's interests. They include: the planner; if applicable, the planner's employer or partners; and the client's family. Recognizing conflicts of interest and heeding professional ethics are central actions to making professional judgments involving multiple stakeholders. For example, the decision to offer a lower fee structure to attract a large client could benefit the client while still bringing in a large portfolio and future revenue stream for the firm. However, even though primary and secondary stakeholders could benefit, the fee structure still must meet all costs involved so that the decision does not adversely affect the firm or other clients served. Furthermore, the planner must be reasonably competent and capable of delivering the management services offered.

Some financial planners might see the above situation as only a subtle, or perhaps even insignificant, conflict of interest. A more straightforward conflict of interest where multiple stakeholders may be impacted is the potential conflict between a planner's desire to "make money" and a client's need to receive quality and cost-effective solutions. This conflict could be manifested by churning (or other practices designed to increase commissions), or by inconsistently setting fees (e.g., higher for some clients and lower for other clients) to increase revenues. Both represent practices that could signify questionable professional judgment on the planner's part, either because such practices do not fully consider all stakeholders, are unethical, or are illegal.

The impact of planning recommendations and client choices about long-term care insurance, umbrella (i.e., excess liability) insurance, estate planning options, and large (perhaps even extravagant) purchases may also demonstrate another dilemma of professional judgment for advisors. In some situations the financial planner may also need to take into account the interests of secondary stakeholders in addition to the primary stakeholder (i.e., the client) when making recommendations. For example, the interests of a beneficiary named in a will might be considered in the planning process. Secondary stakeholders—children or other family members who may in the future question the judgment of the advisor in failing to prudently plan for assets or potential expenses, such as nursing home care—may need to be accounted for. (Conversely, the argument could be made that children subsequently questioning the advisor's judgment in prudently planning for potential expenses are really co-opting an issue that is rightfully the client's.) Situations like this may ultimately result in charges of professional malpractice or malfeasance, and further illustrate that a challenge to professional judgment does not necessarily have to come from an adversely affected primary stakeholder.

Not all financial planners agree that the interests of secondary stakeholders need to influence recommendations for fear of compromising the best interests of one stakeholder over another. Furthermore, it is possible that an individual whom one planner considers a secondary stakeholder another planner may define as a primary stakeholder. For example, a child questioning the judgment of an advisor in prudently planning for potential expenses may be interpreted as an offshoot of a primary stakeholder issue. However, if the parents have decided to spend their assets for their own enjoyment, to the detriment of their child's inheritance, that is the parents' (as the primary stakeholders) prerogative. A planner representing the child's interests in protecting the inheritance would fail to maximize the interests of the primary stakeholders. As long as the task of spending down assets can reasonably and prudently be accomplished, some financial planners would question whether it is the planner's professional duty or obligation to even attempt to represent the child's interests.

What is important, as these examples illustrate, is a commitment to professional ethics, behavior, and an awareness of "normative principles," or accepted practice standards within the profession. Even more important in the context of professional judgment is a "willingness to think" and critically evaluate the issue, the decision, and the potential ramifications for all stakeholders.

Setting

"Setting" refers to the characteristics or dimensions of the problem or decision that the professional must address on the behalf of the stakeholder or client. In describing the setting, Facione, Facione, and Giancarlo identify seven dimensions and note that with interaction effects among the individual dyads, or the two ends of each scale, there is a potential for 128 (or 2^7) different kinds of decisions or problems that a professional might encounter—not to mention all the interim points along each scale! The generalized references (outlined below) offer useful criteria for characterizing professional judgment within financial planning:

1. *high* stakes decisions to *low* stakes problems or issues;

2. *time constrained* issues to decisions that are *time unconstrained*;

3. *novel* problems/decisions to issues that are *very familiar* to the professional;

4. *unexpected* problems/issues to decisions that are *planned*;

5. issues that require *specialized knowledge* to problems requiring *knowledge commonly shared* by the community of professionals;

6. issues that can be handled *solely by the professional* to problems that require *collaboration with other professionals*; and

7. *routine*, commonly addressed problems in the profession to an *unusual* situation that rarely occurs.

These descriptors suggest a variety of financial planning situations that expand and contextualize professional judgement and practice. Estate and tax planning issues for a high net worth client with multi-national assets might represent an unusual situation requiring the collaboration of a planner, accountant, attorney, interpreter, or even a professional in another country. The situation may arise suddenly and be high stakes and time-sensitive in response to a life event. Or, it could be proactively planned for with less urgent time constraints. Planning for a child's education shortly after the child is born might be characterized as a routine issue with relatively low stakes and no immediate time pressure. But a buy-out offer in advance of an employer relocation plan might require immediate action and have very high stakes for the executive.

In the exercise of professional judgment, planners need to be sensitive to the client's setting; however, they must also recognize that they may be influenced by their own setting. An inexperienced planner may view each client with a sense of urgency and time pressure that an older, more established planner may not feel. Planners with dissimilar business models and methods of compensation may attribute different characteristics to the setting for the same client situation. This is not to say that planners are not always acting in the best interests of the client; they may just approach client situations with different expectations and points of view. Consider the executive buy-out offer example from above, except this time approach it from the planner's setting. If asked to manage all of the funds from the buy-out along with the retirement funds, a planner practicing under the assets under management (AUM) model might view this situation with a greater sense of urgency than a planner working on a retainer basis.

These examples illustrate several important considerations when exercising professional judgment in financial planning. First, the characteristics or dimensions of the setting may be the same or different for the client and the planner. A routine issue for the planner may be viewed by the client as high stakes and challenging. Another planning issue may be viewed by both the planner and the client as of signficant importance, with an urgency demanding the immediate attention of the advisor. Second, the setting for many financial planning issues may be further defined by the advisor's business practice model. Third, the complexity of these issues suggests the need for multi-faceted, case-based education for planners that enables them to build and maintain technical competency concurrently with client-centered planning approaches that are sensitive to the client's setting. Finally, and perhaps most importantly, in exercising professional judgment planners must be careful to reflect on how the setting for the stakeholders, as well as *themselves*, may impact the financial planning process.

Problem Framing and Problem Resolution

The difference between problem framing and problem resolution is fundamental to the definition of professional judgment, whether held by the layman or the professional. Problem resolution (represented by some baseline professional competence) is expected of the novice. True acumen at problem framing may only come from broad-based experience that alerts the professional to critical situational data elements and key patterns in the data that lead to problem identification *and* resolution. Facione, Facione, and Giancarlo assert that professional judgment, as characterized by problem framing, may hinge on the nuances of "problem identification, interpretation, differentiation, and diagnosis," which closely parallel the steps within the financial planning process.

When applied to financial planning, problem framing focuses on the planner's ability to use knowledge and experience to discern an ill-defined or complex situation, gain the necessary information, and then generate potential planning solutions. The planner should skillfully build the planner-client relationship to gain information from the client, using both verbal and non-verbal cues. Professional judgment requires a balanced perspective that considers not only all aspects of relevant data, but also the details of the situation, or setting, as well as the broader scope of the situation. Defining the scope of the planner-client engagement, carefully selecting products and services as well as possible alternatives—all consistent with the client situation—would be another example of problem framing. The planner has an obligation to constrain the engagement to the limits of his or her personal expertise, or to seek the assistance of other professionals when necessary. Furthermore, the decisions made and recommendations implemented should bear some resemblance to those made by other advisors under similar circumstances. However, the CFP Board of Standards, Inc., notes that "alternatives identified by the practitioner may differ from those of other practitioners or advisers, illustrating the subjective nature of exercising professional judgment."

Standards of Practice

In defining standards of practice, Facione, Facione, and Giancarlo suggest that there are really several "layers" or dimensions of standards of practice that may be used to assess professional judgment. First, are the obvious criteria that the action or resolution is effective and efficient at satisfying the objective. The third layer defines the action as legal, ethical, and culturally acceptable. In between these micro- and macro-layers is the second layer, represented by *codes of conduct* and *standards of practice* that are unique to the profession and may be used to judge when, where, or how judgments are made.

Also important to this discussion are the qustions of who has the right to impose these standards, or to judge that the standards have been met? In the first layer, or dimension, it would seem reasonable that the planner and the client should be the judges of effectiveness. The opposite end of the spectrum—the third layer of standards—represents a larger, or more macro, social and cultural view. Therefore it would seem reasonable that society at large, or at least the designated representatives of that society (i.e., state and federal regulators and other self-regulatory organization such as the NASD), would be sanctioned to make judgments and to express those judgments in a socially powerful context. Unfortunately, it is once again the in-between level that creates so much ambiguity, because in this realm the credentialing and memebership organizations are the standard bearers and judges.

Therefore, the idea of standards of practice as a characteristic of professional judgment goes beyond the typical code of conduct or professional standards common to most disciplines, including financial planning. As explained in Chapter 2: Ethics, Regulations and Laws, the CFP Board of Standards, Inc., and various financial planning professional associations promote codes of conduct and professional standards. Legal, regulatory, and other compliance standards govern various responsibilities and actions of financial advisors. Additionally, standards of practice focus on the probable consequences and effectiveness of any planning recommendations offered. For example:

- Is the recommended product or service a cost-effective alternative with a relatively high probability of success for the client?

- Is the plan built on valid assumptions representative of the legal, tax, and broader economic environment?

- Does the plan allow for readjustment in response to changing situations?

- Are the client alternatives and proposed solutions socially and culturally acceptable? Financial decisions surrounding divorce, estate planning, and distribution of assets are just a few examples of decisions that carry strong social, cultural or religious implications for the planner-client relationship.

Full and accurate documentation of the planning process, as well as all efforts to implement the plan (when applicable), should be maintained as part of standards of practice. Documentation extends beyond that required for all legal and regulatory requirements to the larger professional responsibility of full accountability and transfer of information to other stakeholders consistent with confidentiality policies.

At issue for the future of financial planning are the questions of acceptance of consistent and broadly applicable financial planning standards of practice to guide the profession and the clarification of who should be sanctioned to make such judgments—in other words, the second and third dimensions of standards of practice as defined by Facione, Facione, and Giancarlo. Most would agree that specifically-defined procedures and protocols that *typically* apply to a particular client situation may not be applicable to financial planning because of the need to individually match recommendations and products to the uniqueness of the client situation. This aspect of subjective professional judgment is further defined by the business practice model of the advisor and the fundamental questions of fiduciary responsibility and full disclosure. For example, should an advisor giving financial planning advice adhere to a fiduciary standard to place the client's interest first? Literature on professional judgment, as well as some financial planners, would argue that the answer is unquestionably "yes." The 1940 Investment Advisors Act requires this standard of a Registered Investment Advisor (RIA) giving investment advice. However, in 2005 the SEC chose not to impose the standard on broker-dealers who claim to provide something less than "financial planning" or who offer planning only incidental to the product sale. The continuing debate over these issues will shape the standards of practice that will guide financial planning into the future.

From Process to Practice

When considered from the Facione, Facione, and Giancarlo framework, it is easy to see why everyone, *and no one*, can really define professional judgment. But the real value of the framework is to call attention to the multidimensional characteristics of stakeholders, setting, problem framing and problem resolution, and standards of practice that define professional judgment. Although there are overriding principles that apply to any profession, professional judgment is contextualized by the individual professional pursuit. Furthermore, professional judgment hinges on a constant attitude that reflects professional skepticism (i.e., a willingness to self-reflect and self-correct in pursuit of professional excellence). Exercising professional judgment challenges advisors not to become complacent with their modes of operation. But having said that, the trap of "paralyzing perfectionism" (i.e., fear of making the wrong decision) can result in inactivity. Confidence to proceed can be gained from a fuller understanding of and consistent application of the systematic financial planning process.

Professional Judgment in the Development of a Financial Plan

What might be considered the core of financial planning occurs when a planner, or team of planners, proceed from identification of strategies that are potentially useful for a client to the integration of the strategies—stated as recommendations—within the plan. This complex, dynamic process is a cognitive challenge requiring knowledge of which pieces of data (both qualitative and quantitative) to consider as well as how to use and weigh those pieces of data in the planning and decision making. The process must be *efficient* in order to attain accurate and complete data, to interrelate and analyze the data, and to identify the best use of the planner's and the client's resources. But the process must also be *effective* in order to focus on the most important data and arrive at a plan that offers the greatest probability of success in an environment where few, if any, factors can truly be controlled. From a worst case scenario, few things are harder to predict than the whims of human nature, the stock market, or the global economy—all of which may contribute to the perceived success or failure of financial planning efforts.

Earlier in this chapter the question was asked "how does professional judgment bridge the *process* of finanical planning with the *practice* of financial planning?" The conceptual model of professional judgment in financial planning shown in Exhibit 5.1 attempts to answer that question. A conceptual model is an abstract representation of the relationship among the most important components of a process, phenomenon, or event A conceptual model attempts to capture information by focusing on (1) the identification of the critical elements, and (2) the relationships among those elements. By picturing only the essentials, conceptual models should be simple but at the same time broad enough to be generalized to a variety of "realities" explained by the model. As such, models are useful to planners providing financial products, modular plans focused on one issue within a core content planning area, or for planners developing comprehensive plans involving multiple goals.

As illustrated by the model in Exhibit 5.1, professional judgment is integral to the financial planning process from the initial identification of the planning goals to the development of the comprehensive plan. These relationships as well as the evolving planner-client relationship will be more fully considered in the next three chapters.

Exhibit 5.1 Professional Judgment in Plan Development

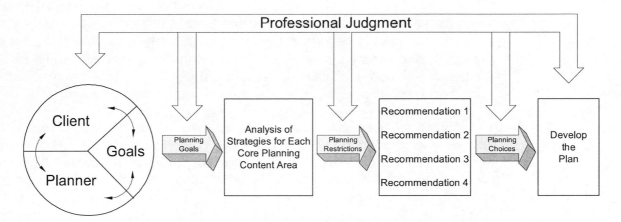

The systematic financial planning process, as illustrated in Exhibits 5.1 and 5.2, suggests that financial planning is linear—and in many ways it is. The integrated plan is built on recommendations that evolve from multiple strategies originating from the core content planning areas. Strategy leads to recommendation, which leads to plan—a very simplified 1-, 2-, 3-step process. But the process may also be recursive (from the Latin "running back") in that finalizing the plan may require the planner to "run back" to analyze competing recommendations, strategies, or other information to formulate the most cost-effective plan that is likely to satisfy the client's goals. What appeared initially to be the best recommendation may subsequently have to be abandoned when considered relative to all planning restrictions or choices. Ultimately, every financial plan evolves from this linear—yet more often recursive—process shown in Exhibit 5.2, The Spiraling Professional Judgment and Planner Client Relationship.

Exhibit 5.2 The Spiraling Professional Judgment and Planner Client Relationship

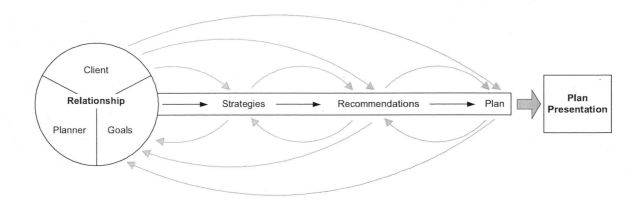

Beyond the initial development of the plan, the financial planning process, as reflected by the ongoing planner-client relationship, is also recursive or circular. The continuing evolution of the planner-client engagement and relationship must be responsive to the client's life changes, events, and transitions. Whether goals are achieved or abandoned, the planner and client will need to "run back" and consider the impact on that individual goal as well as other aspects of the client's financial situation. Although not all planner-client engagements support this relationship, many do and the relationship may even expand to multiple generations within the family. But whether reflected in the initial plan (the micro level) or the planning process that ensues over multiple years or multiple generations (the macro level), the recursive trait cannot be overlooked. Neither can the significance of the planner-client relationship be overlooked either, for this relationship is the foundation of the entire financial planning process and the source of the planning goals that give direction to the plan.

If planners and clients complete all aspects of each step in the process they may be able to minimize what may appear to be "going in circles" while maintaining focus on the two primary issues that ground the financial planning process—the **goal orientation** and the **cash flow orientation**. Both are hallmarks of a successful plan, yet neither can fully protect the client from the eventualities of life. The attention to cash flow (which may include discretionary income as well as other available assets) ensures, but cannot *guarantee*, that the client will be able to afford the goals. The goal orientation ensures that the plan is consistent with the client's values, needs and desires—both now and in the future—because as one goal is accomplished, a new goal may be identified and new recommendations initiated. The attention to cash flow ensures that the pursuit of any one goal does not expose the client to unwarranted risk or leave the client completely unprepared to withstand unexpected negative financial consequences. In fact, it can be argued that the primary purpose of financial planning is to maximize and stabilize cash flow across the client's planning period. Yet, there is an equally valid argument that it is the goal orientation of financial planning that provides the framework and motivation for sustained client commitment. Thus, by its very nature, financial planning must be circular, or recursive, as it attempts to respond to the client's "circles of life"—none of which can be fully anticipated, but are the focus of financial planning.

Chapter Summary

This chapter introduced the six-step systematic financial planning process. The process was characterized as being grounded in the planner-client relationship, controlled by the professional judgment of the advisor, and based on the dual but integrated perspectives of the goals orientation and the cash flow orientation to planning. The process, whether applied to the discreet development of a plan or when applied to a continuing client-planner engagement, is recursive. The four dimensions of stakeholders, setting, problem framing and problem resolution, and standards of practice offer a useful approach to characterizing and contextualizing professional judgment within financial planning. Critical to the understanding of professional judgment within financial planning is the commitment to broadly consider these dimensions throughout the planning process, albeit influenced by the advisor's business practice model and the subjectivity of professional judgment.

Chapter Endnotes

1. Certified Financial Planner Board of Standards, Inc., *CFP Board's Standards of Professional Conduct*, at: www.CFP.net.
2. Facione, P. A. (1990). *Critical Thinking: A Statement of Expert Consensus for Purposes of Educational Assessment and Instruction*, Millbrae, CA: The California Academic Press. ERIC Document ED 315-423.
3. Facione, P. A., Facione, N. C., & Giancarlo, C. A. F. (1997). *Professional Judgment and the Disposition of Critical Thinking*. Millbrae, CA: The California Academic Press. Available from: http://www.insight assessment.com/pdf_files/Prof_Jdgmnt_&_Dsp_CT_97_Frnch1999.pdf.

Chapter Review

The Basics: Review Questions

Discussion Questions

1. List the six steps in the systematic financial planning process.

2. In step 3 of the systematic financial planning process, list and describe the three sub-steps.

3. Define professional judgment. Explain why "everyone and no one" can adequately define it.

4. Why is the development of a comprehensive financial plan more likely to be a recursive, not a linear, process? Is this equally true for a targeted, or modular, plan?

5. How do the seven dimensions of "setting" influence the type of decisions a financial planner might face when working with clients? Give an example of a client issue or situation to illustrate each dimension.

6. When developing a client-based recommendation, what seven key questions should be addressed? What is likely to happen if these seven questions are not given adequate consideration?

7. Describe the difference between problem framing and problem resolution. How might these vary with the expertise or experience of the advisor?

8. How does the identification of the primary and secondary stakeholder differ if the financial advisor has a fiduciary responsibility to the client? To the advisor's employer?

9. Describe the two primary issues that ground the financial planning process. What do both ensure? Why are these perspectives on planning both unique and integrative?

10. Explain the three "layers" or dimensions of standards of practice that may apply to financial planning,

Chapter 6

The Systematic Process: Framing the Relationship, the Situation, and the Goals

1. Identify the fundamental outcomes of the first step of the systematic financial planning process.

2. Explain what client data the planner should collect to understand the client's situation.

3. Explain how the data may be collected and which cautions to consider.

4. Define financial risk tolerance and explain its importance in financial planning decisions.

5. Describe a client intake form and its purpose.

6. Describe the focused interview between planner and client.

7. Explain what it means to frame client goals and objectives.

8. Demonstrate use of the goal ranking form.

Six-Step Systematic Financial Planning Process

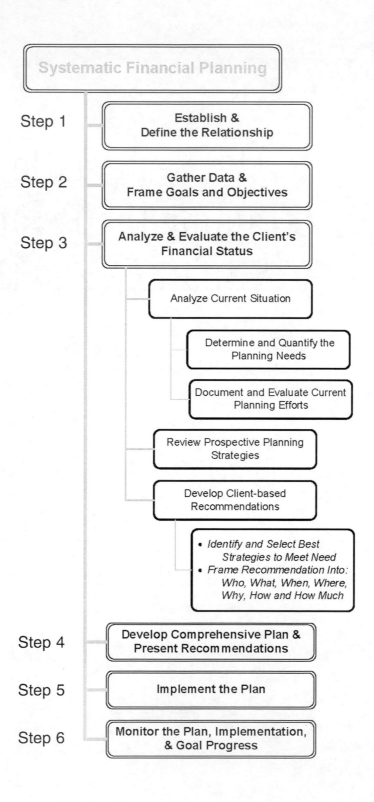

Key Terms

Attitudes and beliefs	Life transition
Client intake form	Needs
Conceptual framework	Objectives
Data collection questionnaire	Personality
Framing	Temperament
Focused interview	Wants
Life cycle event	

Framing: The Wide-Angle View *vs.* the Microscopic View

A check of the dictionary reveals that the word **frame** may be used as a noun or a verb, or as an adjective (i.e. frameable) with multiple meanings assigned. As a noun, a common usage of the word frame refers to the frame that forms the structure of a building (e.g., timber or steel). Used as a verb, frame refers to putting the parts together, as in framing a house, or in the abstract, conceptualizing or designing. Another noun usage refers to a paradigm, view, or frame of reference. All of these definitions are relevant to financial planning goals and objectives, which provide the *core structure* or *frame* for a financial plan. Both the goals and the plan must be **framed**—that is, put together, conceptualized, or designed—through the collaborative efforts of the planner and the client. Finally, how the goal is viewed, framed, or defined will have significant repercussions for the planner and the client. The planning process is grounded on the engagement and relationship that the planner and client forge, and it is from that relationship that the data are gathered. (For more information on framing in the context of behavioral finance, see Chapter 4 - Decision Making.)

The systematic financial planning process was introduced in the previous chapter as a frame of reference, or model for financial planning. In proceeding through each of the six steps, there are different recognized tasks to be completed and decisions to be made. When viewed from this linear perspective, a "stage-gate" (to borrow a production management term) must be passed before progressing to the next step. The stage-gates represent the evolution and enrichment of the planner-client relationship, the planning process, and a sequence of planning tasks that should be completed before progressing on to the next step. This very methodical, or systematic, process ensures that the client's personal and financial objectives are being met in the most effective and efficient means possible. Simplifying the process into the unique steps to be explored, as through the lens of a microscope, allows for greater understanding of the tasks, decisions, and minutiae that must be accomplished in each step, and is the focus of this chapter and the next two chapters. However, readers are cautioned not to overlook the fact that financial planning is recursive—both through the development of the plan and the continuing relationship with the client—and that the wide-angle view provides a much different perspective than when the details are viewed through the microscope! Let's begin with step one.

Step 1: Establish and Define the Relationship

The client must be proactive in seeking the help of a financial planner. Whether it was the planner's marketing efforts that motivated the client *or* whether the client sought out the planner on his own is not as important as the simple fact that the client and planner have agreed to meet. The relationship should begin by outlining both the planner's *and* the client's responsibilities and the extent of the contractual arrangement. Specifically, conflicts of interest, compensation arrangements, length of the agreement period, and the products or services to be provided should be fully disclosed and agreed upon. Professional practice standards (e.g., CFP Board Practice Standard 100-1) and regulatory agencies outline the expectations of this step. For example, the Securities and Exchange Commission (SEC) requires that all Registered Investment Advisors (RIAs) distribute part two of Form ADV (the Uniform Application for Investment Advisor Registration) to clients and prospective clients. In short, step one considers the regulatory, legal, contractual, and professional expectations of the planner-client relationship. Some of these issues are discussed elsewhere in the text (see Chapter 1 - What is Financial Planning and Chapter 2 - Ethics, Laws & Regulations), while others fall within the purview of practice management and are beyond the scope of this chapter.

Step 2: Gather Data and Frame Goals and Objectives

The second step in the planning process involves collecting information and identifying client goals. Client information may be obtained through data collection questionnaires, client and planner interviews, and from original source documents provided by the client. Some planners mail a data collection package to a prospective client prior to the first meeting. In this case, the client will independently complete the forms and return the needed documents by mail prior to the meeting or bring them to the client meeting. A recent innovation allows clients and planners to complete the forms together electronically from different locations. Another method uses joint form completion with the client and planner filling out the data collection forms in the planner's office. However, not all financial planning practitioners use, or approve, of this latter method. When the "data gathering meeting" focuses primarily on completing the form, the discussion is often excessively focused on quantitative data to the exclusion of effective qualitative information gathering about the client's values, goals, dreams, beliefs, and risk tolerance. Increasingly, best planning practices models suggest that clients should be encouraged to independently complete data forms. Then, the forms can be reviewed during the data gathering meeting to ensure full understanding by both parties, but the form completion will not be the focus of the meeting. Regardless of the method(s) utilized, the objective is for the planner to gather vital financial and personal information— both quantitative and qualitative—that encourages discussion. Once the forms are complete, the client and planner mutually agree on the client goals, objectives, and assumptions to guide the planning process.

But a client rarely states a goal in the form of a statement such as "We need $55,000 for Susie's college expenses." Rather, a client may state a general goal like "We want to provide Susie with a college education." Note that either statement can be problematic as the planner attempts to fully understand and quantify the client's goal. For example, the $55,000 cost for education will probably be significantly higher in the future depending on the assumed rate of inflationary increases and the time until the funds are needed. Also, the client may not have fully considered the range of costs attributable to different types of educational institutions or the most appropriate choice for Susie. Therefore, what assumptions are valid for this situation? It will be up to the planner, in conjunction with the client, to quantify the cost and determine the best means to achieve the education goal without sacrificing the client's other goals. From here the planner and client can mutually determine the goals and assumptions upon which the plan will be developed. There are two very important outcomes from these initial meetings: (1) the establishment of trust between both parties; and (2) the procurement of information for the planner to begin analyzing.

Although factually accurate, this brief summary of Step 2: Gathering Data and Framing Goals and Objectives, ignores the nuances of this important foundational step in the planning process. Because of the significance of this step and the variety of approaches utilized in practice, the discussion will focus on the abstract and practical implications of four fundamental questions:

1.   What client data are collected?

2.   How does the planner use the data?

3.   How are the data collected?

4.   What does it mean to frame goals and objectives?

What Data Are Collected?

Time is a valuable commodity to clients and planners. Yet, planners must somehow find a way to gain enough information to fully understand the client, diagnose the situation, and generate a workable plan that is acceptable to the client, and do so effectively and efficiently. And, if that conundrum is not sufficiently perplexing, consider that for most people talking about money is not culturally acceptable. For too many individuals, any talk about money is laden with emotional undertones that may reflect explicit memories (good or bad) or an implicit uneasiness that defies explanation. It is not hard to understand why many planners prefer the safety of products to the psyche of the client, but increasingly planners are considering both. To be effective, the student or novice planner must understand what data to consider and why it might be useful. Then, to be efficient, the student or novice planner must be armed with a client intake form, or questionnaire, and other relevant questions that will garner the needed insights.

A conceptual model of the types of client information typically collected by planners is shown in Figure 6.1. Recall that a conceptual model is an abstraction of reality, or an attempt to explain the relationship among the key elements of a phenomenon, event, or process. In this situation, four influential client factors have been identified as descriptive of the client situation and significant contributors to the client's goals, including:

1. temperament and personality;

2. attitudes, beliefs, and behaviors;

3. financial knowledge and experience; and

4. socioeconomic descriptors.

Furthermore, this information is the primary source of data for the analysis of each of the core content planning areas and is considered throughout the planning process. The information obtained is shaped—directly or indirectly—by the planner's temperament, personality, attitudes and beliefs, and financial knowledge and experience. Certainly, not all planners measure or directly consider all four client situational factors, but increasingly planners are expanding the scope of information used to gain familiarity with the client situation and to build trust with the client.

Figure 6.1 Goals: The Interaction of Situational Factors

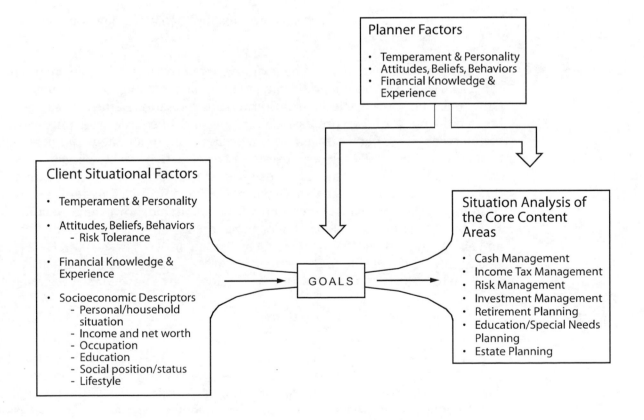

Temperament and Personality

Temperament is commonly defined by mood or disposition. Temperament is generally agreed to reflect inherited, cross-cultural traits that appear early in childhood and shape the personality. Dimensions of temperament focus on characteristics such as emotionality, sociability, sensitivity, adaptability, distractibility, persistence, and activity. **Personality** encompasses both the behavioral and emotional tendencies of an individual and goes beyond temperament to consider other traits such as character and intellect. Psychologists believe that there are five dimensions of personality, typically referred to as the "Big Five":

1. *Extraversion* – exemplified by being energetic, assertive, talkative, or outgoing.

2. *Agreeableness* – represented by signs of sympathy, kindness, and affection.

3. *Conscientiousness* – described as being organized, thorough, disciplined, and achievement-oriented.

4. *Neuroticism* – characterized by being moody, anxious, tense, or displaying other unpleasant emotions.

5. *Openness to New Experiences* – exemplified by having numerous interests and being imaginative.

An increasing number of financial planners are turning to personality profiling as a way to better understand their clients and to facilitate communication. Other planners view the administration and interpretation of these tests as being beyond the range of their professional training and outsource the profiling; some planners simply avoid it altogether. Dimensions of temperament and personality may explain emotional responses to market activity, whereas clients with stronger traits of persistence or conscientiousness may recognize that market downturns are a normal occurrence when working toward a long-term goal (e.g., retirement that is 20 years in the future). That being said, however, the emotional aspects of financial decisions cannot be ignored. For example, some planners and clients immediately liquidated assets to a majority (or even 100%) cash position following the events of September 11, 2001—an understandable risk averse reaction to a situation that could not be elucidated by knowledge or experience.

Attitudes, Beliefs, and Behaviors

Attitudes, beliefs, and behaviors are interrelated concepts in that attitudes and beliefs are thought to affect behavior. Attitudes may reflect an individual's views, opinions, desires, choices, purposes, or values. Although the concept of belief connotes different meanings, in psychology beliefs are recognized as a type of attitude because the belief reflects an interpretation, expectation, or claim about some aspect of life. Values represent strongly held attitudes and beliefs that indicate the individual's perception of what is right or desirable. Values are said to reflect the individual's fundamental meaning or interpretation of life and as such are a significant influence on personal goals and choices. Attitudes, beliefs, or values are considered to be distinct from temperament and personality in that attitudes and beliefs are theorized to potentially change over time, particularly as a result of experience. On the other hand, values are thought to remain consistent over the life cycle, although the order or priority placed on individual values may change over time. Attitudes, beliefs, and behaviors have far-reaching implications for clients and financial planning. For example, consider some of the idioms surrounding money, all of which may reflect deeply held attitudes or beliefs:

- "Money is the root of all evil."

- "Pinch a penny until it screams."

- "Money doesn't grow on trees."

- "Blood money."

- "It takes money to know money."

- "I feel like a million bucks."

- "Born with a silver spoon in her mouth."

Similarly, consider terms that are often freely associated with money (e.g., power, self-worth, independence, freedom, reward, or happiness), but reflect attitudes, beliefs, and values that directly or indirectly affect financial practices.

But note that the effect of attitudes on financial behavior is much more pervasive than simply those attitudes, beliefs, and values associated with money, poverty, or wealth. Consider the following examples:

- The parent who wants to "teach" the value of independence by refusing to pay for four years of a child's college education, although the parent is fully capable of paying the expense.

- The blue collar worker who diligently saves for retirement, becomes a millionaire, and chooses to continue working; or who makes a large charitable gift rather than "enjoying life" and spending the savings.

- The couple with an annual income of $750,000 who save little and continually increase their debt in pursuit of the "good life."

In each case, the behavior may be viewed on a continuum ranging from rational to irrational—contingent on the attitudes, beliefs, values, and experiential map of the individual making the judgment. Although making the *judgment* may be a natural reaction for anyone, the role of the financial advisor is limited to understanding *why* and *how* the attitudes, beliefs, and values of the individual affect financial decisions *and* to helping the client *identify* and *understand why* and *how* the attitudes, beliefs, and values are influential. Showing empathy (which does not necessarily require agreement) to the client in exploring these topics is an important approach for building trust with the client.

Because of the importance attributed to temperament, attitudes, and beliefs, some larger financial planning firms include, or refer clients to, professional staff with psychological or counseling expertise. Other advisors rely on questions, scales, or other assessments promoted by experts such as Olivia Mellan,[1] Kathleen Gurney,[2] George Kinder,[3] and others. Even though building expertise in this area requires further study or collaboration with an expert, appreciating the importance of temperament, attitudes, values, and beliefs and working to recognize them in the work with clients is indeed an important first step.

Although other attitudes related to financial well being, economic trends, or market returns may also be assessed, the client's financial risk tolerance is the attitude most frequently considered because of its importance. This is true because it represents the juncture of the *need to understand the client* for the purposes of client-centered financial planning with the *need to document the client's risk tolerance* for regulatory compliance. For example, using interview-based assessments as a means for determining most attitudes and beliefs is accepted practice among most planners, although some use personality profiles as mentioned earlier. But using questionnaires tends to be the norm for risk tolerance evaluation because a questionnaire produces a documented assessment of risk tolerance for regulatory purposes.

Financial **risk tolerance** is defined as the maximum amount of risk the client is comfortable with taking in a financial situation. Research suggests that risk tolerance is a personal characteristic or attitude that can change depending on the situation being faced or the activity in question. Risk tolerance, and its counterpart risk aversion, is a complicated and elusive concept, one that is typically measured on a continuum. Financial risk tolerance impacts a wide range of financial decisions beyond the obvious applications (i.e., investments, retirement planning, or insurance, where questions of suitability are typical), even extending to non-portfolio decisions. When considered in the context of portfolio management choices, risk tolerance centers on the client's perceived feelings, reactions, or level of comfort with losses in investment values. But a client's risk tolerance may also affect decisions concerning the type of mortgage, comfortable debt level, emergency fund amount, choice of insurance coverage, or estate planning strategy. A client with a high level of risk tolerance can be expected to take greater risks and act with less information than someone with a lower risk tolerance. A financial choice, such as an interest-only mortgage, may be viewed as highly risky to one person and yet be perfectly acceptable to another. Individuals with high levels of risk tolerance generally require higher chances of a gain, tolerate more uncertainty, and require less information about the performance of an investment. Highly risk-tolerant individuals accept volatile events, while lower risk-tolerant individuals require certainty. What appears to be speculation to one client may simply be prudent hedging to another.

As noted above, it is expected that financial planners will assess the risk tolerance of their clients. Some planners use self-developed measures of risk tolerance, but caution is recommended to ensure that this practice meets all compliance requirements. Other planners infer risk tolerance from available client information; however, it is recommended that any attempt to measure risk tolerance should be specific to the activity. For example, using a client's willingness to engage in risky physical behaviors (e.g., sky diving, skiing, hockey, etc.) as a proxy for taking risks in financial situations may lack validity. Some planners use scales included in comprehensive financial planning software, while others purchase psychometric tests from independent firms.[4] Regardless of the method or combination of methods used, it is important for an assessment instrument to be valid—that is, the scale should measure what it purports to measure. A 13-item financial risk tolerance scale that has been shown to offer practitioners a reasonable level of validity and reliability is included in Appendix C. The scale can be used to assess, broadly, a client's propensity to take investment and financial risks.[5]

Financial Knowledge and Experience

Financial knowledge and experience may represent the most extreme difference between the planner and client, with both parties bringing a range of knowledge and experience to the planning engagement—but at different levels. Professional responsibility constrains the planner to offer services within the purview of his or her acknowledged expertise. Thus, whenever necessary the planner should seek the collaboration of other professionals or refer the client to others. Likewise, professional judgment imbues that, if possible, the planner not recommend products or services that are beyond the boundaries of the client's knowledge, experience, or capacity for loss. Inevitably though, certain recommendations will almost certainly present the need for products or services about which the client lacks experience or knowledge. In these cases it becomes even more important to educate the client about the risks and benefits of that product or service. This precaution will not only satisfy the planner's responsibility for client education, but also help the planner overcome potential client objections. The client's inate financial knowledge and experience may influence the initial goal choices, recommendations proffered by the planner, and subsequent reactions by the client. The planning process offers the advisor the opportunity to assess and build the client's knowledge as a foundation for making more fact-based, rational decisions. The advisor, in the role of educator, has the opportunity to use the planning process and other forms of client communication to increase the client's financial knowledge and foster independence of thought and decision making.

Socioeconomic Descriptors

Socioeconomic descriptors represent a broad range of characteristics to describe the client. While these are typically the easiest data sources to collect and interpret, keep in mind that clients may not always be totally forthright. Categories of information include: the demographic profile for the client's household, including relevant medical history or other factors that may influence the client's goals; financial data (i.e., income, assets, liabilities, insurance protection, etc.); and a description of the client's lifestyle, or what might be referred to as social position or status. The latter category may include travel, hobbies, collectibles, leisure activities, or personal property or real estate that support the client's lifestyle.

How Does the Planner Use the Data?

The client and the planner enter the planning relationship with unique characteristics of temperament, personality, attitudes and beliefs, and financial knowledge and experience that shape the planning process. Some simple examples may help to illustrate the impact of these features on the planning process:

- Some clients may cry, scream, or yell in response to a life event, a change in the stock market, or an advisor's recommendation, whereas others will calmly discuss the situation. For some clients, a downturn in the stock market or other financial difficulty will represent a temporary setback, while others will claim the loss as personal and pervasive in everything they attempt to do. A client's attitude may be demonstrated by an emotionally charged statement such as "I knew this would happen to *me*!" rather than by exhibiting a calm, logical application of knowledge of investment market and economic cycles to the situation at hand.

- Some clients will make a decision on a whim, readily accepting the planner's recommendations; others will "nit pick" and challenge the planner until fully convinced that every last detail has been carefully considered from every angle.

- The financial lives of some clients are perennially disorganized. These clients may be easily distracted from their financial plan by the latest "hot" market sector, or the whim to purchase the popular "adult toy." Meanwhile, other clients remain focused on the plan and diligent in reaching specified goals.

As discussed earlier, risk tolerance (or the client's comfort with risk) is an attitude typically linked with investment or portfolio management choices; but it may also impact other financial decisions, such as type of mortgage, comfortable debt level or emergency fund, choice of insurance products and levels of coverage, or estate planning strategies. For example, a risk tolerant individual may not willingly purchase insurance, or may purchase lower amounts of coverage, because of their preference to "gamble," by risking a potential loss, and instead spending the money on goals perceived to be more worthwhile. The risk averse client, who may expect and fear loss, may have a tendency to purchase larger amounts of insurance for the assumed protection offered. When considered in light of portfolio management choices, risk tolerance centers on the client's perceived feelings, reactions, or level of comfort with losses in investment values. Without specific training, a planner's experience may be the best guide for working with the range of temperaments, personalities, and attitudes that clients exhibit The more the planner knows about the client, the greater the chances of developing a plan that will accommodate the client's unique situation.

Just as temperament, personality, attitudes and beliefs, and financial knowledge and experience characterize the client, the same is true for the planner. These factors shape the planner's relationship with the client, the mitigating effect of the planner, and, consequently, the style of planning. The planner's role is to collect and objectively process the client's data. However, two limitations must be acknowledged. First, regardless of all efforts to function as the objective, independent professional, the planner is confined to some extent by personal temperament, personality, attitudes, beliefs and values, and financial knowledge and experience. These "filters" directly and indirectly affect the planning process. Whereas this may be equally true for other professionals, it is more apparent because of the personal nature of the planning relationship and the need to divulge very private information. Second, the planner is privileged only to the information about the *individual* and the situation that the client is willing to share. Clients may withhold information, either knowingly due to lack of trust, or unknowingly because the information is thought to be irrelevant or was simply overlooked. Without the client's full disclosure, the planner will not be able to suggest optimal solutions.

Ideally, the crafting of the client goals and objectives, analysis of the situation, and development of the recommendations should hinge on objectivity rather than subjective inferences. Planners must use care to minimize the impact of personal feelings, interpretative judgments, and opinions that may develop or evolve during the planning relationship. Although these insights may be significant to the planning relationship, it is important that the interpretations be confirmed with the client for validity. Furthermore, it is incumbent on the planner to make every attempt to encourage the client to divulge as much information as can be useful to the planning engagement. As professionals, advisors must fully acknowledge their own limitations of expertise or other paradigms that may adversely affect or bias a client-planner relationship. The necessary steps should be taken to compensate for or override those issues within the professional relationship.

How Are the Data Collected?

As noted earlier, client data are typically collected through some combination of original source documents (e.g., investment statements—see Exhibit 6.1), a client questionnaire, and one or a series of planner-client interviews. However, students and novice planners are cautioned about the limitations of and problems associated with these data collection methods. Once provided by the client, original source documents or copies thereof are conveniently available to the planner; but extreme care must be taken to safeguard the documents and the privacy of the clients. Futhermore the planner's privacy policy statement should be provided to the clients at the time the documents are requested. Usefulness of the questionnaire will be limited by its ease of use, clarity, and applicability to the client. It is important that neither the questionnaire nor the interviews overwhelm the client or cause undue time commitments. Accuracy of the data to be obtained is important and care must be taken to ensure (to the extent possible) that the client is candid and forthright because there may be a tendency not to disclose all information, or to provide answers that are more socially acceptable or "what the planner expects." On the other hand, the planner's role as a direct or indirect "filter" of the information should not be overlooked. Finally, the planner must develop a system for collecting, organizing, and managing the data throughout the planning process as well as safeguarding it in the future.

To summarize, the importance of the client data collection is reflected in the following objectives:

- to allow the planner to gain a more complete understanding of the client;

- to measure the client's financial risk tolerance;

- to empower the planner and the client to clarify goals and set realistic expectations for the outcome; and

- to provide the information needed for the planner to diagnose the situation and identify the most appropriate recommendations given the client's resources and planning situation.

Supporting Documents

The form, shown in Exhibit 6.1 can be used by the planner and client to track the flow of original documents between the parties. Every effort should be made to electronically scan or copy the documents so that the originals are quickly returned to the client. In some instances the documents are used to verify information already provided by the client, while other documents provide technical information to the planner that may be beyond the scope of the client's knowledge. The form can be completed for the household, with individual lines added in each category, as applicable, for each spouse or partner; or an individual form can be completed for each individual.

Exhibit 6.1

Client Supporting Document Tracking Form

Date Requested from Client	Date Received from Client	Date Returned to Client	Supporting Document (for Client 1, Client 2, and joint accounts, as applicable)
			Latest Bank Statement(s)
			Latest Investment Account Statement(s)
			Loan Statement(s) (e.g., real estate, car, boat, etc.)
			Real Estate Deed, Deed of Trust, and HUD-1: Summary of Closing Costs
			Latest Credit Card Statement(s)
			Federal and State Tax Returns for the Last Three Years
			All Insurance Policies (e.g., life, disability, health, homeowners, automobile, etc.)
			Any Current Budget or Record of Spending
			Most Recent Paycheck Stub(s)
			Employee Benefit Statement(s)
			Employee Retirement Plan Statement(s)
			Other Retirement Plan Statement(s)
			Summary of the Retirement Plan Description
			Wills, Trusts, or Other Estate Planning Documents
			Other:
			Other:

The Client Intake Form

While not all financial planners actually use a formalized **client intake form**, or **data collection questionnaire**, the benefits of such a form are simply too important to be overlooked. Because the task of gathering data can be somewhat subjective, it is a good policy to complete an objective data collection questionnaire with each and every client. To the extent it is completed with accuracy and candor, a well-designed form or questionnaire is a tool that helps to capture a client's qualitative and quantitative information. From a purely practical point of view, a client intake form reduces professional liability. Without a well-defined and consistently used data collection method, a client, family member, or legal entity may make a future claim that the planner's recommendation did not match the client's situation, goals, or engagement with the planner. Planners that document—objectively and definitively—the client's responses pertinent to the situation will be in a better position to defend themselves against claims of professional misconduct. Finally, a questionnaire can help pinpoint a client's financial strengths and weaknesses as well as attitudes or expectations that may contribute to, or hinder, a successful planner-client relationship. In summary, the use of a client data gathering questionnaire provides a framework for summarizing a client's goals, attitudes, income, expenditures, assets, and liabilities, all of which are needed to write a comprehensive plan. More importantly, it opens up the discussion on other issues, fears, or concerns beyond the obvious data collected on the interview form.

Data Gathering Tip: Share Completed Forms with Clients?

It is not necessary to share completed forms with a client. Some planners may include a copy of the completed questionnaire as an appendix to the final plan, but this is certainly not a universal practice.

The data collection questionnaire shown in Appendix A offers one way to gather client information. Note that this form is designed to be completed by the client, but it could be adapted for use in a planner guided interview. Each section of the form is summarized below:

Section 1. It is essential that a planner know basic demographic information about the client as well as client contact data. Items such as name, nickname (if any), address, phone numbers, birth date, and Social Security number are important to have in a client file. This type of information will generally be needed whenever investment or insurance products are purchased, and it will be less burdensome to ask a client once rather than several times for this basic information.

Section 2. This section of the form allows a client to share information about his immediate or extended family. This information is useful for tax and estate planning issues, and may offer insights into the client's goals—spoken and unspoken.

Sections 3 and 3a. Employment status and income reporting can be summarized in this section of the data collection form. Note that retirees are given their own sub-section to answer income questions.

Section 4. It is important to note how a client spends leisure time. Leisure activities usually cost money and having a client identify hobbies and activities allows the planner to double check the accuracy of a client's budget. For instance, if the budget does not account for leisure activities this may indicate that the client is not fully accounting for all expenditures. Discussing these activities also allows the planner and client to connect on a personal level that transcends the focus on income and expenses and that offers insights into client dreams or goals that may impact the financial planning process.

Section 5. Goals are the root of financial planning. This section of the form allows a client to identify and rank personal and financial goals. The assignment of time horizons for realizing the goal and for depleting the funding helps the planner and client to establish more realistic expectations.

Section 6. This section of the form provides the necessary information for the planner to conduct a thorough insurance analysis. Information about the client's life, disability, health, long-term care, and property and liability insurance coverage is collected. Note that each allows for multiple policies to meet the needs of different client or household situations.

Section 7. Helping clients manage their assets is an important aspect of financial planning. This section of the form documents ownership of taxable and tax-deferred assets. The additional information requested focuses on the: current value, cost basis, and growth rate; contribution schedule; ownership or titling of the asset; purpose assigned to the asset; and the proposed use of the asset upon the owner's death. Some caution is warranted regarding the client's designation of the purpose and use of assets, although this approach is commonly used within financial planning. As noted in Chapter 4 – Decision Making, the behavioral finance concept of mental accounting may lead to faulty decision making. Consequently, planners need to be cautious about accepting the client's assignment of assets, but at the same time should also exercise professional judgment that is sensitive to the client's views and maximizes the client's interests. The second part of this section informs the planner of the current asset allocation for each of the assets. *Section 7* may challenge the average client, and may require the client to provide investment or other statements for the planner's review and summary of the necessary information.

Section 8. This section summarizes the client's tangible personal assets, and, if applicable, business assets. Consistent with *Section 7*, additional information requested focuses on the: current value, purchase price, and growth rate; ownership or titling of the asset; and the proposed use of the asset upon the owner's death.

Section 9. This section, linked with *Sections 7* and *8*, documents the client's personal debt situation so that the planner can complete a net worth statement. Additional information focuses on the amount of the liability, origination date, monthly payment, interest rate, duration of the loan, and the loan holder. Note that the credit card account listings apply only to clients that do not pay off all credit card balances in full each month.

Section 10. In this section, the client reconstructs annual expenditures to assist the planner with the creation of an income and expense statement.

Section 11. A client's attitudes, values, and expectations are recorded here. The 10 questions provide a snapshot view of the client's attitudes and investment risk preferences. Although the obvious objective is to complete the form, a broader objective of this exercise is to promote conversation in order to increase the planner's knowledge of the client and to encourage discussion of mutually agreed upon planning assumptions.

Section 12. This section continues the attitudinal assessment. Clients are asked to reflect on the economy as well as their personal finance knowledge. Self-assessment questions focus attention on the client's satisfaction with his or her job, income, and overall financial situation. These items assess the client's attitudes and can serve as a foundation for formulating client goals and establishing assumptions that will guide the planning process. (*Scoring note:* Lower levels of satisfaction may indicate a need for more planner-client discussion about the financial situation. Also, research suggests that low levels of self-assessed financial knowledge are positively correlated with lower levels of financial risk tolerance.)

Section 13. Answers to questions in this section are designed to help the planner quickly identify potential retirement or estate planning concerns. The checklist provided can be used to spot weaknesses in a client's financial situation or areas where financial improvements can be made.

Section 14. This section of the data collection form identifies other financial professionals with whom the client has worked and asks the client to reflect on satisfaction with these relationships. Information obtained can help the financial planner understand why a client is seeking help, provide insights into the client's motives or expectations, and identify other professionals who might be involved in the plan implementation.

Section 15. The final item queries the client on the expected primary outcome of the planner-client engagement.

Just as no tool, technique, or strategy is appropriate for every client or client situation, the client intake form provided in the appendix is not necessarily the right one for every client situation. It may be too comprehensive for planners working on an as-needed basis or on single-issue plans, although selected sections may still be useful and exposure to the form may alert the client to future planning issues. Planners often use specialized data collection forms for targeted client situations, such as small business owners or retirement and employee benefit plan participants. Others use forms coordinated with professional software packages to facilitate data entry. Finally, for planners affiliated with product providers, a proprietary client data form may be required to ensure regulatory compliance. After gaining more experience, advisors may edit the forms provided or design their own questionnaire and forms to be used in addition to the proprietary forms required to meet product provider or government agency compliance.

Guided Planner – Client Interviews

Meaningful exploration of a client's financial situation (and its many nuances as described earlier in this chapter) does not typically occur through a *conversation*. A conversation typically involves an exchange of information, such as facts, opinions, and feelings. The same information may be solicited through what is often casually referred to as an *interview*, but an interview is actually defined as a conversation with a *purpose*. Planners who work with clients to jointly complete, or subsequently review, client intake forms have a purpose: to collect accurate factual data. But to expand that preliminary exchange into the realm of goals, attitudes, values, dreams, concerns, or fears surrounding money, or the role of money in the client's life, may necessitate entering into a conversation with a purpose—an interview.

A **focused interview** is an excellent way to explore another person's feelings, experiences, perceptions, attitudes, views, or knowledge.[6] Approaching the client meeting as an interview should not inadvertently change the tone or formality of the exchange. Instead, advance preparation for the discussion can: increase the planner's confidence; encourage more in-depth understanding of the topic and the client's perspectives and motives; and build the planner-client relationship. But to be effective, several issues must be considered from the standpoint of the financial advisor:

1.   An issue-oriented, topical list or set of questions must be carefully planned to serve as a framework or guide for the interview. Although digressions to other topics may occur, the framework will ensure that important topics are not overlooked. Furthermore, with repeated use the planner can perfect the questions and gain experience from typical client responses.

2.   Although planned in advance, the questions must still allow for adaptations to be made regarding the level of language, word choice, or order of questioning to best match the client and the situation. This will contribute to an air of informality and allow the planner to more effectively mirror the client.

3.   The client should be encouraged to openly and freely share information, feelings, perceptions, or observations.

4.   Open-ended questions that are nonjudgmental and respect the sensitivity of the topic should be used. It is important to fully consider the meaning of the question *and* its impact. For example, what may appear to be a straightforward question, "Do you gamble?," may not solicit as truthful a response as "About how many times a week/month would you think that you gamble?" (Similar questions could be designed for arguments about money, going over the limit on a credit card, providing funds to a relative or friend, etc.) Questions beginning with "why" should also be avoided.

5.   Follow-up questions and verbal or nonverbal reinforcements should be used as necessary to encourage the client to elaborate or offer more explanation. Simple questions (e.g., "Can you tell me more about that experience?" or "How did that happen?") or simple statements (e.g., "Um-hum" or "I understand") are not only encouraging, but also will not bias the response. Nonverbal cues (e.g., eye contact, posture, expressions such as a smile, a nod, or silence) may all encourage the client to continue talking and reflecting on the situation.

6.   Rapport, which is characterized by trust or positive feelings, is important to a successful interview. It can be encouraged by identifying common interests or, within the confines of the professional relationship, the sharing of personal information.

7.   The planner, with the consent of the client, must identify an efficient and effective strategy for capturing and summarizing the data for use in

the future. The planner may take notes during the meeting, if this can be done without being distracting. Another option is for the paraplanner or other client services staff member to take notes during the meeting. Or the planner may summarize the information immediately following the meeting. However, the latter method can be problematic— a quality, in-depth interview will produce more detailed information than virtually anyone could entirely recall and accurately record after the interview. (For more information on planner-client communication strategies, see Chapter 3 – Client Communication.)

Consequently, planner-client conversations done for the purpose of data gathering in the context of a guided interview can benefit the relationship and offer new opportunities to increase the planner's expertise. But where do students or novice planners get targeted questions for different planning issues in the first place? Industry literature, continuing education opportunities, and conversations with experienced advisors are all good sources of targeted, but challenging, questions. Consider, for example, the following questions published in the *Journal of Financial Planning*[7] that Ross Levin reports using in fact-finding meetings with clients to explore the issues of needs, wants, accomplishments and future goals (personal and financial) that may be motivating the individual:

1. "What financial things do you currently have that you appreciate the most?"

2. "What are some things that you set out to obtain and have done so?"

3. "If you were to look back over your life today, what, financially, will you have been most grateful for accomplishing?"

4. "What are you most proud of financially?"

These questions, although scripted, are a good example of the type used for a focused interview. Increased familiarity with typical client goals and life cycle events as well as client motives and reactions can serve as the background for developing basic questions that can be further refined with use. Other specialized approaches, such as those promoted by George Kinder[8] or Mitch Anthony,[9] for example, offer planners questions for helping clients gain increased understanding of financial and life planning. Kinder[10] is recognized for the following questions (asked in this order) to help clients explore what he calls "a life worth living":

1. "If you had all the money you needed, what would you do with your life?"

2. "If you had only five to ten years to live, but would be in good health the entire time, what would your life look like?"

3. "If you knew you were going to die tomorrow, what did you miss? What did you not get to do? Who did you not get to be?"

While some planners would argue that these questions are beyond the scope of *any* client conversation they wish to have, or even beyond the scope of financial planning, other advisors are embracing the integration of financial planning and life planning. The shift from a client relationship based on one or more separate *transactions* to one based on complete *transformation* could have significant impact on the practice of financial planning. While the ability to skillfully guide a client through the questions cited above goes beyond the fundamental skills of conducting a focused interview, both are valuable techniques for collecting client data.

What Does it Mean to Frame Goals and Objectives?

Goals are sometimes defined as dreams that become reality. This simple definition implies that motivated or purposeful action is required when pursuing a goal.

Depending upon the issue being considered, a goal may range from the abstract to the concrete. In Chapter 1, a **goal** was defined as a more global statement of a client's personal or financial purpose, while an **objective** was a more discrete financial target that supports a goal. For example, a client may state that he or she desires a "comfortable retirement," but it is only through further discussions and clarification that the planner may be able to discern a definitive objective of accumulating $1.65 million by the age of 55. Blanchard coined the acronym "SMART" to describe goals that are:

- **S**pecific;

- **M**easurable;

- **A**ttainable;

- **R**ealistic; and

- **T**rackable.[11]

This type of analysis offers planners a useful guideline for working with clients and can easily facilitate discussions on assumptions and expectations appropriate for the planning situation and the goal in question. (Framing SMART goals also facilitates consideration of the seven questions that must be answered by any well-written recommendation.)

Many times a planner, through the broader exchange with a client, will uncover a goal that the client was either uncomfortable listing or simply could not fully articulate. These insights increase the planner's understanding of the relationship and help the planner to discover nuances and subtle priorities among the client's goals. Planners should not look at each goal in isolation. Goals may be independent, interrelated, or interdependent. And the best solution for one goal may have a deleterious effect on another goal. For interrelated goals, the first goal may need to be fulfilled as a precursor to fulfilling the second goal. The idea of a personal goal hierarchy or ranking is commonly accepted, as is the duration of the time available for funding the goal. Typically, goals are categorized by some time line for accomplishment, such as:

- *Short-term*: less than two years.

- *Intermediate-term*: requiring from two to ten years.

- *Long-term*: requiring more than ten years.

The exact specifications range from a few months to multiple years or decades. Recognizing and examining these relationships provides a deeper understanding of the client's situation. The communication required to fully identify and frame goals can sometimes be challenging. Nonetheless, the outcomes attained are essential to preparing feasible, actionable, client-oriented recommendations.

Within financial planning, much attention is focused on goals—especially goals that are socially acceptable or supported by tax policy (e.g., accumulating funds for retirement or education expenses). But from a broader perspective, it is also important to consider the *origin* of a client's goals. Although clients' goals can be framed or defined in limitless ways, goals basically emanate from (1) wants and needs, (2) life cycle events, and (3) life transitions. Wants and needs are differentiated by their significance, with **wants** described as desires or pleasures while **needs** are required to sustain life. The interpretation of wants and needs varies widely across the spectrum of income or wealth. **Life cycle events** represent typical biological, socioeconomic, or sociocultural events that occur over the life span of an individual or household. Anthony defines goals as what the client would like to "have, do, or be" during life, while a **life transition** represents a "change or transition" currently faced or expected to occur in the near future.[12] Using this definition, life transition might represent a life cycle event or a random occurrence (e.g., the diagnosis of a chronic disease). Clients may identify a new goal, modify existing goals, or change the hierarchy of the goals as a result of a perceived want or need, life cycle event, or life transition.

The categories listed above for classifying goals are not necessarily mutually exclusive. For example, a divorce may result from an unfulfilled personal need, or be viewed as a life cycle event or a life transition. Rebuilding a vacation home following a hurricane could be viewed as a need (i.e., to receive the insurance reimbursement), a want (i.e., to continue family memories), or a life transition resulting from the "change" to the household as a result of the property damage. Examples of selected needs, wants, life cycle events, and life transitions are shown in Exhibit 6.2; for more examples see the Client Intake Form in Appendix A.

Exhibit 6.2 Selected Examples of Needs, Wants, Life Cycle Events & Life Transitions That May Result in a Client Goal

	Need	Want	Life Cycle Event	Life Transition
Selling/buying/starting a business	√	√		
Vacation / Travel		√		
Second home / Vacation home		√		
Change in marital status (formation, dissolution, widowed)		√	√	√
Military service or deployment				√
Having children or grandchildren		√	√	√
Signing up for Social Security and Medicare			√	√
Change in employment	√	√		√
Children entering or graduating from college			√	√
Hobbies / leisure activities		√	√	
Risk management protection	√			
Funding for education expenses	√	√	√	
Leaving a legacy (for family, charity, community, etc.)		√	√	
Caring for parents			√	√
New car every X years		√		
Boat / motorcycle		√		
Family celebration (wedding, anniversary, Bah Mitzvah, second honeymoon)		√	√	√
Death of family member or friend			√	√
Disability of friend			√	√
Receipt of a large settlement		√		
Pool, spa, tennis court or other home improvement		√		
Moving parents to a care facility			√	√
Financial independence (freedom, security, etc.)	√	√	√	
Financial gift for a family member or friend		√	√	
Funding for retirement	√	√	√	√
Debt reduction or elimination	√	√		

Two significant questions typically emerge after data have been collected and reviewed. Should client financial goals be ranked? And if so, how? Answers to these questions range from easy to complex. In situations where a client is able to prioritize goals, the answer can be relatively straightforward. But in cases where a client has several equally important, but somewhat conflicting goals, obtaining an answer to the question becomes significantly more problematic. Of course the ranking of goals may not be an issue if sufficient funding is available; however, this is rarely the case for most clients.

Exhibit 6.3, the Goal Ranking Form, illustrates one way to prioritize and rank a client's financial goals. The logic behind this table is rooted in goal-based decision making theory. The theory suggests that goals can be prioritized to allow a decision maker to choose the most important goal to be achieved. In principle, once this goal is obtained, or at least fully funded, the next highest ranking goal would be dealt with, and the process would continue until all goals were either accounted for or a client's resources were depleted. This is one approach, but there are alternatives for ranking and funding goals that exceed the available funding. Exhibit 6.3 provides a definition and a scoring methodology for each goal ranking item. In effect, multiple goals can be compared using these items, with a total score generated for each goal. The goal with the highest total score would be ranked number one; the next highest scoring goal would be ranked number two, and so on.

Now, a word of caution is in order. Simply because goals can be ranked does not necessarily mean that the highest ranking goal should be dealt with first. Client goals and objectives and the corresponding recommendations that are developed may be moderated by a planner's knowledge of the client's situational factors. Goals and recommendations may then be subject to further refinement based on the planner's own financial planning knowledge and experience as well as other descriptive factors. These issues are discussed further in the case example that follows.

Data Gathering Tip: The Importance of Specifically Recording Client Goals

It is always good practice to take client information—no matter how it is provided—and put it in a format for practical use. It is unlikely that a client will ever arrive in a planner's office with goals specifically outlined and ranked. Most clients have a general idea of what they would like to accomplish, but few will be able to define their goals precisely during a first meeting. It will take energy, intuition, and persuasion to coax goals and objectives from the client. Recording a client's goals and objectives, as understood by a planner, is a good way to develop a checklist for further discussion. Furthermore, realistically framing, articulating, and ranking goals can only occur as the client's "dreams" are brought into perspective with the analytical and technical knowledge of the planner. A thoughtful and honest interchange between client and planner will be necessary to arrive at the final goals for the plan—and everyone must realize that the goals and the plan are subject to changes in circumstances and the vagaries of the future.

Exhibit 6.3

Goal Ranking Form

What is the goal?

Total possible score range (9 – 33)

Goal Feature	Explanation	Scale	Score
Emotional Importance	How important is this goal to the client's personal well being?	Low Medium High	1 2 3
Financial Importance	How important is this goal to the client's financial situation?	Low Medium High	1 2 3
Need/Want	Does the client define this goal as a need or a want?	Want Need	0 2
How Many Ways Can the Goal Be Achieved?	Are there many alternatives to achieve the goal or just a few ways to satisfy the goal?	Many Ways Few Ways Limited Ways	1 2 3
How Many Times Goal Could be Achieved?	Is the goal recurring or is funding the goal a one-time event?	Often Limited One-Time	1 2 3
Likelihood of Goal Accomplishment	What is the probability or likelihood that the goal will be achieved?	Low Moderate High	1 2 3
Time Horizon for Funding the Goal	When is the funding for the goal needed?	More than 10 years Between 2 and 10 years Within 2 years Within 3 months	1 2 3 4
Is a Delay Possible?	Can the target date for goal realization be delayed?	Yes Maybe No	1 2 3
Time Horizon for Depleting the Goal Funding	For how many years must the funding for the goal last?	Within 3 months Within 2 years Between 2 and 10 years More than 10 years	1 2 3 4
Financial Impact of Goal Failure	How serious are the financial consequences for the client if the goal is not achieved?	Minor Serious Devastating	1 3 5

Adapted from Slade, S. (1994). *Goal-Based Decision Making: An Interpersonal Model.* Lawrence Erlbaum Associates, Inc., Publishers. NJ: Hillsdale.

From Process to Practice

The vignette that follows introduces the Kims, a young professional couple with an 8-year-old daughter named Azalea, and their financial planner, Jane. Their retrospective story, which recounts their financial planning experience, will continue from Chapter 6 through 8. In this first section, the Kims recall the events that characterize Steps 1 and 2 of the financial planning process for them.

Tom and Nyla asked Jane on the way out of her office "Are we done?" "Not quite," Jane said, "but we have made a lot of progress this year." Tom and Nyla Kim had just completed their first annual check-up and monitoring meeting with Jane, their financial planner. The meeting did not go at all as the Kims had expected. There were no questionnaires to complete, no forms to fill out, no disclosure agreements to sign; in fact neither of them even picked up a pen. "Wow," Tom mused as they headed for the car "Did we make it?" As Tom and Nyla drove home, they began reflecting on Jane's final comment. They had made a lot of progress but there had also been a lot of hard work, soul searching, prioritizing of their goals, budgeting of their income, attending several meetings, and participating in several phone calls with Jane over the course of a little over a year.

Tom and Nyla initially met with Jane after a recommendation from a friend who also was one of Jane's clients. Their friend explained that Jane, a graduate of a college financial planning program, was a fee-based comprehensive financial planner who worked with young professional clients who wanted to establish strong, long-term planning relationships. They went to Jane for what they now call "the first of our financial physicals. We wanted to know that we were financially healthy and that there weren't any problems looming on the horizon," Tom recollected. In the beginning Tom and Nyla both felt unsure about their financial future. They had often thought about seeing a professional, but did not know where to go, who to ask, or how to begin. They felt sure that their lack of a clearly defined direction and limited assets meant that professional help was out of their reach. However, when they initially met with Jane, her approach was just what they needed. She did not focus on the financial aspects of their life; instead she asked some very thought-provoking questions, such as "Where do you see yourselves financially in 10 years?" and "How did you come to be where you are now?"

At the end of the first meeting, Jane asked if they would like to continue the relationship. Upon their agreement, she scheduled a follow-up meeting in two weeks and provided them with "fact-finder" questionnaires, called the Client Intake Form (to complete jointly), the Goal Ranking Form (to completely individually and jointly), and the Risk Tolerance Assessment (to complete individually). The completed forms and a list of other needed documents were to be returned to the office a few days before their next meeting. But to the Kims the most important thing Jane said before they left was that she would be available to help if they started to feel overwhelmed with the forms. "It is a lot of work" she said, "but 'totally worth it.' Some clients look back at the Client Intake Form several years later and take pride in how far they have come. It is like throwing another log on the fire. Most people get re-energized because they see the progress and want to make even more." With that, the Kims started their financial planning relationship with Jane—but that was about a year ago.

Two weeks after their introductory meeting, the Kims had completed the intake form and brought the requested documents back to Jane's office. Again, they were surprised at how relaxed Jane was about their prospects. Although they had talked with her and her staff several times over the phone about getting assistance with the forms, they were very happy to see that she was still so upbeat. They had been afraid that with all of their questions and their obvious lack of financial knowledge that Jane might have decided not to work with them.

Tom recalled that as Jane meticulously reviewed the intake form and their other financial documents, that she paid particular attention to the Goals and Objectives section as she began asking questions. These were not questions that made them feel uneasy or that they had not done the right things thus far—just questions. For example, "How do you feel about providing funding for your daughter's college?" and "Will you be staying with family on your proposed international vacation?" Exhibit 6.4 shows an example of the Goals and Objectives section of the Client Intake Form as completed by Tom and Nyla Kim.

Nyla remembered being really impressed by the questions that Jane asked and the fact that she seemed genuinely interested—like she was really paying attention to their lives and not just their money. Jane had explained that her additional questions helped her to get a better picture of her clients—to learn about their values, goals, attitudes, and even their family health histories as a background for understanding what was important in their lives and their financial plan. As the discussion focused on their goals, Jane reviewed the Kims' completed Summary Goal Ranking Form. Jane's original instructions said that the Kims could individually complete a form for each goal and then come to a consensus, or that they could simply discuss each goal and complete the scoring. Either way, Jane needed their summary form. Exhibit 6.5 provides an example of the goal ranking form completed by the Kims (after several hours of discussion) for three of their goals.

Nyla recalled how difficult it was to complete the form, and although the total scores were very close for each goal, Nyla and Tom remembered that discussing each goal and ranking had been very helpful. Each of their goals was very important to them. Ever since Azalea was born, they had talked about wanting to at least partially pay for her to go to college. When they discussed the possibility of not taking the international trip, Tom quickly reminded her of the promise "to go on a honeymoon someday even if we have to take the kids." Furthermore, they were pleased that Jane, even with her extensive financial knowledge, did not presume to know their desires or arbitrarily rank the goals and proceed with the plan development without their input.

Exhibit 6.4 Tom & Nyla Kim's Goals & Objectives Form

Goals/Objectives (Tom & Nyla Kim)	Importance Level (0-5)	Time Horizon to Begin	Time Horizon to Complete
Personal			
Becoming more financially knowledgeable	3	Now	
Improving recordkeeping methods	0		
Starting a family	0		
Advancing in current career	4	Now	
Changing careers	0		
Returning to college	0		
Caring for parents	2	15 years	Unknown
Retiring early	3	25 years	Unknown
Traveling extensively in retirement	0		
Other:			
Other:			
Financial			
Reducing revolving debt	5	Now	Unknown
Increasing periodic savings	3	Now	
Reducing taxes	1		
Evaluating insurance needs	3	Soon	
Increasing investment diversification	1		
Increasing investment return	2	Now	
Starting a small business	0		
Saving for children's education	5	Now	10 years
Purchasing a vehicle	0		
Saving for the down payment on a home	0		
Purchasing a home	0		
Investing an inheritance	0		
Saving for retirement	5	Now	25 years
Giving to charity	2	5 years	Unknown
Transferring estate assets	0		
Other: Vacation	4	Now	2 years
Other:			
Other:			

Exhibit 6.5 Tom & Nyla Kim's Summary Goal Ranking Form

Summary Goal Ranking Form

What is the goal?		Azalea's Education		Retirement		Vacation Trip	
Goal Feature	**Scale**						
Emotional Importance	(1-3)	High	3	Low	1	High	3
Financial Importance	(1-3)	Medium	2	High	3	Low	1
Need/Want	(0-2)	Need	2	Need	2	Want	0
How Many Ways Can Goal Be Achieved	(1-3)	Few Ways	2	Many Ways	1	Few Ways	2
How Many Times Goal Could be Achieved	(1-3)	One-Time	3	One-Time	3	Limited	2
Likelihood of Goal Accomplishment	(1-3)	High	3	High	3	Moderate	2
Time Horizon for Funding the Goal	(1-4)	Between 2 and 10 years	2	More than 10 years	1	Within 2 years	3
Is a delay possible?	(1-3)	No	3	Yes	1	Maybe	2
Time Horizon for Depleting the Funding	(1-4)	Within 2 years 10 years	2	More than 3 months	4	Within	1
Financial Impact of Goal Failure	(1-5)	Moderate	3	Serious	5	Minor	1
Total Possible Range	(9-33)						
Total Score			25		24		17

Adapted from Slade, S. (1994). *Goal-Based Decision Making: An Interpersonal Model.* Lawrence Erlbaum Associates, Inc., Publishers. NJ: Hillsdale.

Overall, Tom and Nyla remembered the goal-setting process as emotionally difficult but informative. Ultimately, they were both very pleased with the relationship they had established with their new financial planner. They recalled leaving the second meeting feeling like they had shared their life story with Jane—with the unexpected benefit that they had actually learned some new things about each other after more than 12 years of marriage. They had three goals for their future, and Jane had left them with the impression that they weren't just dreams—they could be goals!

Chapter Summary

The establishment of the client engagement sets the parameters for the *breadth* of information to be gathered about the client situation. But the *depth* of information gathered about the client's situational factors provides the background for the upcoming client's situational analysis, whether completed for a single issue, a core content planning area, or for a comprehensive financial plan. The Client Intake Form and guidelines for conducting a focused interview were introduced as methods for gathering quantitative and qualitative data. It is through these efforts that the planner comes to know and understand the client and the planning needs. At the outcome of Step 2: Gather Data and Frame Goals and Objectives, the advisor and client should have identified mutually agreeable, clearly defined goals and objectives. The scope of the planner-client engagement (from Step 1) and the planner-client relationship and goals (forged from Step 2) serve as a foundation for the continuation of the financial planning process.

Chapter Endnotes

1. Mellan, O. (1994). *Money Harmony: Resolving Money Conflicts in Your Life and Relationships*. Walker & Co.: NY. or for more information see http://www.moneyharmony.com/say.html

2. Gurney, K. (1988). *Your Money Personality: What It Is and How You Can Profit From It*. Doubleday: NY. Or see http://www.financialpsychology.com/ or http://www.finpsych.com/.

3. Kinder, G. (1999). *Seven Stages of Money Maturity: Understanding the Spirit and Value of Money in your Life*. Dell Publishing: NY.

4. One psychometrically-designed risk tolerance scale that is commonly used in the United States and abroad is available from FinaMetrica® at www.finametrica.com.

5. Grable, J. E., & Lytton, R. H. (1999). *Financial Risk Tolerance Revisited: The Development of a Risk Assessment Instrument*. Financial Services Review, 8(3), 163-181. The risk tolerance scale is also available at http://www.rce.rutgers.edu/money/riskquiz/default.asp for public use.

6. The concept of a semi-standardized or focused interview is borrowed from social science research. An interview to complete the client intake form would be a standardized or structured interview, restricted by the form.

7. Levin, R. (February, 2003). When Everything You Have *is* Enough. *Journal of Financial Planning*. 16 (2), 34-35.

8. Kinder, G. (1999). *Seven Stages of Money Maturity: Understanding the Spirit and Value of Money in your Life*. Dell Publishing: NY.

9. Anthony, M. (2002). *Your Clients for Life: The Definitive Guide to Becoming a Successful Financial Planner*. Dearborn Financial Publishing: Chicago.

10. NAPFA Advisor (August 2003). "Interview: George Kinder & Life Planning." *NAPFA Advisor*, 7-13.

11. Blanchard, K. Blanchard, K., Zigarmi, P. & Zigarmi, D. (1985). *Leadership and The One Minute Manager: Increasing Effectiveness Through Situational Leadership*. William Morrow & Co., Inc.: NY.

12. Anthony, M. (2004). Life Transitions Profile. Financial Life Planning Institute, at: www.financialifeplanning.com.

Chapter Review

The Basics: Review Questions

Discussion Questions

1. What kinds of client information are encompassed within the exploration of client situational factors? Give five examples and explain how each might impact the planning process and, therefore, be important information for the advisor to consider.

2. Why is it important for the financial planner to know if the client is currently working with another financial professional, such as an attorney, accountant, or enrolled agent?

3. How might the financial planning attitudes and practices of a risk tolerant client vary from those of a risk averse client? Consider multiple attitudes and practices beyond those associated with investments. How can these insights inform the planning process for planner and client? How can these heuristics, or stereotypes, negatively affect the planning process?

4. Identify at least five original source documents that an advisor may wish to review. For each identify why the document may be requested and the information to be gained.

5. What is a focused interview? How is it similar and dissimilar from a conversation? Why is verbal and nonverbal communication an important aspect of a focused interview?

6. Why is a goal stated as "to live life with a relatively high level of financial satisfaction" not very useful in terms of a practical financial planning analysis? What might a SMART objective state in support of that goal?

7. Answer the sample focused interview questions from Levin or Kinder. How might your answers vary from the answers given by your spouse, partner, or close friend? How might these differences affect your financial choices?

8. What are the benefits of using a formalized client intake form? Review the form and identify: (1) data you suspect will be most difficult for the average client to provide; and (2) data that you were surprised to see requested. For each answer, explain why.

9. Review the definitions of needs, wants, life cycle events, and life transitions. Identify examples of each, noting those that may not be mutually exclusive. Try to identify examples that are not shown in Exhibit 6.2.

10. According to goal-based decision making theory, how might goals be prioritized to allow an advisor and client to choose the most important goal(s) to be achieved? What criteria contribute to the ranking?

Chapter 7

The Systematic Process: Analyzing the Situation and Developing the Plan

Learning Objectives

1. Explain how to analyze a client's current situation.

2. Identify information needed to determine and quantify the planning needs, document planning assumptions, and document and evaluate current planning efforts for each of the core financial planning content areas.

3. Understand the role of potential products and strategies within the analysis of the client's current situation and be able to provide an example of a product, product strategy, or procedural strategy for each of the core financial planning content areas.

4. Explain, apply, and defend the options available to a planner and client when the costs of funding all recommendations exceed the available discretionary cash flow or other assets.

5. Explain how a financial plan is developed.

6. Explain planner practices that are important to the successful presentation of a plan to the client.

7. Differentiate between holistic judgment, the systematic approach, and triangulation when analyzing the client situation and developing a plan.

8. Demonstrate how to use holistic judgment, the systematic approach (including the planning forms), and triangulation in the development of a plan.

Six–Step Systematic Financial Planning Process

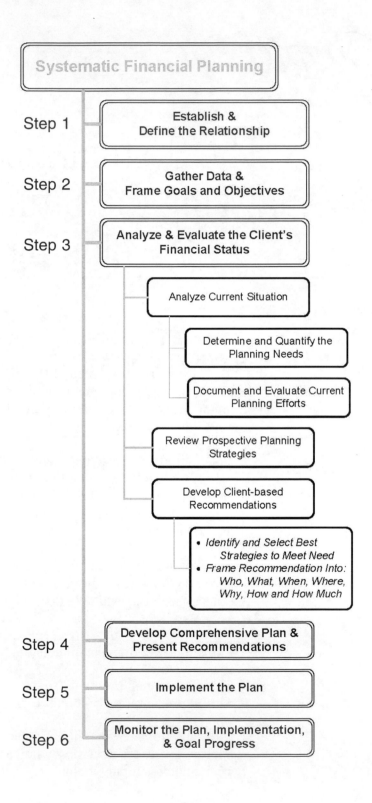

Key Terms

Assumptions	Procedural strategy
Holistic judgment	Product strategy
Impact analysis	Systematic approach to planning
Liability release form	Triangulation

Professional Judgment: The "Black Box" of Financial Planning

Nearly all financial planners agree that developing a list of potential financial planning strategies to address a specific client issue is a relatively straightforward process. Some planners will gravitate towards simple, easy to understand strategies. Others will use their knowledge and experience to create more complex strategies that address multiple goals (e.g., funding a 529 plan with the maximum five-year allowable contributions to reduce the taxable estate). Strategic identification is grounded in knowledge of the products and procedures surrounding the core financial planning content areas. The difficulty in strategizing may occur when a planner is forced to narrow a list of potentially workable strategies into one or more recommendations. This process may become more difficult as the planner integrates multiple recommendations into a workable plan, and even more frustrating if the cost of funding all of the recommendations exceeds the funds identified. In fact, the process actually goes beyond product knowledge into the realm of analytical thinking, problem solving, and inference. Students and novice planners may struggle with the questions of, "How does 'it' happen?" or "What is the process of moving from strategies to the selection of a recommendation or multiple integrated recommendations that make up a plan?" Too often, experienced planners offer little or no explanation, such as:

"I just know….it just comes to me as I think about the client and the options."

"Most of the time I agree with the plan produced by the software."

On the other hand, some planners may be honest enough to admit that, "For some clients I really struggle with the plan development. There just never seems to be an easy answer. Other times, the pieces just fall into place."

Building on the Systematic Financial Planning Process that was introduced in Chapter 5, this chapter considers Step 3: Analyze and Evaluate the Client's Financial Status, and Step 4: Develop the Comprehensive Plan and Present the Recommendations. It explores what happens within the "black box" of developing the plan, or what some planners refer to as professional judgment, expertise, or intuition.

Step 3: Analyze and Evaluate the Client's Financial Status

It may take years of study and experience to fully comprehend the nuances and complexities of doing a thorough analysis and evaluation of a client's situation. This process is a financial planning conundrum built on facts known about the client, inferences gleaned from the planner-client relationship, and assumptions that should be mutually agreed upon by the planner and client. It is—to put it simply—the application of professional judgment in the assessment and diagnosis of the client's financial situation, followed by a review of available alternatives. Then, in conjunction with the client, a course of action that offers the best risk-adjusted probability of success is identified. As illustrated in Figure 7.1, Step 3 is a multi-layered step consisting of three sub-steps: (1) Analyze the Current Situation; (2) Review Prospective Planning Strategies; and (3) Develop Client-based Recommendations.

Analyze the Current Situation

Analysis of the client's current situation requires the planner to review and distill all of the information collected about the client's situation in the context of the marketplace—the tax, economic, political and legal, or regulatory, environment. The analysis, summarized in Figure 7.1, Selected Example Issues for Analyzing the Client's Situation in Each of the Core Financial Planning Content Areas, is designed to answer four questions for each core content area:

1. *What is the client's planning need?* The determination, or *qualification*, of the planning need is based on the advisor's familiarity with the client's situation. Quantitative and qualitative data will be considered, such as income replacement needs, time horizon for a goal, family health history, occupational hazards, and attitudes. This investigation focuses on the current *known* needs as well as any client information that might suggest *unknown* needs, current or future. For example, a 45-year old client may not currently need long-term care insurance, but may be strongly committed to purchasing a policy anyway because of a potential future need created by a family history of Alzheimer's disease. Planning needs may be identified by the client or planner.

2. *What assumptions are relevant to the client's planning need?* **Assumptions** are inferences based on premise, reasoned conclusions, facts, or circumstantial evidence that affect the client's planning need and the quantification of that need. For example, historical stock market returns, recent inflationary increases in the cost of higher education, and average skilled nursing home costs are supported by factual data and may be included in the quantification of the client's need. These assumptions and many others reflect the current or projected marketplace, such as the tax, economic, political and legal, or regulatory, environment. Other assumptions reflect the client's personal situation (e.g., the assumed need for long term care insurance; the likelihood of a child receiving college scholarships or fellowships; or life span projections). Assumptions must be fully disclosed, mutually agreed upon, and realistic.

3. *Can the client's planning need be quantified?* Technical expertise, computations, and other analytical tools are used (where applicable) to

objectively analyze and *quantify* the client's need. For some core content planning areas, such as estimating life insurance needs,, several recognized approaches may be available and supported by different software applications. Quantification of other needs (e.g., the need for long-term care insurance protection), may be far harder to defend and consider multiple, seemingly unrelated amounts, such as the client's projected net worth and the daily benefit amount.

4. *How is the planning need currently being met?* The planner must document the planning efforts currently in place to meet the need, or the absence of any efforts on the part of the client to attempt to address the need. Then, a thorough and objective assessment of the products and strategies currently in use must be completed to project the likelihood of achieving the goal. Results of this evaluation may reveal needed changes or may validate the client's approach and the fact no changes are warranted. (For more information on some standard benchmarks that may be used to evaluate insurance and investment products, see Appendix B.)

Whereas the need to answer these four questions applies to each core content area, the data sources considered and the analytics completed may be quite different. Because of the importance and complexity of the sub-step, Analyze the Current Situation, it must be individually and systematically applied to each of the core content planning areas as summarized in Figure 7.1. A thorough exploration of the analysis surrounding each of these four questions is too extensive for consideration here; however, the table should offer students and novice planners some useful insights to how these analyses could be conducted.

Increased awareness of the issues to consider in the analysis of the client's current situation can inform and frame the data gathering that occurs in Step 2 of the systematic financial planning process. For example, as shown in Figure 7.1, insurance needs must be evaluated against certain client risk classification factors because these risk factors determine the need for, availability of, and cost of insurance. Although planners are not expected to be knowledgeable of the specific company's underwriting methods, a general knowledge of the factors to be considered is critical to effective data gathering and planning. In reviewing the hazards and risks characteristic of a client, planners should consider the following factors:

- **Lifestyle**
    - Using tobacco, alcohol, or drugs
    - Convictions for reckless driving, driving under the influence of alcohol or drugs, or receiving multiple speeding tickets
    - Participating in sensation-seeking activities, including ultralight flying, scuba diving, or mountain climbing
    - Personal character or household financial situation

Figure 7.1 Selected Example Issues for Analyzing the Client's Situation in Each of the Core Financial Planning Content Areas

Financial Planning Core Content Area	Determine the Planning Needs	Document Current Planning Assumptions	Quantify the Planning Needs	Document & Evaluate Current Planning Efforts

Cash Flow Planning "Financial Situation"	• Attitudes about debt
	• Availability of emergency fund
	• Goal commitment
	• Potential career, income and/or asset changes
		• Interest rate changes
		• Asset and liability acquisition
		• Job security
			• Review of:
			  ○ income statement
			  ○ balance sheet
			  ○ financial ratios
			  ○ net worth
				• Uses of debt
				• Discretionary cash flow
				• Cash management system
				• Current/future financial needs and goals

Income Tax Planning	• Attitudes about tax:
	  ○ tax payments
	  ○ charitable giving
	  ○ tax reduction strategies
	  ○ audits
		• Marginal tax bracket
		• AMT triggers
		• Changes in tax code
			• Project current tax liability
			• Identify possible implications from other planning issues
				• Review past tax returns
				• Review current employer withholdings or estimated tax payments

Life Insurance Planning	• Need for:
	  ○ dependent income
	  ○ liability mitigation
	  ○ small business continuation
	  ○ estate planning
	  ○ charitable giving
	• Potential beneficiaries
		• Client's life span (age at death)
		• Spouse or other financial dependents' life spans
			• Human life value approach
			• Capital retention approach
			• Income retention approach
			• Income multiplier approach
			• Needs analysis approach
				• Amount of current coverage
				• Product review:
				  ○ provider quality/rating
				  ○ fees and expenses
				  ○ past performance
				• Annual price per thousand

Health Insurance Planning	• Family health status
	• Pre-existing conditions
	• Couple/partner issues
	• Self-employment issues
		• Life cycle events:
		  ○ young adult
		  ○ retirement
		  ○ Medicare/Medigap
		• Health care inflation rate
		• Family health history
			• Savings to meet deductibles or co-pays
			• Stop-loss limit
			• Lifetime maximum limit on coverage
				• Employer provided
				• Individual or group policy
				• Product review:
				  ○ provider quality/rating
				  ○ cost
				  ○ amount of coverage

Figure 7.1 Selected Example Issues for Analyzing the Client's Situation in Each of the Core Financial Planning Content Areas (cont'd)

Financial Planning Core Content Area	Determine the Planning Needs	Document Current Planning Assumptions	Quantify the Planning Needs	Document & Evaluate Current Planning Efforts
Disability Insurance Planning	• Leave Available: ○ medical ○ personal/vacation • Savings available • Partner/spouse income • Risk tolerance • Occupation • Caregiver availability • Self-employment issues • Occupational hazards	• Projected: ○ severity ○ length • Eligibility for Social Security disability benefits • Family Medical Leave Act eligibility	• Short-term need • Long-term need • Need during any gap in coverage	• Employer-provided • Individual or group policy • Product review: ○ provider qaulity/rating ○ fees and expenses ○ amount of coverage ○ definition of disability
Long-Term Care Insurance Planning	• Current or family health history • Attitudes: ○ care giving ○ caregivers ○ charitable giving • Lifestyle choices • Occupational hazards	• Health care inflation rate • Family health history • Client's life span (age at death) • Spouse or other financial dependents' lifespans	• Review current and projected net worth: ○ $250,000 ○ $250,000 - $1.5 M ○ >$1.5 M	• Employer-provided • Individual or group policy • Product review: ○ provider quality/ rating ○ fees and expenses ○ amount of coverage
Property & Liability Insurance Planning	• Maximum, probable and typical loss exposure • Extended replacement cost endorsement • Building code upgrade endorsement	• Real and/or personal asset acquisition • 80% coverage rule	• Assets — real and financial • Location of property • Need for: ○ GAP ○ endorsements, riders, extensions	• Excess liability/ umbrella coverage • Coverage needs matched to assets • Product review: ○ provider quality/ rating ○ cost ○ amount of coverage

Figure 7.1 Selected Example Issues for Analyzing the Client's Situation in Each of the Core Financial Planning Content Areas (cont'd)

Financial Planning Core Content Area	Determine the Planning Needs	Document Current Planning Assumptions	Quantify the Planning Needs	Document & Evaluate Current Planning Efforts
Investment & Asset Management Planning	• Risk tolerance • Knowledge and experience • Time horizon • Risk capacity • Satisfaction with investments	• Expectations of market conditions: ○ interest rate changes ○ inflation rate ○ financial markets ○ currency valuation • Marginal tax bracket • Projected returns	• Current and projected cost of goals • Required rates of return • Asset allocation	• Portfolio statistics • Sensitivity analysis • Product review: ○ provider quality/rating ○ fees and expenses ○ past performance
Education Planning	• Attitudes (who pays for college costs) • Projected education needs	• Duration of education; time to completion • Education inflation rate • Financial aid availability and cost	• Estimate future education costs	• Current taxable and tax-advantaged accounts • Investments • Asset allocation • Asset ownership
Retirement Planning	• Early, typical, delayed retirement • Early and post-retirement lifestyle • Retirement issues (e.g., attitudes, health, employment, etc.)	• Eligibility for Social Security disability and/or retirement benefits	• Asset allocation • Capital depletion approach • Capital preservation approach • Inflation-adjusted approach	• Projected need vs. savings • Investment types • Use of employer-provided retirement accounts • Other qualified and nonqualified accounts
Estate Planning	• Estate tax attitudes • Family and charitable gifting attitudes • Small business continuation • Legacy issues • Guardianship appointment for children or other financial dependents	• Client's life span (age at death) • Spouse or other financial dependents' life spans • Changes in tax code	• Projected taxable estate value • Use of unlimited marital transfer	• Current estate planning documents: ○ wills ○ letters of instruction ○ power of attorney ○ advanced medical directives • Ownership issues • Trusts (intervivos and testamentary) • Gifting

- **Occupation**

  - Working in a hazardous profession or occupation

  - Piloting commercial, private, or military aircraft

- **Medical condition or history**

  - Gender, age, height, and weight

  - Family medical history

Individuals who because of any of these factors have a higher than standard mortality are considered substandard risks for privately purchased life insurance. These same factors may also affect cost, availability, or need for other types of insurance. Depending upon the company, client insurability factors may result in a denial of the policy application, increased policy costs, or the inclusion of riders that control coverage. Insurance planning in particular exemplifies the need for a broad-based exploration of a client's situational factors, such as the lifestyle, personal, attitudinal, and socioeconomic profile that comprise Step 2: Gather Data and Frame Goals and Objectives. Gathering the client data needed for a thorough and defensible evaluation of the client's situation, whether for the purposes of a single-issue analysis, to support a product sale, or to complete a comprehensive plan, may appear intrusive, but is, in fact, the foundation for the future with that client. Throughout the planning process, the planner or planning team must demonstrate genuine empathy toward the client balanced with rigorous analytical skills.

At this juncture in the planning process, based on the data gathered and the analysis of the client's current situation, the planner has an arsenal of useful information to process, as outlined below:

- Insights into the client's temperament, personality, motivations, risk tolerance, financial knowledge, experience, and perceived level of financial success up to this point. The planner can begin to answer the questions of *who* and *why* as well as the questions *for whom*, *what*, and *how*.

- Clear, mutually agreed upon definitions of the client's goals and desired outcomes of the planning process. The planner can begin to answer the questions of *why*, *what*, *when* and *for whom*.

- For each of the core content planning areas—cash flow management, income taxes, risk management (e.g., life, health, disability, long-term care, property and liability), investments, education or other special needs planning, retirement planning, and estate planning—the planner can begin to answer *why*, *what*, *when*, *where*, *how* and *how much* based on the following results:

  - quantitative data analyses built on mutually agreed upon personal and economic assumptions conducted independently and systematically for each of the core content planning areas;

- qualitative and household needs assessment to identify potential individual, lifestyle, life event, or other factors that might impact the client in any of the core content planning areas;

- the planner's knowledge and professional insights regarding any factors that might impact the client in any of the core content areas, including issues, problems, or concerns beyond the client's awareness;

- the planner's and/or client's scan of the legislative, tax, political, and economic environmental factors that may affect implementation of the plan, either immediately or in the future; and

- the planner's consultation or collaboration with other professionals.

Review Prospective Planning Strategies

With the analysis of the situation complete, the advisor should have a clear understanding of the issues to be addressed and thus should be ready to proceed to the next sub-step, Review Prospective Planning Strategies. This sub-step of the analysis of the client's situation focuses on the identification of possible strategies or available alternatives for meeting the client's needs and goals. With the results of the quantitative and qualitative analysis complete, the planner can begin to fully answer the strategy, recommendation, and implementation questions of *why*, *when*, *where*, *how much*, *how*, and *by whom*.

Strategies reflect the advisor's technical competence and the universe of possible solutions that might be applicable to the client's situation. Simply put, strategies are the "Rolodex" of answers that a planner must identify and then apply to the client's situation (or at least eliminate as an option) until the process yields a limited number of viable alternatives for each core content planning area considered. Strategies may be categorized as product or procedural. A **product strategy** reflects the use of a specific type of product or product feature to meet a planning goal or need. A **procedural strategy** emphasizes a process, service, or type of ownership rather than a product.

Figure 7.2, Products and Product Features for Use When Identifying Strategies, provides a summary of some of the most widely used financial planning products and services and matches these items to their common usage within the financial planning process. For example, a 1035 exchange is shown as a service used by financial planners to implement a tax-free annuity or life insurance exchange. In the table, a 1035 exchange is shown to be useful in three core financial planning content areas: (1) tax planning; (2) insurance planning; and (3) investment planning. Note that the specific relationships among the products, services, and core content areas are somewhat fluid—meaning that although a relationship may be indicated in the table, the actual role of a product or service may be different for each client. The table is intended to serve as a summary of typical products and services used by financial planners—not as a comprehensive list. Examples of product and procedural strategies that incor-

Figure 7.2 Products and Product Features for Use When Identifying Strategies

Product or Product Feature	Potential Role of Product or Service in the Financial Planning Process X = Product or Service Impact in Core Planning Content Area						
	Financial Situation Planning	Income Tax Planning	Risk Management Planning	Investment Planning	Education Planning	Retirement Planning	Estate Planning
1031 Like-Kind Exchange		X		X			
1035 Exchange		X	X	X			
2503(b) and 2503(c) Accounts		X		X	X		X
529 Plan					X		X
Annual Gifting	X	X		X	X		X
Annuities							
Fixed	X	X	X	X	X	X	X
Variable	X	X	X	X	X	X	X
Bond							
Corporate				X			
Government Agency		X		X			
Junk				X			
Municipal		X		X			
Treasury		X		X			
Buy/Sell Agreement	X	X	X			X	X
Certificate of Deposit (CD)	X	X		X		X	
COBRA Provision			X				
Collectibles			X	X			
Coverdell Education Savings Account		X			X		X
Credit Cards	X						
Disability Insurance		X	X			X	
Donor Advised Fund		X					X
Dependent Care Reimbursement Account	X	X					
Durable Power of Attorney	X						X
Family Limited Partnership		X					X
Flexible Spending Account (FSA)	X	X	X				
Hard Assets				X			
Health Insurance			X				
Health Savings Account (HSA)	X	X	X				
Home Equity Line of Credit	X	X					
Home Equity Loan	X	X					
Homestead Exemption			X				X
Incentive Stock Options		X		X		X	
Individual Retirement Account (IRA)							
Roth		X		X	X	X	
Traditional		X		X	X	X	
Letter of Last Instructions							X
Life Insurance							
Term			X				X
Universal			X				X
Variable			X	X			X
Variable Universal Life (VUL)			X	X	X	X	X
Whole Life/Cash Value			X				X
Living Will							X
Long-Term Care Insurance	X		X			X	X
Medicaid			X			X	X
Medical Directive			X				X
Medical Savings Account (MSA)		X	X	X			
Medicare			X			X	
Medigap Insurance			X			X	
Money Market Deposit Accounts (MMDA)	X			X			

Figure 7.2 Products and Product Features for Use When Identifying Strategies (cont'd)

Product or Product Feature	Potential Role of Product or Service in the Financial Planning Process — X = Product or Service Impact in Core Planning Content Area						
	Risk Financial Situation Planning	Income Tax Planning	Manage-ment Planning	Invest-ment Planning	Educa-tion Planning	Retire-ment Planning	Estate Planning
Mortgages							
Conventional	X	X					
Interest-only	X	X					
Refinanced	X	X		X			
Reverse Mortgage	X	X		X		X	X
Shared Appreciation	X	X		X			
Mutual Funds							
Bond	X	X		X			
Commodity				X			
Foreign/Global/International				X			
Money Market	X			X			
Real Estate				X			
Stock				X			
Non-Qualified Retirement Plan		X				X	
Non-Qualified Stock Options		X				X	
Options and Futures				X			
Pooled Income Fund		X				X	X
Property & Casualty Insurance							
Personal Automobile Insurance			X				
Earthquake Insurance			X				
Flood Insurance				X			
Homeowner's Insurance			X				
Umbrella, or Excess Liability, Insurance	X		X				
Qualified Retirement Plan		X		X		X	
Real Estate		X		X		X	
Savings Accounts	X			X			
Savings Bonds (E/EE/H/I)[a]		X		X	X		
Scholarships and Grants		X			X		
Stock							
Domestic			X			X	
Foreign			X			X	
Social Security Benefits							
Retirement		X		X		X	
Survivor / Disability		X	X	X		X	
Tax Credits	X	X			X		X
Titling							
Payable On Death (POD)		X					X
Transfer on Death (TOD)		X		X			X
Trust							
A/B Trust		X					X
Charitable Lead Trust		X					X
Charitable Remainder Annuity Trust (CRAT)		X				X	X
Charitable Remainder Unitrust Trust (CRUT)		X				X	X
Grantor Retained Annuity Trust (GRAT)		X					X
Grantor Retained Unitrust Trust (GRUT)		X					X
Irrevocable Life Insurance Trust (ILIT)			X				X
Qualified Personal Residence Trust (QPRT)		X				X	X
Qualified Terminal Interest Property (QTIP) Trust							X
Revocable or Living Trust		X	X				X
Uniform Gifts to Minors Account (UGMA) or Uniform Transfers to Minors Account (UTMA)		X		X	X		X
Unsecured Line of Credit	X	X					
Viatical Settlement			X				X
Will						X	

[a] The United States Department of the Treasury, Bureau of Public Debt, no longer issues Series E or Series HH Bonds; however, these bonds are still held by the investing public.

Figure 7.3 Selected Examples of Product and Procedural Strategies

Financial Planning Core Content Area	Sample Product Strategy	Sample Procedural Strategy
Financial Situation	Assuming the client is not subject to the alternative minimum tax (AMT), use a home equity loan to pay off high-interest debt or to finance a needed purchase, such as a new auto.	In consultation with the client, identify expenses that could be reduced or eliminated to free up cash flow for meeting other recommendations, which are mutually agreed to be more important.
Income Tax Planning	Purchase tax-managed mutual funds to reduce capital gain and dividend income.	Reduce tax liability by shifting income producing assets to family members in a lower tax bracket.[a]
Life Insurance Planning	Choose declining term policy to meet decreasing needs as children mature.	If estate taxation is not at issue, make some life insurance benefits payable to the estate to insure liquidity.
Health Insurance Planning	Choose a high deductible health plan (HDHP) and fund a health savings account (HSA).	If member of household is self-employed, consider having that person purchase and pay for policy to utilize self-employment deductibility of 100% of premiums.
Disability Insurance Planning	If cost difference is not great, purchase individual disability policy to avoid income tax on policy benefits.	Match short-term disability benefit period with long-term disability elimination period to ensure no gap in benefits.
Long-Term Care (LTC) Insurance Planning	Purchase a joint LTC policy that utilizes a shared pool of benefits.	Consider an adaptable policy, or policies, that provide coverage for the continuum of care from home, to an assisted living facility, and progresses, if necessary, to a skilled nursing facility.
Property & Liability Insurance Planning	Purchase a personal auto policy (PAP) with minimum split-limit coverage of 100,000/300,000/50,000.	Separate children's potential liability claims from the parents' assets by having the children purchase their own auto policies.
Investment & Asset Management Planning	Purchase ETFs or mutual funds, based on the advantages and disadvantages relative to the individual client, to diversify the portfolio.	Increase portfolio rates of return by reallocating the portfolio more aggressively and then following a periodic schedule of rebalancing to maintain the allocation.
Education Planning	Fund a 529 plan.	Title education assets in parents' names to increase flexibility of distribution and use of assets.
Retirement Planning	Balance funding of tax-deferred and IRA accounts (as available) to maximize employer matching funds while planning for future projected tax implications.	Plan to work part-time in the active post-retirement years to supplement income.
Estate Planning	For a high net worth household, establish an A-B, or marital bypass trust, to provide for the spouse and beneficiaries and reduce estate taxes for the second-to-die.	Start or increase annual giving and charitable giving to reduce the gross estate, thereby avoiding or reducing estate taxes and/or probate fees.

[a] The Tax Increase Prevention and Reconciliation Act of 2005 raised the age limit on the "kiddie tax" from age 14 to 18. However, consistent with gifting provisions, the strategy could still be used to reduce tax liability by shifting unearned income to other adult family members in a lower tax bracket than the original asset owner.

porate these typical products and services for each of the core content planning areas is shown in Figure 7.3, Selected Examples of Product and Procedural Strategies.

Initially, the ability to identify multiple strategies in response to the identified planning needs would appear to be highly correlated with the planner's experience and expertise. Recall that professional judgment, as well as professional ethics, constrains the planner to offer services within the purview of acknowledged expertise, to seek the collaboration of other professionals, or to refer the client to others. Like everyone else, financial planners become accustomed to using certain strategies or products or focusing on selected patterns of information. Development of two to four alternatives is becoming common practice; equally common is the practice of planners falling back on using the same old strategies they have used for years. It is these heuristics, or favored solutions, that a planner may turn to when working with a client. The biggest problem with this approach is that the financial planning industry (and more specifically the products and regulations) are almost constantly changing. These changes create additional opportunities for the planner and client, but also create additional confusion.

While commonly used strategies or products may increase efficiency for the planner, and promote depth of knowledge in a diverse universe of products, it may or may not yield the best outcome for the client. Professional judgment and ethical practice standards suggest that advisors acknowledge any limitations, prejudices, or other relationships that may adversely affect or bias the planner-client relationship. Furthermore, advisors are encouraged to continually apply some professional skepticism to compensate for, or override, those issues.

A primary source of confusion for planners today is that they have so many—almost too many—bases of information to consider. As Exhibit 7.1 suggests, there could be as many as eight factors, with multiple data points, that may influence the generation of client-specific strategies. The five factors on or above the horizontal axis characterize the planner and client and, for the most part, represent inferences gleaned by the planner from the available data and interactions with the client. Note that assumptions appear directly across from planning goals and objectives to represent the significance of this relationship.

Of the three factors below the horizontal axis, all represent factual information that may also serve as the basis of assumptions (e.g., client's projected lifespan or tax bracket in retirement). In sum, it is the integration of the facts, inferences, and assumptions that add to the complexity of identifying client-specific strategies. Some financial planning firms control the types of strategies, products, and recommendations that can be used. For example, it is not uncommon for planning firms to restrict the number and types of securities that may be used (known as an "approved product list"), or the type of insurance products that may be offered to a client. These limitations, based on established criteria to screen for performance or due diligence, may make the identification of strategies less complicated, but may also limit a planner's creativity in designing unique strategies to meet a client's needs. These issues, as well as other regulatory or compliance issues, make the planner's business model a significant consideration in the identification and evaluation of strategies.

Exhibit 7.1 Factors Affecting a Planner's Strategy and Recommendation Development

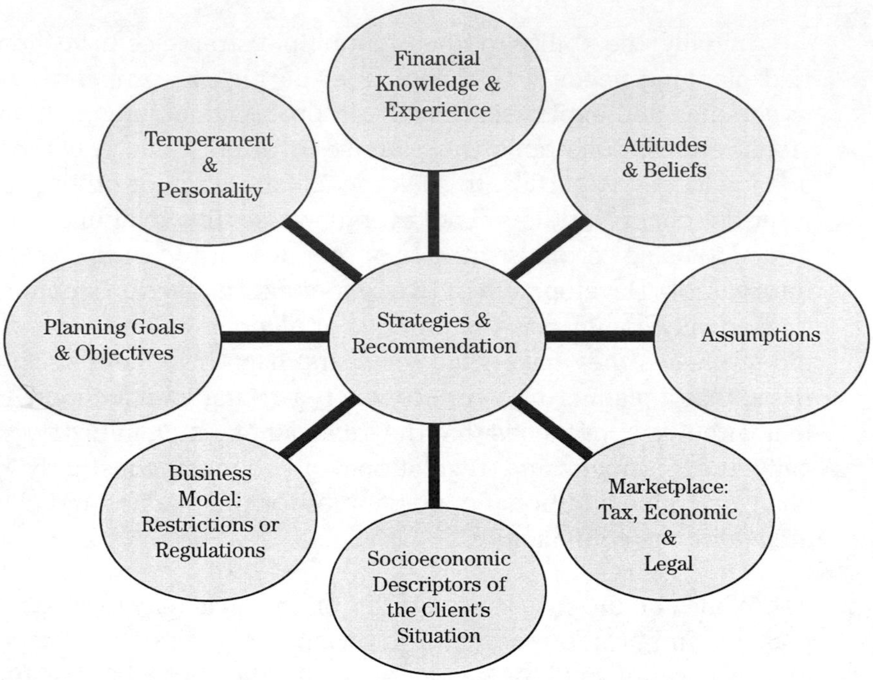

Develop Client-Based Recommendations

With the strategies identified, the planner can formulate the recommendations. The strategies may need to be altered or combined as the planner deliberates the advantages and disadvantages of each potential recommendation and considers the probable outcomes and impacts on the client's situation. As the planner attempts to align the recommendations with the client's goal(s), the total cost of the recommendations must be compared to the available cash flow or other available assets for funding the recommendations. Consider an example of an investment recommendation to fund a future goal (i.e., retirement, education, vacation home) based on a product strategy of an actively managed mutual fund. Facts and assumptions are at issue as the advisor considers increasing the anticipated rate of return (an assumption) in an attempt to limit or reduce the present value cost (a fact). Another relevant assumption, the client's risk tolerance for the goal, must be incorporated. This assumption influences the portfolio allocation and projected returns as well as the client's potential comfort with, and commitment to, the recommendation if the risk tolerance is exceeded.

The process of separating, distilling, and integrating client situational factors, planner factors, and strategies results in the development of one or more client-based recommendations that represent the scope of the planning engagement. This is true whether the advisor is developing a comprehensive plan, or one targeted on either a single issue or the entire core financial planning content area. The recommendations should offer the client cost-effective, adaptable alternatives. Contingent on the scope of the engagement and the degree of specificity implied by that arrangement, the recommendations should address these key questions:

1. Who should implement the recommendation?

2. What should be done?

3. When should the recommendation be implemented?

4. Where should the client, or other party, implement the recommendation?

5. Why should the recommendation be implemented? Why is it important to the client's financial future?

6. How should implementation take place?

7. How much should be purchased, saved, or invested to implement the recommendation? Specifically, what is the cost of the recommendation?

The significance of considering each of these questions in the development of the recommendations should not be overlooked. The questions may seem too simplistic to be meaningful, or answering all seven may seem unnecessary. But routine use of this simple rubric for framing recommendations can be a powerful tool for two reasons. First, careful consideration of the questions helps the advisor to reconsider the logic of each recommendation and the consistency with the client's goals and situation. Second, the rubric helps the advisor to fastidiously consider and articulate the funding and other implementation issues that are critical to sound plan development and motivated client action.

Step 4: Develop the Comprehensive Plan and Present the Recommendations

Well-designed financial plans are characterized by thoughtful analyses, logical consistency, thoroughness, clarity of purpose, and feasible, client-centered recommendations. This is true regardless of the style, format, scope, or length of the documents (i.e., comprehensive or modular) provided to the client. For example, each recommendation should be clearly supported by the analysis of the situation and the criteria used to prioritize the alternatives. The analysis should consider multiple aspects of the client situation and be based on reasonable assumptions acceptable to both planner and client. This is equally true for recommendations that support product sales. If the rationale for the recommendation is not clearly supported, the logical inconsistency will be apparent. This will confuse the client and may call into question the viability of the entire plan.

Thoroughness is represented by the comprehensiveness of the analysis, the number of alternatives considered, and the recommendations identified. Caution is warranted, however, in the way alternative recommendations are presented to the client. Involvement of the client in the decision making is important, but care must be taken to tailor the presentation of alternatives so that it does not overwhelm the client or suggest bias on the part of the planner. (A biased presentation may leave the client feeling manipulated and inadequately informed.) A clear focus on the best interest of the client coupled with the integration of the recommendations into a goal-based workable plan strongly supports clarity of purpose. Furthermore, clarity of purpose in reflecting the client's situation is important in the design and feasibility of the implementation steps. For example, if simplicity of implementation is an issue, this factor should be a primary consideration in the choice of recommendations. If the client acknowledges a tendency to procrastinate, the implementation plan must allow for this trait and incorporate strategies to avert potential oversights. Finally, the plan should project, but not promise, the potential outcomes and consequences of each recommendation.

In summary, both the plan and the presentation to the client must have logical consistency throughout. A well-designed plan is the foundation of an effective presentation to the client. Such plans and presentations are easier for clients to understand and are more likely to motivate client action. But how are well-designed plans developed? What happens in the "black box" when developing a financial plan?

Developing the Financial Plan

The foundation for the development of the plan is the constantly evolving and developing relationship between the planner and the client. That interaction results in the identification of client goals that ground the financial planning process. Those mutually agreed upon goals, in conjunction with the information about the client's situation, serve as the foundation for the analysis of each core content area and the identification of the potential strategies. The integration of applicable strategies, available resources, and knowledge of the client situation results in client-based recommendations.

By this stage of the planning process, there are still critical questions that are unresolved before the plan can be finalized. The development of the plan is the culmination and integration of the cash flow orientation to planning and the goal orientation to planning. Although comprehensive plans are more complex, the synthesis of goals and funding strategies applies to both comprehensive and targeted (or modular) plans. The same is true of analysis in support of product sales, because a client must be convinced that the product fulfills a recognized need or goal *and* is worthy of funding.

As illustrated in Exhibit 7.2, the planner and client may face an "either/or" situation that hinges on the availability of **discretionary cash flow** or other assets for funding the recommendations. Discretionary cash flow is the income that remains at the end of the period, for example an average month or year, after all expenses have been met. Critical to this definition is the designation of *expenses*. Some planners and clients define expenses as those minimally required or necessary to support the chosen standard of living. Clients, however, may choose to define expenses more broadly and could be, in fact, spending excess funds over which they have discretion. In that case the client could either choose not to spend or could reasonably reduce spending, in lieu of other goals. In reality, the determination of discretionary cash flow may vary with the income, values, and lifestyle of the client, but ultimately it must represent the periodic cash flow that is available to the planner to earmark for goal funding or product purchase. If the projected funding, from discretionary cash flow or other client assets (i.e., savings, investments) is not sufficient, the planner, working on the basis of the knowledge of the client situation or directly with the client, must conduct a cost-benefit analysis to determine the best use of the available funds relative to the proposed "ideal" recommendations. Although creative options may be available, generally planners and clients are limited to considering one or more of these options:

- Fully fund the most important recommendation in support of the goal determined by the planner and the client, then prioritize the other recommendations and corresponding goals or planning needs and apply the remaining funds.

- Agree to fund all recommendations, but stagger the implementation over a reasonable period of time that does not adversely affect the client's financial situation. This approach assumes that other assets will become available to facilitate future funding—either as a result of an inflow of income, assets, or the completion of funding for a goal—thus, freeing money to be redirected to another goal(s).

- Reconsider the recommendations and "downsize," or reduce, one or more of the suggested funding alternatives so that all recommendations receive some funding.

- Review mutually exclusive recommendations that might be integrated and met through another multi-purpose planning product or procedure (e.g., Roth IRA or life insurance).

- Prioritize the recommendations and goals, fund those that are most important, and eliminate or postpone other recommendations.

- Increase discretionary cash flow, or available funding, for all or some of the recommendations by reducing spending (e.g., for goods, services, or interest on debt) or by earning more (e.g., by increasing personal income, liquidating assets, or reallocating other assets for higher earnings).

Exhibit 7.2 Alternative Options for Funding Recommendations

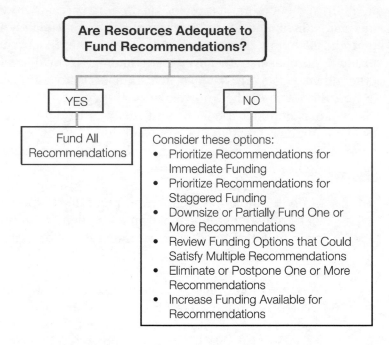

The planner—in the roles of advisor, educator, and mediator—can offer explanations to assist the client with these decisions. In exercising professional judgment, the planner, working with or on behalf of the client, must resolve the issue of competing recommendations in light of the same analysis that supported the development of the original recommendations (e.g., the multi-faceted analysis of the client's current situation, the marketplace scan, and the consultation with other professionals, if warranted).

However, the decision rests with the client and must be consistent with the priorities, values, and beliefs of the client. If the client chooses a course of action that could potentially jeopardize his or her future financial situation, or could raise questions about the professional judgment of the planner, a **liability release form** signed by the client should be considered. However, caution must be used in exercising this practice. To routinely ask a client to sign a liability release (e.g., simply because funds are not available or prioritized to meet all goals or planning needs) may, at best, be interpreted as insulting or rude, and at worst may be detrimental to the planning relationship. Planners might consider reserving this practice for situations when the client is clearly making a decision detrimental to the situation or is specifically repudiating the planner's advice or guidance. A liability release form protects the advisor from future suitability or legal challenges from the client or other primary stakeholder for professional malpractice or malfeasance.

Financial planning recommendations are not made in a vacuum, nor do the projected actions from implementing recommendations occur independently. Implementing one recommendation tends to have a ripple effect throughout a client's financial plan as illustrated in Exhibit 7.3, Typical Recommendations That Have Multiple Impacts on a Client's Financial Situation. Because of this, it is important for financial planners to incorporate an **impact analysis** as part of the planning process. Although the integration across core financial planning content areas is beyond the scope of the engagement of an advisor focused on single issue analysis, the importance of the impact analysis should not be overlooked. Projecting the integration of all recommendations through an impact analysis ensures the financial planner that a client has enough discretionary cash flow and assets to fully fund, and continue funding, all recommendations. Furthermore the impact analysis gives the advisor another perspective on the logic and assumptions upon which the plan is based. A Recommendation Planning Checklist and an Impact Analysis Form are presented later in this chapter. An Implementation Checklist for tracking funding sources for recommendations is shown in Chapter 8. All of these forms can be used to help the student

Exhibit 7.3 Typical Recommendations That Have Multiple Impacts on a Client's Financial Situation

Recommendation	Result
Refinance Mortgage	1. Change Cash Flow 2. Change Net Worth[a] 3. Change Tax Status
Restructure Debt	1. Change Cash Flow 2. Change Net Worth 3. Change Tax Status
Reallocation of Portfolio Assets	1. Change Cash Flow 2. Change Net Worth[b] 3. Change Tax Status
Increase Retirement Savings	1. Change Cash Flow 2. Change Net Worth 3. Change Tax Status 4. Change Estate Situation
Purchase Additional Life Insurance	1. Change Cash Flow 2. Possible Change in Net Worth Depending on Type of Insurance 3. Change Estate Situation
Retitling of Assets	1. Change Cash Flow 2. Change Net Worth 3. Change Tax Status 4. Change Estate Situation
Begin Gifting Strategies	1. Change Cash Flow 2. Change Net Worth 3. Change Tax Status 4. Change Estate Situation

[a] Assuming closing costs are paid from assets rather than current income.
[b] Due to transaction costs or sales charges.

or novice planner fully integrate the recommendations within a plan. Ultimately, this stage of the planning process should end with a realistic plan for achieving the client's financial and life goals, and lay the foundation for what could potentially be a long-term planner-client relationship.

The Plan – Modular or Comprehensive

Chapter 9 - Writing a Financial Plan, thoroughly explores the components and stylistic elements of a financial plan as a deliverable product and outcome of the financial planning process. However, from the context of considering how multiple recommendations are integrated into a plan, it is worthwhile to briefly consider how to convey this information to the client. One of the challenges facing planners who write comprehensive financial plans is how to account for the integrative nature of recommendations, implementation, and monitoring within the plan. The analysis, recommendations, and projected outcomes must be completely integrated into the respective individual sections within the plan as well as across all core content planning areas. The following ideas can be helpful:

1. Describe the current situation for each of the core content areas as if no other recommendations have been made or implemented.

2. Present all recommendations within a core content section (e.g., for instance the retirement planning section) on the basis of the current situation analysis.

3. Describe alternatives or alternative outcomes in client circumstances where a recommendation in one core content area is based on the implementation of a recommendation in another core content area. For example, show alternative recommendations and alternative outcomes when education funding is done with or without gifting from the grandparents.

4. Conclude a plan by illustrating a client's projected situation assuming all recommendations are implemented.

The fourth rule implies that a reanalysis and recalculation of certain client data will occur. At a minimum, the following information should be recalculated to project the client's financial situation in one year (or some other time frame) assuming that recommendations are implemented:

*   available discretionary cash flow;

*   net worth balance;

*   income tax situation; and

*   estate tax situation (when applicable).

Recalculating these measures to reflect the projected outcomes is another way to motivate clients. For instance, if a client can be shown that refinancing debt, reallocating portfolio assets, purchasing additional forms of insurance, and implementing other recommendations will result in positive outcomes, it is more likely that the client will take action. Revised cash flow, net worth, income tax, and estate tax projections can be included within a plan as a separate section or in an appendix, perhaps titled *Key Financial Measures in 200X* to reflect the projected status one year in the future. Some financial planners incorporate future projections (tabular or graphic) for each core content planning area within the respective section of the plan. Different time frames, coordinated to the individual goal or planning need, would be used to project the short-, intermediate-, or long-term impact of the successfully implemented recommendation(s) on the client's future.

Either approach helps the client to grasp how recommendations are integrative within a plan, and to see the potential impact of financial planning. However, it is extremely important that any projections reflect the appropriate disclaimers (e.g., "past performance is no guarantee of future returns," "all projections are based on historical data, which may not be reflected in future returns" or "projections are hypothetical") so as to not mislead the client or to give the impression of "promised" returns or outcomes.

Presenting the Plan

If Starbucks thought that *connecting with the customers* was important enough to develop and deliver a board game to 8,000 managers for training the baristas, then consider the importance of a *connection* between financial advisors and clients when presenting a financial plan.[1] Much of the planner-client relationship discussed so far was forged in the exploration of the client situation, which grounded the goals and informed the planning process. But regardless of the planner's business model, the presentation of the plan is the opportunity to "close the deal" with the client. Whether spoken or implied, the planner is *selling* something—ranging from the obvious (e.g., a product or service) to something more subtle (e.g., client education or a suggested change in a client's attitudes or behaviors). Good presentations are an outcome of training and experience, but a few simple reminders can help a student or novice planner to present the plan clearly and consistently. For additional information on communication techniques, dealing with client emotions, and overcoming client resistance, review Chapter 3 – Client Communication.

1. **Be genuinely warm, open, and welcoming**. Although planners and clients may develop personal friendships or interact socially, most advisors prefer to maintain only a professional relationship with the client when tending to financial planning issues. Nevertheless, the significance of the planner-client *connection* cannot be overstated. The topics addressed in the plan are of utmost importance to the client and may trigger a range of emotions (e.g., delight, guilt, regret, embarrassment, or shame). It is equally important that the planner address those concerns in a respectful, nonjudgmental way. In this situation, acting like a reassuring friend—by effectively reading and conveying verbal and nonverbal cues—is probably more important than actually being a friend. Using the client's name, asking about the client's family, career,

hobbies or other interests—in other words, generally encouraging the sharing of information—are all ways to build a connection.

2. **Practice being an effective communicator.** Smile, nod, lean, and listen—with both eyes and ears—for words and feelings. Good salespeople listen more than they talk. Recognize that most communication occurs not through words, but through the use of paralanguage (i.e., rate, tone, volume of speech), body language (i.e., face, eyes, gestures), and space. Matching messages to a client's preferred information processing and communication style will lead to more meaningful client interactions and ensure that the advisor is tuned in to the client's needs and goals, spoken or otherwise. The use of pictures, charts, and graphs is recommended, especially for visual communicators, but it is important to attempt to connect through all three information processing styles.

3. **Practice empathy**. Financial planners are often called *advisors* but many may unwittingly ignore the universal fact that people do not accept advice, on any topic, unless they are first convinced that: (1) the other party is truly listening; and (2) the other party is genuinely concerned and committed. Empathy validates the client and sends the message, "you are important and I understand."

4. **Make a confident, competent impression by being prepared**. This idea applies to the office environment as well as the planner. The meeting area should be clean and arranged to facilitate the presentation and discussion of the plan. The office, staff, and the planner should present an image representative of the firm, but appropriately matched to the client. The plan and or other supporting documents should be neatly prepared and organized for the presentation, as should any documents that might require a signature. Both the plan and the presentation should be free of errors and have an attractive, but professional, appearance that also represents the image of the firm. The presentation should use a font size and style that is easily legible for all viewers. If presentation equipment is to be used, the equipment and the presentation should be checked to ensure that everything is working properly. Finally, the planner should be familiar with the plan and the analysis upon which it was built so that explanations are clear and the planner can comfortably address any questions. A good joke is lost on a bad delivery; the same goes for a financial plan.

5. **Involve the client, to the extent possible**. Some clients lack the time, interest, or willingness to be fully engaged in the planning and implementation process. Other clients are seeking financial education, confirmation, reassurance, or simply direction. In fact, contingent on the business model of the planner and the products or services provided, the balance of independence/dependence is a defining characteristic of the planner-client relationship. By engaging the client in the planning and decision making process, the planner is more likely to garner commitment followed by action. To put it simply, the client "buys in" and takes ownership with the planner. Advisors that appear to be

approachable and knowledgeable, regardless of their target demographic, are likely to be more successful than those who proudly assert their knowledge or position. The language used by the advisor is one obvious example; be careful to match the language, terms, or acronyms to those comfortable for the client. "Big words" and jargon may sound *professional*, but overuse can show a lack of *professionalism*.

6. **Plan the message and anticipate the response.** Planners should be mentally and emotionally prepared for the meeting, having given some thought to the message to be delivered and the possible client reactions. The presentation must summarize all stages of the planning process and present the recommendations in such a way that the client can adequately judge the merits of the plan. Making the effort to educate the client by means of the plan itself, with any supporting documents, or during the presentation can be an important value-added service. The presentation should not be scripted, and it is important that it be logical and well-organized. The presentation should encourage the client to read the plan, but provide enough information to fully inform the client of the situation analysis and the proposed recommendations. Logical organization also reduces the likelihood of overwhelming a client with data and charts. Detail is important only up to a point, and is contingent on the temperament and personality of the client.

7. **Motivate action with thorough, clearly defined, manageable steps**. Morrow relates a very important analogy to remember.[2] He asks planners to imagine going to a medical clinic for a diagnosis, only to have the personnel respond that life-saving efforts will require that 10 courses of treatment be undertaken at the same time. The patient would likely be in shock. But this is exactly what most planners, especially those who write comprehensive financial plans, often do. They show clients 10 to 20 problems and provide 10 to 20 solutions, including alternatives. Clients feel overwhelmed and apathetic, which may result in lack of action. The communication rule that should be used to overcome client inaction involves summarizing the results of the analysis in simple, logical, and straightforward terms. A summary table, "To Do List," or timeline accompanied by crisp narrative should be provided in the plan. Recommendations should be prioritized to match the client's goals and objectives. It may be helpful to list the most important recommendations in bold type, followed by the secondary recommendations. In this way, the client can better grasp, both intellectually and fiscally, the importance of the recommendations.

8. **Time it right**. It is important that sufficient time be allowed for a full presentation and exploration of the plan. Correctly judging the amount of time is subject to the client's demographic profile (e.g., age, education, family, etc), personality, temperament, lifestyle, and personal finance knowledge and experience. Explaining even a simple plan can be a lengthy process. It is essential that the advisor reads the client's body language and other communication clues to gauge and adjust the tempo of the presentation. Gender, cultural, and ethnic differences in

communication should also be considered. For example, males typically have a "bottom line, get to the point" approach, while women are typically more interested in the details and relationships.

9. **Expect small changes**. It may be unrealistic to expect a client to immediately commit to implementing more than a few recommendations, if any at all. The very nature of comprehensive planning implies that a multitude of interrelated and integrated issues must be considered concurrently. Often this level of analysis is too much for a client to absorb during one meeting. It is reasonable to get client confirmation on one or two implementation policies during the presentation meeting, but clients should not be pressured into making a large number of decisions. Instead, specific follow-up dates should be established. Communication may continue electronically or by phone, or it may be necessary to schedule additional meetings in the following weeks or months. Building planner-client trust and rapport will expand the relationship and the potential for change. Implementation of plan recommendations is most closely tied with a planner's ability to communicate a sense of accomplishment, value, and goal achievement.

10. **Don't make promises.** Regardless of the sophistication of the analysis or the expertise of the planner, under the best of circumstances a financial plan is nothing more than an educated supposition. A well-developed plan built on valid personal and economic assumptions can help the client *prepare* for the unknown with realistic expectations, but it will not help the planner or client to *predict* the unknown. To build a trusting relationship, clients and planners are best served by unbiased presentations that acknowledge that tax, legislative, economic, or personal life changing events may positively or negatively affect the planning projections. For this reason, alone, a long-term relationship with periodic reviews and adjustments offers the client the greatest likelihood of reaching financial goals. How to maintain and foster that relationship through the implementation and monitoring of the plan is the subject of the next chapter.

"Thinking Outside the Box"

Conceptualizing a financial plan may require a great deal of cognitive and emotional energy, a task that is further complicated by the complexity of the financial planning issues and the personal challenges posed by the client. To exercise prudent professional judgment suggests that the planner must fully engage in the process, consider all the data and information, and arrive at a reasonable solution clearly supported by the data. But professional judgment also requires the planner to maintain and practice an attitude of inquisitiveness, skepticism, or what might commonly be described as "playing the devil's advocate." This sort of focused inquiry and *gentle* debate," however, by the planner does not occur in a vacuum. In reality, planners work in group practices where expertise can be shared. Other planners—through formal or informal networks, often facilitated through professional associations—rely on colleagues for advice, counsel, or knowledge on how to deal with a new, complex, or unique client or client situation.

The term "paradigm" is used to describe a viewpoint, perspective, or distinct way of thinking. It is what some call "the pair of glasses through which the world is viewed." Change the glasses, and the view of the world changes. This section introduces several paradigms for thinking about professional judgment or the conceptualization of a financial plan.

Holistic Judgments

The similarities between how financial planners and other professionals, as *expert* practitioners," arrive at conclusions and diagnoses are striking. "Expert" status is typically accorded those who have completed a lengthy educational process and gained significant on the job experience that enables them to demonstrate outstanding problem solving abilities. These professionals pride themselves on being able to make holistic judgments in response to the cognitively challenging and information rich situations encountered in their daily professional practice. Ruscio defined holistic judgments as those that are based not on an independent consideration of data separately or additively, but such that each piece of information must be considered in light of all other available data.[3] In other words, the possible interactions among all pieces of data must be considered—or as Ruscio said, "everything influences everything else" in a complex whole. In a review of the research on the accuracy of holistic judgments (i.e., physicians, medical pathologists, mental health clinicians, weather forecasters, mechanics, venture capitalists, auditors, and financial advisors), Roszkowski and Grable observed that experts were generally not reliable or accurate in their holistic judgments, although this varied by profession.[4] Professionals who utilize more fact-based information and are less dependent on subjective human preferences, tendencies, and conditions demonstrated greater accuracy.

Many financial planners use a form of holistic judgment to generate client recommendations. This approach is premised on the idea that the planner has a thorough knowledge of the client and the client's situation, including client attitudinal and behavioral factors. After making observations about the strengths and weaknesses inherent in the situation, financial planners who use a holistic approach would then compare their observations and conclusions against what they know about the client's circumstances. While a planner may use heuristics, or mental shortcuts, to simplify inputs used to make a decision or design a recommendation, the actual process involved when making a holistic judgment may be subjective and difficult to measure. The success of the judgment may be affected by the patterns of information observed about the client, or the emphasis placed on those patterns.

This is not to say, however, that holistic methods of arriving at client recommendations are totally inadequate. Research has shown that training may be more highly correlated with the accuracy and effectiveness of judgments than experience, and that judgments are more likely to improve in situations where feedback on performance is available and can be considered in future decision making or problem solving. More experienced planners may rely on a combination of training, background, knowledge, and temperament to craft recommendations. But it is possible that students and novice financial planners could benefit from training that:

- focuses attention on the most germane information in the client situation (i.e., the most important patterns of information); and

- provides feedback that enables the student to not only judge the merits of alternative approaches, but also to incorporate that knowledge into future scenarios.

The Systematic Approach

Too often students look for one correct answer. Unfortunately, financial planning does not always lend itself to a single correct response. As acknowledged by the CFP Board of Standards, Inc. there may be multiple solutions that enable a client to reach a goal, an example of subjective professional judgment. Client situations may be addressed in multiple ways by different financial planners. Some recommendations may be equally effective; others may be dismissed as ill-conceived or simply less likely to result in successful goal attainment. It is important for students and practitioners to thoroughly review their methodology used to guide the progression from strategies and recommendations to final plan.

The **systematic approach** to planning promotes the repeated use of planning forms and protocols to guide and document the planning process. Some financial planners will find systematic tools and techniques very useful for framing a protocol for "attacking" the issues presented by the client's situation. Others will conclude that such tools limit creativity and are cumbersome or repetitive to use. Because the approach is very methodical and organized, systematic planning tools can help students and novice planners to:

- organize what may initially appear to be an overwhelming mass of data and analysis into a manageable format;

- focus attention on critical planning needs;

- focus attention on problems or issues that may require research or referral with other professionals;

- focus attention on issues or questions that require additional inputs from the client;

- recognize the need for creative alternatives for meeting the client's goals; and

- gain confidence that relevant issues have not been overlooked.

The Recommendation Planning Checklist, Recommendation Form, and Recommendation Impact Form are three examples of such planning tools. As shown in Figure 7.4, the Recommendation Planning Checklist challenges the

Figure 7.4 Recommendation Planning Checklist

Recommendation Planning Checklist

Cash Flow Analysis to Maximize Client's Discretionary Cash Flow			Recommendation Needed?	
1. Has planner reviewed financial ratios and compared these to benchmarks?	Yes	No	Yes	No
2. Have steps been taken to designate savings or other assets for use as an emergency fund or source of emergency income?	Yes	No	Yes	No
3. Has planner reviewed client budget for possible expense reductions?	Yes	No	Yes	No
4. Has planner verified that the client is able and willing to proactively save money on a regular basis?	Yes	No	Yes	No
5. Have debt reduction or debt restructuring alternatives been reviewed?	Yes	No	Yes	No
6. Have mortgage refinancing alternatives been reviewed?	Yes	No	Yes	No
7. Other client-specific cash management issues to consider?	Yes	No	Yes	No
Tax Analysis To Minimize Taxes and Maximize Client's Discretionary Cash Flow			**Recommendation Needed?**	
8. Have tax projections for 1, 3 or 5 years been done to guide the planning process?	Yes	No	Yes	No
9. Have client income tax withholdings been matched to tax liability?	Yes	No	Yes	No
10. Have client FICA withholdings been matched to FICA liabilities?	Yes	No	Yes	No
11. Has planner reviewed client's tax situation to ensure that other tax reduction opportunities have not been overlooked?	Yes	No	Yes	No
12. Is the client currently subject to AMT? Have projections been made for the next 1, 3 or 5 years?	Yes	No	Yes	No
13. Has planner checked to determine if client is maximizing tax-reduction insurance alternatives?				
a. Flexible spending accounts?	Yes	No	Yes	No
b. Dependent care accounts?	Yes	No	Yes	No
c. Employer provided life, health, and disability benefits?	Yes	No	Yes	No
14. Other client-specific tax management issues to consider?	Yes	No	Yes	No
Insurance Analysis to Limit Client's Household Risk Exposures			**Recommendation Needed?**	
15. Has a life insurance analysis been conducted?	Yes	No	Yes	No
16. Has a disability insurance analysis been conducted?	Yes	No	Yes	No
17. Has a long-term care insurance analysis been conducted?	Yes	No	Yes	No
18. Has a health insurance analysis been conducted?	Yes	No	Yes	No
19. Has a property, casualty, and liability insurance analysis been conducted?	Yes	No	Yes	No
20. Other client specific risk management issues to consider?	Yes	No	Yes	No
Investment Planning Analysis to Maximize Client's Return			**Recommendation Needed?**	
21. Has an investment funding goal been identified?	Yes	No	Yes	No
22. Is the client on track to meet the targeted amount and date?	Yes	No	Yes	No
23. Are the asset allocation and the investment vehicles suitable given the client's time horizon, risk tolerance, and other assumptions?	Yes	No	Yes	No
24. Is the client fully benefiting from tax-advantaged investments?	Yes	No	Yes	No
25. Other client-specific investment planning issues to consider?	Yes	No	Yes	No

Figure 7.4 Recommendation Planning Checklist (cont'd)

Recommendation Planning Checklist

Education or Special Needs Planning Analysis to Maximize Client's Return			Recommendation Needed?	
26. Has an education funding goal been identified?	Yes	No	Yes	No
27. Is the client on track to meet the targeted amount and date?	Yes	No	Yes	No
28. Are the asset allocation and the investment vehicles suitable given the client's time horizon, risk tolerance, and other assumptions?	Yes	No	Yes	No
29. Is the client fully benefiting from tax-advantaged accounts?	Yes	No	Yes	No
30. Other client specific education planning issues to consider?	Yes	No	Yes	No
31. Has a special needs funding goal(s) been identified? Is the client on track to meet the targeted amount(s) and date(s)?	Yes	No	Yes	No
32. Are the asset allocation and the investment vehicles suitable given the client's time horizon, risk tolerance, and other assumptions?	Yes	No	Yes	No
33. Other client-specific special needs planning issues to consider?	Yes	No	Yes	No

Retirement Planning Analysis to Maximize Client's Return			Recommendation Needed?	
34. Has a retirement funding goal been identified?	Yes	No	Yes	No
35. Is the client on track to meet the targeted amount and date?	Yes	No	Yes	No
36. Are the asset allocation and the investment vehicles suitable given the client's time horizon, risk tolerance, and other assumptions?	Yes	No	Yes	No
37. Is the client fully benefiting from tax-advantaged accounts?	Yes	No	Yes	No
38. Are other retirement funds available?	Yes	No	Yes	No
39. Other client-specific retirement planning issues to consider?	Yes	No	Yes	No

Estate Planning Analysis to Minimize Estate Taxes and Ensure Client's Final Wishes			Recommendation Needed?	
40. Has the client begun gifting assets to dependents, other family members, or charity?	Yes	No	Yes	No
41. Are documents in place to distribute property and provide for dependents, heirs or charities?	Yes	No	Yes	No
42. Have steps been taken to minimize estate or inheritance taxes?	Yes	No	Yes	No
43. Have steps been taken to minimize settlement costs, including legal and accounting fees?	Yes	No	Yes	No
44. Are funds available, or plans in place, for the payment of estate taxes and settlement expenses?	Yes	No	Yes	No
45. Are documents in place to guide incapacitation or other end-of-life decisions?	Yes	No	Yes	No
46. Are documents in place to care for, or name guardians for, financial dependents, such as children?	Yes	No	Yes	No
47. Other client-specific estate planning issues to consider?	Yes	No	Yes	No

Cross Planning Analysis: Have the Following Interactions Been Considered?			Recommendation Needed?	
48. Net worth ⬌ insurance?	Yes	No	Yes	No
49. Income taxes ⬌ insurance?	Yes	No	Yes	No
a. Flexible spending accounts?	Yes	No	Yes	No
b. Dependent care accounts?	Yes	No	Yes	No
c. Employer provided life, health, and disability benefits?	Yes	No	Yes	No
50. Life insurance ⬌ estate planning?	Yes	No	Yes	No
51. Long-term care (LTC) ⬌ estate planning?	Yes	No	Yes	No
52. Education funding ⬌ estate planning?	Yes	No	Yes	No
53. Education funding ⬌ income tax planning?	Yes	No	Yes	No
54. Investment planning ⬌ income tax planning?	Yes	No	Yes	No
55. Retirement planning ⬌ income tax planning?	Yes	No	Yes	No

advisor to carefully consider key questions related to each of the core content planning areas. Although the questions may not offer comprehensive or sophisticated analysis of every client situation, the form provides a framework for reviewing and summarizing the client's individual circumstances. An initial negative response to any question should prompt the planner to reconsider the need for additional preparatory work. Any positive answers to the question "Is a Recommendation Needed?" should help the planner to initially identify and summarize the parameters of the client's planning situation. Finally, the section on cross-planning analysis helps to focus the problem solving on fundamental interactions, represented by the "⇔" symbol. As noted earlier, it is not possible to encapsulate a process as broad and dynamic as financial planning in a simple form; this limitation cannot be overlooked. However, the form does offer the advantage of focusing attention on the most common patterns of interaction that should be considered, whether developing a single-issue or comprehensive plan.

Exhibit 7.4, The Recommendation Form, helps the planner focus on the essential issues to be included in an actionable recommendation. This useful planning tool summarizes the answers to the seven critical recommendation questions of *who, what, when, where, why, how,* and *how much* into one simple format for communicating the information to the client. Possibly one of the most beneficial uses of this form is documenting the titling of assets. The form also clarifies the designation of the beneficiary, or contingent beneficiary, as applicable. Initially, the use of the form is simply a tool for the planner to summarize and cost out potential recommendations for use in meeting client goals. Issues related to how much a recommendation will cost and potential benefits associated with the recommendation can also be addressed. As the plan develops, it may be necessary to combine, sort, and rank recommendations from other core content planning areas, and the forms can quickly summarize the costs and benefits of each recommendation.

Exhibit 7.4 Recommendation Form

Planning Recommendation Form

Financial Planning Content Area				
Client Goal				
Recommendation #:	**Priority (1 – 6) lowest to highest:**			
Projected/Target Value ($)				
Product Profile				
Type				
Duration				
Provider				
Funding Cost per Period ($)				
Maintenance Cost per Period ($)				
Current Income Tax Status	Tax-Qualified		Taxable	
Projected Rate of Return				
Major Policy Provisions				
Procedural Factors				
Implementation by Whom	Planner		Client	
Implementation Date or Time Frame				
Implementation Procedure				
Ownership Factors				
Owner(s)				
Form of Ownership				
Insured(s)				
Custodial Account	Yes		No	
Custodian				
In Trust For (ITF)	Yes		No	
Transfer On Death (TOD)	Yes		No	
Beneficiary(ies)				
Contingent Beneficiary(ies)				
Proposed Benefit				

The Recommendation Impact Form, shown in Exhibit 7.5, offers a final opportunity to verify that any potential interactions among the recommendations have not been overlooked. This form would be completed as each recommendation is finalized. Should cash flow or other assets be insufficient for funding all recommendations, completion of the Recommendation Impact Forms might help a planner identify mutually exclusive recommendations that might be integrated and met through another "multi-purpose" planning product or procedure. Use of the forms may also help the student or novice planner to *complicate* the planning process—not in the sense of making it more difficult, but in the sense of more broadly informing the planning process. By seriously considering the impact of each recommendation on the other core content planning areas, the planner may gain new insights to the client situation that otherwise might have been overlooked or never even considered. Likewise, if the advisor cannot reasonably and knowledgeably assess the impact of the recommendations, more research or consultation with other professionals may be warranted. As such, the systematic approach, which justifiably may be criticized for stifling creativity, may actually encourage a broader depth and range of thinking. Ultimately, what is important is that a consistent approach be used to rank and order strategies and recommendations in a way that is comfortable for the advisor. But to be effective, whatever approach is chosen must encourage the professional freedom, and responsibility, to shift paradigms when analyzing and reviewing the client's situation.

Exhibit 7.5 Recommendation Impact Form

Recommendation Impact Form

Recommendation:						
Recommendation #:						
Planner Decision	Accept		Reject		Modify	
Client Decision	Accept		Reject		Modify	
Financial Impact						
	Annual Impact on Cash-flow ($)					
	Immediate Impact on Net Worth ($)					

Planning Issue	Degree of Significance				Notes
	Major	Modest	Minor	None	
Financial Situation – Cash Management					
Tax Planning					
Life Insurance Planning					
Health Insurance Planning					
Disability Insurance Planning					
LTC Insurance Planning					
Property & Liability Insurance Planning					
Investment Planning					
Education or Other Special Needs Planning					
Retirement Planning					
Estate Planning					
Other Planning Need					
Other Planning Need					

Financial Planning Tip: Asset Titling and Ownership

Titling may be one of the more overlooked aspects of a financial plan; however, it is also one of the most important aspects, as ownership means control. There are four primary forms of ownership: (1) individual; (2) joint (i.e., joint tenants with rights of survivorship, tenants in common, or tenants in the entirety); (3) custodial; and (4) trust. Individual ownership or any form of joint ownership should be carefully reviewed for its impact on other aspects of the plan or the transfer wishes of the owners. Custodial ownership is very common with retirement and other tax-qualified accounts where the custodian plays a key role in reporting and control. The trust ownership form is primarily used for asset transfer purposes or for minors (who cannot legally own assets in most states). Planning for the eventual distribution or transfer of assets can have widespread ramifications on how the assets should be held. Keeping track of ownership is also a crucial part of tax planning.

Triangulation

The term "triangulation" is most frequently associated with military practices, navigation, and map making, all of which are based on multiple celestial or terrestrial references. The term also refers to a social science research method designed to improve the validity, or accuracy, of research findings. In its simplest form, **triangulation** refers to study, exploration, or examination from multiple (typically three) perspectives. In research, those perspectives might refer to: multiple data sources or data collection methods; multiple theories of explanation; multiple researchers; multiple methods of conducting the research; or some combination of these research activities. Consider for a moment the obvious parallels with financial planning. Client data ranges from the confirmed fact to the perhaps unconfirmed assumption or observation. Advisors working independently or in teams, representing different business models and product or service orientations, approach a client situation from very different vantage points and offer diverse explanations and solutions. Yet all are focused on *helping clients achieve multiple financial goals and objectives through the application and integration of synergistic personal finance strategies.* Although researchers and financial planners—through their various modes of professional practice—may arrive at alternative explanations of the same situation, both are motivated by the need for accuracy. Triangulation offers another method for pursuing accuracy and exploring the interactions among the data considered.

Therefore, the multiple perspectives might refer to: multiple client data sources or data collection methods (e.g., client provided, planner observed, planner and client confirmed); multiple strategies, recommendations, or financial products; multiple planning team members or collaboration with other professionals (e.g., accountants, attorneys, investment or money managers, product providers); multiple methods of conducting quantitative analysis of the client situation; or some combination of these planning activities. The list that follows, although by no means exhaustive, offers examples of how triangulation might be used to enrich, or expand, the advisor's view:

- *Data or information* – The plan is built on quantitative and qualitative data garnered from the client as well as independently generated analytical or diagnostic results and mutually agreed upon assumptions.

What method is most effective for collecting client data? What types of analysis should be considered as most appropriate to the client situation? How might a client's fundamental motives, values, morals, or ethics affect the interpretation and acceptance of the planner's mathematical computations and logical explanations?

- *Stakeholders* – How would the client, the planner, other members of the client's household, or other professionals react to the recommendation? How would the recommendation serve their interests? How might fees, commissions, other methods of compensation, or other costs influence the choice? How might another professional identify, interpret, differentiate, and diagnose the *same* client situation? What biases, if any, may affect the planner's perspective on this client situation?

- *Competing goals or recommendations* – Is the protection of the future income stream the foremost objective? What are the projected short- and long-term implications of the recommendation on the client's assets? What is the client's net worth? How do the planner, client, or the two in combination, weigh the wants and needs identified in the planning situation?

So Which Approach is Best?

The explanation of the core of the financial planning process throughout the chapter has employed triangulation, or offered new ways of considering the process that might employ triangulation. Holistic judgment *assumes* that all of the data interrelationships known about the client situation are considered in the development of the plan. The systematic approach strips away much of the "noise" in the data and initially focuses attention on the core content planning issues identified within the client situation. Both approaches have recognized advantages and disadvantages. Triangulation builds on both approaches and serves as a solid reminder that no recommendation should be left to intuition, good intention, or stark fact. Use of this method challenges the planner to triangulate three sources of evidence or information upon which to build a sound justification for any conclusion or recommendation. Recall that professional judgment is the application of knowledge *balanced* with the willingness to always review, question, or evaluate the solution.

Process to Practice

The vignette that follows continues to explore the experiences of the Kims with their financial planner, Jane. Recall that the Kims are on the way home from their first annual check-up and monitoring meeting. This installment includes reflections by the Kims and Jane, as they offer some insights on their "real life" experiences with Steps 3 and 4 – from both sides of the desk.

Looking back on their first meetings with Jane, Tom could now jokingly reminisce with Nyla about how difficult it was, initially, to verbalize and prioritize their goals. "With two women, you can't get a word in, and planning for the future is even harder than trying to talk with two women. Should we worry about our retirement or Azalea's education? Should we give her a good education and hope for the best on retirement? You know what they say, 'be good to your kids, they'll pick your nursing home'. . . but saving for it all is a big challenge!"

Nyla's promotion, which occurred just a few months before their first meeting with Jane, had meant an increase of $6,900 of after-tax income. Based on the Kims' responses on the Client Intake Form, the Summary Goal Ranking Form, and the discussion during their second data gathering meeting, the Kims and Jane were able to rank their financial goals as follows:

1. Partially fund Azalea's education through savings over the next 10 years.

2. Increase annual funding so both Tom and Nyla could retire in 25 years.

3. Save for an international vacation in two years to visit extended family.

The Kims finally had a direction for their future! And they had no doubt that with Jane's help, they could do it all.

But the third meeting (called the plan presentation meeting) quickly erased all of their bravado. It was a bit of a shock to learn that *none* of their plans would work, at least not according to Jane! Tom reminisced to Nyla that "it was getting tough to handle. We thought we had done fairly well. We knew we could do better, that is why we sought out Jane, but it was very hard to hear Jane present her findings."

"No, it wasn't all 'hearts and flowers' nor was it all 'dollars and cents' leading up to the plan development," commented Nyla. She remembered that on top of their own predetermined goals, Jane also added some recommendations based on the Recommendation Planning Checklist that she had completed. Jane shared the Recommendation Planning Checklist, shown in Exhibit 7.6, with the Kims to help them learn more about some of the standard "checkpoints" for measuring their financial status. Jane had made the analogy that the checklist results and other financial ratios and analyses reported in their plan could be thought of as comparable to the height, weight, blood pressure, and cholesterol check-ups to measure physical health. In both cases, there are standards for measurement matched to the individual situation. It turned out the Kims weren't as financially healthy as they thought.

Tom recalled being very impressed by all of the effort that Jane had obviously put into analyzing each area of their financial life. It was evident that she truly had been listening to their concerns. She seemed to be making every effort to conduct their financial physical and develop a plan for their future in a man-

Exhibit 7.6 Tom & Nyla Kim's Recommendation Planning Checklist

Abbreviated Recommendation Planning Checklist*

Cash Flow Analysis to Maximize Client Discretionary Cash Flow			Recommendation Needed?	
1. Has planner verified that the client is able and willing to proactively save money on a regular basis?	Yes	**No**	Yes	**No**
2. Have debt reduction or debt restructuring alternatives been reviewed?	**Yes**	No	**Yes**	No
Insurance Analysis to Limit Client's Household Risk Exposures			Recommendation Needed?	
3. Has a life insurance analysis been conducted?	**Yes**	No	**Yes**	No
4. Has a disability insurance analysis been conducted?	**Yes**	No	**Yes**	No
5. Has a long-term care insurance analysis been conducted?	Yes	**No**	Yes	**No**
6. Has a health insurance analysis been conducted?	**Yes**	No	Yes	**No**
7. Has a property, casualty, and liability insurance analysis been conducted?	**Yes**	No	Yes	**No**
8. Other client specific risk management issues to consider?	Yes	**No**	Yes	**No**
Investment Planning Analysis to Maximize Client Return			Recommendation Needed?	
9. Has an investment funding goal been identified?	**Yes**	No	**Yes**	No
10. Is the client on track to meet the targeted amount and date?	Yes	**No**	**Yes**	No
11. Other client-specific investment planning issues to consider?	Yes	**No**	Yes	**No**
Education or Special Needs Planning Analysis to Maximize Client Return			Recommendation Needed?	
12. Has an education funding goal been identified?	**Yes**	No	**Yes**	No
13. Is the client on track to meet the targeted amount and date?	Yes	**No**	**Yes**	No
14. Are the asset allocation and the investment vehicles suitable given the client's time horizon, risk tolerance, and other assumptions?	Yes	**No**	**Yes**	No
15. Is the client fully benefiting from tax-advantaged accounts?	Yes	**No**	**Yes**	No
16. Other client specific education planning issues to consider?	Yes	**No**	Yes	**No**
Retirement Planning Analysis to Maximize Client Return			Recommendation Needed?	
17. Has a retirement funding goal been identified?	**Yes**	No	**Yes**	No
18. Is the client on track to meet the targeted amount and date?	Yes	**No**	**Yes**	No
19. Are the asset allocation and the investment vehicles suitable given the client's time horizon, risk tolerance, and other assumptions?	**Yes**	No	**Yes**	No
20. Is the client fully benefiting from tax-advantaged accounts?	**Yes**	No	Yes	No
21. Are other retirement funds available?	**Yes**	No	**Yes**	No
22. Other client specific retirement planning issues to consider?	Yes	**No**	Yes	**No**
Cross Planning Analysis: Have the Following Interactions Been Considered?			Recommendation Needed?	
23. Net worth ⇔ insurance?	**Yes**	No	Yes	**No**
24. Life insurance ⇔ estate planning?	**Yes**	No	**Yes**	No
25. Education funding ⇔ income tax planning?	**Yes**	No	**Yes**	No

*For illustrative purposes selected questions are not shown, although the analysis was comprehensive.

ner that reflected their financial and life goals. As a result, Jane had also suggested the following recommendations:

1. Pay off credit card debt with cash assets.

2. Purchase a $250,000 term life insurance policy for Nyla.

3. Purchase long-term, 70% income replacement, disability coverage for Tom.

But the bad news came with Jane's explaination that even with Nyla's raise, they did not have enough discretionary cash flow or other assets to fully fund all of *their* goals and *her* recommendations concurrently. During her analysis, Jane had calculated the reduction in discretionary cash flow (i.e., the total cost to implement all of the recommendations) to be $13,100 over the coming 12 months. Tom remembered that this was a much larger amount than the $6,900 available from Nyla's raise. "Where are we going to come up with the additional money?" he remembered thinking. "Does this mean we have to give up everything we enjoy and go back to the way we lived when we were first married and living on only one income?"

As Tom and Nyla continued their conversation in the car they recalled how they *each* felt frustrated and more than a little annoyed that Jane would recommend more goals, knowing that they did not have sufficient funds to meet their own priorities. However, as that meeting continued, Jane sensed the Kims' frustration and encouraged them to discuss their sense of disatisfaction as well as other questions they had as they reviewed the draft of their financial plan.

Next, Jane explained each section of the Kims' plan—even those sections where they were on track and no changes were needed. Tom recalled, "I was relieved to know that at least we were doing some things right!" She also explained each of the approaches used to calculate the amounts of insurance needed by Tom and Nyla. Then Jane explained how she had calculated the education and retirement costs, the assumptions she had considered, and how the projected rate of return, asset allocations, and investments had appropriately been matched to their goals and risk tolerance. Tom and Nyla recalled feeling overwhelmed by all of the information, but still confident that there was some balance of good and bad news. They were convinced that Jane was a knowledgeable professional, but they were very glad that they would have the draft of their plan and all of her analyses to study more carefully at home. Most of all, they were amazed at how patient Jane had been in explaining charts and graphs and answering their questions.

Tom and Nyla recalled feeling some combination of naïveté, stupidity, and embarrassment that their *plan* on how to use the $6,900 salary increase could be so wrong. But Jane quickly reminded them of what Nyla had said: "We didn't really know how to determine the cost of the goals, so we took most of the raise and allocated it as best we could." Before proceeding further, Jane had revisited the underlying planning assumptions and analyses to help them understand why some of the recommendations seemed so different from their initial suggestions. Her assumptions and analyses were accurate and representative of the Kims' wishes. This helped Nyla cope with the decisions, but was little consolation to Tom. The initial suggestions and results of Jane's analysis are shown below:

1. Accumulate $40,000 over the next 10 years to partially fund a 4-year public college education for Azalea.

   - Kims' suggested annual reduction in discretionary cash flow = $2,200

   - Jane's suggested annual reduction in discretionary cash flow = $3,000

   - Number of years = 10

2. Increase annual funding so both Tom and Nyla could retire in 25 years.

   - Kims' suggested annual reduction in discretionary cash flow = $1,700

   - Jane's suggested annual reduction in discretionary cash flow = $4,000

   - Number of years = 25

3. Save for an international vacation in two years to visit extended family.

   - Kims' suggested annual reduction in discretionary cash flow = $3,000

   - Jane's suggested annual reduction in discretionary cash flow = $3,600

   - Number of years = 2

4. Pay off $4,000 in credit card debt with current assets.

   - Annual reduction in discretionary cash flow = $0

   - Number of years = 0

5. Purchase a $250,000, 20-year guaranteed renewable term life insurance policy for Nyla.

   - Annual reduction in discretionary cash flow = $300 (based on quotes received)

   - Number of years = 20

6.   Purchase a long-term, own-occupation, 70% income-replacement disability policy for Tom.

-    Annual reduction in discretionary cash flow = $1,800 (based on quotes received)

-    Number of years = 10 year or more

Tom mused that, "I almost fell over when Jane started talking about spending, really saving, over $10 grand this year to reach our goals." "In fact," Nyla interjected, "there was not enough cash flow remaining to fully fund either the trip or retirement at the level Jane believed necessary, if we saved for Azalea's education." Nyla and Tom both recalled that hearing this was a deflating surprise, but trusted Jane that if $3,000 was really necessary, then that is what they would do.

Jane had explained as she continued presenting the draft of the Kims' plan that in her professional opinion, funding all of their investment goals without regard for their insurance shortfalls could leave them susceptible to unwanted income reductions that, in the event of a death or disability, could undo all of their efforts to save for future goals. Nyla remembers Jane explaining that, "goal funding should follow a logical pattern. First, financial protection needs should be funded." This was the reason Jane recommended that Tom and Nyla strengthen their insurance protection. Paying off the credit card debt and building additional short-term savings with the diverted funds were also financial necessities.

Tom recalled that with Nyla's new salary they felt more comfortable about savings, but had never thought about insurance. Furthermore, they had not considered that Nyla's income now made up a much more significant portion of the total household income. For Nyla not to have life insurance could create an undue hardship on Tom and Azalea, should something happen. Tom and Nyla remembered thinking that the choices among funding Azalea's college, taking her to meet extended family, and protecting their lifestyle by purchasing life insurance were ones that they had never even considered. Nor did they feel prepared to make that choice! Jane explained to them that emotionally it could be very hard to delay or even let go of a goal, but that they had some choices to make.

After some discussion, and having received Tom and Nyla's general consent to pursue all six recommendations, Jane promised to work out the details and send them specific alternatives that Tom and Nyla could study. At their next meeting, they would make final choices about how to implement their plan. "But the *really* good news is " Jane said, "you can take care of those credit card balances you hate so much, without compromising *our* other goals and still save some money. That much we all agree on!"

Nyla also remembered how Jane had outlined the possible alternatives to help resolve the cash flow shortage and still fund all six goals (the three that they had for themselves and the three that Jane suggested). Each alternative, and the Kims' initial reaction, is shown below:

A. *Alternative*: Postpone the projected retirement date; this would allow them to reduce the current funding requirement or delay funding it altogether until after their trip.

    Reaction: Based on their discussions on the time value of money, Tom and Nyla knew this suggestion did not take full advantage of their money working for them!

B. *Alternative*: Reduce the *ideal* amount dedicated to funding retirement with the intent of increasing the funding after the trip.

    Reaction: Tom and Nyla agreed this could be a viable compromise.

C. *Alternative*: Reevaluate and discuss the current rate of return on their retirement and education assets to see if increasing the return assumption could off set the funding and any cash flow shortage.

    Reaction: Jane had cautioned that this should be done very prudently and only as a last resort because increasing expected returns typically increases risk. This increased risk could cause the Kims to abandon the plan, or could cause some regulatory issues for Jane. Tom and Nyla reasoned this may not be the best alternative.

D. *Alternative*: Reduce current expenditures and use this cash flow to fund the retirement goal or pay for one or more of the insurance premiums.

    Reaction: Some reductions were possible, as Tom was convinced that *everyone* could reduce some expenses. But they reasoned their lifestyle was not extravagant, so any reductions would yield minimal savings.

E. *Alternative*: Postpone the vacation to allow more time to accumulate the necessary savings.

    Reaction: Not really what they wanted to do!

F. *Alternative*: Continue to self-insure for some or all of the projected insurance needs.

    Reaction: Tom and Nyla realized this really was not a good choice given Jane's needs assessment, including multiple approaches to calculating Nyla's life insurance needs, and the supporting explanations for why the life and disability insurance was needed.

Nyla remembered how relieved she was when Jane had suggested that fourth meeting to finalize the plan and the implementation; she and Tom were just too overwhelmed with facts, figures, and alternatives to make a decision. Nyla remembered thinking that Jane must have really had her work cut out for her. "All of those dreams and needs, but we have such little money to realize them," she recalled thinking to herself as she and Tom left Jane's office with their plan that day. Then she realized that although Jane had commented at the end of the meeting that "they would work something out," it was really up to Tom and her to make the decisions. But as scary as that seemed, she knew that Jane would be involved to guide their next steps.

Today, almost a year later, as Tom and Nyla continued their drive home, Jane was still involved and the future did not look so scary. In fact, they were regaining some of that bravado they had lost in that plan presentation meeting!

* * * * * * * * * *

As Jane watched Tom and Nyla Kim walk to their car following their first annual check-up and monitoring meeting, Jane recalled how far their planner-client relationship had come in a little over one year. She was also quite pleased, as they were, with the progress they had made. But Jane recalled that getting there had presented its challenges, particularly when she had been developing the plan.

After completing the data gathering meeting with the Kims and completing the analysis of their current financial situation for all core financial planning content areas, Jane knew that she was facing a challenge. Jane, Tom, and Nyla had identified three goals that the Kims were committed to accomplishing. But Jane's initial "gut reactions" to the Kim's financial situation were confirmed by her systematic risk management analyses: Nyla's life insurance coverage was woefully low; Tom had no long-term disability insurance.

Now Jane was faced with identifying potential strategies to accomplish goals for education, retirement, leisure, and risk management—not to mention the outstanding balance of $4,000 of credit card debt to pay for the heat pump replacement. Fortunately, in addition to the projected $6,900 increase in after-tax salary for Nyla, the Kims' balance sheet revealed some good news: their emergency fund savings were $4,000 more than what Jane thought was necessary given the Kims' stable careers and financial situation. Their remaining investment assets were already devoted to funding either college or retirement.

As Jane proceeded to plan development, she knew she needed to rank the recommendations in order of funding priority. One alternative was to simply accept the proposed allocations provided by the Kims and fund each of their three goals accordingly. Using this approach, the Kims had enough money to fund all of their goals, but not in the preferred time frame or in a manner consistent with the risk tolerance or other assumptions they had discussed. This made Jane feel very uncomfortable about the Kims' likelihood of successfully achieving their goals, even if they diverted some of the vacation money from the international trip to other needs. Furthermore, in Jane's opinion, it would be foolhardy to move forward with funding the Kims' financial goals without first making sure that they were covered in case of a financial loss, which meant buying insurance—yet another annual expense for the foreseeable future.

Tom and Nyla had consistently ranked funding Azalea's education as their top priority, although they ranked retirement funding as a close second. So Jane started with the one thing she was sure the Kims wanted—Azalea's college funding. She reviewed Tom and Nyla's risk tolerance, the parameters of their education goal, other available strategies, and then started writing a recommendation:

> *To establish a Real Life Mutual Fund Company 529 Plan account with monthly funding of $250 to accumulate a projected $40,000 to partially fund the cost of a 4-year public college education for Azalea beginning in 10 years.*

To supplement the recommendation, Jane completed the Education Planning Recommendation Form as shown in Exhibit 7.7. As alternatives, Jane repeated the analyses assuming that the Kims (1) continued funding their taxable mutual fund account, or (2) funded a Roth IRA with the idea that the funds could be withdrawn for Azalea's education, if necessary. (The completed Education Planning Section of the Kims' plan is shown in Appendix D). The Kims had mentioned that there *might* be an inheritance. Lots of things could change in 10 years!

Exhibit 7.7 Tom & Nyla Kim's Education Planning Recommendation Form

Planning Recommendation Form

Financial Planning Content Area	Education Planning			
Client Goal	Education funding for Azalea's college			
Recommendation #: 1	Priority (1 – 6) lowest to highest:			6
Projected/Target Value ($)	$40,000			

Product Profie

Type	529 account			
Duration	15 years (10 years of funding)			
Provider	Real Life Mutual Fund Company			
Funding Cost per Period ($)	$250 per month			
Maintenance Cost per Period ($)	$25 set-up fee (one-time only)			
Current Income Tax Status	Tax-Qualified	X	Taxable	
Projected Rate of Return	8.0%			
Major Policy Provisions	None			

Procedural Factors

Implement by Whom	Planner		Client		X
Implementation Date or Timeframe	Within next 60 days				
Implementation Procedure	We will provide you with the appropriate forms to be completed. Upon completion, mail the forms and your check to Real Life Mutual Fund Company. We will monitor account progress for funding adequacy, risk/return objectives and all other investment aspects of the account.				

Exhibit 7.7 Tom & Nyla Kim's Education Planning Recommendation Form (cont'd)

Ownership Factors

Owner(s)	Tom Kim				
Form of Ownership	Individual				
Insured(s)	n/a				
Custodial Account	Yes		X	No	
Custodian	Commonwealth of Virginia				
In Trust For (ITF)	Yes			No	X
Transfer On Death (TOD)	Yes			No	X
Beneficiary(ies)	Azalea Kim				
Contingent Beneficiary(ies)	n/a				

Planning Recommendation Form

Proposed Benefit   By using a 529 plan you will benefit from tax-deferred growth as well as tax-free withdrawals (restrictions apply). Furthermore, we have agreed to maintain a fairly passive approach and this plan has several age-based portfolios that will adjust the asset allocation, thereby reducing the account volatility as Azalea approaches college age. However, the selected plan also offers a static account (one that allows the owner to control the asset allocation) so that additional risk/return adjustments may be made.

Jane would have preferred for the Kims to consider funding a lower cost education goal and using some of that cash flow to fund retirement; so the Roth could be a good option. But, at least initially, she felt that it was more important to meet the Kims' primary goal of dedicating funding for Azalea's education. However, given the total cost they projected for a public 4-year institution, the time horizon, and the amount of their current savings in a taxable mutual fund account, the $2,200 Tom and Nyla had wanted to save annually was simply not enough.

Jane's analysis revealed that the projected annual cost for funding their $40,000 education goal would be nearly $3,000—if all of the cost and return assumptions held true. Given Tom and Nyla's desire to fund the account on a monthly basis, they actually only needed a monthly payment of $220 to achieve their goal. But since the account Jane was recommending required a minimum additional payment of $250, she felt that this was a reasonable trade-off. She finalized this analysis for inclusion in the Kims' plan.

This left Jane with $3,900 in discretionary cash flow to fund their other goals plus the insurance needs. Unfortunately, this was not enough money. Fully funding the education goal could significantly impact the other core content planning areas that the Kims wanted to address. To confirm her thoughts, and to provide documentation for the Kims' plan, Jane completed the Recommendation Impact Form as shown in Exhibit 7.8.

Exhibit 7.8 Tom & Nyla Kim's Recommendation Impact Form

Recommendation Impact Form

Recommendation: Increase education funding for Azalea's college to $250 per month

Recommendation #:	1					
Planner Decision	Accept	X	Reject		Modify	
Client Decision	Accept	X	Reject		Modify	

Financial Impact

Annual Impact on Cash-flow ($)	$3,000
Immediate Impact on Net Worth ($)	$0

Planning Issue	Degree of Significance				Notes
	Major	Modest	Minor	None	
Financial Situation – Cash Management	X				Review automatic investment plan possibilities with client.
Tax Planning			X		State income tax deduction might be available.
Life Insurance Planning		X			Funding the education goal will impact the ability to purchase life insurance.
Health Insurance Planning				X	
Disability Insurance Planning		X			Funding the education goal will impact the ability to purchase long-term disability insurance.
LTC Insurance Planning				X	
Property & Liability Insurance Planning				X	
Investment Planning	X				Funding the education goal will impact the ability to fund the vacation goal.
Education or Other Special Needs Planning	X				Select age-based portfolios to reduce active management time.
Retirement Planning			X		Funding the education goal might impact the ability to fully fund the retirement goal.
Estate Planning			X		Per the plan requirements, Nyla will be designated as the account owner in the event of Tom's death.
Other Planning Need				X	

With this recommendation complete, Jane decided that the best interests of the Kims could be served by proceeding with all of the goals and needs identified. She knew this would take some creative planning, with perhaps multiple scenarios for the Kims to consider, but it seemed to be the best approach.

She felt that Tom and Nyla might not agree with her prioritization of recommendations should she proceed with a comprehensive plan. She knew from working with other clients that sometimes people do not appreciate the immediate need to protect income by funding life and disability coverage. She realized that if the insurance policies were not funded there would be excess cash flow available to fund the Kims' other goals; yet, they would still be underinsured.

This meant that Jane had to help the Kims to make some tough decisions about their financial goals, dreams, and realities. One alternative was to tell Tom and Nyla that the international vacation was out of the question. This was, in Jane's opinion, a financial want, not a need. But Jane realized that this was not a decision that she could, or should, make. Jane knew that a workable and sustainable plan had to reflect the client's wishes, situational factors, and financial goals leveraged with the money available and the advisor's professional judgment. She realized that Tom and Nyla placed a great deal of personal value on the vacation. In terms of lifestyle choices, she suspected they would be willing to sacrifice some current pleasure for long-term well-being—but only up to a point. Canceling all funding for a family vacation, especially of this significance, was beyond that limit in Jane's opinion.

With Jane settled on following through on all six recommendations, she had to decide how to finish the Kims' plan. Rather than developing multiple series of formal recommendations, which might overwhelm her clients and complicate the decision making, she decided to outline some integrated alternatives that the Kims could study. All of the analyses of the financial situation, income tax, risk management, investment management, retirement, and estate planning sections of the plan were complete. A discussion of that much of the plan and a review of the alternative scenarios for meeting the Kims' needs would be more than enough to discuss at their third, or plan presentation, meeting. With that, Jane started to brainstorm how to turn $10,900 of available funds into $12,700 of needs and goals.

Chapter Summary

Following the systematic financial planning process as described in this chapter is one way to develop the skills necessary to conduct a comprehensive analysis of the client's situation for the purposes of a product sale, or the development of a comprehensive or modular financial plan. Following the "black box" analogy, a step-by-step process is fully explained with the objective that important information is not overlooked or overweighted in the decision making process. Analysis in each core content planning area for the client's current situation, using both quantitative and qualitative data, leverages the advisor's professional judgment with the client's financial and life goals. The analysis of the situation should quantify the client's financial strengths and weaknesses, identify any areas where the situation could be improved, and identify potential short-term or future opportunities for planning. After a review of possible strategies, individual recommendations are developed and, when applicable, integrated into a comprehensive financial plan that is presented to the client. Finally, ideas for "thinking outside the box" by using holistic judgment, the systematic method, or triangulation are presented to illustrate and integrate how professional judgment can be applied in response to the question, "How does 'it' happen?"

Chapter Endnotes

1. Business Week (October 24, 2005) "At Your Service: Therapy with Your Latte? It's My Job." *Business Week*, 3956, 16.
2. Morrow, E. P. (2001, October). "Presenting the Financial Plan," Financial Planning, 176.
3. Ruscio, J. (2003). "Holistic Judgment in Clinical Practice," *The Scientific Review of Mental Health Practice*, 2 (1), available at http://www.srmhp.org/0201/holistic.html.
4. Roszkowski, M. J. & Grable, J. (2005). Estimating Risk Tolerance: The Degree of Accuracy and the Paramorphic Representations of the Estimate. *Financial Counseling and Planning*, 16 (1), 29 – 47.

Chapter Review

The Basics: Review Questions

Discussion Questions

1. All products and services that are incorporated into strategies and recommendations have an impact on client goal achievement, but some products and services have greater effects than others. Use Figure 7.2 to identify two to three products and/or product features that, when used, can have wide ranging impacts on a client's financial situation.

2. Explain the five characteristics that describe a well-designed financial plan.

3. Explain triangulation. What purpose does it serve when conceptualizing financial recommendations? How else might it be useful throughout the financial planning process?

4. How can the client's and the planner's financial knowledge and experience be *either* beneficial, detrimental, or *both* beneficial and detrimental when conceptualizing a plan?

5. List and summarize the five most important strategies for making an effective presentation of a plan to a client. Defend your choice of those five approaches. Why are communication strategies so important in the presentation of the plan?

6. Why should a financial advisor conduct an impact analysis as part of the transition from formulation of recommendations to development of the comprehensive plan? Can planners who work with single issues or develop modular plans ignore the integration of recommendations within the planning process?

7. Why is it important that financial planners be aware of their own limitations and planning prejudices when developing financial planning solutions for a client?

8. What are the seven questions that all financial planning recommendations need to address?

9. What interactions might be identified through cross-planning analysis? Give an example of an interaction and explain how it might affect a client's situation and planning outcome. What might have been the outcome had the interaction been ignored?

10. In what circumstances should a financial planner have a client sign a liability release?

Chapter *8*

The Systematic Process: Implementing and Monitoring the Plan

Six–Step Systematic Financial Planning Process

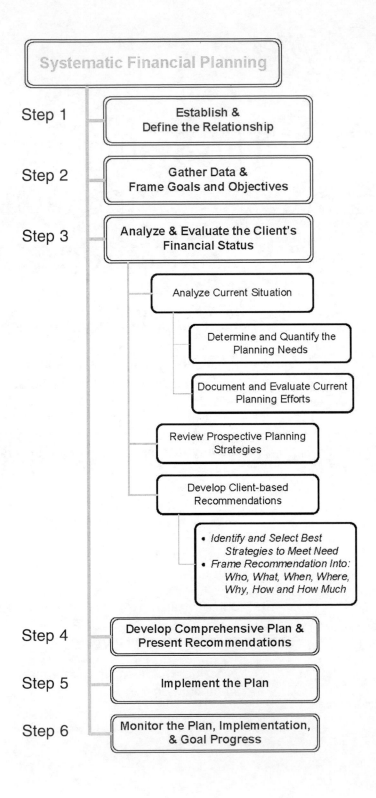

Key Terms

Fee disclosure
Fiduciary liability
Implementation
Implementation checklist

Monitoring
Referral network
Strategic alliance
To-Do List

Integrative Implementation and Monitoring

In response to the question "what is financial planning?," Chapter 1 introduced the idea that financial planning is a profession, a process, and a product. Subsequent chapters have more fully explored how financial planning can be framed as a deliverable product or service—ranging from the *service* of exploring life and financial planning issues—to the product—ranging from a discrete financial product to a modular or comprehensive financial plan. Consistent with this multiplicity of products and services is a variety of business models and compensation methods. The three preceding chapters were built on the premise that financial planning could, and should, be guided by a systematic process. However, the differentiation in business models and deliverables that encompass financial planning is perhaps most evident in Step 5: Implement the Plan, and Step 6: Monitor the Plan, Implementation, and Goal Progress.

It is easy to think that simply because a recommendation has been made that, first, it will be implemented, and that second, it will result in the anticipated outcomes. While this may be true, it would be imprudent to believe that clients always implement recommendations and that advisors' recommendations always work according to plan. Monitoring client outcomes is one method to ensure that recommendations actually *work* in helping a client meet financial goals.

But the seemingly apparent simplicity of implementation (i.e., buy the product or service) and monitoring (i.e., check the success of the product or service) masks a number of complications—ones that are both predicated on, and complicated by, the differentiation of business models and deliverables that encompass the practice of financial planning. The fact that implementation and monitoring represent a series of time spans ranging from immediately following the presentation of the plan to what could be months, years, or even decades in the future further adds to the complexity. Other real challenges are the fact that: recommendations are not implemented in a controlled environment; implementation does not occur in a vacuum; and monitoring may fall on a continuum from consistent to none. Implementing one recommendation tends to have a ripple effect through a client's financial life, which may be anticipated by the advisor but cannot be forecast. The impact analysis considered and projected as part of the plan development in Step 5 may now be the client's reality that is apparent as a result of the implementation and monitoring.

Exhibit 8.1 provides a simple illustration of the integrative nature of plan implementation and monitoring. The process is actually circular beginning with a recommendation. Once a recommendation is implemented, a change in a client's situation will occur. Whether or not the change produces the intended consequences is something that needs to be monitored over time. Future financial planning recommendations will then be based on how well a client is progressing towards meeting the original financial goals or new financial goals that may have evolved. The process continues for as long as the planner-client relationship exists and to the extent that the process is within the scope of the agreed upon (or, in some cases, what may be the renegotiated) planner-client engagement.

Exhibit 8.1 The Integrative Nature of Plan Implementation and Monitoring

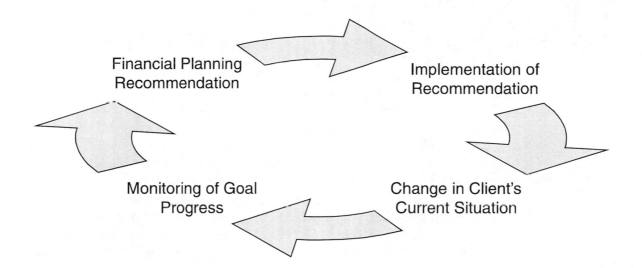

The complexities and distinctive differences in how Steps 5 and 6 may be carried out offers the greatest challenge to the premise that financial planning should be guided by a systematic process. But those same issues further justify the need to have a reliable framework from which to conceptualize these steps within the process. The questions of *who, what, when, where, why, how,* and *how much* can serve as that standard framework and provide further evidence of why it is so important that every recommendation fully answer these questions. However, because implementation and monitoring are so heavily influenced by the business model and practice management of the advisor, the scope of this chapter is limited to a general overview. Recall that the implementation necessary for every recommendation should be explicitly and thoroughly explained in the plan and presented to the client, prior to any implementation efforts.

Step 5: Implement the Plan

Implementation refers to the act of putting a recommendation into action. Offering realistic recommendations is essential to meeting a client's financial goals and objectives. Without a thorough, defensible, and easily understood description of the implementation for each recommendation, it is likely that some clients will fail to implement, or fail to even be convinced of the need or appropriateness of the recommendations. Some advisors would argue that providing clients with a reasonable implementation plan may, in fact, be the most important part of a financial plan. In many cases, that means buying a product or transferring assets to a new custodian to be managed by the advisor. For other business models, selling a specific product or managing assets—whether because of regulatory, philosophical, or other reasons—is simply not a *service* provided; with these advisors, the client is responsible for following the planner's advice to implement the recommendation.

Who Should Implement the Recommendation? What Should be Done? Where Should it be Done?

Once the planner ensures that the client approves of the plan, the implementation step begins. A recommendation is only as good as the ability of the planner, client, or other professionals—working together or independently—to effectively implement the recommendation. In the simplest terms, *who* will do *what* and *where* should it be done? Depending on the planner's business model and the products or services offered by the planner, plan implementation approaches will deviate between planners and perhaps even across clients served by the same planner. Some advisors will take most, if not all, of the responsibility for carrying out various aspects of the plan and request little assistance from the client (assuming such authority is granted). Other planners will inform or assist the client who has primary responsibility for the execution of some or all of the recommendations. Some recommendations may require clients to work with professionals with whom they have existing relationships (e.g., insurance agent, broker, banker), while other recommendations will require the forging of new relationships. Planners often consider themselves as the hub of a wagon wheel as they facilitate the plan implementation in collaboration with the client and multiple other parties (e.g., the client's accountant, attorney, trust administrator, or personal assistant).

Professional referrals have considerable impact on the way some financial planning recommendations are implemented. For example, unless a financial planner is also a licensed attorney, the planner cannot draft legal documents or qualified retirement plan documents. In some instances, even as a licensed attorney the advisor may be limited by broker-dealer or other employer restrictions from "practicing law." Consequently, if there is a need for new, or revised, legal documents, the planner's role may be to:

- make the recommendation and let the client take responsibility for engaging an attorney, whether an existing or new professional relationship;

- provide the client with a list of qualified attorneys whose practice and personality match the client's needs, based on the advisor's broader knowledge of the client's situation and the professional colleagues; or

- refer the client to an attorney within the advisor's referral network or strategic alliance.

Contingent on the planner-client-attorney relationship, the planner *may* act as an intermediary between the client and the attorney with the primary function of facilitating the conversation. For example, the planner knows and can quickly share relevant information that can be useful to the attorney. Conversely, the planner's knowledge can be a source of questions that will benefit and inform the client, who may not know what to ask the attorney or who may feel uncomfortable in doing so.

A **referral network**—a more informal network for making client referrals—or a **strategic alliance**—a more structured collaborative relationship of allied professionals who serve clients—is often used to facilitate plan implementation. Although the number and mixture of professionals varies, typical examples may include certified public accountants (CPAs), enrolled agents (EAs), attorneys (i.e., estate planning, divorce, personal injury), trust officers, charitable giving specialists, brokers, money/wealth managers, psychologists, insurance professionals, and mortgage or real estate brokers. Providing easy and convenient access to a professional is one method to help a client move from recognition that action needs to be taken to actually implementing recommendations. If referrals are made, clients must be notified if fees, or other forms of compensation, are shared between the planner and the referred professionals. Full **fee disclosure**, coupled with full disclosure of any conflicts of interest (e.g., accountant A is part of the network, accountant B is not), is one way to maintain professional referral networks in a way that benefits clients and their advisors. The planner benefits from increased revenues from the shared clients served, but more importantly the planner and clients benefit from a group of like-minded professionals who can collaborate and contribute to a mission of serving clients well. Each of the professionals can play an important role in helping clients implement financial planning recommendations, as both the advisor and the client are assured of the professionalism of the provider in meeting the client's objective.

In conjunction with the question of *who* are the issues of *what* and *where*. The latter may refer, literally, to the place a client must go to access the provider of the product or service recommended (e.g., URL, mailing address). *What* represents the variety of traditional insurance, investment, retirement, and other ancillary financial planning products and services that emanate from the strategies identified in Step 5 to a wide range of "concierge" services. Some planners provide high net worth clients a variety of time and money saving services that alleviate the client's need to shop and negotiate (e.g., for transportation or mortgages, or to handle routine bill payment for themselves or other extended family members).

What in this instance may also refer to the client information that may be shared with other professionals, contingent on the disclosure agreements with the client, or the scope of the agreement giving the advisor the authority to act on the client's behalf. In some instances the client will be the "go-between" among all of the financial service providers; in other cases the client will sign a disclosure document that allows the financial planner to contact other providers (e.g., tax preparer, lawyer, trust administrator) directly. This may be done simply for convenience, or to reduce delays in plan implementation for a client who is frequently unavailable. Situations like this require the utmost of care and trust in the planner-client relationship and the boundaries of the authority must be clearly documented.

Some core content planning areas offer unique implementation challenges requiring careful coordination of responsibilities and attention to the details of *who, what,* and *where.* As one example, without follow-through an advisor's recommendation to establish a trust may not be fully and successfully executed to benefit the client. Bear in mind that the scope of the attorney's work is most likely limited to the preparation of the trust documents. Thus, from the perspective of the attorney, the transfer of assets to fund the trust is the responsibility of the client. However, the client may lack the knowledge or time to complete the transfer. Consequently, to avoid a lapse in execution, the planner may need to either provide full instructions to the client and facilitate the process *or* act on behalf of the client to effect the transfer. In either case, someone must be knowledgeable about and be responsible for the details necessary to accomplish the advisor's plan—the establishment and proper funding of the trust to accomplish the client's goal. The actual implementation process is contingent on the advisor's expertise, business model, and scope of the planner-client engagement.

A more common example—such as implementing health insurance recommendations—may be a more relevant challenge. With most other forms of insurance a planner can generally execute, or at least facilitate, the implementation; but because of the prevalence of employer-provided "group" health plans, the planner may have no or only limited access. To further complicate the implementation, coverage changes are generally limited to an annual open enrollment period, unless selected client exceptions apply. Consequently, the planner's role may be urging the client to use the plan as a guide, reminding the client (e.g., a postcard, email or telephone call), or, in some cases, implementing the change.

As these scenarios illustrate, the actual implementation process is contingent on several factors, including the advisor's business model, the advisor's expertise, and the client's expectations. Perhaps most important is the advisor's responsibility, per the agreement, to assist and motivate the client to *act in the client's best interest.*

Why Should it be Done? When Should the Recommendation Take Place?

Regardless of the range of products or services provided by the advisor or whether the client is solely or partly responsible for implementing recommendations, ultimately actual implementation rests with the client. While it is often assumed that clients acting in their own best interests will put plans into action, this is not always the case. The implementation issues of *why* and *when* may become inextricably intertwined. Regardless of the reason for inaction, lack of implementation is the single greatest deterrent to successfully meeting financial goals. As such, it is imperative that planners take steps to examine, and in some cases supervise or facilitate the timeliness and effectiveness of client implementation, if such responsibilities are part of their business plan and agreed-upon engagement with the client.

One of the advisor's primary goals is to effectively use the plan and the plan presentation to educate the client on two subjects: (1) *why* the recommendations are viable solutions to the client's concerns; and (2) *when* implementation should occur to best meet the client's objective in a timely method. Just because a client pays for a plan does not mean the client is motivated to take action. Both the plan and the presentation should clearly communicate to the client that without proper implementation, the capacity to reach long-term financial goals will be jeopardized. Thus, it is essential that a financial planner adopt a proactive position regarding plan implementation.

Two methods of conveying differences in implementation to the client are a two-by-two matrix and a timeline. The two-by-two matrix divides goals into one of four categories:

(1) immediate implementation and immediate completion;

(2) immediate implementation and delayed completion;

(3) delayed implementation and immediate completion; or

(4) delayed implementation and delayed completion.

The meaning of "immediate" or "delayed implementation" is fairly obvious; however, the meaning of "immediate" or "delayed completion" is not as transparent. A goal that is immediately completed (regardless of any delay in implementation) might be, for instance, writing a will. The idea of immediate completion is that there is very little or no continuous action required to achieve the desired result; it is basically "one and done." Once the initial action has taken place, the recommendation or goal should be realized. However, if the results do require periodic or continuous action, and/or monitoring, then the goal would be categorized as a delayed completion goal. Typically these goals require more commitment and effort by both the client and planner to see them come to fruition. Exhibit 8.2 shows a sample matrix that could be used.

Exhibit 8.2 Recommendation and Goal Classification Matrix

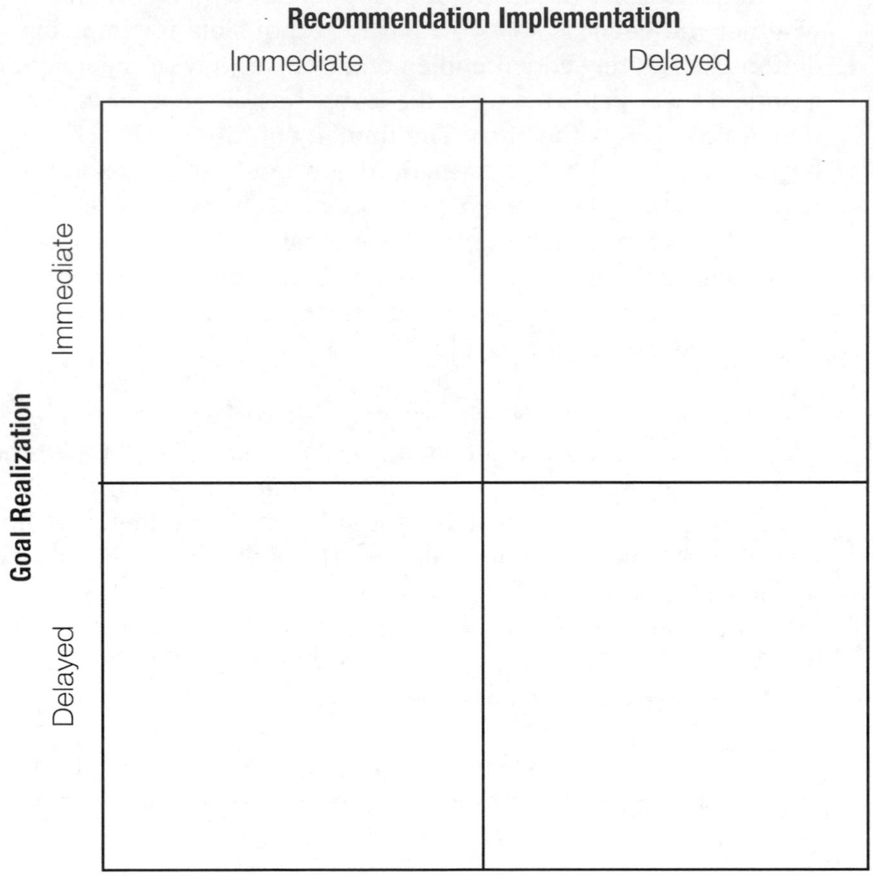

Recommendation Implementation

Immediate   Delayed

Goal Realization — Immediate / Delayed

Another method for illustrating some of the complexities surrounding the timing ("*when*") of the implementation process is a timeline. The old adage states "a picture is worth a 1,000 words." Exhibit 8.3 graphically illustrates the concepts of immediate or delayed implementation as well as examples of how goals might be satisfied over different time horizons.

Keeping clients motivated to take action in the short-term as well as over the longer term is a personal characteristic that separates the best planners from others. Furthermore, it takes careful attention to the details to keep the implementation and the outcome of the plan on track. It is important to help clients realize that:

- a recommendation may be implemented and completed almost immediately (e.g., filing a change of beneficiary form for a retirement account);

- a recommendation may be implemented and completed within *60 days* (e.g., processing a 401(k) salary-deferral of 10% of the participant's gross salary, which qualifies the participant for the company provided match of an additional 3% of annual salary, to save for retirement);

Exhibit 8.3 Recommendation Implementation Timeline

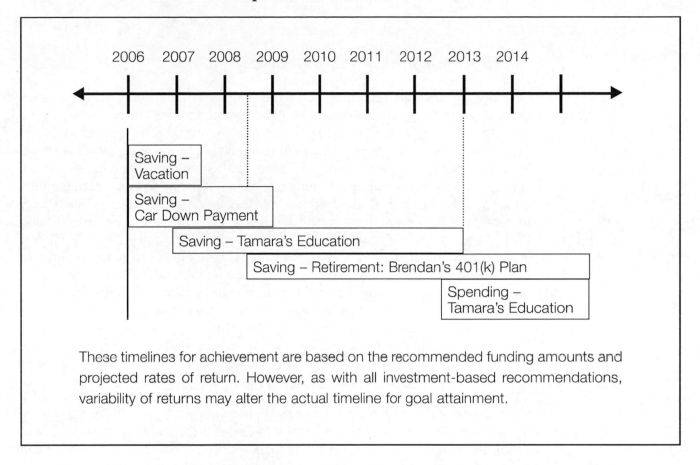

These timelines for achievement are based on the recommended funding amounts and projected rates of return. However, as with all investment-based recommendations, variability of returns may alter the actual timeline for goal attainment.

- another recommendation may be implemented and the goal satisfied within *60 months* (e.g., contributing $500 per month for the next five years to fund a 529 plan for the client's education costs); or

- a series of recommendations may be implemented over *60 years* or more (e.g., funding and distributing retirement savings).

The advisor's technical and analytical skills are instrumental to explaining *when* and *why* to the client, but those same skills may not necessarily prepare the advisor to understand or help the client understand *why* the client is choosing *not* to implement. Recall that temperament, personality, beliefs, and attitudes are significant influences in a client's financial life. Some clients will immediately begin to implement recommendations without any nudging based on: their belief that they will be rewarded by their progress; their perception of increased control of their financial situation; or other intrinsic or extrinsic factors. Other clients may know *why* they should implement, logically, but emotional or other barriers to *when* may be the greatest deterrent. These clients may have the desire to implement, but postpone taking action for any number of reasons, such as:

- procrastination;

- avoidance of difficult or uncomfortable issues and decisions (e.g., estate planning, beneficiary designations, gifting, etc.);

- competition with other life arenas;

- lack of time or knowledge; or

- simply forgetting to follow through.

One way to motivate action involves the planner collaborating with a client's other advisors (e.g., tax professional, attorney) in an effort to continually reinforce that certain actions are necessary to successfully reach financial goals and objectives (e.g., development of legal documents, filing taxes, or funding retirement accounts). Frequent communication with clients is a second, and often, simple way to motivate action. Calling clients occasionally to confirm that implementation has occurred as well as meeting periodically with clients may increase a client's commitment. Third, notes of congratulations and recognition for implementation and goal achievement also may work well with some clients. What may be most influential is framing all of these efforts from the context of how the client will potentially benefit from the implementation and the impact on client goal achievement. To help clients put their attitudes, competing spending habits, or procrastination into perspective, the advisor may confront the client with the question, "How would you feel if _____ is not accomplished?" However, because of the potentially emotionally-charged response (e.g., shame, embarrassment, defeat, etc.), this approach should be used with care and reserved for strong, trusting client-planner relationships.

Sometimes a client must be faced with a significantly negative consequence in order to fully convey the importance of *when* and *why* implementation should occur. For instance, if the client elects to take actions contrary to the advice and guidance of the planner, or if the client does not implement recommendations in a timely manner, the planner may ask the client to sign a waiver of liability. When presented with a liability release form that protects the *advisor* from future legal challenges for professional malpractice or malfeasance, the client may then fully comprehend the magnitude of the consciously chosen action or inaction. But caution must be used in exercising this practice. A liability waiver should be used only when the client's *conscious* refusal or *inaction* could potentially jeopardize the client's future financial situation or even raise questions about the professional judgment of the planner. (As noted in the previous chapter, routinely asking a client to sign a liability release just because funds are not available or prioritized to meet all goals or planning needs is an action that must be used judiciously, relative to the individual client situation.)

In extreme situations the planner may resort to terminating the planner-client relationship unless client action is taken to implement *selected* recommendations. However, this approach also must be used with caution. Apparent attempts to force a client to take action may be viewed as a conflict of interest— *even if the action is in the best interest of the client*. This is especially true in situations where the action would result in increased commissions or other planner compensation.

The increasing emphasis on fiduciary relationships and the encouragement of the wise exercise of professional judgment in serving clients has heightened planner concern over **fiduciary liability** and the potential for civil suits for professional negligence. The client's signature on a liability release acknowledges that the planner made a recommendation that was declined by the client and, thus, relieves the planner of further responsibility. Recall the earlier discussion of primary and secondary stakeholders (e.g., the client's spouse or children) who might, for example, question the planner's exercise of fiduciary duty to the client when long term care insurance was not proposed, despite a family history of Alzheimer's disease. When working with clients to implement recommendations initially, as well as later in the subsequent monitoring step of the process, it is important to clearly and accurately document all advisor or staff communication with the client. These repeated documentation efforts to convince a client to implement a recommendation, as well as other notes regarding the client's plans and wishes, could provide important evidence of the planner's professional judgment in the future. In summary, efforts to motivate client action, and to fully explain *when* and *why* the recommendation is important to the client's financial future, can be equally important for the protection of the client *and* the planner.

How Should Implementation Take Place? How Much Should be Purchased, Saved, Invested to Implement the Recommendation?

Beyond the complex dilemma of deciphering client motivation, are the final two implementation issues: *how* and *how much*. Often the best answers to these practical, and perhaps technical, issues are convenience and cost. These queries may appear simplistic, given the range of business models, recommendations and products and services employed, but cost and convenience are important regardless of how the implementation is handled. The following list offers some very simple examples of strategies that may help clients adopt new financial management practices:

- specific **"To-Do" Lists** (as shown in Exhibit 8.4) or timelines that clearly explain the *how* and *how much* for each recommendation; these lists can help the planner *and* the client to divide what may appear to be an overwhelming list into manageable tasks that can be easily tracked;

- cash management tactics (e.g., electronic transfers, an asset management (sweep account) or electronic access to bank or investment account information) that simplify how the recommendations are put into practice;

- "low maintenance" investment products such as index mutual funds, other passively managed investments, or age-based portfolios for use by clients with little or no need for continuing advisor support; and

- when applicable to the planner-client engagement, periodic meetings with the planner, which will facilitate the implementation of the plan.

Exhibit 8.4 "To-Do" List

This "To-Do" list reflects the recommendations presented in your plan.
Don't hesitate to call our office for clarification or assistance with any actions recommended.

Immediate Action

☑ Visit a financial planning firm to get a roadmap for achieving your life goals.

❑ Pay off all credit card balances of $7,800 with money from the inheritance.

❑ Adam, contact the Human Resources/Personnel Department of your school district and increase retirement contributions by $180 bi-weekly. Acquire a copy of the beneficiary designation for your plan and send it to our office.

Within 3 months

❑ Complete the paperwork with our office to rollover your 401(k) from your previous employer to a Traditional IRA.

❑ Have your attorney update your wills, draft a durable power of attorney, and establish a YourState advance directive. Provide our office with copies.

❑ Contact your corporate benefits provider on-line to determine the cost of increasing your group term coverage by an additional $300,000. Compare the premium to the low-load, direct-purchase on-line quote provided by our office. Complete the transaction to increase the coverage. Provide our office with a copy of the beneficiary designation form.

Within 6 months

❑ Use your tax refund to help build your cash reserve, or emergency fund.

❑ Complete a comprehensive household inventory, including digital records. Meet with your insurance agent to review coverage for needed endorsements, riders, or extensions. Add an umbrella, or excess-liability, policy for $1.5 million.

One of the most effective ways to motivate client action involves systematically summarizing recommendations so that implementation can be easily accomplished. The use of an **implementation checklist** within each core financial planning content area, whether in a modular or comprehensive plan, is recommended. However, checklists could also be completed for certain segments of time. For example, a client with staggered goals or goals with staggered or changing funding schedules might best be served by having one checklist for each of several 6-month periods. And in some instances, just one checklist may be sufficient. An implementation checklist shown in Exhibit 8.5, provides an answer to the seven critical questions that a recommendation should address to facilitate the implementation: *what, who, when, where, why, how,* and *how much.*

Exhibit 8.5 Implementation Checklist

Recommendation: What	Who	When	Where	Why	How	Annual Cash Flow Impact (How Much)	Immediate Net Worth Impact (How Much)
Total Impact of Recommendations on Cash Flow and Net Worth							
Annual Discretionary Cash Flow After Recommendation Implementation							
Net Worth After Recommendation Implementation							

Financial planners are often adept at answering *how much,* but frequently are much less comfortable with helping the client address the fears and concerns associated with *how.* The results of the analysis of the client's goals, built on defensible assumptions and sound analytical approaches, will yield an answer to the question of *how much should be purchased, saved, or invested.* The planner's technical knowledge and the implementation checklist can provide the client with concise implementation instructions for *how* to put the recommendations into action. Note, however, that fears and concerns about *how* may have a more significant impact on the client than initially recognized by even an experienced advisor. Explicitly, the client may be apprehensive about not having sufficient financial knowledge, experience, or perseverance to implement the plans. Implicitly, the client's experiential map or attitudes about money may be a source of anxiety. What the advisor may interpret as reluctance to implement may actually be the client's lack of confidence to implement—regardless of the amount of income available or the logical benefit to the client. At this juncture of the financial planning process, advisor sensitivity to the impact of these client situational factors is an important first step to gaining the skill and confidence to explore the issues with the client. Such efforts to fully understand and respect the client's issues contribute to a more trusting planner-client relationship.

Managing client expectations is another area of concern to the planner. Too often the client assumes that if the plan is perfectly executed, the planner's recommendations will result in a perfect outcome. But the client may not fully understand that the planner: built the recommendation on the best (but not perfect) information available at the time; used professional judgment to determine the best (but not foolproof) course of action; and framed both the action and the expected outcome on the basis of assumptions (some of which may ultimately prove to be invalid). Some of the assumptions originated with the client (e.g., the fact that the child was a highly talented musician and, therefore, would surely receive an academic scholarship). Other assumptions originated from historical data (e.g., the commonly accepted assumption of a future 7% annual increase in the average annual tuition at four-year colleges).

Managing client expectations during the implementation and monitoring of a plan hinges on three important concepts. First, the client must acknowledge that the plan is based on the information provided to the planner; consequently, withholding relevant information, giving "socially acceptable" answers, or otherwise knowingly or unknowingly misleading the advisor will not result in a sound plan. Second, the client must be fully informed of the function and formulation of hypothetical projections within the financial planning process. Third, the client must be educated about financial trends and economic issues to provide a valid and reliable context for gauging plan results. The latter can be accomplished through planner-client interactions, such as periodic monitoring meetings, newsletters, or website postings.

Step 6: Monitor the Plan, Implementation, and Goal Progress

The sixth and final step in the systematic financial planning process involves ongoing **monitoring** of:

- the plan as a malleable element within the client's life that is responsive to the changing situation and goals of the client;

- the implementation of the recommendations to date;

- the viability of the products and services incorporated into the implementation and their continued usefulness to meet the client's needs; and

- the outcomes associated with the recommendations and the progress toward goal achievement.

It is important to recognize that monitoring incorporates periodic evaluations and ongoing monitoring of some products and services, such as investment management services. Review of product performance and returns, company ratings of providers, risk levels, expenses, and the need for portfolio rebalancing are just some examples of the ongoing monitoring that must be done relative to the original assumptions. But the extent of these monitoring activities—whether periodic or ongoing—varies with the advisor's business model and agreed upon engagement with the client. However conducted, this last step in the financial planning process is important for several reasons.

First, monitoring compels a planner to stay in touch with a client. Periodic contact from the planner can motivate a client to continue to take action to meet financial goals and objectives, which can benefit the client's financial situation and benefit the advisor from a continuous revenue stream. Annual plan reviews are typical, but the frequency and extent of the reviews vary with the client-planner relationship. Conducting annual reviews of the changes in the client's current situation as well as issues related to each of the core content planning areas may seem redundant, or even intrusive in some cases. But it is important to remember that a comprehensive financial plan must be built on a thorough knowledge of the client that extends beyond changes in gross income to a broader exploration of other issues that may impact current and anticipated lifestyle decisions. Proactive planners will try to anticipate their clients' changing needs when appropriate, and facilitate the dialogue to identify potential responses. It is equally important to encourage clients to proactively initiate reviews or changes in the plan in response to upcoming needs (e.g., planning in anticipation of a divorce; a marriage, with or without a pre-nuptial agreement; or the birth of a child).

Second, periodic monitoring of a client's situation ensures that previously made recommendations and products are still appropriate and useful for the client's situation. The periodic monitoring step of the process begins with a review of the client's current situation and the original planning assumptions and goals. Significant changes may require a reevaluation of a client's planning needs or priorities, including an analysis of the client's situation, identification of prospective strategies, and development and presentation of recommendations. Depending on the extent of the changes, new recommendations may be needed for an isolated goal or core content planning area, or for several goals integrated across multiple areas of the plan.

Periodic monitoring also allows for the review of products for which ongoing monitoring is not necessary, or is not provided by the advisor. Product reviews during monitoring are conducted for a purpose similar to those provided in Step 3 (i.e., to evaluate the client's current planning efforts). Criteria to be considered would include: product and provider performance; product and provider ratings; fees and expenses; and other features unique to the product in question. (For more information on some standard benchmarks that may be used to evaluate insurance and investment products, see Appendix B.) Finally, periodic reviews provide opportunities for the advisor to continue to educate the client and to manage client expectations relative to the performance of savings, investments, or investment-based insurance products.

Third, monitoring keeps the planner and the client on track to make time-sensitive changes or to implement recommendations that were delayed until a future date (e.g., redirecting funds from a 529 plan to retirement savings because the college savings goal has been met). Time-sensitive changes may also be precipitated by changes in the marketplace (e.g., economic, tax, legal, or regulatory environment), the client's personal situation, or the availability of new planning products and strategies. These changes may necessitate both macro-level changes (e.g., revising a plan to accommodate divorce, remarriage, or career change) and micro-level changes (e.g., revising the amounts contributed for selected investments; revising the asset allocation strategy; starting the funding of a new Roth 401(k); replacing a poorly performing mutual fund). Without consistent monitoring, a client's plan can inadvertently become obsolete, and an obsolete plan defeats the purpose of proactive planning.

For the greatest likelihood of client success, a financial plan must be responsive to change. The plan must *mature* in concert with the client and the life cycle progression just as it must be *responsive* to unforeseen events or the need for different products or services. On any given day, clients might call about a job loss, a promotion, an inheritance, or a profoundly disabling accident or stroke; the list of possibilities is endless. It is during the monitoring stage that a good planner can really demonstrate the value-added benefit of the planner-client relationship. But for this to happen, both the *personal* relationship and the *business* relationship of the planner and client must support this kind of trust-based exchange.

Obviously, some aspects of the monitoring step of the financial planning process pertain only to planners who are soliciting an ongoing relationship—for services, products, or servicing of products—with their clients. Consequently, the process described as monitoring can widely vary. Some advisors are consistently involved with their clients, offering counsel on how to achieve financial and life goals. This kind of relationship is not necessarily characteristic of any business model; nor is it always consistent with the client's expectations. For planners that conduct their practice like a medical model (i.e., with a treat-as-needed approach), or for these doing modular plans (e.g., on a single problem, issue, or core content planning area), monitoring will be beyond the scope of the planner-client engagement. The planner may not have the opportunity to follow-up with a client with these business models because implementation and monitoring are the responsibility of the client, who may or may not re-engage the advisor for a review and evaluation of progress. In a more sales-based or product-delivery model, service may not include monitoring of the situation once a product is sold to meet the need. Monitoring may be limited to periodic reviews of the client's progress on a multiple-year schedule. Nevertheless, periodic client communication (e.g., a newsletter, periodic postings to a web site, or targeted personal communication) can be a good reminder for future services or referrals—both of which are extremely important to the planner's success.

Thus, it is important to recognize that the advisor's business model and the scope of the agreed upon planner-client relationship generally set the parameters for monitoring. This is particularly evident when the question of *who* will do the monitoring (either periodic or ongoing) is being considered. Monitoring may be the responsibility of:

- the client;

- the planner, *or* the planner in coordination with other product or service providers (recall the idea of the planner as the hub of wheel that coordinates implementation and monitoring);

- a variety of product or service providers with no coordination; or

- no one.

Having no monitoring of the implementation or success of the recommendations provided to a client is not consistent with the intent of the financial planning process. Unfortunately, though, it is a reality. And that reality, according to many observers, is detrimental to the client and the advisor, both of whom are missing the opportunities inherent in the long-term recursive flow of the financial planning process.

From Process to Practice

The vignette that follows continutes to explore the experiences of the Kims with their financial planner, Jane. This installment includes reflections by the Kims and Jane as they offer some insights on their "real life" experiences with Steps 5 and 6—from both sides of the desk.

As Tom and Nyla continued their trip home from the annual check-up and monitoring meeting, they laughed that it was a wonder that Jane had even worked with them in the first place! But after four meetings just to get them started, they reasoned that she had too much invested not to see them through. But the meeting today had confirmed their initial impressions: it had all been worth it.

Recalling that fateful implementation meeting, Tom and Nyla remembered how Jane's normally upbeat demeanor had been uncharacteristically serious. She told them that she was willing to compromise her desires to protect their current and future financial position and would do everything she could to help them realize their goals—*if* they were fully willing to accept the possible consequences of postponing the insurance purchases. They remembered her saying that "finding a meeting point amidst the fundamental disconnect between the needs that *I* have identified and the needs that *you* have identified is a huge part of what financial planning is all about."

But to everyone's surprise, after evaluating Jane's different alternatives for funding, downsizing, and staggering the implementation of the recommendations, the puzzle of what to do quickly fell into place. By the end of the initial meeting, they had decided on a plan for the next year (as shown in Figure 8.1, Tom and Nyla's Implementation Checklist). Jane had everything that she needed to complete the plan with formal recommendations, and the Kims had everything they needed to take responsibility for the plan implementation.

Although getting the plan in place had been a bit challenging for everyone, implementing it could not have been easier. Jane's idea to stagger the implementation had been a great approach for several reasons. First, it allowed Tom and Nyla to immediately make progress, but did not consume too much time or effort on their part. Jane's implementation checklist had certainly expedited the establishment of the 529 plan and the savings plan for the trip. The purchase of

Nyla's life insurance was soon complete, as well—all because the details were there.

Second, postponing the increase in their retirement savings by only six months turned out to be a very reasonable compromise. Tom and Nyla knew there would be opportunities to continually and gradually increase the funding. With the promise of Jane's careful attention to the plan in the future, they were confident that they could still consider retirement in 25 years. They also rationalized that when Azalea became independent, they could significantly increase their retirement savings.

Third, although they knew they were taking a significant risk by postponing Tom's disability insurance for a year, given their other demands and the importance of the timing of their trip, they decided they were willing to take that risk. The flexibility of Tom's career was also a significant consideration. In the end, they reasoned that the value of their memories from the trip could not be discounted so heavily. Their trip account value was steadily increasing as was their excitement. Although they knew their international vacation was still over a year away, they had already started planning an itinerary. Everything they had learned from planning their finances with Jane had made them strong proponents of planning ahead!

Today, the results of their first annual check-up and monitoring meeting further confirmed that view. According to Jane, everything was on course and only minor modifications needed to be implemented. She recommended that Tom and Nyla automate their 529 monthly contributions, just as a convenience. She also recommended that they rebalance Tom's retirement account due to recent out performance in selected areas of the market. Because Nyla's retirement plan custodian had added some new mutual funds, Jane also wanted to change the asset allocation for Nyla's retirement account. With Tom and Nyla's approval, Jane agreed to prepare a new implementation checklist to explain the details. After lighthearted and then serious discussion of the Kims' personal and financial situation, the first annual check-up and monitoring meeting was over. No questionnaires to complete, no forms to fill-out, no disclosure agreements to sign, no hard decisions to make—in fact neither of them even picked-up a pen!

* * * * * * * * * *

As Jane watched Tom and Nyla Kim walk to their car following their first annual check-up and monitoring meeting, she recalled how far their planner-client relationship had come in a little over one year. She knew they had laid a foundation for the future.

Returning to her office, Jane mused that the Kims might turn out to be her best clients—not because of the fees from her services, but because with clients like them she would need no advertising. They were very complimentary of the newsletters she sent and reportedly recommended Jane and her new on-line calculators to all of their friends!

After a year of working together, Jane and the Kims had finally admitted some of their frustrations along the way, but had also acknowledged that the final plan was consistent with the values and attitudes of all parties. Jane knew she had a strong preference for funding recommendations that she defined as a *need* rather than a *want*; however, in this case she realized how important it was to balance ideals against what she perceived to be a very strong client aspiration (i.e., a vacation to strengthen family ties). Another planner, working with the same clients, might just as easily have discounted the Kims' vacation goal in favor of increased retirement funding or the immediate need to purchase insurance protection. But Jane was confident that she and the Kims had accomplished what she thought financial planning was all about—the merger of a client's goals, available cash flow and assets, and the advisor's professional judgment into the development of a synergistic plan for the future.

Figure 8.1 Tom & Nyla Kim's Implementation Checklist

Tom & Nyla Kim's Implementation Checklist						(Months 1 - 6)	
Recommendation (What)	Who	When	Where	Why	How	Annual Cash Flow Impact (How Muoh)	Immediate Net Worth Impact (How Muoh)
Pay-off $4,000 in combined credit card balances	Tom and Nyla	Immediately	Service Bank, Nichols, Guarantee National	This action will eliminate high interest debt by using liquid, low interest assets to increase your cash flow.	Use additional funds (beyond the projected need for the emergency fund) in your money market account.	+$600	None
Establish 529 Plan for Azalea's college funding	Tom, Nyla and Jane	Within one month	Real Life Mutual Fund Company	529 plans have the benefit of tax-deferred growth as well as tax-free withdrawals (restrictions apply).	Complete the provided forms and mail them to Real Life Mutual Fund Company. Begin with monthly contributions of $250.	-$3,000 (dependent upon availability of tax deductions)	None
Save $300/month for international vacation using a savings account at local bank	Tom and Nyla	Within one month	First Local Bank	Beginning to fund trip will help reinforce your commitment to the goal.	Open a savings account specifically dedicated to this goal; when the money market deposit account (MMDA) minimum balance has been achieved, transfer the balance.	-$3,600	None
Purchase a $250,000, 20-yr term life policy	Nyla	Month 1	On-line Life Ins., Inc.	Life insurance will help protect your family in the event of your death.	On-line forms are available. Our office will assist in their completion, if needed.	-$300 (count 5/6 toward year 1)	None
Total Impact of Recommendations on Current "Planning Year" Cash Flow and Net Worth						-$6,250	$0
Annual Discretionary Cash Flow After Recommendation Implementation						$650	
Net Worth After Recommendation Implementation						$147,800	

Figure 8.1 Tom & Nyla Kim's Implementation Checklist (cont'd)

Tom & Nyla Kim's Implementation Checklist						(Months 7 - 12)	
Recommendation (What)	Who	When	Where	Why	How	Annual Cash Flow Impact (How Much)	Immediate Net Worth Impact (How Much)
Review "trip" savings account balance to see if MMDA minimum is met	Tom and Nyla	Ongoing	First Local Bank	Transferring balance to higher yielding account will increase returns.	Contact bank to transfer the balance (if minimum balance has been achieved).	None	None
Increase contribution to tax-qualified retirement accounts	Nyla	Month 7	Your employer's HR Dept	Using a salary deferral plan to save for retirement, you decrease current tax liability and your savings will grow tax-deferred. This also allows you to reallocate your investments without incurring tax liability.	Visit your HR Department and increase your salary deferral from 4% to 5%	-$400 (count ½ toward year 1)	None
Increase contribution to tax-qualified retirement accounts	Tom	Month 7	Your employer's HR Dept		Visit your HR Department and increase your salary deferral from 5% to 7%	-$960 (count ½ toward year 1)	None
Additional Impact of Recommendations on Current "Planning Year" Cash Flow and Net Worth						-$680	$0
Total Impact of Recommendations on Current "Planning Year" Cash Flow and Net Worth						-$6,930	
Annual Discretionary Cash Flow After Recommendation Implementation						-$30	
Net Worth After Recommendation Implementation						$147,800	

Figure 8.1 Tom & Nyla Kim's Implementation Checklist (cont'd)

Tom & Nyla Kim's Implementation Checklist						(Months 13 - 24*)	
Recommendation (What)	Who	When	Where	Why	How	Annual Cash Flow Impact (How Much)	Immediate Net Worth Impact (How Much)
Continue funding 529 Plan for Azalea's college funding	Tom and Nyla	Ongoing	Real Life Mutual Fund Company			-$3,000 (dependent upon availability of tax deductions)	None
Reduce trip savings amount to $175/month	Tom and Nyla	Month 13	First Local Bank	Given amount invested in year one, goal can still be attained with reduced level.	Reduce amount of monthly savings from $300 to $175.	-$2,100	None
Maintain contribution to tax-qualified retirement accounts	Nyla	Month 13	Your employer's HR Dept			-$400	None
Maintain contribution to tax-qualified retirement accounts	Tom	Month 13	Your employer's HR Dept			-$960	None
Purchase a 70% income replacement long-term disability policy	Tom	Month 13	Ensure Your Life, Inc.	Disability insurance will replace some of your income in case you become disabled.	Contact Mr. Mathers at the local Ensure Your Life office.	-$1,800	None
Pay life policy premium	Nyla	Month 15	On-line Life Ins., Inc.	Life insurance will help protect your family in the event of your death.	Mail check to On-line Life Ins., Inc.	-$300	None
Total Impact of Recommendations on Next "Planning Year" Cash Flow and Net Worth						-$8,560	$0
Total <u>Additional</u> Impact of Recommendations on Next "Planning Year" Cash Flow and Net Worth						$1,630	
Annual Discretionary Cash Flow After Recommendation Implementation						-$1,660**	
Net Worth After Recommendation Implementation						$147,800	

* This list is for informational purposes only; we will review your progress at your annual check-up and make any adjustments at that time.

** Given your historical annual salary increases, this shortfall should be covered by your projected after-tax raise during months 13-24. The annual expense projections and funding alternatives can be adjusted, if necessary, at the annual check-up and monitoring meeting.

Chapter Summary

A financial plan has been called a roadmap to a client's future. Just as following a map enables a traveler to reach a destination, implementing and monitoring within the financial planning process keeps both the planner and client on course. In some instances a financial planner can control all aspects of implementation; in other cases a planner can only prompt a client to take action. What is needed is for the client to commit and take action on recommendations in a timely manner, because without proper implementation a financial plan becomes nothing more than an impressive book on a client's bookshelf. Similarly, an atlas is useless if the traveler never consults it. Client goals and objectives may never be met without implementation. In the end, implementation of plan recommendations is most closely tied with a planner's ability to communicate methods for accomplishment, the value (economically and personally) of the products or services, and real potential for successful goal achievement. The importance of monitoring should not be an overlooked aspect of the financial planning process. In fact, plan monitoring, conducted via ongoing assessments of products and services leveraged against a revised assessment of the client's situation, is the primary way successful advisors provide service to clients over time. Monitoring will almost always result in future opportunities to serve a client through product delivery, services, or consultation. Truly comprehensive financial planners do not discount the importance of plan monitoring.

Chapter Review

The Basics: Review Questions

Discussion Questions

1. Explain why Steps 5 and 6 may offer the greatest challenge to the premise that financial planning should be guided by a systematic process.

2. Describe how failing to implement one or more plan recommendations may jeopardize a client's goal.

3. Identify approaches a financial planner can use to motivate action when a client is solely responsible for implementation.

4. How can a referral network benefit both the client and the planner? What disclosures, if any, are necessary?

5. How can providing a client with a "To-Do" List or timeline improve the likelihood that a client will implement plan recommendations?

6. Why is the concept of time, or consideration of *when* to implement or when to monitor, so important for the client to appreciate?

7. Explain why monitoring plan outcomes is so important within the comprehensive financial planning process.

8. In what circumstances might a financial planner have a client sign a liability waiver? What is the purpose of this form?

9. Why is it important to manage a client's expectations during implementation and monitoring?

10. List the four objectives of monitoring and cite at least three "real life" client examples to illustrate each objective.

Chapter 9

Developing A Product: Writing A Financial Plan

Overview

Writing a comprehensive financial plan can be an intimidating task, especially for those who have never written more than client letters, brochures, or a few pages of client analysis. In actuality, writing a plan does not have to be onerous. Preparing a financial plan, whether modular or comprehensive, is similar to engaging in a sporting activity. First, planners need to know the rules of the game. Fortunately, there are a few simple tenets that can be employed whenever writing, but the most important is the adage "know your audience." Second, planners need to assess their strengths and weaknesses in relation to the game through a combination of practicing their skills and gauging their competencies. For example, it is important that planners understand their own preferred learning and information processing style as a foundation for interacting with clients, whether orally or in writing. Third, the game—in this case writing—must be played and the score tallied. For some novice financial planners, this is the hard part. Writing takes time, energy, and a workable outline, all of which may contribute to points earned. Does the plan capture the client's situation and reflect values, goals, needs, and desires as well as the expert wisdom of the advisor? Can the client clearly and easily comprehend the analyses, recommendations, and the implementation approach? Does the plan encourage the client to take action? Does the plan meet the standards consistent with the firm's business model? If the answer to these questions is yes, the plan was effectively written and the game was played well.

The final question is will the game be played again? If the answer is yes, then more practice will be needed to continue to improve. For example, some plan sections that seem to be effective with most clients, or that provide basic client education, may be repeated almost verbatim in future plans, while other sections that are client specific may have to be revised as the planner crafts plans that address different client situations and challenges. Practicing a sport makes the players better; similarly, the more plans that are written by a planner, the easier it becomes to do.

Key Terms

Acceptance letter
Client engagement letter
Code of ethics
Executive summary
Investment policy statement
Mission statement

Observations
Privacy statement
Statement of principles
Vision statement
Voice
Writing style

Writing Style and Voice

Writing a comprehensive financial plan is the optimal way to systematically describe a client's needs, wants, desires, and goals within the context of a reasonable plan for making those dreams become reality. The challenges of writing an effective plan lie hidden within the nuances of that statement. Writing plans, or even purchasing software to do much of the writing, requires the planner to identify and develop a personal **writing style**. Style is nothing more than a distinctive approach that is consistently used to communicate. Norman Mailer, the Pulitzer Prize winning author, stated that writing style is a reflection of the author.[1] The good news is that a financial planner need not be Norman Mailer to write a good plan. All that is necessary is to follow some essential writing guidelines grounded on one fundamental premise—know your audience, or in this case, know your client.

A useful starting point in determining one's writing style is revisiting the learning and information processing style comparisons presented in Chapter 3 - Client Communication. The three primary modes for processing information or experiences are visual, auditory, and kinesthetic. Although the theory and applications surrounding this topic are quite complex and worthy of more study, the simple approach of processing information through the eyes, ears, experiences, or actions can help guide a planner's communication with clients. Individuals that are visually oriented will find that pictures, graphs, charts, and other visual aids are quite helpful in addition to the written word when reviewing complex issues. Hearing information may offer only a temporary insight for visual learners. On the other hand, auditory learners will quickly and easily grasp even the complex issues without ever looking at the written plan; consequently, for these clients talking with the planner is critical. Kinesthetic, or experiential, learners benefit from engagement with the content. Internet-based calculators, software simulations, or a well-defined "to do" list for plan implementation may appeal to this type of learner. Clearly, not every communication exchange can match the preferred information processing style of the participants. But recognition of these styles can increase communication effectiveness and challenge planners to creatively adapt their various forms of client communication, including financial plans, to appeal to all styles of learners.

Before writing one word of a financial plan, however, it is important for financial planners to recognize their own preferred information processing style. Financial planners tend to write plans based on the assumption that their clients process information the same way they do. However, one approach, by itself, seldom meets the learning needs of most clients. Instead, each planner should attempt to balance aspects of all preferred information processing styles by employing a variety of the methods used for client communication. Some communication may, by necessity, require one approach; but one approach should not dominate all forms of client communication on a routine basis. Instead, supplement the primary learning approach with aspects from one or more of the other learning style preferences. This ensures that all learners are "getting the message" since the visual, auditory, and kinesthetic needs of all clients are being met (at least to the extent that is possible). Employing a combination of learning styles also helps the client to feel "understood" by the planner. The sample section of a financial plan in Appendix D illustrates how text can be augmented with visual components, such as graphics and font styles.

In addition to writing style, the second most important consideration is the **voice** to be conveyed in the plan. The voice, or image of the writer and his or her message, is conveyed through the: (1) point of view or perspective used by the author; (2) choice and use of pronouns; and (3) choice of active or passive verb forms. As background for considering these issues, first consider the voices that a planner might need to invoke:

- a knowledgeable expert with technical expertise;

- an objective professional serving in a fiduciary role;

- a trusted confidante and friend;

- a counselor, coach, referee, challenger, or educator;

- a business person or service provider with good customer relationship skills;

- a trusted family friend; or

- a motivator and "voice of reason" for financial issues.

Although it is neither possible nor necessary to convey all of these voices within the plan, both the plan and the voice used should project an image of the planner and the planning firm.

The point of view or perspective chosen by a writer may be described as impersonal or personal. The impersonal voice is business-like, objective, serious, fact-based, and devoid of any consideration of the experiences, feelings, or opinions of the author or the reader. In contrast, the personal voice communicates a more private or personalized message that employs the use of pronouns that directly address and involve the reader. Consistent with these points of view is the idea of "person" and the use of *first*, *second*, or *third person* voice. The first person voice, where the author is the speaker, provides a direct, personal account by using the term "I." With the second person voice, the author as speaker directly addresses the reader by using the word "you." As for the third person voice, the author provides a more objective or distanced explanation, but pronouns (if used) may be in the subjective or objective case. Exhibit 9.1 summarizes the accepted use of singular and plural pronouns when used in the subjective, objective, or possessive voice. Some authors choose the impersonal voice and the gender-neutral pronoun "one," which can be used as a third person substitute for a first person pronoun (e.g., I, we, me), or used in the possessive form as in the example "It is important to perfect one's writing style."

Exhibit 9.1 Subjective, Objective, and Possessive Case Usage

Case	Singular Usage	Plural Usage
Subject or Subjective		
√ First Person	I	We
√ Second Person	You	You
√ Third Person	She or He	They
Object or Objective		
√ First Person	Me	Us
√ Second Person	You	You
√ Third Person	Her or Him	Them
Possessive		
√ First Person	My	Our
√ Second Person	Your	Your
√ Third Person	Her or His	Their

Plural first and second person possessive usage is the most common style used when writing a financial plan. For example, it is conventional to state something like "*Our* firm prides itself in meeting *your* financial goals." Some financial planners prefer to use a subjective plural pronoun style such as "*We* believe that *you* will meet your goals by 2018." In some cases, financial planners use first person plural subjective pronouns to describe themselves, but then use the first names of their clients within the plan. For example, a plan might state "Jim and Mary, *we* recommend that a $250,000 policy be purchased for your disabled son, Todd." Or, consider the contrasting but more impersonal statement "It is recommended that *one* purchase a $250,000 policy." First person singular should probably be avoided unless the planner is truly a one-person firm. The excessive use of "I" (i.e., repeatedly saying, "I recommend," "I conclude" etc.) could suggest an air of arrogance or even set a controversial tone, although this was not the intent of the planner. If the plural usage is selected, then the singular usage should be avoided. However, it is likely that the plan will switch between subjective and possessive pronoun use when appropriate.

The choice and use of active or passive verb form is the third factor that contributes to voice. Active voice is recommended as it results in shorter sentences that are more forceful and direct. Consider the following examples of passive and active voice:

> "Based on the recommendation, a $1 million term policy was purchased by Yogini."

> "Based on the recommendation, Yogini purchased a $1 million term policy."

Unless the object of the action or verb is more important than the subject or person doing the action, use the active voice. Note how the first sentence emphasizes the $1 million term policy, while the second sentence shifts the emphasis to Yogini. The choice of the active voice also makes the voice of the plan more personal.

The selection of point of view, pronoun and case usage, and active or passive verb usage depends entirely on the stylistic effect or voice the planner prefers to use. A plural possessive approach will present a more objective and slightly more impersonal image. Consistent with this style, the planner might use more passive sentences or use the gender-neutral pronoun "one." On the other hand, a more active style that incorporates pronouns with first names will make the plan read more informally, but also more personally. Once chosen, the overall voice should be consistent throughout the plan. However, there may be subtle shifts between the elements of the plan that provide definitions or explanations to educate the client and the sections that reflect on how the client's goals and assumptions influenced a recommendation. Attention to voice will help the planner develop a consistent style that does not jolt the client between "hard core" facts versus a message that conveys a sincere understanding of the client's needs. Attention to the voice used when making observations and recommendations is also extremely important. The planner is the expert, but it is important to temper the role of expert with the roles of coach, educator, and friend.

Plan Style and Format

There are many details that go into designing and writing a plan that should not be overlooked. Factors such as how the plan is bound, the type of paper used, the use of fonts and color, and the mix between text and graphics all play a role in how the final plan will look, feel, and read. General formatting issues need to be carefully considered (e.g., how much text versus how many graphs, charts, or tables will be used). There is no universal answer except "know your client." A well-designed plan lends credence to a planner's recommendations—both literally and figuratively. For example, if a financial planner deals primarily with engineers and other professionals who tend to be very analytical and well educated, the plans may tend to emphasize written text over graphical summaries. These clients may spend more time studying an abbreviated summary of the plan and examining the *exact* details of the spreadsheets included in the appendix than reading the plan itself. Conversely, other clients may only glance through the appendix or simply ignore "all those pages of numbers." A planner who works with less sophisticated clients may want to emphasize graphical displays that summarize and interpret the plan content over written text or spreadsheets filled with data. In both cases, the planner may use the plan to educate the client, but the scope of the educational effort should also be tailored to the client's needs.

Finally, a client might think that if the plan is attractive and well organized that it is also likely that the contents of the plan have been carefully developed. Thus, formatting is an important aspect of an effective financial plan. Remember, anything that can assist a client in accessing and interpreting a plan will enhance the probability that the client will buy into the ideas presented and, most importantly, ultimately implement the recommendations. Here are some basic rules to follow to increase the effectiveness of the plan:

1. A functional format with easy to read fonts is advisable. At a minimum, a 12-point black font in either Times New Roman or Arial is recommended. Font sizes or styles may be altered to separate sections or to designate headings, but it is important to remain consistent from section to section if different fonts or font sizes are used.

2. Consistency in the formatting, writing style, and voice from one plan section to another is important. Clients expect uniformity in presentation, and the best way to achieve this is to choose a format and writing style and stick with it.

3. The mix between black and white and color within a plan is a major formatting issue. The use of color appeals to visual learners. Color also adds a sense of vitality and attractiveness to a plan that can otherwise be thought of as technical or impenetrable.

4. The choice of plan cover is also important. Some planners prefer to use a loose-leaf binder to organize a plan. This is a good choice for those that see a plan as a "living document" that will be added to on a frequent basis. Other planners prefer to actually bind a plan. This approach makes a plan look and feel more like a book, which often presents an image of utmost professionalism. However, some planners may interpret a book-bound plan as being inflexible in purpose and use. Still other planners use punch-hole binding methods or spiral binding. The choice of binding is an individual decision, and there is no correct or incorrect practice standard currently in use. However, a spiral bound plan with a plastic sheet cover will impart a different feel than the same plan bound in a faux-leather binder.

5. Check and recheck the plan! Financial planners are encouraged to take extra time to edit all material within a plan for errors, omissions, and grammar. *How* something is said may be as important, or even more important, than *what* is said! Also carefully check all the facts and numbers for accuracy throughout the plan.

6. Each core content section within a comprehensive financial plan should stand alone if read separately, just as a targeted, or modular, plan must do. This means that a client should be able to read a section on education planning, for example, and understand the: current situation as described by the planner; analysis conducted; recommendations made; and how the recommendations will be implemented and monitored in the future.

7. Needless to say, plans must be well written. To do this, planners should avoid technical jargon and financial planning acronyms. Technically complicated topics and terms should be simplified and defined. There is no point in trying to impress a client with technical jargon; in fact this practice can make the plan seem more impersonal. Keep it simple, but whenever appropriate, use the text, or accompanying background articles, to educate the client. Supplement the text information with a glossary of terms or other supporting education articles in the appendices.

8. Write as if the plan were a cookbook rather than a financial document. The plan needs to reasonably follow the financial planning process. This means that a logical progression from planning goals and objectives, definition of terms, current situation assessment and analysis, recommendations, and implementation to monitoring should be used.

9. Use a combination of pre-scripted and client specific information. Approximately one-half of any written plan may consist of pre-scripted material (e.g., explanations of core content topics within the plan, definitions of terms, and explanations of financial products and strategies). While it is true that, for instance, definitions within a plan may be exactly the same for every client, this does not mean that recommendations can be universally applied to each client. Recommendations and implementation strategies may be similar among clients, but it is important that each recommendation within a plan be matched to the client's unique goals, objectives and situation. Recommendations should always reflect a client's personal circumstances, existing market conditions, laws and regulations, and the current state of the economy.

10. Document, document, document! Footnotes should be used to document material in the plan referenced from other sources. The use of references suggests that the planner is well read, which may enhance the planner's professional image. Also use footnotes or other referencing system to help the client easily locate supporting spreadsheet or software results in the appendices.

Components of a Financial Plan

Sometimes students and novice financial planners think of the written plan as the end product rather than the means to help a client reach financial goals and objectives. A well-written financial plan provides a client with a dynamic financial road map to enhanced financial wellness. By its very nature, a well-written comprehensive plan is integrative, realistic, and synergistic. A plan is integrative if one section builds upon, or links with another section. The same is also true for a single issue, or modular, plan, except the progression from analysis of current situation to recommendation is limited to only one planning topic, whereas the comprehensive plan addresses a broader array of topics. In a comprehensive plan, the effects of one recommendation must be considered relative to the outcomes of another recommendation. Both the analysis and recommendations of modular and comprehensive plans must be realistic for the client's situation, the mutually agreed upon assumptions, and the legal and economic environment.

The writing process allows a planner to bring multiple strategies and client solutions into one integrated presentation. A realistic plan is one that can be implemented with or without the planner. A well-written plan is also synergistic if, when read as a complete plan, the whole is greater than the sum of the individual parts. In other words, an effective plan is one that provides a financial life roadmap to a client. The roadmap, when presented in its entirety, shows more information than simply looking at each piece of a person's financial picture separately.

Continuing with the road map analogy, it is equally important for plan writers to have a workable outline to guide the progression and development of the plan. To proceed without an outline that is perfected to match the way the planner or firm serves clients would be analogous to beginning a cross-country trip without a map. But the broad variation in providers of planning services is also evident in the plans produced. For example, the Letter to Client and the Copy of the Client Engagement Letter, or some of the information included, may not be applicable for those advisors who are delivering a financial plan only as a method to establish product needs. Certainly, including these documents when the planner is actually in a continuing financial planning engagement may be helpful, but may not be applicable when the financial plan is ancillary to a product sale. Although the applicability or sequencing of some components of a plan may vary, many plans follow a general outline similar to that shown in Figure 9.1. What follows is a description of each plan component and a discussion of the purpose or reason for including the component in a comprehensive plan.

I. Cover Page

It is important for a financial plan to have a well designed cover page. The cover is the first thing a client will see, and as such, the cover will give the first impression of the quality and content of the plan itself. Typically a cover page includes the firm's logo (if applicable) and the following information:

- the firm's name and address;

- the planner's name;

- a brief firm or planner vision statement;

- a phrase such as "A Comprehensive Financial Plan Prepared for [Client's Name]";

- the term "confidential" clearly indicated;

- any applicable disclosure statements as required; and

- the date of the plan.

II. Letter to Client

A cover letter serves many purposes depending on the type of planner-client relationship or the business practice model used. One purpose may be to reintroduce the planner and the firm to the client, but also to reiterate the planner's commitment to helping the client achieve financial objectives. The process used to develop the plan may be quickly reviewed. The planner's or firm's core values or commitment to client relationships may also be restated. Consistent with

Figure 9.1 Comprehensive Financial Plan Outline

I. Cover Page

II. Letter to Client

III. Copy of the *Original* Client Engagement Letter

IV. Table of Contents

V. Other Introductory Materials (optional)

    a. Mission/vision statement

    b. Statement of principles or core values

    c. Ethics statement, privacy statement

    d. Review of assumptions

    e. Investment policy statement

VI. Client Profile, Summary of Goals and Assumptions

VII. Executive Summary *or* Observations and Recommendations

VIII. Individual Core Content Planning Sections

    a. Cash Flow Analysis

    b. Net Worth Analysis

    c. Tax Analysis

    d. Insurance/Risk Management Analysis

        i. Life insurance

        ii. Health and disability insurance

        iii. Long-term care insurance

        iv. Property and liability insurance

        v. Umbrella insurance

        vi. Other insurance needs

    e. Investment Analysis

    f. Retirement Analysis

    g. Estate Planning Analysis

    h. Specialized Analyses

        i. Educational funding

        ii. Planning for special needs

        iii. Refinancing scenarios

        iv. Saving for special objectives

IX. Implementation and Monitoring Section

X. Client Acceptance Letter or Client Engagement Letter

XI. Appendices

    a. Calculations and projections

    b. Educational materials

that message, the letter may outline the future relationship between the firm and the client, if applicable, such as the:

- timing of periodic reviews;

- expected client preparation for review meetings (e.g., updating the client information form by mail or online);

- provision of quarterly reports or other client updates;

- availability of the planner or other staff for client assistance;

- mailing of newsletters; or

- access to other services provided by the firm.

Another purpose that a cover letter may serve, such as when the planner and client do not have an ongoing relationship, is simply to convey specific required information. In these cases, the cover letter may only include some compliance or legal disclosure statements. Some advisors feel these disclosures carry a stronger message when they are included in the more personal cover letter addressed to the client. Yet other advisors believe that the importance of these compliance matters warrants omitting the Letter to Client altogether and including these disclosures on a separate disclaimers page in the "Introductory Materials" section to reduce the likelihood that these messages will be overlooked.

Whichever format is used, these compliance messages are typically reiterated in the plan after having been initially introduced in the client engagement letter (if applicable to the planner-client relationship). Compliance statements may relate to the planner's role in ensuring the confidentiality of the client's data, and in some cases may even extend to protecting the confidentiality of the planning relationship. Investment performance disclaimers (e.g., "Past performance is no guarantee of future returns" or "All projections are based on historical data, which may not be reflected in future returns") may be included in the cover letter. Additional disclaimers regarding relationships with other financial professionals may also be needed. For example, the client may be reminded that "Prior to implementing the advice provided in this report, please confirm suggestions with your tax professional or attorney." The letter should be dated and signed by the planner.

III. Copy of the Original Client Engagement Letter

A **client engagement** letter is a one-to-three page document that outlines the responsibilities and duties of the planner and the client. Although this may sound similar to the cover letter, there are distinct differences. The client engagement letter, when applicable to the planner-client relationship, is more contractual while in most cases the cover letter is simply informational. In fact, as shown in Figure 9.2, the client not the planner signs the client engagement letter, thereby agreeing to the services and costs explained and engaging the planner to provide the products or services outlined. If the engagement letter is completed prior to the development of the plan, it may not appear in the plan, or a copy may be included simply for information. Note that some planners require that clients sign and return the letter prior to plan delivery to confirm the scope of the agreed upon services. This letter may also be found at the end of the plan, as noted in Figure 9.1.

An engagement letter should detail how and when future client reviews and evaluations will occur. Special attention should also be given to informing the client that (1) past performance is not a guarantee of future returns, and (2) all analyses and recommendations are based on information provided by the client. The engagement letter may also outline the components of the financial plan. Finally, legal disclaimers, especially those related to tax and legal issues, should be included when appropriate. Figure 9.2 provides an example of a client engagement letter:

Figure 9.2 Client Engagement Letter Sample

Mr. and Mrs. Jonathan T. Sample
111 East Avenue
Dayton OH 45402-4300

Dear Jon and Annie:

Re: Financial Planning Engagement

This letter will confirm the terms of our recent conversation regarding the financial counseling services we will provide. You will furnish complete and up-to-date information of your personal circumstances and your financial and investment objectives. We will make this task easier by providing information forms for you to complete and then clarifying that data in our interviews.

Once all your information is assembled, we will analyze your present financial situation. That analysis will include a review of your assets and liabilities, current and projected income, current insurance program, and investments.

We will provide written analyses and recommended actions in the form of a financial review. Your written financial review will refer to such things as: the holding or sale of securities and other assets; your projected income, cash flow, and tax consequences; and retirement, estate, and insurance planning.

Our recommendations will be made based on the written data provided by you and will include considerations of your stated personal, financial, and investment objectives—so please use care in providing the data. It is usually not necessary for us to see your actual stock certificates, etc.

All information given to us and all recommendations and advice furnished by us to you will be kept confidential and will not be disclosed to anyone, except as we may agree in writing or as may

Figure 9.2 Client Engagement Letter Sample (cont'd)

be required by law. You may later request that a copy of our plan be delivered to another professional advisor.

When you receive your written financial review, it will be your decision alone to implement the recommendations, either completely or in part. So there will be no future misunderstanding, it is for the written financial review alone that you will pay a fee under this agreement and this plan shall contain all our financial services recommendations to you through the date of its delivery.

After you have evaluated your financial review, there are three aspects of follow through:

(1) Service Assistance.

     This involves delivery of documents to, and conferences with, your other advisors as well as attention to the completion of forms and agreements to accomplish your objectives. There is no additional fee for this service.

(2) Product Sales.

     This involves the voluntary acquisition by you of investment, real estate, or insurance products to accomplish your objectives. This agreement and fee does not provide for any product-related activity.

(3) Plan Implementation Assistance.

     Implementation of any aspect of your plan by product acquisition is entirely at your option. We recognize that in many areas, you will already have satisfactory business relationships and we will assist you with them. However, if you request our assistance in directly making any financial acquisitions and decide to make purchases through us or our associates, they would (or we would) receive commissions where commissions are due.

We emphasize that you are not obligated to make any purchase through our associates. You are free to select any brokerage firm, insurance or real estate agents, or other vendors you desire for the implementation of product recommendations.

We are not authorized or qualified to give you legal advice or prepare legal documents for you. You should look to your own attorney for these services.

We are not authorized or qualified to prepare or amend the filing of personal income, gift or estate tax returns for you. You should look to your own accountant for these services.

We are not authorized or qualified to act as trustee, and acting upon the advice of your attorney you should select appropriate individuals or trust companies to provide this service.

We regard the responsibility for preparing your written financial review as a very important personal relationship with you. So that you may feel informed about dealing with us, we want you

Figure 9.2 Client Engagement Letter Sample (cont'd)

to have our brochure and a disclosure statement that describes our firm, its history and our key personnel. Execution of this engagement letter acknowledges your receipt of this material.

While we do not expect to ask anyone else to fulfill any of our responsibilities under this agreement, it may become necessary to do so. If that situation should arise, we will obtain your prior written consent. Assignment will cancel this engagement.

If at any time you feel that you are dissatisfied with this agreement, you may cancel it. If you do so within five days of acceptance, you will receive a full refund. Thereafter, any fees that you have paid in advance will be charged for the time and effort we have devoted up to then, and the balance refunded.

Furthermore, you agree (as we do) that all controversies between us concerning any transaction or the construction, performance, or breach of this or any agreement between us, whether entered into prior, on or subsequent to this date, shall be determined by arbitration as permitted by law. Such arbitration shall be conducted in accordance with the Commercial Arbitration Rules of the American Arbitration Association then applying. The award of the arbitrators or their majority shall be final and binding and not subject to review or appeal.

You may wish to receive an annual update of your written financial review and a more frequent periodic review because of changes in the tax laws or in your personal financial situation. These are available as a separate service of our firm. We feel that continued monitoring is essential to accomplishing all of your objectives.

Our practice for this continued service is to charge 60% of the initial planning fee, commencing the first quarter of the next calendar year. Should you request our continued service and updated financial plan, we will bill you 15% of this year's fee on a quarterly basis commencing next January. In future years, this amount may be adjusted to meet changing circumstances.

Our fee for preparing your financial review is determined based on anticipated work to be done. We appreciate that our clients wish to know the exact fee amount before retaining us. Since we cannot accurately determine that amount until learning about their family and financial circumstances, it is our practice to establish the fee after an initial, no obligation session.

One half of the fee is payable after the information gathering interview, and the remainder upon receipt of your financial review. The total fee for your financial review will be: $\_\_\_$.

If you understand the above terms and agree to them, please sign both copies of this letter and return one copy to us. You may include, or forward later, your deposit of one-half of the initial fee.

We look forward to working with you for the achievement of your financial goals.

Understood and Agreed to by: _____

    This _____, _____.

Source: PracticeBuilder Financial, Financial Planning Consultants, Inc. 2507 N. Verity Parkway, P.O. Box 430, Middletown, OH 45042-0430, www.FinancialSoftware.com. Used with Permission.

While this particular sample letter clearly defines the scope of the relationship and outlines the rights and responsibilities of the interested parties, when the engagement is limited to delivery of a financial plan, other engagement letters could look substantially different contingent on the scope of the planner-client relationship. If implementation of planning recommendations is expected to happen in conjunction with the plan, then the engagement letter would include additional information about how, and by whom, the implementation would occur. Additionally, if an advisor provides a plan as part of an ongoing, perhaps retainer relationship, concierge services might be explained in the letter of engagement and would be available to the client as needed.

IV. Table of Contents

The table of contents helps the client navigate the financial plan by conveying the overall organization of the plan, the availability of supporting documents, and the relevant page numbers. An increasing number of planners are color coding sections within a plan, which are then coordinated with color coding in the table of contents. Planners are also using color coded tabs to coordinate the sections of a plan, with colored page numbers that correspond with the section font color in the table of contents. These are all good ideas, although care must be taken that these methods do not distract from the overall image of the plan. Anything that will assist a client to read and understand the plan, seriously weigh the recommendations presented and, more importantly, implement the recommendations, is beneficial to the planner and the client.

V. Other Introductory Materials

The inclusion of other introductory materials (e.g., the firm's mission and vision statements, statement of principles, ethics statement, privacy statement, or client investment policy statement) provides a mechanism for fostering client confidence in the planner and the firm. The introductory materials (with the client-specific investment policy statement excluded) do not change from one client to another. Although the inclusion of these statements is optional, this should not be interpreted to mean that the information is not as valuable as material presented later. Since only the privacy statement is required, the information in this section is provided solely to enhance the credibility of the planner. This is an opportunity to communicate or reinforce the planner's total commitment to the client. Because this information may have been included in a brochure, marketing, or information packet, or other client communication provided earlier in the relationship, some planners choose not to include the introductory materials (or if included, to summarize them in some way).

A planner's **mission statement** defines the strengths and expertise of the planner relative to the market segment that the planner or firm has chosen to serve. A planner's mission statement may be very simple. For example, a mission statement can be as straightforward as "Providing comprehensive financial planning services to middle income clients." A mission statement is different than a **vision statement**, which typically summarizes a planner's ultimate aspirations and likely reflects some broadly defined values or principles that govern the operation of the business. While a mission statement defines a target market, a vision statement describes what efforts a planner or planning firm is going to take to accomplish the firm's mission. The mission and vision statements should resonate with the firm's clients and contribute to the clients' decision to choose the firm, as demonstrated by the following vision statement example:

> *We strive to bring our clients financial peace of mind. Our goal is to identify optimal recommendations to help guide our clients in reaching their financial goals and objectives. We do this by building trusting, long-lasting client relationships that always focus on the best interests of our clients—not our own. It is our goal to give the best guidance and advice to help our clients consistently make sound financial decisions in pursuit of their hopes and dreams.*

Increasing public concern over impropriety in the financial services industry has led some planners to include a summary statement of principles or code of ethics in the introductory section of a plan. The statement of principles may reflect core firm values, such as customer service, teamwork, and professional expertise, as exemplified by the following statements excerpted from a student-developed statement of principles for a hypothetical firm:

- We expect a high level of customer service and satisfaction from our staff.

- We believe that planning through teamwork provides better service.

- We believe that expert knowledge in all financial areas is essential.

Financial planners who are Certified Financial Planner™ (CFP®) certificants, and all students enrolled in CFP® Board of Standards registered undergraduate, graduate, and certificate programs must adhere to the CFP Board of Standards, Inc., Code of Ethics and Professional Responsibility. This ethical code is comprised of seven principles: integrity; competence; objectivity; fairness; confidentiality; diligence; and professionalism. A number of professional groups that attract planners and other financial service professionals support a similar set of core values that should guide all business transactions. It is highly recommended that planners adopt and promote the Board of Standard's Code or a similar code of ethics.[2] Planners who are not CFP® certificants should still adhere to and publish their commitment to an ethical code developed personally or in conjunction with a professional group.

A **privacy statement** is not only a prudent document to include in a plan, in certain circumstances it is the law. Federal legislation (the Gramm-Leach-Bliley Act of 1999) and subsequent rulings by the Securities and Exchange Commission (SEC) mandate that any firm that has access to private and confidential client data must disclose to each client how the firm will use the data. In the case of financial planning firms, client data must remain totally confidential. Data should be shared *only* with members of the planning firm and regulators, or other financial professionals with appropriate disclosure and consent by the client. A firm's privacy statement should communicate these policies to clients. Depending on the planner's business model and affiliation, a privacy statement is required at the initiation of the business relationship with subsequent annual privacy notices. Although the privacy statement was likely provided prior to the delivery of the financial plan, as required by law, some planners choose to include a statement within the plan.

The **investment policy statement** (IPS) is not contractual, but should be a written document signed by the planner and the client to acknowledge their agreement to the parameters guiding the investment or management of client funds. Because of the communication between planner and client that is required to develop a comprehensive IPS, it is likely this process occurred prior to the development of the plan. However, in some firms the plan may precede the IPS because the plan is developed as a foundation for establishing the kind of portfolio needed to maximize the liklihood of achieving the client's goals. The statement may be included because of its vital link to the planning process, and as a reminder to the client and planner of the importance of adhering to the established guidelines.

VI. Client Profile, Summary of Goals, and Assumptions

The client profile typically summarizes the demographic profile of the client household, lists the primary goals identified as a foundation for the planning process, and reviews the client-planner planning assumptions. Whereas the demographic profile may seem redundant and unnecessary, it is a final verification of basic client information such as names, address, employment, ages of all household members, and perhaps health status or other pertinent personal information. The statement of primary goals serves to clearly articulate and perhaps rank the goals as identified by the planner and client. Since these goals not only served as the foundation for the planning process, but also strongly influenced the choice of financial strategies to be implemented now or in the future, it is important that they are clearly defined.

Finally, one of the most important sections within a financial plan is a summation of the assumptions used by the planner when writing the plan. It is important to note that although called *assumptions*, this section may include *factual* information about the household or other planning issues as well as other situational information, as explained in Chapter 7 and illustrated by the following list of educational assumptions:

- Bradley will start college in the fall of 2020.

- A savings account earmarked for Bradley's college has an account balance of $5,384.

- Today, tuition, room and board and fees at a state-supported 4-year institution total $15,000 per year.

- The tuition inflation rate is 7% per year, calculated on a calendar year basis.

- You are comfortable with a moderately aggressive risk tolerance when investing for this goal, but agree that the risk exposure will need to change as the time horizon for the goal shortens.

- Scholarships or other financial assistance are not expected to be available to Bradley.

The assumptions and facts serve as the basis for conducting the analysis and formulating recommendations by setting realistic parameters, or constraints, on the planning process. While working assumptions will generally appear in each section of the plan when used, it is also a good idea to summarize all assumptions at the outset of the plan. This summary can be used as a reference during client meetings and as a tool to help a client understand the factors impacting an analysis. Finally, clearly delineating the assumptions gives the client one last opportunity to validate or further clarify the planning situation.

VII. Executive Summary or Observations and Recommendations

The **executive summary** may also be called "observations and recommendations." This section summarizes or highlights for the client: the key goals and objectives dealt with in the plan; the relevant assumptions made; the resulting recommendations; the implementation steps to be taken; and the projected financial outcomes made possible by the plan implementation. Many clients may never read an entire plan, but instead, make final judgments on a planner's approach after reading the executive summary. However, it may be necessary to edit this plan section after presentation of the plan to the client to accommodate mutually agreed upon recommendations, specific implementation strategies, and the timeline for implementation. An executive summary should include the following six points:

1. Purpose of the Plan;

2. Methods Used in Analyzing the Client Situation;

3. Results of the Analysis;

4. Recommendation(s);

5. Implementation Strategies for Action; and

6. Timeline for Implementation.

The most common question about executive summaries involves how long a summary should be. The answer, unfortunately, is not an easy one to provide because it depends on the complexity of the client's objectives and the complexity of the solutions provided. Usually, an executive summary can be written in one to two pages; however, a more complex plan may require five or more pages. An excerpt from an executive summary example is shown in Figure 9.3.

Some planners prefer to call this summary section "Observations and Recommendations," "Review of Recommendations," "Preview of Recommendations," or some other title that sounds less technical than "Executive Summary." The choice of terms is yet another reflection of the tone or voice that the planner or firm wishes to project through the plan. In this case,

Figure 9.3 Sample Executive Summary

Executive Summary

The purpose of this comprehensive financial plan is to provide a framework for helping you reach your financial goals and objectives. The plan consists of a section for each of the following topic areas: financial situation; tax planning; insurance planning; retirement planning; education planning; and estate planning.

A comprehensive review of your financial situation was conducted during November 2005 using information provided by you to our firm. Three primary financial goals were identified: (1) clarifying your financial situation as a recent widow; (2) funding retirement beginning at age 62; and (3) pre-funding education costs for your two children.

Several financial strengths were identified during the analysis. It was determined that your net worth is excellent given your age and income level. You are also contributing 10% of your income to your firm's 401(k) plan, and you currently have an own-occupation disability policy in place.

Our analysis also indicates that four specific areas need immediate attention. First, you need to purchase an additional $500,000 in life insurance coverage. Second, in order to achieve an age 62 retirement you will need to save an additional $4,000 per year in a tax-advantaged Roth IRA. Third, tax withholdings ought to be reduced in order to increase yearly discretionary cash flow. Fourth, $36,000 should be allocated to a Section 529 education funding plan to fully cover the college education costs for your children. The following actions are recommended:

√ Purchase a $500,000, 20-year guaranteed renewable term life insurance policy though the XYZ company.

- Date to be Completed: Within the next 30 days

√ Establish and fund a Roth IRA with $4,000 annually using the ABC Mutual Fund.

- Date to be Completed: Before the end of the calendar year

√ Adjust W-4 withholdings through your payroll department by claiming three exemptions.

- Date to be Completed: Immediately

√ Establish two Anystate-sponsored 529 Plans and pre-fund the accounts with $18,000 for each child.

- Date to be Completed: Within the next 60 to 90 days

the section may still include most, if not all, of the information included in the Executive Summary, or the section may be limited to some general observations about the client's situation followed by a listing of recommendations. The client's goals could serve as the organizational structure for the observations and recommendations, or the observations and recommendations could be organized according to the individual core planning sections.

The breadth and depth of information included in this part of the plan varies with the approach used for developing the entire plan. For example, if this section includes more detailed information (such as shown in Figure 9.3), the plan might not repeat this information in a later section of the plan focused solely on implementation and monitoring. However, if the "Observations and Recommendations" section includes a more general statement of the recommendations, then more detailed implementation information would be necessary at some other point(s) in the plan. The objective is not to needlessly repeat information, but to develop an approach that seems logical and easy for the planner to explain and the client to understand. A general review of the recommendations may provide a "big picture" description of the plan, followed by much more detailed information in each individual content section. An "Action Plan," "To Do List," or timeline would logically conclude the plan and offer the detailed information needed for plan implementation. In other words, the message would progress from general to specific. This approach can be equally effective as the more detailed "Executive Summary" shown in Figure 9.3.

VIII. Individual Core Content Planning Sections

The core elements of any financial plan are the individual content sections. The plan components shown in Figure 9.1 represent the suggested sections that should be included in a comprehensive financial plan. As the outline indicates, comprehensive financial planning encompasses a number of critical areas including: cash flow and net worth analysis; tax planning; insurance analysis and planning; retirement and estate planning; investment planning; and special needs planning, which can include education savings preparation. Because each client is unique, a comprehensive plan may also include sections devoted to charitable giving, trust management, long-term care planning, and family business continuation planning, in addition to other specialty topics. It is the core sections that drive a client to action. Furthermore, it is here that the client's current situation is analyzed and described and recommendations are made to improve client outcomes. It is extremely important that the format of each section be similar; using a section outline is one way to ensure that consistency.

The outline in Exhibit 9.2 includes elements that are typically found in a financial planning core content section. This outline assumes that a client's background in personal finance is limited. Each section starts with a brief explanation of the topical area (e.g., life insurance planning or estate planning) and provides definitions of terms or explanations of products included in the discussion of that particular core content section. Once this section has been written for each core content area, it can be used again or easily adapted for use in other plans. In an effort to control the length of the introductory section, and to allow for greater flexibility in meeting the needs of individual clients, planners are increasingly using the appendix to include articles that are particularly relevant to the client. This enables a planner to respond to a unique interest of a client or to provide fundamental client education.

A review of any planner or client assumptions integral to the analysis for the topic should also be provided. Again, explanations of standard assumptions or other client education information can be duplicated from one plan to another. This should be followed by an analysis and explanation of the client's current financial situation.

The tools and approaches used to assess and quantify the planning needs within each of the core content areas of the plan can be quite complicated and technical. Results from this analysis must then be coupled with a review of the client's in-place planning efforts, assuming some strategies have been implemented. The challenge for the planner is to thoroughly, but succinctly, explain the analysis of the client's current situation in such a way as to educate and motivate the client. It is important for the planner to exhibit technical expertise in the plan, but to do so in a balanced approach that does not overwhelm or belittle the client. It is here that a combination of textual and graphical communication should be employed. The use of graphs, charts, and tables is one way to illustrate analyses, make comparisons between products or planning strategies, and generally supplement the verbal explanations. Spreadsheet or other software results may extend for several pages. Some planners include these directly in the core content section, while others prefer to summarize the analysis in the section and place lengthy analytical results or output in the appendix at the end of the plan. If the latter approach is used, the plan must clearly note the availability of the results and direct the client to the corresponding documents.

Once the client's current situation has been described, financial planning recommendations should be presented. Depending on the planner-client engage-

Exhibit 9.2 Financial Plan Section Outline

I. Overview of core content area and definitions
II. Restatement of planner-client assumptions
III. Review of the analysis of client's current situation
    1. Observations about the current situation
    2. Assessment of the planning needs
    3. Assessment of the current planning efforts
IV. State financial planning recommendations (who, what, when, where, why, how, and how much)
V. Compare projected recommendation outcome(s) to the current situation
VI. Suggest alternative recommendations and outcome(s) where appropriate
VII. Provide implementation and monitoring plan
    1. Explain the source of the cash flow or assets to be used to fund the recommendation
    2. Give specific implementation advice

ment, it may be appropriate to provide one or more alternative recommendations. Alternative recommendations offer the planner and client choices for reaching the client's goals, and such an approach can more fully engage the client in the planning and implementation process. Certainly an optimal solution should be identified by the planner, and some clients may be satisfied with that "expert" opinion, without question. However, other clients may wish to be more fully involved in the planning process and the choice of an alternative(s). Finally, and perhaps most importantly, implementation and monitoring strategies for each core content area should be explained.

A few items are worth remembering when working with the outline presented in Exhibit 9.2. First, each core content section should include observations derived by the planner. **Observations** are general statements about a client's financial situation. Observations typically flow from the review of the client's situation. It is not sufficient to say that a situation is "good" or "bad." Rather, the planner needs to objectively and factually document how the situation is currently impacting or is likely to impact the client's goals and objectives. Observations provide the perfect opportunity to add specificity to the written plan. Observations also give the planner an avenue for congratulating a client on past financial decisions and behaviors. Acknowledging the client's successful money management strategies is very important. Making supportive statements to the client balances recommendations that may be counter to the client's typical strategies or that may in fact challenge the client to change some financial attitudes or behaviors. Recall the role of a coach who patiently and consistently offers praise for the productive actions on the field and quickly takes action to curb behavior leading to fouls or penalties. In the role of financial coach, the planner, too, must consistently offer balanced feedback.

Special attention should always be given to the careful crafting of recommendations, which help clients better understand what they must do to improve their financial situation. Recommendations must be specific and actionable. Ambiguous recommendations lead to client confusion. An actionable recommendation is one that the client can afford to implement. Furthermore an actionable recommendation answers the seven fundamental questions (who, what, when, where, why, how, and how much) listed below:

1. *Who* should implement the recommendation?

2. *What* should be done?

3. *When* should the recommendation be implemented?

4. *Where* should the client, or other party, implement the recommendation?

5. *Why* should the recommendation be implemented? Why is it important to the client's financial future?

6. *How* should implementation take place?

7. *How much* should be purchased, saved, or invested to implement the recommendation? Specifically, what is the cost of the recommendation?

A planner ought to provide reasonable and actionable answers to these questions for each recommendation. However, the importance of working with the client to arrive at mutually agreeable, realistic recommendations must be considered. Care should be taken that the sheer amount of money or time initially required to implement the recommendations does not overwhelm the client. As is the case within the whole plan, it is essential that these questions be answered clearly and specifically, as illustrated by the following simple recommendation:

> *In order to reach your goal of accumulating an emergency fund equal to four months of current living expenses in your XYZ money market account, you need to automatically transfer, via bank draft, $150 from your checking account for the next 15 months. Cecillia, please initiate the request by calling XYZ, Inc. within the next 30 days.*

In some cases the answer to the question *who* may require the client to take action, while another recommendation may involve action on the part of a spouse, human resources professional, or another professional (e.g., an attorney or accountant). Fully knowing *what* the recommendation encompasses is critical to the client feeling comfortable in taking action, and may hinge on the planner's ability to explain the planning process and the results of the analysis of the client's situation. *When* is particularly important since not all recommendations can, or should, be funded immediately. For instance, should the client implement the recommendation immediately or in five years? The choice can make a lasting difference in client outcomes.

Clients need specific advice when answering the question of *where* a recommendation should be implemented. The answer to this question will depend on the strategy and situation. Often a planner's firm will provide the best combination of products and services required for implementation. However, even if the planner's firm does not provide some of the products or services recommended, the firm is still likely to be involved in the process, and should continue to be involved for future monitoring. *Why* can be answered by showing how the recommendation is based on the analysis and leads to the fulfillment of a goal or objective. *How* and *how much* may seem repetitive, but it is important to be specific in noting both of these details to the client.

If the situation warrants further exploration, or if the issues have not been fully addressed in the answers to the seven questions, it may be helpful to compare the projected outcome—assuming the planner's recommendation is implemented—with the outcome if the client's current situation continues without change. Effective comparisons can have a dramatic impact on the client. It is important when doing comparisons to clearly document the method used, to apply any client-planner assumptions, and most importantly, to conduct a fair comparison. All projections should be legitimate and conservative. Tables, charts, or graphs may be useful to illustrate the comparisons as shown in Exhibit 9.3.

Exhibit 9.3 Sample Graph with Comparison of Projected Outcomes

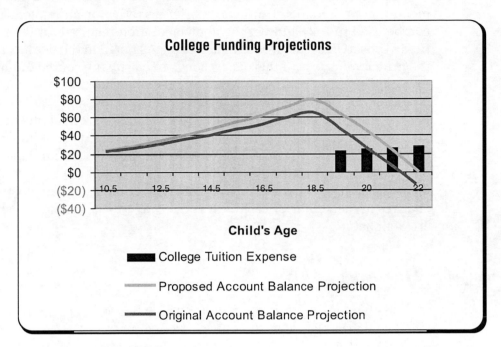

As noted earlier, it may be helpful to include an explanation of alternative recommendations, which again could be a source of comparison with other recommendations or with the current situation. Incorporating alternative recommendations can help the client choose the most appropriate path to goal achievement. Again, the planner is cautioned not to overwhelm the client with options or analysis. However, having the data in support of various options can help to educate a client and provide background information for making difficult choices, as illustrated by the following excerpt (without the referenced tables) from a student-produced plan:

> *Doug and Nancy, we know that your ideal goal is for both of you to retire on January 1, 2025, and continue to fund 100% of current living expenses. However, if you were able to meet this goal, you also wanted us to analyze another retirement goal, which is for Nancy to fully retire on January 1, 2020 and for Doug to semi-retire and work as a consultant until 2025, when he would fully retire. To accomplish this goal, we must consider several alternative strategies. You could use the balances from the Jordon Value Fund, Quest Growth Fund, and the ARC Index Fund for retirement savings, as opposed to using them as recommended to fund a 529 plan for Hannah's college education. The result on Hannah's college fund is shown in Table 11. You would also need to divert cash flow as shown in Table 12 recommended to fund other goals, to save more for retirement. Along with our recommendations to reallocate your retirement portfolio and to invest in Roth IRAs, these changes could provide the necessary cash flow to fund your alternative retirement goal. However, by doing this you will sacrifice other goals, such as fully funding Hannah's education.*

Carefully developed recommendations leave few questions about the implementation procedures. However, a brief narrative or an implementation table can be used to fully address the implementation required for the recommendation(s) posed in each core content section. As noted in the outline in Exhibit 9.2, the primary purpose of this discussion is to clarify the source of funds or assets to be dedicated or realigned to fund the recommendation. A secondary purpose is to describe any other details regarding responsibility for the implementation. Figure 9.4 is one example of an effective format for communicating fundamental information about the implementation and the projected impact of the recommendations on discretionary cash flow (DCF). Notice how the table format can easily track multiple recommendations in support of one goal and document the cost or benefit of each recommendation in the last column. Tracking changes in discretionary cash flow is one way to ensure that recommendations are actionable.

IX. Implementation and Monitoring Section

The implementation and monitoring section of a comprehensive financial plan can be thought of as the official summary of the written document. Not to be confused with the discussion of implementation and monitoring for each core content section, this section of the plan summarizes, integrates and prioritizes all of the strategies and actions required to implement the plan. At this point all of the plan recommendations are presented Situations where one recommendation affects other plan recommendations must be acknowledged and thoroughly explained. A narrative section, perhaps supported by data-based charts or other graphics, may be helpful to explain and illustrate the alternatives. The client's priorities and the planner's expertise must be integrated in order to prioritize the final methods that will be used to rank and fund the recommendations. For more straightforward situations where there are no competing recommendations, a simple "to do list," checklist, or timeline could be used to summarize the implementation. Another method for writing this section involves taking all of the implementation tables (such as Figure 9.5) and combining them into a more comprehensive implementation checklist.

The approach chosen should match the planner's preferences, the planner's knowledge of the client, the complexity of the situation, and the variety of strategies and parties involved in putting the plan into action. This section gives the client another view—perhaps in conjunction with, or in place of, the "Executive Summary" or "Observations and Recommendations" section—that brings a multi-faceted, perhaps complex, plan into a more manageable review. The foremost purpose of this section is to ensure that action occurs, regardless of the party responsible. An effective implementation summary can be used by the planner and client to orchestrate the plan in a timely manner. Furthermore, it can be used to guide future meetings with the client with respect to: monitoring plan implementation; progress toward goals; or needed changes in the plan as a result of changes in the economy, the market, the client's situation, or changes in the client's goals.

Figure 9.4 Retirement Planning Implementation Checklist

Recommendation	Who	When	How	Strategy	Effect on Annual DCF
Contribute the $4,000 annual maximum to a Roth IRA.	Doug and Nancy	Before the end of 2006	Contact your broker to open the Roth IRA accounts, or our firm will be glad to assist with opening these accounts. Funding will come from both your excess discretionary cash flow and money currently held in your money market account.	Saving for retirement by using a tax-advantaged investment account that offers the added benefit of tax- and penalty-free withdrawals under certain circumstances.	Post-tax -$8,000
Increase the salary deferral into your 401(k) plan from 3% to 6% of your salary.	Nancy	Before the next pay period	Contact the benefits administrator at Brady & Associates and increase your salary deferral from 3% to 6%.	Increasing contributions to this tax-advantaged account will enable you to take full advantage of your employer's matching contribution benefit and will increase your annual savings by another $600.	Pre-tax -$1,200
Change your current 401(k) plan allocations to match our recommended asset allocation models.	Doug and Nancy	Within the next 60 days	Contact your employer's benefits administrator or visit their website and reallocate your current holdings to match the Recommended Retirement Asset Allocation shown on page 28 of the plan. Also reallocate your future contributions according to the Recommended 401(k) Asset Allocation.	Increasing the rate of return on your retirement portfolio to match your stated risk tolerance will increase the likelihood of reaching your retirement savings goals.	$0

Net Effect of Retirement Planning Recommendations	**-$9,200**
Discretionary Cash Flow (DCF) After Implementing Recommendations	**$7,345**

X. *Client Acceptance Letter or Client Engagement Letter*

Depending on the business model followed, a letter formalizing the planner-client relationship may appear at the end of the plan. It is prudent practice to ask clients to sign a letter accepting the financial plan as prepared and presented. Some planners refer to this as an acknowledgement of delivery. This letter may formalize the business agreement, but more importantly it verifies that the plan truly reflects the mutually agreed upon assumptions on which the plan is based as well as the goals identified by the client. Furthermore the client's acceptance of the plan reiterates the point that the plan is based on the information provided by the client. An example of an **acceptance letter** is shown in Exhibit 9.4. This letter may be used in addition to the client engagement letter; or the client engagement letter may appear at the end rather than at the beginning of the plan. Again, depending on the business model followed, these letters may be used to formalize the business agreement, or may be included only as record of an earlier transaction or as a confirmation that the plan reflects the client's current situation as presented to the advisor.

Exhibit 9.4 Sample Acceptance Letter

Mr. Jonathan T. Sample
111 East Avenue
Dayton, OH 45402-4300

Dear Jon and Annie:

Re: Acceptance of your Financial Analysis

The planning process is an evolution that started with gathering information, comparing your planning assumptions and objectives, analyzing where you are headed, and defining the major problems or obstacles you may face.

Your plan contains recommendations for your consideration as well as a suggested Implementation Checklist.

However, at some point it is necessary to "freeze" the current plan and proceed with implementation follow-through.

If you are satisfied with the basic plan, please sign below and return a copy for our files. You might also call to schedule a session to start plan implementation.

Plan accepted by: _____   Date: _____

Source: PracticeBuilder Financial, Financial Planning Consultants, Inc. 2507 N. Verity Parkway, P.O. Box 430, Middletown, OH 45042-0430, www.FinancialSoftware.com Used with Permission.

XI. Appendices

Appendices are included to educate the client by supplementing, or expanding, the plan. As such, they typically include supporting printouts of all calculations or spreadsheets used in the analysis, copies or reprints of educational articles, and a glossary of key terms used in the plan.

Every calculation used in a financial plan should be documented. First, showing the calculations helps a client understand the mathematical framework of the plan. Second, sharing the calculation method increases the transparency of the analysis. This reduces a planner's exposure to claims of unsuitability of the recommendations if (1) the calculations are correct, and (2) the assumptions used in the calculations are the same as those listed in the plan. Presumably, the client will have already agreed to the assumptions before the plan is written. By using these assumptions it becomes difficult for a client to later claim that calculation inputs were unreasonable or incorrect.

It is important to note that some financial planners prefer to include all calculations in each core content section of the plan. Using this method, a planner would include not only basic income, expense, and discretionary cash flow figures in the cash flow section of the plan but also a comprehensive income and expense statement and budget projection. Because of the recent concerns about identity theft, the section might also include an explanation of the procedures used to secure the federally-mandated free credit reports or a summary of strategies to safeguard personal information. The comprehensive financial plan outline shown in Figure 9.1 assumes that all complex calculations are grouped in an appendix. This approach reduces the level of complexity within each core content section by limiting the focus to the current situation, recommendations, and implementation. However, it is extremely important that footnotes or other references be used to clearly direct clients to specific pages in the appendix to illustrate how selected numbers were derived. Supplemental client information, such as described above, also would appear in an appendix.

Becoming a Proficient Writer

Stephen King, one of America's most prolific authors, states that "If you want to be a writer, you must do two things above all others: read a lot and write a lot. There's no way around these two things that I'm aware of, no shortcut."[3] This is true for those who want to begin writing financial plans and those that want to improve the plans they write. Whether a planner writes comprehensive or single issue plans, does original drafts, uses professional software packages, or employs some combination of these approaches, the craft of writing can always be improved by reviewing how others write plans.

It is widely acknowledged that almost all writers initially borrow and adapt a style from others who have a history of writing success. As noted in this chapter, the general outline is adapted in various ways to meet the needs of different planners and different business practice models. The outlines and examples provided illustrate just a few of the many ways information can be presented to clients. As in almost all professional activities, this simply means that there are multiple ways to analyze and describe a situation. What is important is this: every planner must choose a format and style that he or she is comfortable with and expect that style to emerge over time as more plans are written and delivered to clients. Although software-produced plans may offer a number of advantages, many advisors still desire the flexibility to adapt the plan to better match the needs of their practice or their clients.

Becoming a proficient financial plan writer takes time and practice. A detailed outline can be helpful as a planner initially gains experience and develops the writing style that seems most effective in communicating with the targeted clients. Attention to grammar, style, and readability must be a primary concern. Checklists (such as the one shown in Figure 9.5) can also be used to review the plan to ensure that all of the critical issues are covered. Finally, there is really only one way to truly become more proficient at writing financial plans. The secret is deceptively simple—practice the craft of planning and writing!

Figure 9.5 Financial Plan Review Checklist

Have the Following Actions Been Taken?	Yes	No
Has material been edited for color, font, and formatting consistency?		
Are header/footer messages, such as the firm's name or logo with the date of the plan, included?		
Is a carefully designed cover page used?		
Does the appearance of the plan, including the written word, reflect your professional image?		
Is a cover letter, engagement letter, or plan acceptance letter included?		
Is a detailed table of contents included?		
Are the optional introductory materials chosen and included?		
Is an executive summary included?		
Is a carefully compiled profile of the client included?		
Is there a summary of the client-specific goals, objectives, and planning assumptions?		
Are each of the required core content planning sections included?		
At a minimum, does each core content section address the situation, recommendations, and implementation?		
Is there a good balance between the text and the charts, graphs, and tables in summarizing and illustrating the analysis? Have all charts, graphs, and tables been checked for accuracy?		
Is there a "To Do List," "Action Plan," timeline, or other explanation of the requirements for and responsibilities of implementing and monitoring the plan?		
Are the appendices clearly labeled?		
Are all spreadsheets or other supporting software results included? Have all coordinating plan and appendix page references been checked?		

Chapter Summary

A well-crafted financial plan is one of the best tools for capturing the interest, trust, respect, and commitment of a client. A financial plan, whether comprehensive or modular, can systematically encompass the financial planning process and integrate an articulation of a client's needs, wants, desires, and goals with a realistic plan for reaching those goals. The plan provides the client and the advisor with a synergistic financial road map to enhanced financial wellness. In addition to cementing a client relationship, standard materials can be used to establish consistent internal procedures for working with all clients. It is this consistently applied procedure that many use to differentiate a profession from an industry.

This chapter described the components to include in a financial plan. While this may be viewed as a best case example, not all sections may be applicable for all planner-client engagements or business models. It is also acknowledged that each planner or firm will develop their own "signature" plan outline, elements, style, and content standards, that best suits their needs, the needs of their clients, and meets the compliance standards for their business model. However, following the recommendations in this chapter can be helpful to students and novice planners as they develop "signature" plans of their own.

Chapter Endnotes

1. Mailer, N. (2003). *The Spooky Art: Some Thoughts on Writing*. New York: Random House.
2. At the time this text was going to print, the CFP Board of Standards had just released a proposal for the revision of their Code of Ethics. Given that the changes had just opened for public vetting, the decision was made to retain the previous version of the Code within this book. To ensure understanding of any possible changes that occurred since publication, readers are encouraged to independently research the final version.
3. King, S. (2000). *On Writing: A Memoir of the Craft*. New York: Scribner.

Chapter Review

The Basics: Review Questions

Discussion Questions

1. How does preferred information processing style influence writing style?

2. What factors contribute to the planner's voice in a financial plan? Why is this important?

3. Why is the choice of font size and style so important when writing a financial plan?

4. What factors should be considered in judging the effectiveness of a financial plan?

5. How does the introductory client letter differ from a client engagement letter?

6. List the seven questions to address when developing an actionable recommendation.

7. Why are appendices included in a financial plan? Explain what information is typically found there. Why might educational materials be included?

8. What makes a recommendation actionable?

9. What is an investment policy statement? Why might a copy be included in a financial plan?

10. Why should the planning assumptions be summarized at the beginning of a financial plan?

Appendix A

Client Intake Form

Section 1: Confidential Client Data

Personal Information

	Client 1		Client 2	
Name		Name		
DOB		DOB		
SSN		SSN		

Contact Information

	Client 1		Client 2	
Home phone		Home phone		
Office phone		Office phone		
Mobile phone		Mobile phone		
Email		Email		
Residence				

Children (or Other Financial Dependents) Information

Name		DOB		Relationship		At home?	
Name		DOB		Relationship		At home?	
Name		DOB		Relationship		At home?	
Name		DOB		Relationship		At home?	

Employment Information

	Client 1		Client 2	
Employer		Employer		
Occupation		Occupation		
Address		Address		
Duration		Duration		
Position		Position		
Annual salary		Annual salary		

Section 2: Please tell us about your family. This information will give us a better understanding of who is affected by your financial decisions (please consider children and other financial dependents, which may include immediate and/or extended family).

Are there any special considerations that relate to the future of your children—perhaps their future education or living conditions? *(Exceptionally bright? Special talents? Disabilities? Prior marriages?)*

_____

_____

_____

_____

Is there anyone you are supporting now, or will be supporting in the future, that you want to consider in your planning? If yes, please list below:

_____

_____

_____

_____

Are there any highly unusual aspects of your family situation that warrant additional consideration or special planning? If yes, please explain below:

_____

_____

_____

_____

Section 3: If you are currently employed, please tell us about your job below:

	Client 1	Client 2
Do you anticipate employment changes?	_____	_____
If so, when (date)?	_____	_____
When do you plan to retire (date)?	_____	_____
Annual salary:	_____	_____
Annual bonuses/commissions:	_____	_____
Are you self-employed?	_____	_____
Annual self-employment income:	_____	_____
Other earned income:	_____	_____

Section 3a: If you are currently retired, please tell us about your current situation below:

	Client 1	**Client 2**
Number of years retired:	_____	_____
Annual Social Security income:	_____	_____
Annual pension income:	_____	_____
Annual income from annuities:	_____	_____
Annual income from investments:	_____	_____
Annual other income:	_____	_____
Do you anticipate working again?	_____	_____

Section 4: Leisure activities are important to consider when planning your financial future. Please help us identify the activities that you enjoy by answering the questions below:

How do you use your leisure time? *(Outside organizations, activities, clubs, etc.)*

_____

_____

What other activities do you enjoy? *(Sky-diving, long/short vacations, bingo, etc.)*

_____

_____

What activities would you like to begin in the future? *(Traveling, volunteering, etc.)*

_____

_____

Section 5: Please tell us what you consider to be your primary goals and objectives for the future. The generic goals provided below are typical for people throughout the lifecycle and are geared to assist us with goal setting.

Rank your goals/objectives using the following scale and time horizons.*

Importance Scale

0 – Not applicable at this time   3 – Important

1 – Not important   4 – Very important

2 – Somewhat important   5 – Crucial

Time Horizon

S/T – 1-3 Years

I/T – 4-7 Years

L/T – 7+ Years

Goals/Objectives	Importance Level (0-5)	Time Horizon to Begin	Time Horizon to Complete
Personal			
Becoming more financially knowledgeable			
Improving recordkeeping methods			
Starting a family			
Advancing in current career			
Changing careers			
Returning to college			
Caring for parents			
Retiring early			
Traveling extensively in retirement			
Other:			
Other:			
Financial			
Reducing revolving debt			
Increasing periodic savings			
Reducing taxes			
Evaluating insurance needs			
Increasing investment diversification			
Increasing investment returns			
Starting a small business			
Saving for children's education			
Purchasing a vehicle			
Saving for the down payment on a home			
Purchasing a home			
Investing an inheritance			
Saving for retirement			
Giving to charity			
Transferring estate assets			
Other:			
Other:			
Other:			

* It is recommended that clients complete the form individually as well as jointly.

Section 6: It is important to know the exact amount of your current insurance coverages to fully evaluate if you are over-, under-, or adequately insured. Please provide the following information:

Life Insurance Information	Policy 1	Policy 2	Policy 3	Policy 4
Insurance company				
Policy owner				
Insured				
Beneficiary(ies), primary				
Beneficiary(ies), contingent				
Face value				
Group or individual policy				
Cost per year				
Premiums paid[a]				
Pre-tax or post-tax dollars?				
Term or cash value policy?				
Policy Provisions				
Renewability[b]				
Inflation protection				
Declining value (term)				
If Cash Value Policy, Please also Provide the Following Information				
Cash value (beginning of year)				
Cash value (end of year)				
Tax-equivalent rate of return				
Current dividend (if applicable)				
Current death benefit/face value				

a: Premiums could be paid by: owner, employer, trust, etc.
b: Renewability options include: annually renewable, guaranteed renewable, non-cancellable.

Have you ever been turned down for life insurance? (Circle)   Yes   No

If yes, what was the reason? _____

Disability Insurance Information	Policy 1	Policy 2	Policy 3	Policy 4
Insurance company				
Policy owner				
Insured				
Group or individual policy?				
Cost per year				
Premiums paid (self or employer)				
Pre-tax or post-tax dollars?				
Policy Provisions				
Type (short-term or long-term?)				
Disability definition[a]				
Waiting period (days)				
Benefit period (years)				
Total annual benefit				
Total benefit (life of policy)				

a: Disability definitions include: any occupation, similar occupation, own occupation.

Have you ever been turned down for disability insurance? *(Circle)*   Yes   No

If yes, what was the reason? _____

Do you anticipate any changes in the coverage or need for coverage for any of the policies listed above?
_____

Do you anticipate making changes to any of these policies that would alter any recommendation based on the above information?
_____

Health Insurance Information	Policy 1	Policy 2	Policy 3	Policy 4
Insurance company				
Policy owner				
Primary insured				
Group or individual policy?				
Cost per year				
Premiums paid (self or employer)				
Pre-tax or post-tax dollars?				
Policy Provisions				
Individual or family policy?				
Annual deductible amount				
Annual stop-loss limit ($)				
Lifetime maximum benefit				

Have you ever been turned down for health insurance? *(Circle)*   Yes   No

If yes, what was the reason? _____

Do you anticipate any changes in the coverage or need for coverage for any of the policies listed above? _____

Do you anticipate making changes to any of these policies that would alter any recommendation based on the above information? _____

Long-term Care Insurance Information	Policy 1	Policy 2	Policy 3	Policy 4
Insurance company				
Policy owner				
Primary insured				
Group or individual policy				
Cost per year				
Premiums paid (self or employer)				
Pre-tax or post-tax dollars?				
Policy Provisions				
Individual or joint policy?				
Elimination period				
Eligibility (number lost ADLs)				
Per-day benefit amount				
Lifetime maximum benefit				
Single or shared benefit pool				
Inflation rider (fixed or variable?)				
Inflation rider (simple or compound?)				

Have you ever been turned down for long-term care insurance? *(Circle)*   Yes   No

If yes, what was the reason? _____

Do you anticipate any changes in the coverage or need for coverage for any of the policies listed above?

_____

Do you anticipate making changes to any of these policies that would alter any recommendation based on the above information? _____

Homeowners/Renters Insurance Information	Policy 1	Policy 2	Policy 3	Policy 4
Insurance company				
Policy owner				
Property insured				
Cost per year				
Amount of dwelling coverage				
Deductible				
Amount of liability coverage				
Deductible/co-payment				
Special property endorsements				
Inflation rider				

Personal Automobile Insurance Information	Policy 1 / Vehicle 1	Policy 2 / Vehicle 2	Policy 3 / Vehicle 3	Policy 4 / Vehicle 4
Insurance company				
Policy owner				
Primary insured				
Other insured(s)				
Cost per year				
Liability Coverage				
Coverage per person				
Coverage per accident				
Property damage coverage				
Coverage per person				
(Uninsured/underinsured)				
Coverage Per Accident				
(Uninsured/underinsured)				
Property Damage Coverage				
(Uninsured/underinsured)				
Medical coverage per person				

Comprehensive and Collision Coverage		
Collision deductible		
Comprehensive deductible		
Uninsured/underinsured deductible		
Additional Coverage		
Towing/labor		
Rental reimbursement		

Have you ever been turned down for either homeowners or auto insurance? *(Circle)*   Yes   No

If yes, what was the reason? _____

Do you anticipate any changes in the coverage or need for coverage for any of the policies listed above? _____

Do you anticipate making changes to any of these policies, or the property covered, that would alter any recommendations? _____

Do you own, and have coverage for watercraft, motorcycle, or other off-road vehicle? *(Circle)*   Yes   No

Additional Insurance:

	Client 1		**Client 2**	
	Coverage/Cost	Group or Individual?	Coverage/Cost	Group or Individual?
Umbrella liability				
Professional liability				

Is your primary residence currently covered by a homestead exemption? *(Circle)*   Yes   No   Unknown

Have you ever been turned down for any other insurance product? *(Circle)*   Yes   No

If yes, what was the reason? _____

Section 7: To better understand your current financial position, we would like to review your available assets. Please tell us about your taxable and tax deferred assets.

Taxable Investment Assets: Client 1 (Also list jointly owned accounts) Description*	Current Value ($)	Cost Basis ($)	Current Annual Contri-bution ($) (if applicable)	Projected Annual Contri-bution Increase (%) (if applicable)	Primary Purpose	Current Total Return (%)	Current Annual Yield (%) (Y/N)	Use Cash to Settle Estate?

* Suggested taxable account descriptions include: checking; savings; certificates of deposit (CD); money market mutual funds; money market deposit accounts; United States Savings Bonds; stocks; bonds; mutual funds; real estate; and other.

Section 7: To better understand your current financial position, we would like to review your available assets. Please tell us about your taxable and tax deferred assets. (cont'd)

Taxable Investment Assets: Client 2 (Also list jointly owned accounts) Description*	Current Value ($)	Cost Basis ($)	Current Annual Contribution ($) (if applicable)	Projected Annual Contribution Increase (%) (if applicable)	Primary Purpose	Current Total Return (%)	Current Annual Yield (%) (Y/N)	Use Cash to Settle Estate?

* Suggested taxable account descriptions include: checking; savings; certificates of deposit (CD); money market mutual funds; money market deposit accounts; United States Savings Bonds; stocks; bonds; mutual funds; real estate; and other.

Section 7: To better understand your current financial position, we would like to review your available assets. Please tell us about your taxable and tax deferred assets.

Tax Deferred Investment Assets: Client 1 (Also list jointly owned accounts) Description*	Current Value ($)	Cost Basis ($)	Current Annual Contribution ($) (if applicable)	Projected Annual Contribution Increase (%) (if applicable)	Primary Purpose	Current Total Return (%)	Current Annual Yield (%) (Y/N)	Use Cash to Settle Estate?

* Suggested tax deferred account descriptions include: 401(k); 403(b); 457; profit sharing; Keogh; Simple; SEP; traditional IRA; Roth IRA; 529 plans; Coverdell Education Savings Accounts (ESAs); fixed annuities; variable annuities; whole life; universal life; variable life; and VUL.

Section 7: To better understand your current financial position, we would like to review your available assets. Please tell us about your taxable and tax deferred assets.

Tax Deferred Investment Assets: Client 2 (Also list jointly owned accounts) Description*	Current Value ($)	Cost Basis ($)	Current Annual Contribution ($) (if applicable)	Projected Annual Contribution Increase (%) (if applicable)	Primary Purpose	Current Total Return (%)	Current Annual Yield (%) (Y/N)	Use Cash to Settle Estate?

* Suggested tax deferred account descriptions include: 401(k); 403(b); 457; profit sharing; Keogh; Simple; SEP; traditional IRA; Roth IRA; 529 plans; Coverdell Education Savings Accounts (ESAs); fixed annuities; variable annuities; whole life; universal life; variable life; and VUL.

Investment Asset Allocation (%): Client 1											
Description (Please list accounts in same order)	Total Value ($)	Large-Cap	Mid-Cap	Small-Cap	Intl. Stock	Corp. Bonds	Govt. Bonds	High-Yield Bonds	Real Estate	Gold	Cash
Taxable											
_____											
_____											
_____											
_____											
_____											
_____											
_____											
_____											
_____											
_____											
_____											
_____											
_____											
Tax Deferred											
_____											
_____											
_____											
_____											
_____											
_____											
_____											
_____											
_____											
_____											
_____											
_____											
_____											

Investment Asset Allocation (%): Client 2											
Description (Please list accounts in same order)	Total Value ($)	Large-Cap	Mid-Cap	Small-Cap	Intl. Stock	Corp. Bonds	Govt. Bonds	High-Yield Bonds	Real Estate	Gold	Cash
Taxable											
Tax Deferred											

Section 8: We would also like to learn about the types of personal assets you own. Use the following form to record your asset information:

Personal/Business Assets Description*	Current Value	Purchase Price	Owner	Use Cash to Settle Estate? (Y/N)	Appreciation Rate (if applicable)

* Suggested personal/business asset descriptions include: primary residence; secondary residence; vacation home; automobile; boat; RV; land; passive business interests; active business interests; and other.

Section 9: Now we would like to review your debts and liabilities. Use the following form to identify your financial liabilities:

Personal/ Business Liabilities Description*	Current Amount Owed ($)	Monthly Payment ($)	Interest Rate (%)	Fixed or Variable	Origina- tion Date	Maturity Date	Person Liable for Repayment	To be Paid-off at Client's Death?

* Suggested personal/business liability descriptions include: primary residence; secondary residence; vacation home; automobile; boat; RV; land; passive business interests; active business interests; and other.

Section 10: Please take a few minutes and indicate how much you spend on a monthly basis on the following items. If you are spending money on something not indicated, please make a note of that item.

Housing		Household/Personal		Loan Payments	
Mortgage / rent	$	Groceries	$	Credit cards	$
Property taxes	$	Personal care	$	Loan payments	$
Home repairs	$	Clothing	$	Other payments	$
Home insurance	$	Domestic help	$		
Utilities	$	Dependent care	$	**Alimony and Child Support**	
Telephone	$	Professional dues	$	Alimony	$
		Education	$	Child support	$
Transportation		Allowances	$		
Auto payment	$	Child care	$	**Variable Expenses**	
Auto insurance	$			Dining out	$
Gas/diesel/ethanol	$	**Personal Insurance**		Bank charges	$
Maintenance	$	Health insurance	$	Recreation	$
License	$	Life insurance	$	Dues	$
Parking/tolls	$	Disability insurance	$	Movies	$
Bus/train	$	Long-term care	$	Events	$
		Medical/dental	$	Hobbies	$
Taxes and Withholding		Prescription drugs	$	Vacation/travel	$
Federal income taxes	$	Other	$	Gifts	$
State & local taxes	$			Charitable giving	$
FICA taxes	$	**Savings**		Other	$
Other withholdings	$	Pre-tax retirement	$	Other	$
		Roth IRA	$	Miscellaneous	$
Other Items		After-tax retirement	$	Miscellaneous	$
Other	$	Unallocated savings	$	Miscellaneous	$
Other	$	Emergency savings	$		
Other	$	Interest & dividends	$		
Other	$	Capital gains	$		

Section 11: Understanding your feelings toward investments can help us guide you when making investment choices. Please provide a response to each statement below that best matches your opinion today:

Client Statement		Strongly Disagree	Disagree	Neutral	Agree	Strongly Agree
1. Keeping pace with inflation is important to me.	Client 1					
	Client 2					
2. I am comfortable borrowing money to make a financial investment.	Client 1					
	Client 2					
3. Diversification is important to investment success.	Client 1					
	Client 2					
4. The return I am making on my current investments is acceptable.	Client 1					
	Client 2					
5. I need to earn more spendable income from my investments.	Client 1					
	Client 2					
6. I am comfortable with the volatility I experience with my portfolio.	Client 1					
	Client 2					
7. Reducing the amount of taxes paid on my investments is a top priority.	Client 1					
	Client 2					
8. I am willing to risk being audited by the IRS in return for higher returns.	Client 1					
	Client 2					
9. I am willing to risk being audited by the IRS in return for paying less tax.	Client 1					
	Client 2					
10. My friends would tell you that I am a real risk taker.	Client 1					
	Client 2					

Section 12: We would also like to learn about your expectations about the future. Please provide your opinion to the following statements:

1. Over the next five years, do you expect the United States economy, as a whole, to perform better, worse, or about the same as it has over the past five years?
    a.   Perform better
    b.   Perform worse
    c.   Perform about the same

2. How satisfied are you with your current level of income?

    1   *2*   *3*   *4*   *5*   *6*   *7*   *8*   *9*   *10*
    Lowest Level   *Highest Level*

3. How satisfied are you with your present overall financial situation?

    1   *2*   *3*   *4*   *5*   *6*   *7*   *8*   *9*   *10*
    Lowest Level   *Highest Level*

4. Overall, how satisfied are you with your current job or position?

    1   *2*   *3*   *4*   *5*   *6*   *7*   *8*   *9*   *10*
    Lowest Level   *Highest Level*

5. Rate yourself on your level of knowledge about personal finance issues and investing.

    1   *2*   *3*   *4*   *5*   *6*   *7*   *8*   *9*   *10*
    Lowest Level   *Highest Level*

Section 13: One way that we can help you is by identifying specific areas in your financial life that need immediate attention. Take a few minutes to answer the following questions about retirement and estate planning.

	Client 1	Client 2
If you are currently working, at what age would you like to retire?	_____	_____

Again, if you are working and were going to retire today, approximately how much annual after-tax income would you need to live comfortably? _____

If currently retired, is your current income sufficient to meet your needs?
(Circle)   Yes   No

If no, please explain. _____
_____

Estate Planning Information	Client 1	Client 2
Do you have a will?		
If so, was it drafted more than five years ago?		
Do you have a living trust?		
Do you have a living will?		
Do you have a durable power of attorney?		
If so, whom have you named?		
Have you named a health care proxy or completed an advanced medical directive?		
If so, whom have you named?		
Are you or your partner named as a beneficiary of a trust?		
If so, from whom or where?		
Do you or your partner expect to receive an inheritance?		
If so, when?		
Approximate value?		
Have you made any gifts to relatives?		
Have you received any gifts from relatives?		
Have you made substantial gifts to charities?		
Do you plan to make substantial gifts to charities in the future?		
If you or your partner were to pass away today, would you plan to pay off your mortgage?		
Would you and your partner continue to fund education for a child if you were to pass away prior to funding college expenses?		
Would you like to continue funding retirement savings, assuming that you are still working, in the event that you or your partner were to pass away before retirement?		
Do you and your partner plan to pay off all of your non-mortgage debt in the event of death?		

Section 14: It is possible that you either have worked with or are currently working with someone in the financial services profession. Please inform us of your existing advisors, so that we may coordinate advice when appropriate:

Do you have a CPA, accountant, enrolled agent, or tax preparer? *(Circle)*   Yes   No

    If yes, who? _____

    How long have you worked with this person? _____

    Would you recommend this person to others? _____

    May we contact this person or firm directly on your behalf? _____

      If yes, an additional form will be required granting that authorization.

Do you have an attorney or other person you depend on for legal advice? *(Circle)*   Yes   No

    If yes, who? _____

    How long have you worked with this person? _____

    Would you recommend this person to others? _____

    May we contact this person or firm directly on your behalf? _____

      If yes, an additional form will be required granting that authorization.

Do you have any other financial advisors? *(Circle)*   Yes   No

    If yes, who? _____

    How long have you worked with this person? _____

    Would you recommend this person to others? _____

    May we contact this person or firm directly on your behalf? _____

      If yes, an additional form will be required granting that authorization.

Are there any other financial professionals of whom we should be aware? *(Circle)*   Yes   No

    If yes, who? _____

    How long have you worked with this person? _____

    Would you recommend this person to others? _____

    May we contact this person or firm directly on your behalf? _____

      If yes, an additional form will be required granting that authorization.

Section 15: Summary

What primary outcome do you expect when hiring us as your financial planning firm?

_____

_____

_____

_____

_____

_____

_____

_____

_____

_____

_____

Thank you for taking the time to complete this confidential client questionnaire. We realize that this is a lengthy process that took a lot of effort, and we are available to assist where needed. We are certain that the information will enable us to collaborate with you to develop a financial plan based on your financial and life goals.

Welcome to our financial planning family!

Appendix B

Financial Planning
Benchmarks

Overview

As noted in Chapters 7 and 8, planning assumptions are based on inferential knowledge that a planner either surmises from information that is readily available or concludes on the basis of fact. There are other times when the planner must rely strictly on fact. Because of the rapidly changing marketplace and regulatory environment for financial planning, data that is perceived to be facts is often accompanied by phrases such as "past performance does not guarantee future results" or other disclaimers to avoid misleading or "promised" expectations. The next best thing to a fact is often a "benchmark," which, by definition is a widely accepted standard that can be used for comparison. But care must be taken to ensure that the chosen benchmark is appropriate—that it correlates or has relevance to the data to which the benchmark is compared. For benchmarks, advisors typically rely on third-party objective data or averages as a proxy for "facts." Using these benchmarks, the advisor can defend professional judgment in:

- the evaluation of a client's previously selected planning strategies or products;

- the selection or placement of other new or replacement strategies or products; or

- the monitoring of products previously recommended and currently in use.

Assumptions (which are often based on benchmarks) and benchmarks are important throughout the planning process. But caution is warranted—historical "fact" ceases to be "fact" when used as an assumption on which future projections are made. When a planner uses a benchmark as a point of historical comparison on which to gauge the relative performance of a product, the past performance of both the benchmark and the product are "facts." However, when a planner uses historical product performance information as the basis for projecting future performance, the planner is now inferring, or making an assumption, based on the historical fact; hence, the use of the disclaimer mentioned above. A word of caution: occasionally planners, either explicitly or implicitly, overstate the persistence (or likelihood of continuation) of performance.

Personal Financial Wellness Benchmarks: Ratios

It is said that people only pay for three things—what they have already bought, what they are currently buying, and what they plan to buy. The trick to having more money is to remove just one thing from the pile. Unfortunately, recent history proves that given the dismal average savings rate, the one thing that individuals usually remove is what they plan to buy.

A financial ratio is used to help the planner and the client better understand the current financial position. Financial ratios provide a quantitative measure of a client's financial status that can be compared to a benchmark. As such, ratios may be used to diagnose problems, or identify issues not immediately evident from the basic financial statements.

Financial planners do not agree about whether to use ratios as benchmarks to assess a client's financial health. These benchmarks—like any others, if taken out of context, misapplied, or incorrectly chosen—can offer beneficial or misleading interpretations of a client's situation. However, if caution and professional judgment are exercised, ratios can provide an appropriate starting point for analysis. For example, simply looking at the numbers on a client's financial statements generally tells a limited story; but further analysis of the income and expense and net worth statements, by applying a series of financial ratios, can offer useful insights.

Nine commonly used financial ratios are presented in Exhibit B.1. The first two ratios summarize a client's balance sheet data and roughly gauge how much of the client's assets are currently financed. The emergency fund ratio compares data from both financial statements, while the remaining six ratios summarize the client's income and expense statement and gauge how well current income meets savings and credit payment obligations.

The **current ratio** is a measure of client liquidity. This ratio determines if sufficient current monetary assets are available to pay off all outstanding short-term debts. The recommended minimum for the current ratio is a number greater than one, which means that if all current liabilities were paid the client would still retain some monetary assets.

Clients often wonder if they have too much debt. The **debt ratio** provides a guideline to help answer this question. In effect, this ratio shows the percentage of total assets financed by borrowing. A typical benchmark of 40% is used for this ratio. In other words, the typical client should strive to have no more than four dollars in liabilities for every ten dollars in assets. As is the case with most financial ratios, the interpretation of this benchmark is flexible, depending on the client's unique circumstances and stage in the life cycle. For example, clients in earlier stages in their careers may not have much choice except to exceed the optimal percentage because of car loans, school loans, revolving credit accounts (for purchases such as furniture and appliances), and other household formation spending.

The **emergency fund ratio**, sometimes referred to as the month's living expenses covered ratio, is critically important because it indicates how long a client could live in a crisis situation without liquidating other assets or being forced into an unfavorable employment situation. A benchmark of 3 to 6 months of expenses is recommended. The rationale for having a range rather than a single value is based on a number of factors. The factors that dictate the suggested

Exhibit B.1 Commonly Used Financial Ratios

Ratio	Formula	Benchmark
Current Ratio	$\dfrac{\text{Monetary assets}}{\text{Current liabilities}}$	> 1.00
Debt Ratio	$\dfrac{\text{Total liabilities}}{\text{Total assets}}$	< 40%
Emergency Fund Ratio	$\dfrac{\text{Monetary assets}}{\text{Monthly living expenses}}$	3-6 months
Savings Ratio	$\dfrac{\text{Personal savings and employer contributions}}{\text{Annual gross income}}$	> 10%
Credit Usage Ratio	$\dfrac{\text{Total credit used}}{\text{Total credit available}}$	< 30%
Long-Term Debt Coverage Ratio	$\dfrac{\text{Annual gross income}}{\text{Total annual long-term debt payments}}$	> 2.50
Debt-to-Income Ratio	$\dfrac{\text{Annual consumer credit payments}}{\text{Annual after-tax income}}$	< 15%
"Front-end" Mortgage Qualification Ratio	$\dfrac{\text{Annual mortgage (PITI) payment*}}{\text{Annual gross income}}$	< 28%
"Back-end" Mortgage Qualification Ratio	$\dfrac{\text{Annual mortgage (PITI) and credit payments*}}{\text{Annual gross income}}$	< 36%

* Principal, Interest, Taxes, and Insurance; see below.

value include job stability, number of household earners, types and amount of available credit, current credit usage ratio, and current savings ratio.

One of the most important questions clients ask financial planners is "Am I saving as much as I should?" The **savings ratio** can be used to answer this question. This ratio sums a client's personal savings and employer contributions to retirement plans, and divides by the client's annual gross income. A benchmark of 10% or greater is recommended. In other words, at least 10% of gross earnings should be saved annually. (*Note*: This ratio is very subjective and should not be blindly applied; rather, great care should be taken to match a client's total savings need to their total goal funding need.)

The **credit usage ratio** is not only a factor in determining the adequacy of the emergency fund ratio, but is also one of the key factors in determining credit score. High credit usage, such as balances above 50% of the credit limit, is usually considered negative. This is because creditors may think more credit is being used than that which can be repaid. (Note: For clients with very high credit scores, as little as 20% credit usage may have a minor negative impact.)

The **long-term debt coverage ratio** reflects how many times a client can make debt payments based on current income. This formula may be calculated in several ways. A common method involves dividing annual gross income by total annual long-term debt payments. Examples of long-term debt payments include mortgage payments, automobile loan payments, student loan payments, or other debts that take more than one year to repay. If a client's monthly credit card payment is large enough that servicing the debt could take more then one year, this amount may also be included in the denominator of the formula. A long-term debt coverage ratio of at least 2.50 is recommended. The inverse of this formula tells an interesting story. The inverse of a long-term debt coverage ratio of 2.50 is .40. This means that a client should allocate no more than 40% of income to cover long-term debt payments.

Related to the long-term debt coverage ratio is the **debt-to-income ratio**, which measures the percentage of "take-home" pay that is committed to consumer credit repayment (defined as *all* revolving and installment non-mortgage debts). A ratio of less than 10% of take-home, or disposable, income is optimal, although up to 15% is usually considered safe. A ratio between 15% and 20% is generally considered a questionable practice, while consumer debt repayments in excess of 20% of take-home pay are usually considered to represent a serious problem. Because automatic payments, salary deferral retirement plans, and other employee benefits may further reduce after-tax (or disposable) income, it is important that planners use care when calculating this ratio. However, interpretation of this ratio is rather clear: when clients commit 15% to 20% (or more) of take-home, or disposable, income to consumer debt repayment, little is left for meeting all other financial obligations.

Lenders also use ratios to determine repayment ability for mortgage qualification. Variations of debt-to-income ratios, in this case referred to as **mortgage qualification ratios**, are used to determine how much of a client's annual gross income is used to pay for monthly mortgage and consumer debt payments. There are two mortgage qualification ratios widely used—the front-end ratio and the back-end ratio. The front-end ratio, or the **mortgage debt service ratio**, is typically limited to 28% of gross income. This ratio results from a comparison of the projected total mortgage payment for principal, interest, taxes and insurance (PITI) to gross household income. The second qualification ratio is called the back-end ratio, or the **debt repayment ratio**, and is limited to 36% of gross income. This rule states that a client should pay no more than 36% of gross income on the projected mortgage PITI, plus other regular monthly consumer debt payments (e.g., credit cards, student loans, or automobiles). These qualification ratios are applied throughout the mortgage industry for conventional loans, although the range may vary by lender or type of loan. Of important note: for a client to qualify for a *maximum* mortgage, the two ratios implicitly limit the other consumer debt payments to 8% of gross income. This corresponds closely to the original debt-to-income ratio that suggests a consumer credit payment limit of 10% of take-home income.

Insurance Industry Benchmarks: Ratings

Very often financial planners will use third-party, or market data, as a means of comparison or measurement. For example, as a means to evaluate insurance policies held by the client or for any policy recommended to the client, planners would compare the information available on the current or proposed policy provider with the ratings information available from third-party evaluation services. Five firms currently assess the financial strength of insurance companies and rate overall company quality as measured by default risk. These third-party evaluators, along with their best and worst ratings, are summarized in Exhibit B.2 Insurance Company Ratings, as shown below. In general, planners and clients alike should be encouraged to use insurance products from companies rated "A" or higher by the five rating agencies.

Exhibit B.2 Insurance Company Ratings

Rating Agency	Best Rating	Worst Rating	Web Presence
A.M Best	A++	F	www.ambest.com
Fitch	AAA	DDD	www.fitchratings.com
Moody's Investor Service	Aaa	C	www.moodys.com
Standard & Poor's	AAA	CC	www.standardandpoors.com
Weiss Ratings, Inc.	A+	F	www.weissratings.com

Fixed-Income Benchmarks: Ratings

As reported in Exhibit B.3, bonds are classified on the basis of default risk (i.e., the probability that the issuing company will not be able to pay the principal as agreed). Ratings are particularly important to bond investors, but also offer valuable insights into the bonds held by various mutual funds or pension funds. For clients with corporate or municipal bonds, ratings should be tracked to monitor potential rating and price changes.

Exhibit B.3 Bond Rating Agencies and Descriptions

Moody's	Standard & Poor's	Fitch	Rating Description
Investment Grade Bonds			
Aaa	AAA	AAA	Highest investment bond rating
Aa	AA	AA	Very high investment grade rating
A	A	A	Medium investment grade rating
Baa	BBB	BBB	Lower investment grade rating
Speculative Grade Bonds – Junk Bonds			
Ba	BB	BB	Highest grade junk bond
B	B	B	Speculative grade junk bond
Caa	CCC	CCC	Low grade junk bond
Ca	CC	CC	Default grade junk bond
C	C	C	Issue that pays no interest
	D	D	Issue in default

Financial Market Benchmarks: Indices

Indices track the performance of a select group of equities, bonds, or in some specialized cases, equities and bonds. Indices are typically reported in the media as an indicator of general market conditions or movements; but indices are also useful as a benchmark or standard of measurement for an individual security or portfolio. It is important to select the benchmark that most closely matches the type of security being scrutinized and that reflects a similar level of risk. In addition to benchmarking individual assets, many advisors will also benchmark an entire portfolio. To gauge the overall portfolio performance, the advisor would combine several indices in a proportion similar to the assets in the portfolio. Information should easily be available to track the performance of most securities over time. Although there are numerous indices that track different market segments (nationally, regionally, and internationally), some of the most commonly used indices are listed in Exhibits B.4 and B.5. However, it is important to note that a decision to purchase or sell a security should not be based solely on performance relative to the benchmark index, but should consider other aspects of the client's situation as well.

Exhibit B.4 Most Widely Used Financial Market Indices (by Provider)

Company	General Market Segment	Most Quoted Index	Web Presence
Standard & Poor's	Stocks	Standard & Poor's 500	www.standardandpoors.com
NASDAQ[1]	Stocks	NASDAQ Composite Index	www.nasdaq.com
Russell	Stocks	Russell 2000	www.russell.com
Wilshire	Stocks & real estate	Wilshire 5000	www.wilshire.com/Indexes/
Dow Jones	Stocks	DJIA Industrial 30[2]	http://djindexes.com/mdsidx/
Morgan Stanley	Stocks & bonds	MSCI EAFE[3]	www.msci.com/equity/index.html
Lehman Brothers	Bonds	LB Aggregate Bond	www.lehmanbrothers.com

1 National Association of Securities Dealers Automated Quotation System
2 Dow Jones Industrial Average
3 Morgan Stanley Capital, Inc., Europe, Asia and Far East

Exhibit B.5 Most Widely Used Financial Market Indices (by Sector)

Market Sector	Corresponding Index by Provider				
	S&P/Barra	**Russell**	**Morgan Stanley Capital**	**Wilshire/ Dow Jones**	**Lehman Brothers**
All U.S. stocks	Composite 1500	Russell 3000	Market 2500	Wilshire 5000	—
Large-cap U.S. stocks	S&P 500	Russell 1000	Large-cap 300	Wilshire 750	—
Mid-cap U.S. stocks	S&P 400	Russell Mid-cap	Mid-cap 450	Wilshire 500	—
Small-cap U.S. stocks	S&P 600	Russell 2000	Small-cap 1750	Wilshire 1750	—
World equity market	S&P Global 1200	—	AC World Index[1]	—	—
International stocks (non-emerging market)	S&P 700		AC World Index excluding US		
Emerging market stocks	IFCI	—	Emerging Markets	—	—
All U.S. bonds	—	—	—	—	U.S. Universal
U.S. corporate bonds	—	—	—	—	U.S. Corporate
U.S. municipal bonds	—	—	—	—	U.S. Municipal
U.S. mortgage-backed	—	—	U.S. MBS Index[2]	—	U.S. MBS
U.S. high-yield (junk)	—	—	—	—	U.S. High-yield
World bond market	—	—	—	—	Multiverse
International bonds	—	—	—	—	Global Aggregate
Emerging market bonds	—	—	—	—	Global Emerging Markets
International high-yield	—	—	—	—	Global High-yield
Real Estate (REITS)	S&P REIT Composite	—	—	Wilshire REIS[3]	

1 All-capitalization levels
2 Mortgage Backed Securities
3 Real Estate Securities Index

Appendix C

Assessing Your Financial Risk Tolerance[1]

Instructions: Circle your first response to each question.
The response should be almost instinctual; in other words
do not "over-think" your response.

1. **In general, how would your best friend describe you as a risk taker?**

    a.   A real gambler
    b.   Willing to take risks after completing adequate research
    c.   Cautious
    d.   A real risk avoider

2. **You are on a TV game show and can choose one of the following. Which would you take?**

    a. $1,000 in cash
    b.   A 50% chance at winning $5,000
    c.   A 25% chance at winning $10,000
    d.   A 5% chance at winning $100,000

3. **You have just finished saving for a "once-in-a-lifetime" vacation. Three weeks before you plan to leave, you lose your job. You would:**

    a.   Cancel the vacation
    b.   Take a much more modest vacation
    c.   Go as scheduled, reasoning that you need the time to prepare for a job search
    d.   Extend your vacation because this might be your last chance to go first-class

4. **If you unexpectedly received $20,000 to *invest*, what would you do?**

    a.   Deposit it in a bank account, money market account, or an insured CD
    b.   Invest it in safe, high quality bonds or bond mutual funds
    c.   Invest it in stocks or stock mutual funds

5. **In terms of experience, how comfortable are you investing in stocks or stock mutual funds?**

    a.   Not at all comfortable
    b.   Somewhat comfortable
    c.   Very comfortable

6. **When you think of the word "risk" which of the following words comes to mind first?**

    a. Loss
    b. Uncertainty
    c. Opportunity
    d. Thrill

7. **Some experts are predicting prices of assets such as gold, jewels, collectibles, and real estate (hard assets) may increase in value; bond prices may fall; however, experts tend to agree that government bonds are relatively safe. Most of your investment assets are now in high interest government bonds. What would you do?**

    a. Hold the bonds
    b. Sell the bonds, put half the proceeds into money market accounts, and the other half into hard assets
    c. Sell the bonds, and put the total proceeds into hard assets
    d. Sell the bonds, put all the money into hard assets, and borrow additional money to buy more

8. **Given the best and worst case returns of the four investment choices below, which would you prefer?**

    a. $200 gain best case; $0 gain/loss worst case
    b. $800 gain best case; $200 loss worst case
    c. $2,600 gain best case; $800 loss worst case
    d. $4,800 gain best case; $2,400 loss worst case

9. **In addition to whatever you own, you have been given $1,000. You are now asked to choose between:**

    a. A sure gain of $500
    b. A 50% chance to gain $1,000 and a 50% chance to gain nothing

10. **In addition to whatever you own, you have been given $2,000. You are now asked to choose between:**

    a. A sure loss of $500
    b. A 50% chance to lose $1,000 and a 50% chance to lose nothing

11. **Suppose a relative left you an inheritance of $100,000, stipulating in the will that you invest ALL the money in ONE of the following choices. Which one would you select?**

    a. A savings account or money market mutual fund
    b. A mutual fund that owns stocks and bonds
    c. A portfolio of 15 common stocks
    d. Commodities like gold, silver, and oil

12. **If you had to invest $20,000, which of the following investment choices would you find most appealing?**

   a. 60% in low-risk investments, 30% in medium-risk investments, 10% in high-risk investments
   b. 30% in low-risk investments, 40% in medium-risk investments, 30% in high-risk investments
   c. 10% in low-risk investments, 40% in medium-risk investments, 50% in high-risk investments

13. **Your trusted friend and neighbor, an experienced geologist, is putting together a group of investors to fund an exploratory gold mining venture. The venture could pay back 50 to 100 times the investment if successful. If the mine is a bust, the entire investment is worthless. Your friend estimates the chance of success is only 20%. If you had the money, how much would you invest?**

   a. Nothing
   b. One month's salary
   c. Three month's salary
   d. Six month's salary

SCORING
(Using the scale below, add the points for each response.)

1. a = 4; b = 3; c = 2; d = 1
2. a = 1; b = 2; c = 3; d = 4
3. a = 1; b = 2; c = 3; d = 4
4. a = 1; b = 2; c = 3
5. a = 1; b = 2; c = 3

6. a = 1; b = 2; c = 3; d = 4
7. a = 1; b = 2; c = 3; d = 4
8. a = 1; b = 2; c = 3; d = 4
9. a = 1; b = 3

10. a = 1; b = 3
11. a = 1; b = 2; c = 3; d = 4
12. a = 1; b = 2; c = 3
13. a = 1; b = 2; c = 3; d = 4

Scoring instructions: Add the point values that correspond with your response and compare to the scale below to determine your financial risk tolerance.

Score	Risk Tolerance Level
0-18	Low tolerance for risk
19-22	Below-average tolerance for risk
23-28	Average/moderate risk tolerance
29-32	Above-average tolerance for risk
33-47	High tolerance for risk

1 Grable, J. E., & Lytton, R. H. (1999). "Financial risk tolerance revisited: The development of a risk assessment instrument." Financial Services Review, 8 (3), 163-181. Also available at http://www.rce.rutgers.edu/money/riskquiz/default.asp; results will be automatically tabulated and interpreted.

Appendix D

Education Planning

"The following financial plan excerpt is provided as an example for illustrative purposes only. Data and calculations are based on specific case assumptions, some of which are not shown in the illustration. The analysis, strategies, and recommendations are fictional and subject to alteration based on changes in assumptions."

Planning for Azalea's education is your primary goal. As we discussed, education expenses are very costly, but higher education is the gateway to opportunity. Like other financial goals, the key is to start saving early! You are already saving, sporadically, in a taxable account designated for Azalea's education. As background for this section, consider the latest available information from The College Board (http://www.collegeboard.com/) for the 2005-2006 academic year:

- The average cost of tuition, fees, and room and board was $12,127 for 4-year public schools, an average increase of 6.6%, while private school costs averaged $29,026 or a 5.7% increase.

- Tuition and fees, alone, totaled $5,491 for public schools and $21,235 for private schools, with average annual increases of 7.1% and 5.9%, respectively.

- The 7% increase in public school tuition is less than for the three previous academic years, when increases averaged 9%, 13%, and 10%, respectively.

- The 5.9% increase in private school costs is similar to 2004-2005, but the rate of growth has "slowed considerably."

- Private, institutional, federal, and state grants as well as federal and state tax credits and deductions cover approximately 33% of tuition, fees, room and board costs for a private college and 27% of public college costs for 4-year, full-time students.

- The average debt for 2003-2004 graduates was $25,622 for public schools and $22,581 for private schools, as reported by the Center for Economic and Policy Research, based on College Board data. For more information see http://www.cepr.net.

Finally, if financial aid is a consideration in your education goal planning, the account owner should be the parent and not the child. Financial aid formulas treat college assets in the parent's name more favorably than money saved in the child's name. For example, today, financial aid formulas typically include only 5.6% of parental assets versus as much as 35% of the child's assets.

Education Goal

The goal is to accumulate at least $40,000 toward funding the cost of a 4-year public school education for Azalea beginning in 10 years.

Assumptions

Based on our discussions and the information you provided, we have agreed to the following planning assumptions:

- Currently, $1,550 in a taxable mutual fund account, jointly owned by Tom and Nyla, is designated for Azalea's college expenses.

- For taxable account projections, the federal income tax rates on annual distributions are 15% on capital gains and 25% on nonqualified dividends and other income. It is assumed that no dividends are "qualified" for the lower income tax rate treatment.

- Tuition, fees, and room and board are estimated as $12,200 (in today's dollars) per year for a 4-year public college.

Azalea will begin college in 10 years, or the fall of 2017.

- You wish to save for this goal through July 2017, the month before Azalea begins college.

- All future planned contributions will remain level during the funding period.

- College expenses will increase 7% annually.

- The stated risk tolerance for this goal is moderately aggressive.

- You want to maintain ownership of, and access to, the account.

- You prefer a dedicated account for Azalea's education.

- Scholarships will not be considered as a source of funding.

- Azalea will be expected to contribute to her education funding through high school or college employment and personal savings.

Analysis

Based on our discussions and the information you provided, the following three alternatives were analyzed to partially fund Azalea's education:

- Continue funding the taxable account with a suggested fixed end-of-year contribution of $2,200 per year.

- Establish a new 529 Plan account with fixed monthly contributions of $250 or a total of $3,000 per year. Distributions from this account are tax-free if used exclusively for qualified education expenses.[1]

- Fund a Roth IRA with fixed monthly contributions of $250 or a total of $3,000 per year, with the intention that the money could be withdrawn for Azalea's education. This account would generally be tax-deferred rather than tax-free even for qualified expenses.

It is important to note that the federal income tax consequences for the 529 Plan and the Roth IRA could be the same, assuming both are used exclusively for qualified education expenses and the total distributions from the Roth IRA did not exceed the total contributions. In other words, whereas no taxes would be owed on any portion of a distribution from a 529 Plan, taxes would be owed on the "earnings" portion of a distribution from a Roth IRA although the 10% additional tax "penalty" would not apply. State tax consequences could vary. (Please consult your tax advisor for a full explanation.) The graphs below compare the tax-free account (the 529 Plan) and the taxable account for meeting your education goal funding.

As shown in the following graph, the tax-free account would yield approximately $15,000 more than the taxable account at the beginning of the disbursement period due to the differences in funding and taxation. (The spreadsheet documenting the results is shown on page xx.[2]) Note also that if the tax-free account is used, then the taxable account—with the $1,550 balance—would be closed and the proceeds deposited into the tax-free account. Any taxes due upon liquidation of the taxable account (which should be a very small amount due to the size of the account) would be paid with outside funds to maintain an equivalent opening balance for either account.

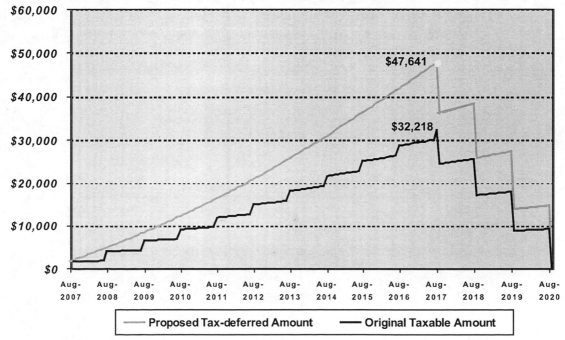

Current Taxable Account Scenario

Assuming you deposit $2,200 at the end of each year, Azalea's projected year one college expenses of $24,000 would be underfunded by approximately $16,000. (See pie chart.) This approach would only provide one-third of the required amount for year one. Results for the other three years are shown in the Education Planning Assumptions and Analysis Table (Figure D.1).

Proposed Tax-Deferred[3] Account Scenario

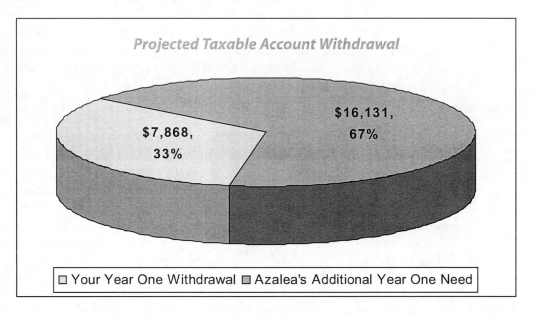

Projected Taxable Account Withdrawal

$7,868, 33% $16,131, 67%

☐ Your Year One Withdrawal   ▨ Azalea's Additional Year One Need

To overcome some of this projected shortfall, funding should be increased to the equivalent of $3,000 per year, or contributions of $250 per month. With this increase in funding the account should cover over 49% of the $24,000 of expenses for year one. A similar level of withdrawal will also be available in future years, as shown in the Education Planning Assumptions and Analysis Table shown below (Figure D.1).

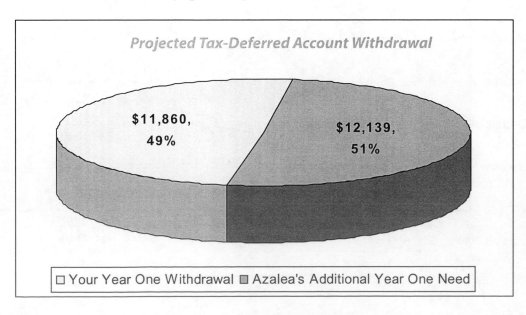

Projected Tax-Deferred Account Withdrawal

$11,860, 49% $12,139, 51%

☐ Your Year One Withdrawal   ▨ Azalea's Additional Year One Need

Summary of Alternatives

Our analysis, based on the assumptions, projects that Azalea's tuition, fees, and room and board for a 4-year public school will cost $106,555 as shown in the table below. To meet your goal of saving $40,000 by the time Azalea enters college, funding of $250 per month will be required, assuming our tax and return projections are accurate. The following table outlines all information on which the calculations for the taxable and tax deferred (and potentially tax free) account projections were based.

Figure D.1

Education Planning Assumptions and Analysis

College Begins	2017	Years until College	10
College Ends	2021	Total Years in College	4

Present Value Cost per Year	$12,200	Total Current Funding	$1,550
Annual Education Inflation Rate	7.00%		

Future Value Cost per Year	Year 1	Year 2	Year 3	Year 4
Total: $106,555	$23,999	$25,679	$27,477	$29,400

Additional Periodic Funding	Existing		Proposed	
Annual	$2,200		n/a	
Monthly	n/a		$250	

Assumed Rates of Return (Nominal) *	Year 1-7	Year 8	Year 9	Year 10+
(rates compounded monthly in calculations)				
Total Return	8.00%	7.25%	6.75%	6.50%
Return from Capital Gain	6.00%	5.25%	4.25%	3.50%
Return from Dividend	2.00%	2.00%	2.50%	3.00%

Assumed Income Tax Rates			Nonqualified Dividends, Other Income	
	Capital Gains			
	15%		25%[1]	

Education Planning Projections (Existing Taxable Account; $2,200/yr)

Projections by Year	08/01/17	08/01/18	08/01/19	08/01/20
Account Values	$32,218	$25,653	$18,157	$9,638
Withdrawal Amounts	$7,868	$8,419	$9,008	$9,638
Percentage of College Expense Covered	33%	33%	33%	33%

Education Planning Projections (Proposed Tax-qualified Account; $250/mo)

Projections by Year	08/01/17	08/01/18	08/01/19	08/01/20
Account Values (prior to withdrawal)	$47,641	$38,177	$27,193	$14,527
Withdrawal Amounts	$11,860	$12,690	$13,579	$14,527
Percentage of College Expense Covered	49%	49%	49%	49%

1   To err on the side of safety, it is assumed that no dividends are "qualified" for purposes of determining after-tax returns. This should slightly understate the return and therefore understate the subsequent account balance. Actual after-tax returns should be higher because at least some of dividends distributed by most investment companies are "qualified." Your tax advisor will be better able to determine the exact amount of "qualified" dividends you receive.

By increasing the level of funding, the account has the potential to grow to just under $48,000—exceeding the $40,000 targeted amount. However, by slightly overfunding the account, there is a better chance of achieving the goal. You have indicated that a $250 per month commitment is not unreasonable given Nyla's recent salary increase. Note also that the projections are based on a continuous fixed contribution over the 10-year savings period, with no planned increases. The graph below summarizes a comparison of how much money is projected to be available on an annual basis versus the annual projected college expense. (The spreadsheet documenting the results is shown on page xx.[4]) The available withdrawal from the account differs for each of the four years, as illustrated below, to help keep pace with inflation. The higher account balance in the tax-deferred (and potentially tax-free) account, as compared to the taxable account as previously presented, allows for nearly $18,000 in additional disbursements over the life of the account.

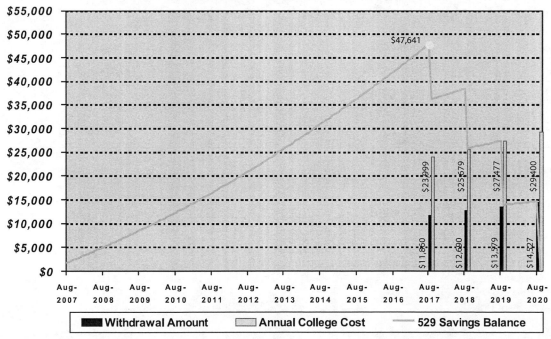

Recommendation & Implementation

√   To establish an AnyState College Savings Plan with a Real Life Mutual Fund Company age-based account with monthly funding of $250 to accumulate a projected $40,000 to partially fund the cost of a 4-year public college education for Azalea beginning in 2017.

With the AnyState College Savings Plan, we feel that the age-based portfolio is your best option. Because the asset allocation for the portfolio is coordinated with Azalea's time horizon for entering college, her portfolio will gradually shift from a riskier asset allocation to a more conservative one. As noted in the

Education Planning Assumptions and Analysis Table, the rates of return are assumed to decrease in response to these changes. The age-based portfolio approach reduces the monitoring required by the owner; however, a static account (i.e., one that allows the owner to control the asset allocation) is available so that additional risk/return adjustments may be made, if deemed necessary. In addition to the automatic asset allocation adjustments, automatic periodic rebalancing of the portfolio is also available.

To fund this plan, deposit $250 per month from Nyla's salary increase (the minimum additional contribution accepted by this plan) beginning this month and continuing until July 2017—the month prior to Azalea starting college. Additional funds may be contributed randomly throughout the year, should you or your extended family on friends wish to donate to the account on Azalea's behalf. In general, the maximum annual amount that can be given gift tax-free by any individual to the 529 Plan for Azalea is $12,000 (in 2006); however, a special provision allows a gift to the 529 Plan exceeding the annual exclusion to be pro-rated over five years.

Our reasons for recommending the 529 Plan account are as follows:

- In addition to the previously mentioned federal tax advantages and the additional advantages described in the forthcoming Planning Tools and Other Background Information section, you will be able to deduct up to $2,000 annually in account contributions from your AnyState taxable income. (Check with your tax advisor for details regarding this deduction.)[5]

- This account does not have an annual fee; however, a "set-up" fee will be due on account establishment.

- The taxable mutual fund account offers no tax advantages and does not provide the automatic reallocation or rebalancing of the portfolio, as available with the 529 Plan.

- The dual-purpose Roth IRA offers only tax-deferral, not tax-free distributions (unless distributions are made after age 59½, death, or disability). Nor does it give you the desired dedicated account for Azalea's education. No state tax deductions apply for the Roth contributions. Furthermore, adjusting the portfolio to appropriately match the time horizon for the goal will require more active management. Typically, no account establishment fees apply, but nominal annual maintenance fees will be incurred.

The recommendation and implementation details are summarized in the **Education Recommendation Planning Form** (Figure D.2).

Finally, although this recommendation was based on the desire to simplify the account management and monitoring, it will still be important to periodically review this education savings plan. Annual reviews will help to ensure that the plan earnings are on target, and that adjustments are being made to reflect changes in your personal situation or to take advantage of changes in the eco-

Figure D.2

Education Planning Recommendation Form

Financial Planning Content Area	Education planning			
Client Goal	Education funding for Azalea's college expenses			
Recommendation #: 1	Priority (1 – 6) lowest to highest:		6	
Projected/Target Value ($)	$40,000			

Product Profile

Type	529 account			
Duration	14 years			
Provider	Real Life Mutual Fund Company			
Funding Cost per Period ($)	$250 per month			
Maintenance Cost per Period ($)	$25 set-up fee (one-time only)			
Current Income Tax Status	Tax-Qualified	X	Taxable	
Projected Rate of Return	Variable (8.0% for first 7 years)			
Major Policy Provisions	None			

Procedural Factors

Implement by Whom	Planner		Client	X
Implementation Date or Time Frame	Within next 60 days			
Implementation Procedure	We will provide you with the appropriate forms to be completed. Upon completion, mail the forms and your check to Real Life Mutual Fund Company. We will monitor account progress for funding adequacy, risk/return objectives and all other investment aspects of the account.			

Ownership Factors

Owner(s)	Tom Kim			
Form of Ownership	Individual, but per the plan, Nyla will be designated as the account owner in the event of Tom's death.			
Insured(s)	n/a			
Custodial Account	Yes	X	No	
Custodian	AnyState			
In Trust For (ITF)	Yes		No	X
Transfer on Death (TOD)	Yes		No	X
Beneficiary(ies)	Azalea Kim			
Contingent Beneficiary(ies)	n/a			

Proposed Benefit

By using a 529 Plan, you will benefit from tax-deferred growth as well as tax-free withdrawals (restrictions apply). Furthermore, we have agreed to maintain a fairly passive approach and this plan has several age-based portfolios that will adjust the asset allocation, thereby reducing the account volatility as Azalea approaches college age. However, the selected plan also offers a static account (i.e., one that allows the owner to control the asset allocation) so that additional risk/return adjustments may be made.

nomic, financial, legal, or tax marketplace. The integration of this recommendation and goal, with the other aspects of your financial life, is summarized in the **Recommendation Impact Form** shown below (Figure D.3).

Figure D.3

Recommendation Impact Form

Recommendation: Increase education funding for Azalea's college to $250 per month

Recommendation #:	1					
Planner Decision	Accept	X	Reject		Modify	
Client Decision	Accept	X	Reject		Modify	

Financial Impact

Annual Impact on Cash Flow ($)	$3,000
Immediate Impact on Net Worth ($)	$0

Planning Issue	Degree of Significance				Notes
	Major	Modest	Minor	None	
Financial Situation – Cash Management	X				Review automatic investment plan possibilities with client
Tax Planning			X		State income tax deduction might be available
Life Insurance Planning		X			Funding the education goal will impact the ability to purchase life insurance
Health Insurance Planning				X	
Disability Insurance Planning		X			Funding the education goal will impact the ability to purchase long-term disability insurance
LTC Insurance Planning				X	
Property and Liability Insurance Planning				X	
Investment Planning	X				Funding the education goal will impact the ability to fund the vacation goal.
Education / Special Needs Planning		X			Select age-based portfolios to reduce management time
Retirement Planning			X		Funding the education goal might impact the ability to fully fund the retirement goal
Estate Planning			X		Per the plan requirements, Nyla will be designated as the account owner in the event of Tom's death
Other Planning Need				X	

Planning Tools & Other Background Information

There are several tools that may be used to save for Azalea's education. What follows is a brief summary of the most commonly used options. A list of other alternatives that could be considered is also provided, as well as a review of the tax considerations.

Taxable Account (Current Funding Tool)

Tom and Nyla, you have been using a taxable mutual fund account to save for Azalea's education. A taxable account is simply an account (i.e. savings account, brokerage account) in your name(s) designated as savings for Azalea's education. Taxes are due on the earnings annually, and taxes are due on the capital gains when the assets are sold. Because this account has no specific planning or tax benefits, there are no annual or lifetime contribution limits.

Advantages

- Numerous investment options (i.e. stocks, mutual funds, bonds, cash investments, etc.)

- Owner(s) controls the account and has unrestricted access and use of the account

- No penalty for funds taken out for purposes other than education

Disadvantages

- Earning and distributions are taxable in the year earned

- Taxes will be due on any capital gains when the account assets are sold

- Since the owner is able to access the funds, it may be difficult to avoid the temptation of taking money out of the account for purposes other than Azalea's education

- The account is included in the owner's gross estate, which could have estate tax implications

- Diversification is harder to achieve due to the minimum initial deposit requirements for some mutual funds

529 Plan (Proposed Funding Tool)

Established under Section 529 of the Internal Revenue Code, 529 plans are tax-advantaged accounts for paying qualified higher education expenses (i.e. tuition, fees, room and board, books, and supplies). Earnings grow tax-free and qualified withdrawals are tax-free. These plans have high contribution limits and other family members or friends may contribute to the account. Also it is important to note that there are two types of 529 plans: prepaid tuition plans and college savings plans. With pre-paid tuition plans, contributions are guaranteed to match the inflation rate of education costs, similar to paying tuition costs in advance. The plans are typically restricted to in-state institutions, but adjustment may be necessary for those out-of-state. With college savings plans, earnings are based on the performance of the market and the mutual fund-type accounts.

Advantages

- Earnings grow tax-free and qualified withdrawals are tax-free

- Considered as an asset of the parent (or other owner) for college financial aid purposes

- Owner/contributor maintains control of the account (i.e., change of beneficiary, owner, distribution amount or frequency, or sub-account options)

- Contributions are not included in the contributor's gross estate because contributions to the account are treated as a completed gift

- Contributions may be "front-loaded" (i.e., five years worth of annual exclusion gifts may be made in a single year)

- High contribution limit (i.e. typically $250,000 or more per beneficiary), with no income phase out

- State income tax incentives (e.g., tax deductions or tax credits) may be available (check with your tax advisor)

- No age or time restrictions on use of asset

Disadvantages

- 10% penalty for early or nonqualified withdrawals, in addition to taxes on the earnings

Custodial Accounts (UGMA/UTMA)

Under the Uniform Gift to Minors Act (UGMA) or the Uniform Transfers to Minors Act (UTMA) individuals can establish custodial accounts that are controlled by the custodian until a minor child reaches the age of majority (usually 18 or 21 as determined by state law). Like a taxable account, these accounts usually allow a broad range of investments and unlimited annual or lifetime contributions. However, funds placed in these accounts are considered an irrevocable gift. Thus, at the age of majority, the child will gain control of the account and have unrestricted use.

Advantages

- Numerous investment options (i.e. cash, stocks, bonds, mutual funds, etc.)

- Unlimited contributions

Disadvantages

- Beneficiary (minor) gains control of the account at the age of majority

- Limited income tax benefits since tax law changed in 2006

- Considered the property of the student for college financial aid purposes

- Annual funding limited to the tax-free gift threshold ($12,000 per person in 2006).

- Restricted use of funds for the benefit of the minor before the beneficiary reaches the age of majority

- Account is included in the custodian's gross estate (if custodian was also the donor), which could have estate tax implications (consult your tax or legal advisor)

Coverdell Education Savings Account (ESA)

The Coverdell Education Savings Account (formerly known as the Education IRA) is another tax-deferred (and potentially tax-free) account and can generally be distributed tax-free if all funds are used for approved education expenses. These funds may be used for college expenses as well as elementary and secondary education savings. Other family members or friends may contribute to the account. However, contributions cannot exceed $2,000 per beneficiary per year for 2006. Furthermore, the $2,000 contribution amount may be limited by your income level. Tom and Nyla, under the current law, you qualify to make the full $2,000 contribution.

Advantages

- Earnings grow tax-deferred and qualified withdrawals are tax-free

- Numerous investment options (i.e. stocks, mutual funds, bonds, cash investments, etc.)

- Funds may be used for elementary, secondary, and higher education

- Contributions are not included in the contributor's gross estate

Disadvantages

- Considered the property of the student for college financial aid calculations

- Contributions limited to $2,000 per year per beneficiary (additional restrictions may apply), which may be insufficient to meet college costs

- Contribution amounts may be phased out for those with higher incomes

- 10% penalty for early or nonqualified withdrawals, in addition to taxes on the earnings

- Age restrictions apply; the assets must be deposited before age 18 and used by the account beneficiary before age 30, or rolled into the account, without penalty, of another eligible family member

Other Funding Alternatives

Given the 10-year time horizon to save for Azalea's education, these options are not as relevant to your situation. However, the viability of any of these alternatives could be reconsidered in the future:

- Use Series EE and Series I Savings Bonds as savings tools. These bonds offer the benefit of tax-exempt earnings when used for qualified expenses; but earnings are low.

- Use a home equity loan or 401(k) or other retirement account loan (if available).

- Use a Roth or traditional IRA to concurrently save for education and retirement. The 10% penalty does not apply to early withdrawals for qualified education expenses (e.g., tuition, fees, room and board, and equipment and supplies).

Tax Considerations

Two federal income tax credits and an adjustment for interest on education loans are available to individuals funding a dependent's college education; phase outs and income restrictions apply. Both of the credits can be coordinated with funds withdrawn from a Coverdell ESA or a Section 529 plan, but tax-free withdrawals and credits cannot be applied to the same expenses. The two credits cannot be taken for the same child in the same year; the taxpayer must choose which credit to apply.

- The Hope Scholarship Credit provides a credit of up to $1,650 (in 2006) per year for the first two years of a student's qualified higher education expenses.

- The Lifetime Learning Credit provides a credit up to $2,000 per year for qualified higher education expenses or non-credit career advancement courses. This credit is available for an unlimited number of years.

- Up to $2,500 of interest on education loans may qualify as an adjustment to income in the year paid.

Other Considerations

In addition to the college savings vehicles mentioned above, we want you to be aware of some other important areas of financial assistance. Each college or university will have its own financial aid system in place and will provide guidelines on application procedures.

- Scholarships

- Financial Aid

  - Pell Grants

  - Perkins Loans and Stafford Loans (subsidized and unsubsidized) available to students

  - PLUS Loans available to parents and others

Tom and Nyla, you may want to consider these and other options as the time approaches for Azalea to begin college. Azalea's high school counseling department also may offer assistance on how to pursue financial aid.

Additional Information

For further information visit: www.savingforcollege.com

Chapter Endnotes

1. These expenses include: tuition, fees, books, supplies, and equipment required for attendance at an eligible educational institution. Additional details about qualified expenses and eligible institutions can be found in IRS Publication 970 or discussed with your tax advisor.
2. The referenced results would be available in the plan section or appendix, but are not included here.
3. If distributions are handled correctly, the goal is that such distributions will ultimately be tax-free because they will have been used to pay for qualifying expenses.
4. The referenced results would be available in the plan section or appendix, but are not included here.
5. Currently 29 states and the District of Columbia offer either state tax deductions or state tax credits to residents whom invest the their "home state's" 529 plan.

Index